COUNSELING TECHNIQUES

Counseling Techniques

IMPROVING RELATIONSHIPS WITH OTHERS, OURSELVES, OUR FAMILIES, AND OUR ENVIRONMENT
Second Edition

ROSEMARY A. THOMPSON, Ed.D., NCC., LPC., NCSC.

BRUNNER-ROUTLEDGE
--
New York & Hove

Published in 2003 by
Brunner-Routledge
29 West 35th Street
New York, NY 10001
www.brunner-routledge.com

Published in Great Britain by
Brunner-Routledge
27 Church Road
Hove, East Sussex
BN3 2FA
www.brunner-routledge.co.uk

Brunner-Routledge is an imprint of the Taylor & Francis Group.
Printed in the United States of America on acid-free paper.

Cover design by David Sierra.

10 9 8 7 6 5 4 3 2 1

Library of Congress Cataloging-in-Publication Data
    Thompson, Rosemary, 1950—
        Counseling techniques : improving relationships with others, ourselves, our families,
    and our environment / Rosemary A. Thompson.— 2nd ed.
            p. cm.
        Includes bibliographical references.
        ISBN 1-58391-330-0 (pbk.)
        1. Psychotherapy. 2. Counseling. I. Title.

    RC480.T449 2003
    616.89'14--dc21

                                                                              2003004127

Dedication

This book is dedicated to my husband Charlie, who at 17 began to nurture, strengthen, and support all our most rewarding relationships as a couple.

Contents

12.   Stress and Stress Reduction Techniques   333

13.   Trauma, Loss, Grief, and Post-Traumatic Stress Debriefing   357

14.   Psychodynamic Techniques   383

15.   Eclectic Techniques for Use with Family Systems   401
      and Family Development

      References   439

      Index   467

Preface

As counseling and psychotherapy evolved, a kaleidoscope of helping initiatives emerged to meet the needs of the human condition. Each given time period had its clashes of prominent theorists and ideologies. In the 1940s, Freud and psychoanalytic theory was perhaps the initial major influence on all other formal systems of counseling and psychotherapy. Many other perspectives evolved as an extension of or rebellion against psychoanalytical principles, such as the ego psychologists or neo-Freudians of the 1950s and the convincing ideas of Carl Jung, Alfred Adler, Karen Horney, Erich Fromm, Harry Stack Sullivan, Erick Erickson, and Wilhelm Reich, who felt that interpersonal aspects have a more significant influence on the development of the individual. Existential therapy evolved as the third-force in psychotherapy as an alternative to psychoanalysis and behavioral approaches, with the person-centered approach developed by Carl Rogers and Gestalt therapy of Fritz Perls.

Essentially, the 1960s was touted as the decade of person-centered therapy with the emphasis on feelings, and the importance of relationships, and focus on the congruency between the ideal and the real self. The 1970s was the decade of behaviorism and behavior therapy, focusing on measurable and observational data to monitor client growth and change. The 1980s emerged as the decade of cognition and cognitive therapy, focusing on the client's ability to change perceptions, attitudes, and thinking regarding the human condition. The 1990s rapidly emerged as what some have termed *the age of dysfunction* and the decade of eclecticism. As we enter the 21st century, counseling and psychotherapy will have to sustain their worth in response to the constraints of managed care. Solution-focused and brief therapy models will prevail as a means to meet the needs of the growing diversity of clients. There is also a movement toward theoretical integration of all theories. Finally, online counseling, a fairly new method for providing therapy, has introduced a variety of modalities including cybertherapy, cybercounseling, e-therapy, and distance therapy. This will probably generate considerable debate and controversy within the next decade in terms of creditability and ethics.

In this second edition, the reader will find a more enriched and inclusive book that expands and strengthens the therapeutic process. Collectively, each chapter has been updated and strengthened with additional counseling techniques and strategies. For example, Chapter 10 introduces the psychoeducational life skill instructional model to enhance social, emotional, and cognitive skills to maximize human potential. An emphasis on "ownwork" (i.e., homework assignments) as a follow-through to group work is also outlined. Chapter 14 is a new chapter that recognizes outcomes studies of psychodynamic techniques. Chapter 6 adds the rich dimension of expressive techniques such as drama therapy, dance therapy, music therapy, creative writing, and poetry. Twenty-three additional strategies have been added to the chapter on cognitive techniques. Chapter 15, "Eclectic Techniques for Use with Family Systems and Family Development," addresses the implications of play therapy, art therapy, and expressive techniques with children. A special section has been added that confronts the mental health needs of children and adolescents reflecting the *Surgeon General's First Report on Child and Adolescent Mental Health.*

Ultimately, no single theory can account for or reflect the full range of human experiences. Further, adhering to exclusive models in counseling and psychotherapy could be perceived as limiting therapeutic options. Interventions must be considered within the context of culture, ethnicity, interpersonal resources, and systemic support. Thus, any single theory and associated set of techniques is unlikely to be equally or universally effective with the wide range of client characteristics, coping repertoires, and interpersonal as well as intrapersonal skills.

In addition, through research, advocacy, and articulation, helping professionals are beginning to recognize and acknowledge the following trends in counseling and psychotherapy:

- A collaborative continuum of care between helping professionals has emerged that reflects the following services: outpatient clinics, intensive case management, home-based treatment services, family support services, day treatment programs, partial hospitalization, emergency/crisis services, respite care services, therapeutic group home or community residence, crisis residence, and residential treatment facilities.
- Homework assignments, treatment planning, and follow-through designed to put increased responsibility on the client have become an expectation. Treatment planning that reflects many alternatives and combines methods in a logical and systematic way to maximize a more positive therapeutic impact is imperative.
- Counseling and psychotherapy has emerged as an educational-developmental

model that is holistic, reflecting the interdependence of physical and psychological well-being and the realization that both coping skills and coping opportunities occur in systems (i.e., individuals live, grow, develop, or become defeated in family systems, organizational work groups, communities, culture, and environment).

- The utilization of professional counselors in all aspects of the health care delivery system, addressing the mental health and developmental needs of all people, is supported in both public and private sectors. In addition, the most rapidly growing field in counseling and psychotherapy is human services counseling.
- Bringing multicultural awareness into all aspects of the helping profession with sensitivity to values, beliefs, race, ethnicity, gender, religion, historical experience within cultures, socioeconomic status, political views, and lifestyle has been integrated into therapeutic practice.
- Promoting standards for professional development, accreditation, licensure, and ongoing professional growth and development is systematically promoted, structured, and monitored.
- Counselors, mental health professionals, and therapists are launching into cyberspace for instant access to other counselors and therapists around the world as well as to a host of other counseling and mental health resources. This represents a new terrain with a tremendous opportunity for interaction, shared professional growth, and visibility in a more global community.

It is clear that the mental health and counseling profession has grown and changed extensively during the preceding decades. The resourceful, responsive, and responsible therapist will have the benefit of a therapeutic repertoire gleaned from the visions and perspectives of his or her predecessors, reflecting a full spectrum of counseling techniques to meet the demands of an increasingly, diverse and demanding clientele.

This book is unique in that it collectively assembles more than 300 techniques to provide helping professionals with critical skills to meet the demanding needs of today's clients. The primary focus, central to all therapies, is improving relationships—those with others, our families, our environment, and ourselves. Fundamentally, a counseling technique is presented as a strategy. A strategy is an intervention. An intervention is a counselor or therapist's intention to eliminate or illuminate a self-defeating behavior. Counseling techniques that are included in this book are intended to be broadly applicable to a wide range of client problems, from enhancing relationships to dealing with grief, loss, stress, and family dysfunction. Each technique provided in this book is followed by a *counseling intention,* as outlined in Chapter 2, followed by a brief description.

A final value of this book lies in the greater understanding that may be gained from *perspectives for the therapist,* the small reflections that flow through the pages of the book that can bring existential meaning to the work of the helping professional. This brings content and consciousness together, as well as provides hope and meaning for the reader.

A CAVEAT ON USING COUNSELING TECHNIQUES

Specific techniques implemented by the counselor to elicit client change are an important component of the counseling process. Techniques in counseling and psychotherapy, however, are offered with the precaution that the acquisition of techniques alone merely produces a technician skilled in gimmicks, not a therapist whose intention is to effect change. The counseling experience is much more than the counselor's use of technique; the human dimension of the relationship as well as the readiness and responsiveness of the client are also very important.

Fundamentally, a technique may be conceptualized as a preferred strategy of the counselor and may be drawn from many available sources. The skillfulness with which the intervention is implemented is critical. A counseling technique must be organized around a fundamental principle of treatment and directed toward the ultimate goal of wellness. It should contribute to the total process, becoming an integral part of the therapeutic goal by becoming an assimilated force in the counseling relationship. Lambert (1989) suggested that the technically skilled counselor could have a major impact on the counseling process and therapeutic outcome.

Although a technique may or may not be associated with a specific theory of counseling, each theory or model has its own repertoire of techniques integrated into the total therapeutic process. Most counseling interactions are universal, regardless of theoretical orientation. A successful technique must be flexible, appropriate, and pragmatic. Flexibility is a prerequisite to attending to diverse populations with varying expectations and needs. Furthermore, a technique that is too prescriptive and rigid will hamper the interaction between client and therapist, and may significantly impede progress.

This is perhaps best illuminated with the early work of Lieberman, Yalom, and Miles (1973) regarding encounter group experiences. They reviewed the activating techniques of encounter group leaders and compared them to outcome. Two important findings were revealed: (1) The more structured the exercises the leader used, the more competent members deemed the leader to be, and (2) the more structured the exercises used by the leader, the less positive were the results. These findings may seem like a contradiction, because initially group members do want the group leader to lead and often equate a large number of structured exercises with competence. Yet, in the long run, many structured exercises become counterproductive, because they foster a dependent group who relies on the leader to supply too much to the process; members become resistant to working on their own issues.

Simkin and Yontef (1984) provided two guidelines for integrating techniques in the counseling session: (1) It has the aim of increasing awareness, and (2) it is within the bounds of ethical practice. Byrum (1989) further outlined 10 components critical to a client's understanding and acceptance of techniques:

1. State the purpose of the technique.
2. Introduce the technique in familiar language that the client can understand.
3. Support the use of the technique or the rationale.
4. Relate the technique to the client's experience.
5. Indicate how the technique has worked for other clients.
6. Indicate that the technique is voluntary and that the client has the right to decline to participate in the experience.
7. Give an overview of what will happen.
8. Take the participant through the process.
9. Process the experience with the clients.
10. Provide for action planning and follow-up. (pp. 79–89)

Finally, I would be remiss if I did not acknowledge that many of these techniques have been gleaned from many resources and I have tried to credit counselors, psychotherapists, and researchers as much as possible. I have been both a student and a counselor in the fields of psychology and psychotherapy for the last three decades and have been influenced by many counseling initiatives. I consider myself a counseling historian in that I have tried to archive and bring the ideas of leading therapists collectively to the forefront to further the profession. I hope the book will be helpful for aspiring students, counselors, therapists, psychologists, social workers, counselor educators, school counselors, human service counselors, health care professionals, mental health counselors, case managers, juvenile justice authorities, drug and alcohol counselors, the religious community, and any helping professional who works with people in an effort to help them function more effectively both interpersonally and intrapersonally.

From this perspective, it becomes clear that techniques used in counseling or psychotherapy are guided by ethical responsibility and are not intended to be used haphazardly or capriciously. This book does not assume full coverage of all the practical procedures with which counselors need to be familiar in selecting and assessing clients, implementing appropriate counseling techniques, and evaluating the therapeutic process. Counseling techniques are intended to be broadly applicable to a wide range of client problems—depression, phobias, sexual inhibitions, crisis intervention, and family dysfunction. Moreover, this is not a comprehensive handbook covering all the strategies and tactics that a helping professional might want to assimilate in his or her therapeutic repertoire. However, with more than 250 systems of counseling and psychotherapy, and an emerging collection of counseling techniques, this book is perhaps a beginning.

Chapter 1

Professionalism in Counseling and Psychotherapy

Perspective for Therapist: On psychotherapy

But, ineffably, psychotherapy heals. It makes some sense of the confusion, reins in the terrifying thoughts and feelings, returns some control and hope and possibility of learning from it all. Pills cannot, do not, ease one back into reality; they only bring one back headlong, careening and faster than can be endured at times. Psychotherapy is a sanctuary; it is a battleground; it is a place I have been psychotic, neurotic, elated, confused, and despairing beyond belief. But, always, it is where I have believed—or have learned to believe—that I might someday be able to contend with all of this. . . . No pill can help me deal with the problem of not wanting to take pills; likewise, no amount of psychotherapy alone can prevent my manias and depressions. I need both. It is an odd thing, owing life to pills, one's own quirks and tenacities, and this unique, strange, and ultimately profound relationship called psychotherapy.

Kay Redfield Jamison, *An Unquiet Mind*, 1995, p. 89
(Reprinted with permission)

A pivotal debate exists among counselors and therapists on the efficacy of particular practices and theoretical approaches in counseling and psychotherapy. The continuum of discussion focuses on adhering to a single therapeutic model, pursuing a theoretical integration of models, or adopting a more eclectic approach to therapy in an effort to meet the changing needs of diverse client populations. The pervasive question is, "Do practicing counselors and therapists clearly understand how they use counseling theories and other cognitive schemata to guide their therapeutic perspective and their therapeutic interventions?"

Technical eclecticism has been touted as the fundamental thrust of counseling and psychotherapy in the 21st century primarily because of the time constraints of managed care (Lazarus, Beutler, & Norcross, 1992). Technical eclecticism advocates the selective combination of the most efficient techniques, regardless of their theoretical origin, to achieve optimal therapeutic results for a specific client (Lampropoulos, 2000, p. 287). Beutler and his associates have been using *personality-matched eclecticism* for more than 30 years (Beutler & Clarkin, 1990; Beutler, Goodrich, Fisher, & Williams, 1999). Collectively, the researchers have developed an eclectic model called *Systematic Treatment Selection.* It has become an advanced eclectic approach using systematic, empirically based treatment selection. It has been developed to allow eclectic recommendations for specific disorders such as depression (Beutler, Clarkin, & Bongar, 2000) and alcoholism. For implementing eclectic approaches, Lampropoulos (2000) makes the following training recommendations for therapists: (a) educate them to identify and be aware of their relationship styles; (b) train them to explore and attempt varying therapeutic styles, when necessary; (c) train them to recognize important criteria for adopting different relationship styles; (d) educate them to identify and maintain an optimal level of fit or difference in the relationship; and (e) train them to make appropriate referrals when there is a clear incompatibility and mismatch in the relationship that cannot be fixed (p. 291).

The pragmatic emphasis of managed care is loosening therapists' attachment to schools of therapy and forcing conceptual refinement of practice. Other developments are also deemphasizing schools of therapy, with a movement to integrate the psychotherapies (Norcross & Goldfried, 1992). Only theories and techniques that correlate with cost-effectiveness and quality are likely to survive in the managed-care environment (Cummings & Sayama, 1995). Other developments are also forcing the deemphasis of schools of therapy. The movement to integrate the psychotherapies has been gathering momentum and support (Norcross & Goldfried, 1992).

COUNSELING THEORY, PHILOSOPHY, OR CONCEPTUAL MODEL?

*Learn your theories as well as you can, but put them
aside when you touch the miracle of the living soul.*

Carl Gustav Jung

Many researchers and practitioners have taken on the arduous task of attempting to define the theoretical aura that surrounds counseling practice. The image of a "theoretical aura" reflects the continuum of debate about whether counseling and psychotherapy are guided by a theory, a philosophy, or a conceptual model. Caple (1985) stated that a *theory* is a formally organized collection of facts, definitions, constructs, and testable propositions that are meaningfully related. Ginter (1988) emphatically asserted that "therapy cannot exist without theory" (p. 3). A theory serves as a conceptual map and the fundamental foundation of a counseling practice, meaningfully relating therapeutic constructs, counseling intentions, and client outcomes. Within the theory are specific functions. Boy and Pine (1983, p. 251) outlined six functions of theory that make counseling pragmatic:

1. It helps counselors find unity and relatedness within the diversity of existence.
2. It compels counselors to examine relationships they would otherwise overlook.
3. It gives counselors operational guidelines by which to work and helps them in evaluating their development as professionals.
4. It helps counselors focus on relevant data and tells them what to look for.
5. It helps counselors assist clients in the effective modification of their behavior.
6. It helps counselors evaluate both old and new approaches to the process of counseling.

Thus, theory is the basis from which new counseling approaches are constructed. To separate theory from the context of the theorist can distort our perception not only of the theory but also of its application to the client and his or her world. Thus, Hansen, Stevic, and Warner (1986) outlined four requirements of an effective theoretical position:

1. It is clear, easily understood, and communicable. It is coherent and not contradictory.
2. It is comprehensive, encompassing explanations for a wide variety of phenomena.
3. It is explicit and generates research because of its design.
4. It is specific in that it relates methods to outcomes. (p. 356)

Brammer and Shostrom (1977) further stressed the value of a theoretical framework for the counselor:

Theory helps to explain what happens in a counseling relationship and assists the counselor in predicting, evaluating, and improving results. Theory provides a framework for making scientific observations about counseling. Theorizing encourages the coherence of ideas about counseling and the production of new ideas. (p. 28)

Here, counseling theory can be very practical by helping to make sense out of the counselor's observations. But is it practical? Does it serve as a formative perspective that is routinely consulted to meet the needs of every new client who is counseled? As Kelly (1988) stated, "The ultimate criteria for all counseling theories is how well they provide explanations of what occurs in counseling" (pp. 212–213). Theory is, at best, a hypothesis or a speculation about people's behavior, their developmental unfolding, and their capacity for adjustment. Counseling theories are not facts, but rather can be beliefs, convictions, or dogma held by the therapist regarding human behavior. This less-than-desirable perspective will continue to emerge if theory is not linked to practice through outcome accountability.

THE THEORETICAL VOID: VALIDATING RESEARCH AND PRACTICE

To many, counseling research based on theory has not demonstrated outcome accountability. Falvey (1989) illuminated the practitioner's problem by noting that practitioners tend to ignore research findings because those findings do not provide consistent, relevant guidelines for understanding therapeutic change in applied settings. Strupp (1981) and Falvey (1989) emphasized the importance of linking research and practice. Strupp and Bergin (1969) stressed that psychotherapy research should be reformulated as a standard scientific question: What specific therapeutic interventions produce what specific changes in specific patients under specific conditions? Patterson (1986) responded to this dilemma in the profession and outlined the specifics for such a proposal. As a frame of reference, counselors or therapists would need:

• A taxonomy of client problems or a taxonomy of psychological disorders (a reliable, relevant diagnostic system).
• A taxonomy of client personalities.
• A taxonomy of therapeutic techniques or interventions.
• A taxonomy of therapists (therapeutic style).
• A taxonomy of circumstances, conditions, situations, or environments in which therapy is provided.
• A (set of) guiding principles or empirical rules for matching all these variables. (p. 146)

At present, skeptics continue to note that clinical research in counseling and psychotherapy has had little or no influence on clinical practice. This is particularly distressing because the primary goal for counseling and psychotherapy as disciplines has been to produce practitioners who would integrate theory into practice to produce new knowledge and understanding. Linden and Wen (1990) suggested that the limited influence of research on practice stems from its failure to provide conclusive evidence regarding the relative effectiveness of psychotherapeutic interventions with different clients and problems:

> *When addressing the reasons for a lack of conclusive evidence, it has been argued that the outcome literature is essentially noncumulative and not informative enough for clinicians, that studies lack the power to detect effects, and that the current review and publication process is more of a hindrance than a help for accumulating a solid data base on therapy outcome. The lack of accumulated knowledge has been attributed to a tendency among researchers to conduct mostly analogue studies and typically small-scale, independently initiated, and uncoordinated studies.* (p. 482)

Many counseling theories cannot meet the criteria of outcome accountability and perhaps would more accurately be called counseling models (Blocher, 1989; Ginter, 1988, 1989). A *model* serves to identify treatment goals and procedures that are assessed as appropriate for client concerns. An incessant concern raised among critics, however, is that counseling models often lack the formal theoretical delineation that can be empirically validated (Blocher, 1987). From this perspective, counseling models provide more of a philosophical viewpoint than a theory. Corsini (1989) captured this sentiment with a list of 250 different systems of psychotherapy. Kelly (1991) aptly stated that research is needed to ascertain if theory-based counseling leads to better outcomes. Corsini and Wedding (1989, p. 256) observed that in counseling or psychotherapy, just as in education or politics, ideological enclaves evolve. Some enclaves (models of therapy) consist of people who believe that they have the right, final, complete, and only answer—and that all other systems are incomplete, tentative, weak, or simply mistaken. The reading and writings of people within these enclaves tend to reinforce their views by recounting their successes, proving to one another the superiority of their way of thinking, acting, and behaving. As alternative positions develop, schismatic groups form; the new configuration of beliefs or tenets are either expelled from the original enclave or take off on their own.

Kelly (1991) characterized the existing theories of counseling as being only partial perspectives on the complex labyrinth that is the human world:

> *Picture the situation of three persons standing outside a labyrinth whose structure is unknown to and hidden from them. Each of these persons is in possession of a map that purports to depict the structure of the labyrinth and to show the way to reach its center. In comparing their maps, the three discover, with some surprise, that the maps bear no resemblance to one another. After a few futile moments spent in attempting to convince one another of the unique value of their own maps, the three decide to enter the labyrinth and to navigate it, each relying on his or her own map.*

> *They enter the labyrinth, part company, and, after a period of time, meet again at the center of the labyrinth. In discussing what their experience portends regarding the overall structure of the labyrinth, the three conclude that the structure must somehow involve a composition of the divergent details displayed on their three maps. Moreover, because the labyrinth is nothing if it is not an integrated whole, the three conclude that the overall structure of the labyrinth must involve an integrated composition of these divergent details.*
> (p. 109)

Thus, the debate over whether the practice of counseling and psychotherapy is empirically anchored in theory or is merely a represention of one's philosophy or conceptual models continues to divide practitioners. The complex labyrinth that Kelly (1991) described gives us partial maps that can be equally useful in producing effective treatment; however, a significant fraction of clients may be hindered from changing because of the limited nature of theories that guide their treatment. It also is the counselor's or therapist's responsibility to understand that one model of counseling may be too limited when working with an increasingly diverse population (Allen, 1988).

In the long run, conceptual frameworks are helpful, but individuals are too diverse, too complex, and too nebulous for therapists to expect that the ultimate, most comprehensive theoretical model will be discovered. This assumption is supported by the theory of chaos, which maintains that human behavior is so complex that no single traditional scientific discipline will enable us to understand the behavior and the causes. The concept of chaos requires a multidisciplinary approach because "complex behavior implies complex causes" (Gleick, 1988, p. 303).

Fortunately, most contemporary counseling texts leave the reader with personal choice, inviting creativity, pragmaticism, adaptability, and a foundation for further study. Perhaps Corey (1986), in "Theory and Practice of Counseling and Psychotherapy," best captured the more flexible theoretical position needed by counselors who struggle with their own modus operandi:

> *It is hoped that the reader will remain open and will seriously consider both the unique contributions and the limitations of each therapeutic system. No single model fully accounts for all the dimensions of the various therapies. The danger of presenting one model that all students are expected to advocate to the exclusion of other fruitful approaches is that the beginning counselor will unduly limit his or her effectiveness with different clients. Valuable dimensions of human behavior can be overlooked if the counselor is restricted to a single theory.* (p. 2)

LIMITATIONS OF EMBRACING THE CLASSICS

Like most disciplines, as counseling and psychotherapy evolved, their growth mirrored the zeitgeist of the period. The 1960s was the decade of person-centered therapy, with an emphasis on feelings; the 1970s marked the decade of behaviorism and behavior therapy, with a focus on quantifiable, observable data; and the 1980s was the decade of cognition and cognitive therapy, seeking to change the way we think about the blight of the human condition. The 1990s appeared to be the decade of eclecticism and eclectic therapy in response to client diversity. The 2000s are still in the process of becoming.

Traditionally, counselors and therapists have been painstakingly trained in classic counseling approaches such as psychodynamic, person-centered, behavior, or cognitive-behavior therapies. As counseling and psychotherapy continue to evolve, the works of Freud, Rogers, Perls, and Skinner are perhaps becoming more important as historical referents to counseling and therapy than as absolute frameworks of counseling practice. Each approach and its tenets have survived critical debate. For example, although psychoanalysis accounts for unconscious resistance, defense mechanisms, or early recollections, the lengthy techniques of free association and interpretation do not lend themselves to an efficient or accountable therapeutic relationship between client and therapist. Person-centered research indicates that the "necessary and sufficient" conditions of empathy, congruence, and unconditional positive regard are necessary but not sufficient for change in counseling (Bergin & Lambert, 1978). And, in a meta-analysis of 143 studies, Shapiro and Shapiro (1982) found cognitive and behavior treatments have more favorable outcomes. There also is some consensus that changes achieved by clients in rational-emotive therapy (RET) are not adequately explained by rational-emotive theory (Dryden, 1987). The classic debate again emerges with Weinrach (1991): "RET is a philosophy and a theory of psychotherapy. As a philosophy, it explains the nature of the human experience. As a theory, it defines emotional disturbance; identifies factors that contribute to it; and offers cognitive, emotive, and behavioral ways to treat it efficiently" (p. 374). Yet Ziegler (1989) maintained that RET is a personality theory.

Thus, adhering to exclusive models in counseling and psychotherapy could be perceived as limiting therapeutic options when working with clients, especially when options are considered in the context of culture, ethnicity, interpersonal resources, coping skills, and systemic support. Okum (1990) related how this has been detrimental to the practice of counseling and psychotherapy:

Each of the major models of psychotherapy has devotees who believe that their view is the only correct view. This type of doctrinarism has probably done more harm to the development and credibility of the psychotherapy field than any other single variable, because it has

> *reinforced turf competition and dichotomous thinking such as right*
> *or wrong, science or art, good or bad. Therapists afflicted with this*
> *doctrinarism are unlikely to select treatments that can be flexibly and*
> *effectively tailored to the needs of clients who are experiencing dis-*
> *tress related to today's sociocultural context.* (p. 3)

Any single theory, including its associated set of techniques, is unlikely to be equally or universally effective with the wide range of client characteristics or dysfunctions. Nance and Myers (1991) argued that counselors or therapists who work from only one theoretical model may be unable to work with a heterogeneous group of clients because they find themselves unable to adapt to a wide range of presenting problems. This is clearly illuminated from a multicultural perspective. Multicultural counseling practice takes into consideration the client's specific values, beliefs, and actions and how they related to race, ethnicity, gender, religion, historical experiences with the dominant culture, socioeconomic status, political views, lifestyle, and geographic region (Wright, Coley, & Corey, 1989). Socioeconomic diversity among the poor, for example, can include single mothers, elderly persons, unskilled laborers, unemployed workers, migrant farm workers, immigrants, and homeless people. Within this framework, adhering to a single theoretical model clearly would be anachronistic.

THEORETICAL INTEGRATIONISM, PLURALISM, OR SYSTEMATIC ECLECTICISM

With the inherent limitations of embracing a single theoretical model, many writers are proposing (a) theoretical integration, (b) pluralistism, or (c) eclecticism as an alternative to meet the diverse needs of clients. Theoretical Integrationism—integrating theoretical conceptions from other theories—is based on the premise that when various theories converge therapeutic procedures will be enhanced. Most efforts toward integrating theories have attempted to combine psychoanalytic and behavior theories (Goldfriend, 1982; Wachtel, 1977, 1987), with a focus on behavior and insight. This approach also has its limitations and critics (Lazarus & Mayne, 1990; Messor & Boals, 1981). Others have merged behavioral and Gestalt therapies (Fodor, 1987), cognitive and interpersonal therapies (Safran, 1990), or general psychotherapy principles with theories of information processing (Mahoney & Gabriel, 1987). The limitations of empirical efficacy and issues of accountability also encumber integrationism.

Okum (1990) proposed the concept of *pluralism* as an alternative to single theory or theoretical integration, to provide an opportunity for an open system, multifaceted perspective of current and emerging theoretical models of psycho-therapy. Pluralism acknowledges and attends to the different levels and diversity of the human experience and the accompanying systems that operate with the client's worldview. Okum (1990, p. 407) maintained that pluralism allows for consideration of both the mind and body, conscious and unconscious, biology and culture, quantitative and qualitative, subjective and objective, masculine and feminine, insight and behavior, historical and ahistorical, directive and nondirective, autonomy and connectedness, content and process, linear and cybernetic causality, along with the other major polarities associated with the dichotomous thinking of the major models of psychotherapy. Pluralism opens up the possibilities of varying and different levels of human experience as well as possibilities of varying and different levels of therapeutic change. It acknowledges the equal value of the different models, takes personal preference into account, and encourages a careful assessment of what model is best utilized for what person with what problem in particular circumstances.

A pluralistic approach embraces the notion that many appropriate ways exist to treat a client; several different theoretical perspectives might explain the client's problem(s), and at least several different therapists could be effective for each client. Fundamentally, a therapeutic pluralistic approach accounts for diversity on the part of the client, the therapist, the treatment, and the theoretical rationale.

Many researchers have identified a major shift toward eclecticism in the practice of counseling and psychotherapy (Andrews, 1989; Corsini, 1989; Garfield & Bergin, 1986; Ivey & Simek-Downing, 1980; Kelly, 1988; Nance & Myers, 1991; Norcross & Prochaska, 1983; Simon, 1989; Smith, 1982). Yet, eclecticism was defined as a construct as early as 1958 by English and English: "Eclecticism in theoretical system building, is the selection and orderly combination of compatible features from diverse sources, sometimes from incompatible theories and systems; the effort to find valid elements in all doctrines or theories and to combine them into harmonious whole. The resulting system is open to constant revision even in its major outlines" (p. 18).

In 1982, Smith conducted a survey of 422 members of the American Psychological Association, and 41% identified their orientation as eclectic. Norcross and Prochaska (1983) found that 30% of their sample of members of the Division of Clinical Psychology declared an eclectic orientation. The rise in eclectic counseling is viewed by many as a constructive response to the wide range of client differences. Eclectic practice coincides with the current knowledge based on a growing body of empirical research that no one theoretical approach produces reliable counseling outcomes with a heterogeneous group of clients. Many researchers also have articulated the advantages of developing an eclectic approach (Brabeck & Welfel, 1985; Brammer & Shostrom, 1982; Rychlak, 1985) from the perspective that no single theory is comprehensive enough to be applicable to all individuals under all circumstances. Eclecticism reflects our growing knowledge of people and the dynamics of change in counseling. Nicholson and Berman (1983) have contended that "eclecticism is finally being appreciated for what it is—an essential perspective for dealing with the complexity of human problems" (p. 25). The research literature is filled with nomenclatures such as creative synthesis, emerging eclecticism, technical eclecticism, theoretical eclecticism, systematic eclecticism (Herr, 1989), pragmatic technical eclecticism (Keat, 1985), eclectic psychotherapy (Norcross, 1986), and 'adaptive counseling and therapy—an integrative eclectic model' (Howard, Nance, & Myers, 1986). For example, Simon (1989) distinguished between technical and theoretical eclecticism and suggested that general systems theory (GST) could provide the framework for pulling everything together. Simon (1991) defined technical eclecticism as a kind of eclecticism "based on the assumption that the primary task of an eclectic theory is to indicate in a systematic manner which particular intervention or style of intervening should be used in which particular counseling situation" (pp. 112–113). McBride and Martin (1990) proposed a "theoretical eclecticism" as opposed to "syncretism, or unsystematic, atheoretical eclecticism." Hershenson, Power, and Seligman proposed an "integrated-eclectic" model, a mental health counselor–specific eclecticism (1989a), and the need for a "skilled-based, empirically validated" model (1989b).

In addition, many counselors and therapists are eclectic in their use of theory and techniques. An eclectic approach is the reported emphasis of some 25% of counselor education programs nationwide (Hollis & Wantz, 1986). Lazarus (1985, 1993), Lazarus and Folkman (1984), and Lazarus and Mayne (1990) maintained that systematic, technical eclecticism offers by far the greatest promise for the future, both of practice and research.

From the diversity of eclectic and integrationist viewpoints, national and international societies, groups and professional associations of eclectic counselors and therapists have been formed, and journals are emerging that are devoted to the dissemination of systematic eclecticism (Lazarus & Mayne, 1990). However, embracing an eclectic approach to counseling and psychotherapy is not without its skeptics. Smith (1982) has cautioned: Although the eclectic model allows for openness and flexibility, it also encourages an indiscriminate selection of bits and pieces from diverse sources that results in a hodgepodge of inconsistent concepts and techniques.

Thus, rejecting a single-theory approach and adopting an eclectic stance does not always improve the therapist's intentions (p. 802). Slaveney and McHugh (1987) warned that eclecticism could promote a "methodological porridge in which all ideas are considered equivalent" (p. 4). Ward (1983) further argued for an integrative model of counseling: "Without guidelines to structure counseling and to govern the appropriate selection and applications of theoretical demands, strategies and techniques, the eclectic faces the danger of operating haphazardly, inconsistently, and less effectively than is desirable" (p. 154). In an attempt to address these concerns, Cavanagh (1982) proposed a "healthy" eclectic approach to counseling that requires the counselor to have (a) a sound knowledge and understanding of counseling theories, (b) an integrative philosophy of human behavior, and (c) a flexible means of fitting the approach to the client. The critical prerequisite skills for a well-informed and integrative eclectic counselor are both the mastery of theory and an acute perception of knowing what approach to use with whom.

Perhaps the greatest support for eclecticism comes from the recognition of the uniqueness and individuality of each client. Thus, according to Ivey and Simek-Downing (1980), the immense variety of clients faced in daily practice do not fit easily into theoretical pigeonholes. One client responds well to one approach, but another may resist the same techniques and leave counseling. Evidence is mounting that the professional of the future will require more than a single set of methodological and theoretical answers to meet the needs of an increasingly diverse clientele (p. 1). Fundamentally, no single theory can fully account for the myriad phenomena characterizing the range of human experiences. Within the context of contemporary society, a systematic eclectic approach may be a constructive response to a wide range of client differences. Counseling approaches and client outcomes can be viewed as a matrix of possible interactions with the mutual goal of personal well-being and interpersonal adjustment. Systematic eclecticism embraces the perspective that no single theory-bound approach has all the answers to all the needs that clients bring to the therapeutic setting. Eclectic practice should resemble a "systematic integration" of underlying principles and methods common to a wide range of therapeutic approaches, integrating the best features from multiple sources.

GOALS OF PSYCHOTHERAPY

Psychotherapy can be defined by its goals, its process (stages), its tools, and the principles for using those tools. Future-oriented psychotherapy's intent is to help patients do something positive for themselves after they leave the office. The goals of most psychotherapy relationships fall into six categories (Beitman, 1997):

1. *Crisis stabilization.* A person is distraught because his wife has suddenly left him for another man, for example.
2. *Symptom reduction.* A person has been depressed for several months, which is interfering with his work and social functioning.
3. *Long-term pattern change.* A woman repeatedly develops intimate relationships with abusive men.

4. *Maintenance of change, stabilization, and prevention of relapse.* A woman with a chronic medical disease, a disabled husband, and recurrent depressive episodes requires continuing support to help maintain current functioning.
5. *Self-exploration.* A person with reasonably good social and work functioning wants to understand himself more fully.
6. *Development of coping strategies to handle future problems.* A person learns to handle emotions that increase the likelihood of wanting to drink alcohol excessively but wants to generalize this coping strategy to other situations.

General Principles

Effective therapists seem to possess both a solid grounding in the basics of psychotherapy and a disciplined flexibility. Disciplined flexibility requires structured ways to adjust psychotherapeutic ideas to the therapist's personality as well as to the individualized needs of patients—to move easily, but prudently, among various strategies for change. *Theory and technique are molded to the individual personality of each therapist.* No matter how leaders of schools might attempt to create therapists who strongly resemble each other, most practitioners seem to adjust their selections of school-bound ideas to their own interpersonal styles and worldviews.

CRITICAL CLIENT VARIABLES

In the real world, the success of psychotherapy is anchored in the lives of the client's functioning and the strength of the client's social support networks. Several critical variables play a more important role than theory and technique in influencing the outcomes:

1. The client's readiness to change (Prochaska, DiClemente, & Norcross, 1992).
2. The nature and strength of the client's social network (Bankoff & Howard, 1992; Marziali, 1992; Moos, 1990).
3. Indexes of severity, chronicity, and complexity of symptoms; motivation; acceptance of personal responsibility for change; and defensive operations (Anderson & Lambert, 1995; Safran, Segal, Vallis, Shaw, & Samstag, 1993).
4. Strength of the working alliance between the client and the therapist (Horvath & Greenberg, 1994).
5. Number of sessions (Howard, Orlinsky, & Lueger, 1994; Lambert, 1996).
6. Perseverance, depth of affective experiencing, specific problem versus pervasive problem, and acute difficulties versus chronic problems, well-established correlates of potential client improvement (Robertson, 1995).

Theory and technique are also shaped by the cultural context in which the therapy is being practiced. Psychotherapy is strongly influenced by its sociopolitical context and may sometimes influence the culture in which it grows. *Therapists adjust to influences patients bring to the psychotherapy relationship.* Generally, therapists strive to match client characteristics and problems with the most potentially effective interventions rather than attempting to force patients into therapist-imposed restrictive formats. *Effective therapists learn to move easily among the commonly accepted change strategies.* Three meta-strategies guide the application of change strategies.

1. Key-change strategy: Sometimes the available evidence suggests that one strategy offers the quickest, most efficient avenue to change.
2. Shifting-change strategy: Therapy begins with the most easily used change strategy. If it is not effective, the therapist switches to another strategy.
3. Maximum-impact strategy: With some complex cases, therapists must work simultaneously on several patterns.

Instead of hoping for a sequential effect, therapists may need to work for a synergistic effect, as multiple changes mass together to bring about a desired state. The use of these strategies relies on the principle of using the least amount of energy to produce the greatest output (Prochaska & Prochaska, 1994). *Effective therapists reflect on and analyze their own thinking*: Effective therapists seem to reflect upon their own responses to patients to differentiate their own neurotic responses from patient-induced ones. They attempt to use this understanding to help patients and also to help themselves grow as individuals and as therapists. Overall, the guiding strategy of psychotherapists is an ethical one: Everything therapists do is intended to help their patients (Prochaska & Prochaska, 1994).

In summary, the resourceful, responsive, and responsible therapist of the next millennium would have within his or her therapeutic repertoire a full spectrum of counseling techniques and educational therapies to meet the demands of an increasingly diverse clientele. This perspective supports the observations of Garfield and Bergin (1986): "A decisive shift in opinion has quietly occurred; and it has created an irreversible change in professional attitudes about psychotherapy and behavior change. The new view is that the long-term dominance of the major theories is over and that an eclectic position has taken precedence. I would go even further and state that all good therapists are eclectic" (p. 7).

Perhaps the greatest outcome from this quiet revolution in counseling and psychotherapy is the shifting paradigm of openness and receptiveness to new approaches and creative integration of past and future perspectives. New theoretical developments are occurring that should be integrated into our theoretical frameworks, such as the following:

- Guidano and Liotti's (1983) constructivist cognitive therapy, which integrates cognitive and attachment theories.
- Greenberg and Safran's (1987) information-processing theory of affective experiencing and change processes.
- Ivey's (1986, 1989, 1990) and Ivey and Goncalves's (1988) cognitive-developmental theory of counseling and human development. In the developmental counseling and theory (DCT) model, personality styles or disorders are seen as generated in a life-span development context and reflect the logical result of failed developmental progression (Ivey & Rigazio-DiGilio, 1991).
- Attneave's (1990) network model, which recognizes that an individual's change can best occur when family and larger systems support that change—the critical roles of social networks, culture, gender, and value orientations of the client network need to change for optimum success.

To integrate or clarify counseling theories, a more germane approach may be to look at the new and unfamiliar rather than to embrace the past. Freud, Skinner, Perls, and Rogers are perhaps best regarded as important historical referents rather than absolute guides to counseling practice. Freud was more interested in developing a theory of mind than a model of therapy; Rogers brought empathy and interpersonal relationships into a therapist's repertoire; Ellis and Beck focused on cognitions and irrational thinking; and Perls brought emotion and integration into the context of counseling and psychotherapy. In Sexton and Whiston's (1991) review of the empirical basis for counseling, they found little evidence that adhering to a theoretical model was related to client change. Counseling theories may assist counselors in organizing information, but those same theories do not substitute for an understanding of the elements of the counseling process and the ability to implement appropriate strategies to best meet client needs.

CONCLUSION

There is a professional obligation to ensure that every client receives optimal benefits from therapeutic services. Planned, systematic clinical approaches with accountable outcomes must be the therapeutic norm rather than the therapeutic exception. Perhaps more important, however, we must relinquish the present competition among helping professionals. Negative competition and defensiveness are not helpful to the professional practitioner or to the client consumer. Interdisciplinary collaboration and the acceptance of individual diversity will create a climate of openness and growth for all who embrace the helping relationship and the responsibilities that come with it.

Further, a mature counseling profession has entered the millennium. Several factors—including professionalism, accountability, credentialism, health care consumerism, and public demands for quality mental health care—indicate a need for more definitive statements or standards of practice in counseling. In response to this need. Anderson (1992) identified five discernable forces influencing the counseling profession: (1) a growing demand for quality mental health counseling, (2) increasing public awareness of specific issues in mental health care and general health care consumerism, (3) increasing demands for quality assurance, accountability, and containment of mental health care costs, (4) progressing state-by-state wave of credentialism and licensure, and (5) increasing national emphasis on counselor professionalism. Existing laws, standards of practice, and codes of ethics have shaped the expectations and views that counselors have professional conduct (Anderson, 1992, p. 22). Gibson and Mitchell (1990) maintained, "A profession's commitment to appropriate ethical and legal standards are critical to the profession's earning maintaining and deserving the public's trust. Without this trust, a profession ceases to be a profession" (p. 451). At a minimum, comprehensive standards should include (1) professional disclosure statements, (2) treatment plans, (3) clinical notes, (4) formative evaluations, (5) documentation of consultation or supervision, (6) professional performance evaluation and peer review, (7) psychotherapy for impaired practitioners, and (8) awareness of and responsive to ethical and legal foundations of the profession (Anderson, 1992, p. 22).

Chapter 2

Client-Therapist Relationships

COUNSELING INTENTIONS, INTERVENTIONS, AND THERAPEUTIC FACTORS

> *We all have a load; and we have to work with the load we've got,*
> *with the way we are. We could all use some time to think about*
> *ourselves. The routine time is fifty minutes, but that's ten minutes of*
> *getting started, twenty minutes of therapeutic alliance, ten minutes*
> *of work, and ten minutes of preparation to get back to reality.*
>
> Elvin Semrad, *The Heart of a Therapist*, 1983, p. 101

INTRODUCTION

Within the therapeutic relationship, counselors and therapists often provide assistance in a short amount of time with the presenting problem remediated contingent upon the client's resources and the degree of counselor's expertise. For the most part, counselors and therapists find themselves gathering information, exploring feelings, generating alternatives, or merely providing unconditional support in a safe and secure environment. Budman (1981) concisely outlined the universal components of the therapeutic process as:

- Naming the problem.
- Meeting client expectation.
- Establishing counselor credibility.
- Techniques for relief.

Sexton and Whiston (1991) provided a conceptual three component model of counseling. Their model consists of (1) existing factors, that is, those characteristics clients and counselors bring to counseling such as race, sex, and psychological characteristics; (2) counseling process; and (3) intended outcome. Their model evolved after reviewing over 120 studies and significant meta-analysis (Lambert, Shapiro, & Bergin 1986; Luborsky, Crits-Christoph, Mintz, & Auerbach, 1988) in an effort to assess trends related to counseling that may be important to practitioners, students, and counselor educators.

Of all the characteristics in the model, the counseling process is perhaps the most critical. It begins with the relationship between counselor and client upon which organizational and experiential elements of the counseling session, as well as specific techniques and interventions, are based (Sexton & Whiston, 1991, p. 331). The existing factors and the counseling process result in the intended outcome of counseling—client action and behavioral change. Sexton and Whiston (1991) stressed that counseling effectiveness should be defined by the ability of an element in the counseling process to effect the client's change according to research that is data based.

Fuhriman and Burlingame (1990) conducted a formidable and exhaustive meta-analysis of 167 studies comparing individual and group process research. They found broad therapeutic themes and dimensions in individual and group process. They termed their quest as a "comparative odyssey and a clearer realization of the commonalities and similarities of individual and group treatment of client maladies" (p. 36). The core therapeutic dimension capsulated focuses on the differences and similarities in group and individual counseling on the following dimensions: interactive client-therapist relationships, therapeutic interventions, and therapeutic factors. This is followed by factors that promote the efficacy of group counseling, curative factors in the group process, and counselor-therapist intentions in the counseling/therapeutic process. From these distinct dimensions are specific attributes that differentiate individual and group process.

INTERACTIVE CHARACTERISTICS
OF THE CLIENT-THERAPIST RELATIONSHIP

Characteristics That Are the Same for Individual and Group

The therapeutic relationship is the core of the helping process. The following characteristics are the same for both the individual and the group process. Relationships are reciprocal and collaborative. The importance of the counseling relationship is supported by empirical literature (Luborsky et al., 1988). The client's involvement in the counseling process (Kolb, Beutler, Davis, Crago, & Shanfield,

1985), the client's openness in the relationship with the counselor, and the client's warmth and acceptance of the therapist are significantly related to positive or productive outcomes (Bent, Putman, Kiesler, & Nowicki, 1976).

> ***Reciprocity.*** Reciprocity is manifested through warmth, role implementation, comfortableness, trust, openness, expression of feelings, liking, respect, positive regard, and interpersonal attributes (Fuhriman & Burlingame, 1990; Ohlsen, Horne, & Lawe, 1988; Orlinsky & Howard, 1986).
>
> ***Engagement.*** Extent of engagement, involvement, and commitment by client and therapist is a contributing factor to the bonding component of the relationship. Substantial evidence supports therapists and client's engagement as a central construct of the therapeutic relationship (Fuhriman & Burlingame, 1990; Orlinsky & Howard, 1986).
>
> ***Transference.*** With transference, the client responds to the therapist as though he or she were a significant figure in the client's past, frequently a parent. Both individual and group processes use the construct of transference as a significant variable of the therapeutic relationship. Transference can be positive or negative. Transference and counter-transference of the therapist also are important constructs.

Characteristics That Are Unique to the Group Experience

The group is a social microcosm. The alliances between group members, between members and the therapist, and between the member and the group as a total unit yield multiple possibilities.

> ***Cohesion.*** Cohesion is a multidimensional, interactive construct that has a curative influence in the group. Researchers have conceptualized cohesion as acceptance, unity, tolerance, support, attractiveness, liking, affection, involvement, belonging, solidarity, closeness, attention, and acceptance. (Fuhriman & Bulingame, 1990, p. 23)

Fuhriman and Burlingame (1990) found more empirical support for directive interventions efficaciously on the process and outcome of treatment. Evidence is clear that after a certain minimum level of activity, the content, meaningfulness, and client's personality characteristics supersede a simple baserate explanation for the efficacy for an intervention. Interventions and activities aimed at stimulating or facilitating one or more therapeutic factors (e.g., self-disclosure, insight, catharsis) mediate client improvement (p. 38).

THERAPIST INTENTIONS: EIGHTEEN THERAPEUTIC CHARACTERISTICS

Within the therapeutic relationship, counselors and therapists want to provide assistance effectively and efficiently. For the most part, counselors find themselves gathering information, exploring feelings, generating alternatives, or merely providing support in a secure environment. One means that counselors and therapists might use to clarify their intended purpose and to provide a focus for interventions could revolve around Hill and O'Grady's (1985) 18 therapeutic intentions:

1. *Set limits.* To structure, make arrangements, establish goals and objectives of treatment, and outline methods.
2. *Get information.* To find out specific facts about history, client functioning, future plans, and present issues.
3. *Give information.* To educate, give facts, correct misperceptions or misinformation, and give reasons for procedures or client behavior.
4. *Support.* To provide a warm, supportive, empathic environment; to increase trust and rapport so as to build a positive relationship and to help client feel accepted and understood.
5. *Focus.* To help counselee get back on track, change subject, and channel or structure the discussion if he or she is unable to begin or has been confused.
6. *Clarify.* To provide or solicit more elaboration; emphasize or specify when client or counselor has been vague, incomplete, confusing, contradictory, or inaudible.
7. *Hope.* To convey the expectations that change is possible and likely to occur; convey that the therapist will be able to help the client; restore morale, and build the client's confidence to make changes.
8. *Catharsis.* To promote a relief from tension or unhappy feelings; allow the client a chance to talk through feelings and problems.
9. *Cognitions.* To identify maladaptive, illogical, or irrational thoughts or attitudes (e.g., "I must perform perfectly").
10. *Behaviors.* To identify and give feedback about the client's inappropriate or maladaptive behaviors and/or their consequences; to do a behavioral analysis, point out discrepancies.
11. *Self-control.* To encourage the client to own or gain a sense of mastery or control over his or her own thoughts, feelings, behaviors, or actions; help the client become more appropriately internal in taking responsibility.
12. *Feelings.* To identify, intensify, and/or enable acceptance of feelings; encourage or provoke the client to become aware of deeper underlying feelings.
13. *Insight.* To encourage understanding of the underlying reasons, dynamics, assumptions, or unconscious motivations for cognitions, behaviors, attitudes, or feelings.
14. *Change.* To build and develop new and more adaptive skills, behaviors, or cognitions in dealing with self and others.

15. *Reinforce change.* To give positive reinforcement about behavioral, cognitive, or affective attempts to enhance the probability of change; to provide an opinion or assessment of client functions.
16. *Resistance.* To overcome obstacles to change or progress.
17. *Challenge.* To jolt the client out of a present state; shake up current beliefs, patterns, or feelings; test validity, adequacy, reality, or appropriateness.
18. *Relationship.* To resolve problems; build or maintain a smooth working alliance; heal ruptures; deal with dependency issues; uncover and resolve distortions.

Other important intentions include:

1. *Objectivity.* To have sufficient control over feelings and values so as not to impose them on the client.
2. *Implementation.* To help the client put insight into action.
3. *Structure.* To structure the ongoing counseling sessions so that continuity exists from session to session.
4. *Inconsistencies.* To identify and explore with the client contradiction within and/or between client behaviors, cognitions, and/or affect.
5. *Goals.* To establish short- and long-range goals congruent with the client's potential.
6. *Flexibility.* To change long- and short-term goals within a specific session or during the overall counseling process as additional information becomes available.
7. *Behavioral change.* To develop specific plans, that can be observed, for changing the client's behavior(s).
8. *Homework.* To assign work to the client to reinforce change.
9. *Problem solving.* To teach the client a method for problem solving.

Hill, Helms, Spiegal, and Tichenor (1988) followed through on the initial efforts of Hill and O'Grady (1985), which delineated counselor intention, by providing client reactions to support their initial proposal. These responses were gathered after immediate intervention rather than reporting on more global strategies or reactions for the session. Client reactions were as follows:

> *Supported:* "I felt accepted and liked by my counselor."
> *Understood:* "I felt that my counselor really understood me and knew what I was saying or what was going on with me."
> *Hopeful:* "I felt confident, encouraged, and optimistic; like I could change."
> *Relief:* "I felt less depressed, anxious, or angry."
> *More clear:* "I got more focused about what I was really trying to say."
> *Feelings:* "I felt a greater awareness of or deepening of feelings or was able to express myself in a more emotional way."

Negative thoughts or behavior: "I became aware of specific thoughts or behaviors that cause problems for me or others."

Better understanding: "I realized or understood something new about myself, which helped me accept and like myself better."

Took responsibility: "I felt more responsibility for myself, blamed others less, and realized my part in things."

Challenged: "I felt shook up, forced to question myself, or challenged to look at issues I had been avoiding."

Got unstuck: "I felt freed up and more involved in what I was doing in counseling."

New perspective: "I got a new understanding of another person, situation, or the world."

Educated: "I gained a greater knowledge or information or learned something I didn't know."

Learned new ways to behave: "I got specific ideas about what I can do differently to cope with particular situations or problems."

Miscommunication: "I felt that my counselor didn't really hear me, or understand me. I felt confused or puzzled about what my counselor was trying to say. I felt distracted from what I was saying."

Felt worse about myself: "I felt sicker, more depressed, out of control, dumb, incompetent, ashamed, or self-conscious. I worried that my counselor would disapprove or not be pleased with me or like me. I wanted to avoid something painful. I was overwhelmed about what might happen."

Felt a lack of direction: "I felt that my counselor didn't give enough guidance. I felt impatient, bored, or dissatisfied with having to go over the same thing again"

Ineffective counselor intervention: "I felt attacked, criticized, judged, ignored, put down, or hurt by my counselor. I felt angry, upset, or disturbed about what my counselor was or was not doing. I questioned my counselor's ability or judgment. I felt pressured because my counselor was too directive and wanted things to go a certain way. I felt doubtful or disagreed with what my counselor said."

No particular reaction: "I didn't have a particularly positive or negative reaction to the counselor's statement. The counselor's statement was too short or unclear for me to react. I thought the statement was social conversation." (Hill, Helms, Spiegal, & Tichenor, 1988, pp. 257–306)

THERAPEUTIC INTERVENTIONS: STRATEGIES THAT ARE THE SAME FOR INDIVIDUAL AND GROUP PROCESSES

Therapeutic interventions consist of therapist and client actions intended to facilitate the change process and therapeutic factors in counseling and psychotherapy.

Outcome is enhanced when clients develop a problem-solving attitude (O'Malley, Suh, & Strupp, 1983) and become actively engaged in experiences that help them master problematic situations (Luborsky et al., 1988). Lambert et al. (1986) found that counselors who let the client ramble did not focus the counseling session, and failed to integrate these issues and themes into counseling contributed to negative client outcomes. Sexton and Whiston (1991) also reported that 50% of the benefit of counseling seems to occur within the first 6 months of weekly sessions in which the client was involved, developed a problem-solving attitude and learned to master problematic situations in his or her life, and experienced a wide range of emotions while maintaining a positive expectation for change.

Confrontation. Confrontations focus attention on discrepancies between verbal and nonverbal behavior. Empirical evidence from both individual and group research reveals that confrontations are consistently associated with client improvement.

Interpretation. Interpretative intervention is normative and prescriptive in individual and group treatment and is defined as explanatory interventions to provide clients with insight. The overall effectiveness also may be a function of how interpretations interact with other variables such as content focus, patient characteristics, and timing (Beutler, Crago, & Arizmendi, 1986; Fuhriman & Burlingame, 1990; Orlinsky & Howard, 1986).

Content focus. The therapist is perceived as responsible for the topical boundaries of therapist-client interactions, with support in the literature for focusing on client affect, cognition, and the therapeutic relationship. Content focus on the here-and-now receives more conceptual attention in group treatment.

Concrete rationale. Concrete rationale focuses on the importance of conveying a concrete rationale, including a vocabulary for defining and describing client problems and pregroup preparation.

Guidance. Guidance and advice giving in both individual and group context receives mixed reviews in the literature, from highly valued to less valued.

Therapist self-disclosure. Disclosure of a personal fact or experience by the therapist is often a technique to maintain therapist transparency; however, it is viewed as less appropriate when clients are more psychologically impaired.

Exploration. Exploration in the form of probes is an intervention to collect information and to focus on important aspects of the client's experience. Fuhriman and Burlingame (1990, p. 34) found in group studies that exploratory interventions are most often incorporated into investigations of group structure where high-structure conditions include not only experiential activities but also more directive interventions such as focused questions and probes.

Reflection. Reflection as an intervention involves repeating or rephrasing of the client's statement or nonverbal manifestations to clarify communication and to check for understanding.

Encouragement. Encouragement is used to establish and to maintain the supportive alliance of the therapeutic relationship, can range from minimal encouragers to more direct maneuvers of support, approval, and encouragement.

Experiential activities. Interventions can be advanced as a "novel" means of fostering client improvement.

Pretherapy activities. Pretherapy activities, a growing professional trend advocated in both individual and group therapy, provide pretherapy preparation exercises that train the client to participate in treatment more effectively. Role preparation appears to affect early therapeutic processes positively and also seems to be linked to later client improvement (Fuhriman & Burlingame, 1990, p. 36).

Within-therapy activities. The analysis of the impact of specific within-therapy activities for both individual and group therapy are not easily clarified. Fuhriman & Burlingame (1990), however, cited a number of studies that reveal that therapeutic structure is preferred: (1) for clients who are severely disturbed (Dies, 1983), (2) for more dependent and externally oriented clients (Bednar & Kaul, 1978; Dies, 1983; Stockton & Morran, 1982), and (3) at early stages of treatment to negotiate particular developmental factors (Bedner & Kaul, 1978; Dies, 1983; Stockton & Morran, 1982, pp. 47–68).

THERAPEUTIC FACTORS

Common Factors in Individual and Group Processes

Therapeutic factors are the mainstay of the therapeutic process. According to Garfield and Bergin (1986), research indicates that counseling effectiveness can be explained best by "common factors," variables shared by many approaches and exhibited by a variety of skilled counselors and therapists regardless of their therapeutic school:

Insight. Insight is an integral process in both individual and group process where the client makes connections between new information generated in therapy and present circumstances.

Catharsis. Catharsis is a significant therapeutic process in both individual and group treatment. The nomenclature is synonymous with emotional ventilation, affective arousal, and release of tension, and it is sometimes used synonymously with abreaction.

Reality testing. Reality testing as feedback and confrontation is significantly and positively associated to the client's outcome. The impact of feedback and confrontation, however, may differ in individual and group therapy. Bloch and Crouch (1985) maintained that "group therapy is unique in providing a forum for the mutual exchange of honest, explicit feedback. By contrast, feedback in individual therapy can only come from an authority figure—a radically different experience than from one's peers" (p. 51).

Hope. The instillation of hope and the expectation for improvement are the catalysts of the therapeutic process. Hope is also a variable that interacts with client improvement and premature termination. The instillation of hope is magnified by the vicarious learning that occurs in the group experience.

Disclosure. Self-disclosure is a prerequisite for growth and change. In regard to the group experience, Fuhriman and Burlingame (1990) cite Stockton and Morran's (1982) research, which documented that client self-disclosure is related to (1) reciprocal disclosures from other members, (2) greater liking and attraction, (3) higher levels of cohesion, and (4) a more positive self-concept.

Identification. Identification involves relating oneself to others, resulting in a perception of increased similarity. The process of clients identifying with their therapist emerges as a primary ingredient in all theoretical orientations; the client can relinquish old values or behaviors and replace them with new values based on their inherent identification with the therapist. At the group level, client identification with both the therapist and other group members fosters greater client improvement.

Factors Unique to the Group Process

Fuhriman and Burlingame (1990, p. 47) proposed four putative sources of learning unique to group treatment: (1) participating in a developing social microcosm, (2) giving and receiving feedback in the group, (3) consensually validating, and (4) reciprocal functioning of members in the group.

Vicarious learning. Learning by observing others (or the process) often termed "spectator therapy," has a unique and potent therapeutic aspect for the group process. Vicarious learning that occurs when members observe the therapist perform a difficult social interaction is often helpful in groups of shorter duration.

Role flexibility. The group process provides members greater role flexibility because they can reciprocally function as helper and helpseeker. Fuhriman and Burlingame (1990, p. 49) conceptualized three consequences of role flexibility in group treatment: (1) enhancement of a member's self-esteem from responsible contributions to the therapeutic process, (2) dilution of the therapist power base so the client does not stay in a "one down" position with the therapist, and (3) attribution of change to self resulting in a healthier organization of treatment effects.

Universality. Universality is based on the notion that others are struggling with similar issues, that "we all are in the same boat," and that one's experiences are not unique. Universality is the most highly valued therapeutic factor in self-help groups.

Altruism. Altruism consists of unselfishly offering support, reassurance, suggestions, and insights to group members. Caring for others also empowers clients to relinquish their own self-absorption in exchange for curative factors of helping others. Altruism also has more therapeutic attributions in self-help groups.

Family reenactment. The group experience provides a microcosm of interpersonal interaction that resembles one's family. The group fosters an environment where a member can correctively relive and rework early familial conflicts. Yalom (1985) outlined several aspects of the group experience that resemble one's family of origin: male-female cotherapists (parental authority figures), member-member rivalry for therapist attention (sibling rivalry), and individual client-therapist interactions (early parental interaction patterns). Kerr and Bowen (1988) maintained that the family is always being dealt with even when just one person is present.

Interpersonal learning. Interpersonal learning involves clients' increasing their ability to socialize with others, and to behaviorally and attitudinally adapt to interaction within the group. Individuals who stay in a group longer may have more time to experience opportunities for social skill acquisition, which group therapy is uniquely capable of providing (Fuhriman & Burlingame, 1990, p. 51).

Yalom (1985) and Hansen, Warner, and Smith (1980), as well as others, also have stressed the "curative" and "therapeutic factors" responsible for producing change in productive groups:

Development of social skills. The development and rehearsal of basic social skills is a therapeutic factor that is universal to all counseling groups.

Imitative behavior. Group members learn new behaviors by observing the behavior of the leader and other members.

Group cohesiveness. Group membership offers participants an arena to receive unconditional positive regard, acceptance, and belonging that enables members to fully accept themselves and be congruent in their relationships with others.

Catharsis. Learning how to express emotion reduces the use of debilitating defense mechanisms.

Existential factors. As group members face the fundamental issues of their life, they learn that they are ultimately responsible for the way they live, no matter how much support they receive from others.

When trying to compare individual and group techniques, it is important to remember that other variables influence both modalities. These variables include the differences among therapists, clients, techniques, and interventions. From the perspective of accountability, it may become necessary to control for theoretical approach, counseling intervention, coping skills on the part of the client, and therapist style before the individual and group process can be validated. Nonetheless, a compendium of strategies, techniques, and divergent approaches are a beginning.

GROUP-FOCUSED FACILITATION SKILLS

Many helping professionals want to be able to identify group-helping behaviors to provide structure for service delivery. Gill and Barry (1982) provided a more comprehensive classification of counseling skills for the group process. Such a classification system can assist the therapist or counselor by delineating an organized, operational definition of group-focused facilitation skills. A classification of specific group focused facilitation skills has a number of significant benefits such as clear objectives, visible procedures, competency-based accountability, and measurable outcomes.

Researchers have classified group counseling skills from their own group counseling experiences. Ivey (1973) proposed a taxonomy of group skills consisting of ten skills appropriate to both individual and group counseling. He added four "phases" of skill focus: group, individual, self, and topic. Lieberman, Yalom, and Miles (1973) generated a list of what they considered to be critical group facilitation skills under the auspices of four basic leadership functions: emotional stimulation, caring, meaning attribution, and executive function.

Dyer and Vriend (1977) identified 20 behaviors for group leaders that could be viewed as important competencies for counselors both in one-to-one interactions and in a group setting. Ohlsen (1977) outlined a classification system of 10 facilitative behaviors for group leaders. Many of these earlier classification systems evolved from experiential rather than empirical data, with group leaders using individual counseling techniques to help one person at a time within a group setting. Gill and Barry (1982) recommended a more group-focused classification system, providing a more practical and integrative framework of what should be done. They outlined specific behaviors that are appropriate, operational, developmentally related, group-focused, and composed of progressive interdependent stages.

Gill and Barry (1982) proposed that if counselors wish to use the group as a medium for learning and change, dynamics such as group member interaction, group support, group decision making and group problem solving should receive greater emphasis. They suggested the following criteria for building a system of group-focused counseling skills:

Appropriate. The behavior can reasonably be attributed to the role and function of a group counselor.

Definable. The behavior can be described in terms of human performances.

Observable. Experienced as well as inexperienced observers can identify the behavior when it occurs. The behavior can be repeated by different people in different settings.

Measurable. Objective recording of both the frequency and quality of the behavior can occur with a high degree of agreement among observers.

Developmental. The behavior can be placed within the context of a progressive relationship with other skills, all contributing to movement of the group toward its goals. The effectiveness of behaviors at one stage in the counseling process is dependent on the effectiveness of the skills used at earlier stages.

Group-focused. The target of the behavior is either the group or more than one participant. The behavior is often related to an interaction between two or more participants. The purpose of the group is to facilitate multiple interactions among participants to encourage shared responsibility for helping, to promote participation, or to invite cooperative problem solving and decision making. (Gill & Barry, 1982, pp. 304–305)

Waldo (1985) further differentiated the curative factor framework when planning activities in structured groups. In a six-session structured group, activities can be arranged in relation to the group's development so that group dynamics can foster curative factors:

Session 1: Establishing goals and ground rules (installation of hope) and sharing perceptions about relationships (universality).

Session 2: Identification of feelings about the past, present, and future relationships (catharsis, family reenactment).

Session 3: Demonstrating understanding of other group members' feelings (cohesion).

Session 4: Feedback between group members (altruism).

Session 5: Confrontation and conflict resolution between group members (interpersonal learning).

Session 6: Planning ways group members can continue to improve relations with others, and closure (existential factors).

Each session involves lectures and reading materials (imparting information), demonstrations by the leader (initiative behavior), and within and between meeting exercises (social skills and techniques) (Waldo, 1985, p. 56). This model provides a conceptual map that can be used for structured groups on conflict resolution, decision making, interpersonal relations, or any intervention that needs to be structured to educate, learn, and integrate important life skills.

THE EFFECTIVENESS OF PSYCHOTHERAPY

Perspective for the Therapist: On the wisdom of Freud

Look into the depths of your own soul and learn first to know yourself, then you will understand why this illness was bound to come upon you and perhaps you will thenceforth avoid falling ill.

Sigmund Freud, *One of Difficulties of the Psychoanalysis:*
Collected Papers (1924–1950)

Seligman (1995) maintained that clients benefited substantially from psychotherapy, that long-term treatment did considerably better than short-term treatment, and that psychotherapy alone did not differ in effectiveness from medication plus psychotherapy. Furthermore, no specific modality of psychotherapy did better than any other for any disorder. Lambert (1992) and Asay and Lambert (1999) estimated that only 15% of change can be attributed to specific techniques used by various therapies; the other 85% of clients' improvement can be attributed to factors such as the therapeutic relationship, placebo effects, and other client factors. Further, Seligman revealed that an "effectiveness" study of how patients fare under the actual conditions of treatment in the field can yield useful and credible "empirical validation" of psychotherapy and medication. There were a number of clear-cut results, among them:

- Treatment by a mental health professional usually worked. Most respondents got a lot better.
- Averaged over all mental health professionals, of the 426 people who were feeling *very poor* when they began therapy, 87% were feeling *very good, good,* or at least *so-so* by the time of the survey. Of the 786 people who were feeling *fairly poor* at the outset, 92% were feeling *very good, good,* or at least *so-so* by the time of the survey. These findings converge with a meta-analysis of efficacy (Lipsey & Wilson, 1993; Shapiro & Shapiro, 1982).
- Long-term therapy produced more improvement than short-term therapy. This was true for patients both in psychotherapy alone and in psychotherapy plus medication. There was no difference between psychotherapy alone and psychotherapy plus medication for any disorder.

- Although all mental health professionals appeared to help their patients, psychologists, psychiatrists, and social workers did equally well and better than marriage counselors.
- Family doctors did just as well as mental health professionals in the short term, but worse in the long term. Some patients saw both family doctors and mental health professionals, and those who saw both had more severe problems.
- Long-term treatment by a mental health professional was advantageous not only for the specific problems that led to treatment, but also for the ability to relate to others, coping with everyday stress, enjoying life more, personal growth and understanding, and self-esteem and confidence.
- Alcoholics Anonymous (AA) did especially well, and significantly better than mental health professionals. People who went to non-AA groups had less severe problems and did not do as well as those who went to AA.
- Active shoppers and active clients did better in treatment than passive recipients.
- No specific modality of psychotherapy did any better than any other for any problem. These results confirm that all forms of psychotherapies do about equally well (Luborsky, Singer, & Luborsky, 1975).

These findings are significant because the research provided empirical validation of the effectiveness of psychotherapy. It revealed the efficacy of self-help groups such as AA, the determination of clients actively seeking therapy, as well as the importance of long-term therapy.

GOOD THERAPISTS' VIEWS OF HOW THEY ARE HELPFUL

Therapists' reflections on how they are helpful to their clients focused on the personal domains of interpersonal and relational and less on the cognitive domains of theoretical and technical abilities. The strength of the therapeutic alliance between therapist and client is the most powerful predictive factor for a positive outcome in psychotherapy. Coady (1991) found that there was more explicit recognition that therapist characteristics and behaviors interact with client characteristics and behaviors to determine the quality of the relationship. Therapist attributes such as warmth, friendliness, and empathy are important catalysts to positive change on the part of the client. Other common factors include the therapeutic alliance, empathy and support, positive expectations about therapy, emotional catharsis, problem exploration and insight, exposure and confrontation of the problem, and learning of new behaviors (Grencavage & Norcross, 1990).

Coady (1996) concluded that therapist helpfulness consisted of five general themes which consisted of a total of 34 categories as listed in Table 2.1. These categories embody the importance of basic values (e.g., acceptance, self-determination, respect), basic interviewing skills (e.g., attending), and basic rela-

TABLE 2.1
Good Therapists' View of How They Are Helpful

Themes and Categories

1. Exhibit Personal/Professional Qualities of Self
  Authentic and honest
  Caring and empathic
  Curious and interested
  Humorous
  Attentive and intuitive
  Non-impositional
  Accepting and nonjudgmental

2. Emphasize Development of Therapeutic Relationship
  Value relationship development with clients
  Develop an atmosphere of safety
  Follow client's pacing
  Encourage collaboration
  View clients as equals
  View each client and problem as unique
  View therapy as mutual growth experience
  Personally empathize with client issues
  Establish parameters for termination

3. Focus on Client Empowerment
  Maintain strengths perspective of clients
  Refrain from fixing client problems
  Encourage client self-determination
  View therapy as a small part of clients' lives

4. Attend to Impact of Self
  Critically evaluate own impact
  Guard against imposition of own agenda
  Monitor appropriate personal/professional boundaries
  Seek client feedback

5. Apply Therapeutic Strategies/Interventions
  Normalize client problems
  Maintain focus on feelings
  Use self-disclosure
  Explore influence of larger systems
  Address basic needs first
  Present ideas/suggestions tentatively
  Become more directive in crisis situations
  Help client to develop self-awareness
  Abandon what is not working
  Draw on a range of therapeutic models and techniques

Source: Coady, N. A reflective/inductive model of practice: Emphasizing theory building for unique cases versus applying theory to practice. In G. Rogers (Ed.), *Social work field education: Views and visions* (p. 139–151). Dubuque, IA: Kendall/ Hunt. (Reprinted with permission)

tionship skills (e.g., empathy, authenticity). It is evident that such factors are central to the development of a strong therapeutic alliance. Therapists' emphasis on the importance of skills and attitudes that build good human relationships fits with client reports of what is most helpful in therapy (Coady, 1996).

In addition, at a minimum, a comprehensive standard for counseling and psychotherapy should include (1) a professional disclosure statement about what therapy can and cannot accomplish, (2) treatment plans along with benefits and limitations, (3) clinical progress notes and perhaps journal assignments for the client to review his or her own progress, (4) formative and summative evaluations, (5) documentation of consultation or supervision, (6) professional performance evaluation and peer review, (7) psychotherapy for impaired practitioners, and (8) awareness of and responsiveness to ethical and legal foundations of the profession (Anderson, 1992, p. 22).

CONCLUSION

Techniques presented in this book focus on improving relationships—relationships with ourselves, with our peers, with our families, and with our environment. Inevitably, clients engage in a relationship with a therapist because of current conflict or unfinished business with relationships in the past or the present. For example, we know that numerous dysfunctions or self-defeating ways of relating typically are learned in childhood:

• How to remain superficial.
• How to build facades.
• How to play interpersonal games.
• How to hide from ourselves and others.
• How to downplay risk in human relating.
• How to manipulate others (or endure being manipulated).
• How to hurt and punish others, if necessary. (Egan, 1975)

An important point to realize is that every behavior is a communication, and often behavior that is self-defeating or dysfunctional carries with it an underpinning of poor interpersonal relationships. This is acutely apparent when we examine the void in relationships among our young people today. The growing concern over adolescent suicide rates, alcohol and other drug abuse, alienation, depression, family dysfunction, teen pregnancy, gangs, and violence among American youth demonstrates the critical need for responsible adults to establish close, caring relationships with our young people. Children drop out of school because of poor relationships with teachers and authority. Children begin drinking when they start driving and dating because of the uncertainty and anxiety about interpersonal relationships with the opposite sex. Children have unintended pregnancies because of their need to have a relationship with someone who will depend on them. Children join gangs because of their need to belong and to have power and authority. Children attempt suicide because of difficulties in relating to others, feeling alone, and feeling depressed about either their relationships or lack of them. True, we are a technologically advanced society, but we are all walking around with broken hearts. This malady of poor relationships is pervasive and cuts through all ethnic, racial, and social strata. It is relentless, and it is devastating.

This book seeks to provide helping professionals with critical skills to assist their clients' interpersonal functioning. The focus is on improving relationships— with our peers, our families, our environment, and ourselves. Each technique is followed by the counseling intention and a description. The techniques in this book are not all-inclusive, but they do represent a beginning.

Chapter 3

Eclectic Techniques for Group Therapy

Many theorists such as Garfield and Bergin (1986), Corsini (1989), Andrews (1989), Kelly (1988), and Norcross (1986) collectively asserted that the rise of eclectic counseling and the development of meta-theoretical eclectic models are viewed as a pragmatic response to the wide range of client differences. Any single theory and associated counseling techniques are unlikely to be universally effective with increasingly diverse client populations that reflect an equally diverse array of support systems.

Group counseling is an interpersonal process where members explore themselves in relationship to others in an attempt to modify their attitudes and behavior. Reality testing within the group gives the individual a unique behavior-modifying experience. Carroll and Wiggins (1990, p. 25) identified general goals for helping members in the group:

- Become a better listener.
- Develop sensitivity and acceptance of others.
- Increase self-awareness and develop a sense of identity.
- Feel a sense of belonging and overcome feelings of isolation.
- Learn to trust others as well as self.
- Recognize and state areas of belief and values without fear of repression.
- Transfer what is learned in the group to the outside by accepting responsibility for solving one's own problems.

In broad terms, four types of groups can be identified: (1) support groups including self-help groups of all kinds, which offer relief as opposed to change; (2) psychoeducational or skill-building groups aimed to induce change in social, emotional, and cognitive skills; (3) interpersonal groups that attempt to change long-standing interpersonal or intrapersonal patterns and concerns; and (4) psychotherapy groups which focus on deeper disturbances in intrapsychic and/or interpersonal functioning.

According to Pollack and Slan (1995) a number of questions should be asked of group participants:

1. What kind of help do they need and want? Are they favorably disposed toward a group intervention?
2. Can they talk in the presence of others? Can they reveal themselves? Do they wish to?
3. Are they willing to help others by offering feedback as well as by receiving it?
4. Will they attend reliably?
5. Do they understand and accept limitations on social contact with other group members?
6. Are they willing to take risks?
7. Can they share the spotlight?
8. Can they tolerate the anxiety and tension that group work often elicits?
9. Do they accept the curative factors and goals of group therapy?

Scheidlinger (1995, 1997) revealed that within the group the therapeutic process, experiential factors (i.e., corrective emotional experience) and meaningful attributions (i.e., insight) work hand in hand: "(1) structuring the group's composition, time, meeting place, and remuneration procedures; (2) structuring the conduct of the sessions with reference to confidentiality, agenda, physical contact, therapeutic techniques (i.e., Gestalt exercises, role-play, rational-emotive techniques); empathically accepting and caring for each client, embedded with a belief in the client's potential for change and growth; (4) encouraging the open expression of feelings and concerns; (5) fostering a climate of tolerance and acceptance of variance in feelings and behaviors and on peer helping, coupled with a stress on self and interpersonal scrutiny and awareness in which all members are encouraged to participate; (6) controlling within acceptable limits the drive, expression, tension, and anxiety levels in individual patients; (7) controlling group-level manifestations (i.e., scapegoating, inappropriate contagion) in the interest of both individual clients and group morale; and (8) using verbal interventions ranging from simple observations through confrontation to interpretations, aimed at reality testing and at eliciting meaning and connections" (Scheidlinger, 1997, pp. 151–152).

R. Dies (1994) stresses "contracting" with group members to stem "fears of attack, embarrassment, emotion contagion and harmful effects" (p. 64). Some specifics of the contract include issues of confidentiality, extragroup interaction, and boundary issues. Early discussion of these expectations serves as an antidote to apprehension and increases client optimism for clinical improvement (R. Dies & K. Dies, 1993). Group members can establish control over their negative con-

cerns about group treatment and increase the feeling of group cohesion and com-
monality (R. Dies, 1994).

This chapter is a compilation of group counseling techniques that facilitate
group process, encourage self-awareness, and foster greater communication among
group members. Fuhriman and Burlingame (1990) found that directive interventions appeared to have more empirical evidence of efficacious effect on the process and outcome of treatment. Learning by observing others has a unique and
potent therapeutic aspect for the group process and often is termed spectator therapy.

Technique: *Risk Taking and Trust Building*

Counseling Intention   Trust building.

Description   For any group to be successful, there must exist a sufficient sense
of comfort among the individuals for them to speak freely without fear of attack,
to express opinions and values that they cherish without fear of being ridiculed.
One of the ways to overcome the fear of speaking out is to provide activities
whose primary purpose is to build cohesiveness within the group. Following the
risk-taking/trust-building activity, it is essential to process the experience, to draw
from the participants their feelings and thoughts about the activity.

> *Trust Fall:* Partners stand, one with his back turned, his arms extended side-
> ways, he falls backward and is caught by his partner. Reverse roles and
> repeat.
> *Trust Walk:* One partner closes her eyes and is led around blind—through
> and over things. Reverse roles and repeat (Canfield & Wells, 1976).
> *Trust Run:* Outside, one partner closes his eyes and is led by the other in a
> vigorous run. Reverse roles and repeat.
> *Tug-of-War:* Partners imagine a line between them on the floor and have a
> tug-of-war with an imaginary rope. One partner is to be pulled across the
> line.
> *Mirroring:* Partners stand facing each other. One becomes the mirror image
> of the other's bodily movements. With hands in front, palms toward part-
> ner, they move expressively. Then reverse roles and repeat.
> *Circle Pass:* Group participants stand in a tight circle. A volunteer or partici-
> pant who wants to develop additional trust in the group, is rolled around
> inside the circle.
> *Machine:* One at a time, each participant stands up and imitates a part of a
> machine, using his body for active parts and his voice for machine-like
> sounds. After one person is up, the next goes up, and so on. The facilitator
> can ask the machine to quicken or slow down.

Eye-Contact Chain: Participants form two lines, facing each other about a yard apart. They hold hands, and the persons at the two ends hold hands. This forms a chain similar to a bicycle chain. Without talking, everyone looks in the opposite person's eyes. The group takes one step to the right, then each looks the next person in the eyes. The group takes steps to the right until everyone has returned to the original position.

Personal Interview: Dyad members interview each other. A rule of thumb should be that any question one person asks, he or she should be willing to answer. Each person has the right to decline to answer any question with which he or she feels uncomfortable.

Technique: *Opening Activities for Beginning Groups*

Counseling Intention   To break the ice; to help participants get to know one another.

Description   The following activities provide a low-risk, structured activity to engage members in the process of getting to know one another.

Paired Introductions   Members pair in groups of two. Partners get to know each other and in turn introduce their partners to the group. Variations:

1. Partners get to know each other and instead of introducing each other to the group they join another pair of two and introduce their partners (this is sometimes less threatening).
2. The leader can limit the topics that individuals use to introduce themselves, such as, "Tell your partner about yourself without mentioning anything about family, job, or school."

One-Minute Autobiography   Members group in quartets. Using a timekeeper, each person is given one minute to tell about himself. Again, dialogues can be restricted (e.g., nothing about job, school, family, place of birth, or hobbies). Limits such as these move members into sharing their values, goals, attitudes, and beliefs rather than staying in the comfort of talking about jobs, family, and school.

Deeper Reaches   In groups of four, members are given five minutes each to share deeper reaches of themselves: In the first three minutes, tell others in your group what has brought you to this point in your life; one minute is used to describe your happiest moment; the last minute is used to answer questions from others. The leader may model disclosure for the group to increase their comfort level.

Long and Winding Road   Each person draws on a sheet of paper a picture of his life using stick figures and symbols (newsprint and colored markers can also be used). The road can be divided into developmental stages (childhood, adolescence, adulthood) depicting critical stepping stones in his or her life that brought him or her to where he or she is today.

Name Circle   Members sit in a large circle. The leader begins by stating the name of the person seated on his right, followed by her own name. The person to the leader's right repeats the leader's name, his own name, and adds the name of the person seated to his right. The process is repeated around the entire circle.

Known/Not Known   Sheets of paper or poster board are placed on the walls with headings of "Things I Know" and "Things I Want to Know" (about the content or purpose of the group). Nonverbally, members circulate around the room and write their concerns on the paper. Concerns are processed.

Technique: *Group Consensus on Where to Begin*

Counseling Intention   To provide a structure for the group as to where to begin (Dyer & Verend, 1977).

Description   As leader, define self-defeating behavior. Group members anonymously write on an index card a self-defeating behavior they would like to change. The leader collects completed cards and redistributes them, instructing members to take any card but their own. Members read their new card aloud and the group assigns a rating to the problem from 1 to 10 (1 = low/10 = high). The leader tallies and ranks the problems for the group. The highest collectively rated problem is identified. The individual who wrote it is identified, and the group counseling begins with the focus on that person's concerns.

> *Perspective for the Therapist: On risk taking*
>
> *The Dilemma*
> *To laugh is to risk appearing a fool.*
> *To weep is to risk appearing sentimental.*
> *To reach out for another is to risk involvement.*
> *To expose feelings is to risk rejection.*
> *To place your dreams before the crowd is to risk ridicule.*
> *To love is to risk not being loved in return.*

> *To go forward in the face of overwhelming odds is to risk failure.*
> *But risk must be taken because the greatest hazard in life is to risk*
> *nothing. The person who risks nothing does nothing, has nothing, is*
> *nothing. He may avoid suffering and sorrow, but he cannot learn,*
> *feel, change, grow or love.*
> > *Only a person who risks is free.*

> > Janet Rand
> > (Reprinted with permission)

Technique: *Affirmations of Trust*

Counseling Intention　To build physical, intellectual, and emotional trust.

Description　Each member is instructed to distribute as many statements from the "Trust Is" poem that best describe his or her trust in another member in the group—to write the other person's name, the number of applicable statements, and his or her own signature on a slip of paper and to give it to the member. Each member is instructed to do this for every other member of the group. Members can discuss their reactions to this experience and focus on its goals.

Technique: *Controlling and Influencing Communication*

Counseling Intention　To facilitate communication and confront issues of control, dominance, or resistance.

Description　Using a ball or other inanimate object, instruct group members that only the person in possession of the ball is permitted to speak. A member who wishes to say something must gesture nonverbally to the individual in possession of the ball to receive it. This exercise may be used either as an icebreaker or with focus topics such as reaction to the group experience, dealing with ambiguity, dealing with life stressors. Focus topics are limited. Members who control, influence, dominate, or withdraw from communication in the group also could be processed.

> *Perspective for the Therapist: Creating trust*
>
> *Trust must be developed during the early stage of the group. One of the best ways of building trust is to create a group climate characterized by respect for the opinions and feelings of the members. It is essential that members openly express their feelings concerning the degree of trust they experience in their group.*

> > Marianne Schneider Corey and Gerald Corey,
> > *Groups Process and Practice*, third edition, 1987, p. 123

Technique: *One-on-One Risk Taking on a Scale of 1-to-10*

Counseling Intention   To encourage group self-disclosure.

Description   Self-disclosure is a form of risk behavior that proceeds to different levels. Groups or individuals can explore their own risk boundaries by listing or exchanging disclosure statements on a scale of 1 to 10. An individual lists, or partners exchange a statement that represents an attempt to disclose feelings, emotions, attitudes, and experiences that represent a level of risk. Rank the levels of each statement on a scale from 1 to 10 (10 = high risk, 1 = no risk).

Technique: *After Death*

Counseling Intention   To become in touch with existential perspectives.

Description
1. Ask group member to contemplate and share with another person (in pairs) what they believe happens after physical death.
2. Ask them also to consider and share how their views influence the way they live their lives.

Technique: *Breathing and Vocalizing, Yawning and Sighing*

Counseling Intention   To get in touch with deep breathing.

Description   The group can sit or stand for this exercise. Ask them to do a huge, silent yawn. Then to yawn and allow a modest sound to come out and finally to yawn very noisily. Next, show the group how to breathe in through the nose and give a sigh; then breathe in and sigh longer; and finally to exaggerate this by making a loud noise.

Technique: *Deep Breaths*

Counseling Intention   To get in touch with deep breathing.

Description   Ask the group to stand for this activity. Demonstrate how to breathe in through the nose to a count of three, hold the breath for three, and breathe out to a count of three. Explain that, when breathing naturally, we pause between inhalation and exhalation.

Technique: *Enclosed Feelings*

Counseling Intention   To express latent feelings.

Description
1. Have each group member take a turn at being encircled by a group of five or six people.
2. Instruct the circle to link arms. The person in the middle is to be "a feeling in need of expression" and the circle is representative of those prescriptions that prohibit its full expression.
3. Have each group member define how the roles can best be played to represent his or her own unique struggle.
4. Process the experience.

Technique: *Energy Warm-up*

Counseling Intention   To increase group cohesiveness.

Description   Instruct the group that they have one minute in which to touch four corners of the room; the floor, and six pairs of knees. Indicate when 50 seconds have elapsed, and when the time is up. Invite the group to retrace their steps exactly. Can they remember whose knees they touched, and in what order?

Technique: *Family Sculpture*

Counseling Intention   To evaluate family dynamics in a nonthreatening manner.

Description   Ask group members one at a time to sculpt their families in terms of who feels closest to whom. Ask how each feels about himself or herself and who is repulsed by whom. Allow other group members to assume the auxiliary ego roles of family members; instruct the family sculptor to give each "statue" one line to say to the family or individual members. Process the experience.

Technique: *Fantasy Trips*

Counseling Intention   To confront unfinished business.

Description   Have members imagine they approach a door, open the door, descend down a flight of stairs, and encounter another door. When they open it, they see a scene or mirror with a face (other than their own) or see a person standing there. They must say something to the person or situation that they have wanted to say for a long time. The person answers. They have a dialogue and the members retrace their steps. Share and process the experience.

Technique: *Feedback with Role Reversal*

Counseling Intention   To enhance perceptions of others.

Description   Ask group members to form groups of two. Ask them to become aware of those parts within themselves that might interfere with experiencing their partner. Ask them:

1. To share those issues that might hinder them from making a connection.
2. To give their partners feedback in the here-and-now with regard to the way they are perceiving and feeling that person.
3. To reverse roles with each other and continue giving feedback (reverse back).
4. To reverse roles and support or correct any perceptions.
5. Share and process the experience.

Technique: *Feelings*

Counseling Intention   To gain a greater understanding of self.

Description   Ask group members to consider privately:
1. What brings you most joy?
2. What brings greatest pain?
3. What do you find yourself feeling most of the time?
4. Have them share the answers with the group.

Technique: *Group Body*

Counseling Intention   To reveal perceived roles of group members.

Description
1. Ask the group members to identify a part of the body that best represents what function they individually provide for the group.
2. Ask the members to take the role of the body part, identify themselves to others, and physically position themselves in relationship to others (e.g., the head is at the head, the heart, lungs center appropriately, etc.). Let the roles interact with one another.
3. Share and process the experience.

Technique: *Group Dance*

Counseling Intention   To enhance communication nonverbally.

Description
1. Instruct group members to move to music, then periodically stop the music and ask members to freeze in their positions.
2. Ask them to make a statement congruent with their body message.
3. Share and process in the group.

Technique: *Group Feedback*

Counseling Intention   To gain knowledge of impediments to realizing one's full potential.

Description   Have the group divide into small groups of five to eight. Have each member receive feedback from all small group members on:

1. What is seen as his strongest attribute?
2. What gets in his or her way of maximizing that attribute to its fullest potential?

After hearing from each member, allow each individual to respond before moving to the next group member. Share and process the experience.

Technique: *Group Sculpture*

Counseling Intention   To examine close and distant relationships in a group.

Description
1. Ask group members to sculpt the group and individual members in terms of their feelings of closeness and who feels distant from whom.
2. Instruct the sculptor to give each statue one line to say to the group/or other individual group members.
3. Share and process the experience.

Technique: *Growing Old*

Counseling Intention   To empathically connect with aging issues.

Description
1. Ask two people to pretend they are very old.
2. Insert cotton wool balls in their ears, dim the lights, and ask them to converse with each other.
3. Give them a topic, such as "What is going on in your life?"
4. Process issues of life, change, deterioration, relationships, and mortality.

Technique: *Hand Examination*

Counseling Intention   To increase interpersonal exploration.

Description   Instruct two people to nonverbally examine each other's hands. Ask them to decide which one will examine first and to allow them at least three minutes to touch and look at the partner's hands, before instructing the other partner to be the examiner. Ask each to verbally share the experience and relate specifically what they were able to discover about their partner.

Technique: *Healthy Family*

Counseling Intention   To explore family dynamics functional and dysfunctional.

Description

1. Instruct the group to picture in their mind a scene that symbolizes a healthy family interaction.
2. Ask each person to identify a family member role that they would like to assume, and to share their thoughts with the rest of the group.
3. Ask for volunteers.
4. Let the interaction flow. When the action has reached a natural conclusion, invite members of the group to share.
5. Move other members of the group in and out of the role-playing situation (i.e., replace characters or introduce new characters such as aunts, uncles, or grandparents).

Technique: *Here-and-Now Feedback*

Counseling Intention   To identify feelings of the moment.

Description

1. Instruct individuals in pairs to experience each other in the here-and-now.
2. Have them give each other feedback and relate the feelings that are evoked within while in the other's presence. If they find themselves talking of the past or future, or about someone else, ask them to simply stop talking until they can refocus on the here-and-now.
3. Share and process the experience.

Technique: *Heroes and Heroines*

Counseling Intention   To explore expectations and admirations.

Description

1. Ask individuals to consider who they admire, respect, or love from literature or history.
2. Ask each person to do a self-presentation of the famous figure to the rest of the group.
3. After the self-presentation, instruct the client to choose a group member to role-play the figure.
4. Have a conversation with the historic or literary figure.
5. Share and process the experiences.

Technique: *Holidays*

Counseling Intention   To gain an understanding of expectations for the holidays, both realistic and idealistic.

Description   Direct members to move around the room and recall a family holiday. Have them pack a suitcase with all the things that were important to them at that time. Have each group member reveal what he or she has in their suitcases. What was the object of strength in their case, or what would they have liked to be in that case that they did not have at the time?

Techniques: *Introductions through Parents' Eyes*

Counseling Intention   To understand family scripts and messages about self.

Description   Instruct the group members to use paper and crayons to draw one of their parents (abstract or real form):

1. Talk about the parent in paper-crayon depiction.
2. Do a self-presentation of the parent, focusing particularly on the relationship with their son or daughter (the group member).
3. Have the pairs return to the group and ask each member to assume the role of their partner's parent, and to introduce themselves and their "child."

Technique: *Last People on Earth*

Counseling Intention   To assess members' resourcefulness and problem-solving skills.

Description   Instruct the group that a holocaust has struck the Earth, and they find themselves to be the sole survivors.

1. Help them establish the time, place, and circumstances.
2. Ask them to enact how they would behave and what they would do.
3. When the drama has reached a natural conclusion, have the members share.

Technique: *Living Newspaper*

Counseling Intention   To enhance verbal and nonverbal communication skills.

Description
1. Divide the group into small groups of four or five people.
2. Give each group a newspaper, asking them to select one article they will enact for the rest of the group.
   a. Set the scene of the event.
   b. Introduce the characters via a self-presentation.
   c. Provide a warm-up to the circumstances.
   d. Establish the time.
   e. Tell the story through action.
3. Share and process the experience.

Technique: *Nature Walk*

Counseling Intention   To express feelings via symbols.

Description   Ask group members to take a nature walk and bring something back that best represents how they are feeling about themselves. Share and process the experience.

Technique: *Obituary*

Counseling Intention   To reflect on self, values, accomplishments, and regrets (Simon, Howe, & Kirschenbaum, 1972).

Description   Ask members of the group to separate themselves from one another and find a comfortable place to write. Instruct them to write their own obituaries, indicating the cause, date, time, and place of death. List any surviving family members, life accomplishments of the deceased, and other relevant data. Allow time for contemplation, writing, and rewriting.

Choose one of the following methods of sharing:

1. Post the obituary on a wall or bulletin board for other members to read.
2. Have each member read his obituary to the group.
3. Share the experience of the role of a survivor.

4. Enact the funeral and ask the auxiliary ego, in the role of minister, priest, rabbi, or friend, to read the obituary.
5. Share and process the experience thoroughly.

Technique: *Object Presentation*

Counseling Intention   To understand self in relation to physical objects.

Description   Ask group members to become an object that best represents how they feel about themselves. Let the objects interact as a group or in dyads.

1. Choose:
   - An object they admire.
   - An object they detest.
   - An object they find useful.
   - An object they find useless.
2. Process the experience.

Technique: *Picture Frame*

Counseling Intention   To project feelings and emotions.

Description   Bring into group an empty picture frame (or an imaginary one will do) and ask each group member to imagine a scene or picture for the frame. Instruct the group to create a scene that best fits the situation, such as a family picture, members of the family, a counseling session, or a scene from their lives. After a few moments of silence, allow the members to verbally share their picture in the group. Share and process.

Variation: Have group enact their pictures by setting the scene and using group members to represent the various parts, or choose only one to enact.

Technique: *Poems*

Counseling Intention   To reveal more about self.

Description   Ask people to experience themselves, and write a poem that best describes how they "are." Ask members to read their poems to one other person, or to the entire group as an introduction. Share and process.

Technique: *Role Party*

Counseling Intention   To assess the role members select for themselves.

Description   Instruct the group to assume roles and interact with one another as if they were attending a party together. Establish the time, place, and circumstance. Do one, some, or all of the following:

- Be your hero or heroine.
- Be part of your body.
- Be a Hollywood celebrity.
- Be a character from literature.
- Be a figure from history.
- Be yourself and bring something you have created (e.g., picture, object, or song).
- Share and process the experience.

Technique: *Significant Other Presentation*

Counseling Intention   To project roles or scripts of family members.

Description   Ask each person in a dyad to do a self-presentation of someone who knows him or her fairly well. Allow time for them to warm up physically, emotionally, spiritually, and intellectually to their respective roles.

Ask them to talk about themselves through the eyes of this role. For example: Mark chooses to assume the role of his boss, and as his boss, talks about their employer-employee relationship.

Share and process the experience.

Variation:
1. Ask them to assume the role of someone who dislikes them.
2. Ask them to assume the role for their favorite teacher, student, supervisor, parent, child, a friend, or a sibling.

Technique: *Talk to Yourself*

Counseling Intention   To reveal portions of one's self to the group.

Description   Instruct the group members to imagine they are sitting in a chair, and one at a time, address the chair as if they were having a heart-to-heart talk with themselves. Ask them to talk to themselves at different ages (e.g., 2 years, 10 years, 18 years, 40 years, and 80 years old). Share and process the experience.

Technique: *The Funeral*

Counseling Intention   To confront one's own mortality and life span.

Description   Ask the group members to separate themselves from others in the group and to contemplate their own deaths. Have them visualize the date, time, place, and cause of death. Ask them to picture their funerals.

1. Who is there?
2. What they are saying and feeling?
3. Does the deceased leave behind any unfinished business?
4. Share and process the experience thoroughly.

Technique: *Three Questions*

Counseling Intention   To conduct a personal evaluation of oneself.

Description   Instruct the group to find a comfortable place for themselves either lying on the floor or couch or sitting in a chair. Ask them to answer for themselves the following three questions:

1. Who am I? (That is, what makes them uniquely different from others and what they have in common with others?)
2. Where do I fit? (That is, what are the collectives of people with which they have an affiliation, and who are the people that feel special and vital?)
3. How well am I functioning? (Consider the various roles enacted through the day, week and month and have them conduct a personal evaluation on them.)
4. Share and process the experience.

Technique: *Unfinished Business*

Counseling Intention   To have an opportunity to say things that were not said.

Description   Have group members consider someone with whom they have unfinished business—someone they wish would have said or done something with:

1. Someone close to you
2. Someone with whom you work
3. Someone with whom a communication problem exists for them or you
4. Someone who died
5. Have them pretend the person is in an empty chair and talk to the person about the unfinished business.
6. Process the experience.

Technique: *Sculpting Repressed Feelings*

Counseling Intention   To help a member express difficult feelings.

Description   If someone in a group is experiencing difficulty expressing personal feelings to another member (to the point that it is interfering with his or her personal growth), nonverbal sculpting of repressed feelings may be helpful. The individual who is having difficulty expressing feelings moves with the other participant to the center of the group circle. The recipient is to assume the role of a lump of clay. The individual who is having difficulty expressing feelings becomes the sculptor. The sculptor molds the statue of clay to reflect the way in which the sculptor is experiencing the individual and his or her behavior. Feedback should include facial expression, gestures, and posture.

After the sculpting, the statue holds the position. Next, the group leader instructs the sculptor to sculpt himself in relation to his feelings toward the other member and hold the position. Process both members' positions, feelings, and relation to one another. Encourage group members to share their insights.

Technique: *Positive Perceptions*

Counseling Intention   To focus the group on sending positive messages.

Description   Each group member is to write a positive personal message to each other member of the group. The messages are intended to make the person feel positive about herself. Positive messages could reflect a positive attitude, appearance, success, or special message. Members can sign their positive perception or have the option of leaving it blank. Variations could include sending messages only to individuals for whom they have significant positive feelings. Another alternative could be providing two messages to the individual, one positive perception and one self-defeating perception.

Technique: *Best Friend*

Counseling Intention To project and introduce oneself in a less threatening manner.

Description Individual or group members are asked to identify someone who knows them better than anyone else. He or she can be a mother, father, sister, brother, wife, or husband. He or she will be called the "best friend." Have them write out what their best friend would say about them: "He is a person who likes . . ." "One thing that he or she dislikes is . . . " "If he or she could do one thing in life, it would be . . . "

Place a chair in the middle of the room or group. Each member stands behind the empty chair and introduce themselves as they would expect their "best friend" would do it. Process what was learned by everyone from this projected experience.

Technique: *Choose an Object*

Counseling Intention To project a perception of self (Canfield & Wells, 1976).

Description A collection of objects of varying size, weight, composition, color, and sensation are placed in a container so that others cannot see the objects. Members are to move to the container and select one item that he or she can identify with from those within the container. Each member must identify with a single object. Members explore their respective object and their identification with their object. Others give feedback to each other as to whether the projected identifications matched or did not match their perceptions of each other.

Technique: *Introspection for Individual Assessment and Feedback from Others*

Counseling Intention To compare perceptions of self and those held by others.

Description Each individual completes the Introspection Continuum Table 3.1) according to the instructions. He or she writes his or her name on a second sheet and gives it to his partner to complete in terms of how that person sees him or her. Each member then compares her personal introspective continuum with the one completed by another member and discusses her reactions to the similarities and differences. Processing the experience could focus on why descriptions are different or similar from other people's descriptions in terms of congruency.

TABLE 3.1

Introspection Continuum Scale

The following words were selected to enable you to record your perceptions of yourself. Place an "X" on one of the spaces between each pair of words. The distance from the "X" to a word indicates the degree to which it represents your view of yourself.

I AM

Impulsive	_____	_____	_____	_____	_____	Cautious
Relaxed	_____	_____	_____	_____	_____	Tense
Interesting	_____	_____	_____	_____	_____	Boring
Self-confident	_____	_____	_____	_____	_____	Self-conscious
Secure	_____	_____	_____	_____	_____	Insecure
Happy	_____	_____	_____	_____	_____	Sad
Productive	_____	_____	_____	_____	_____	Lazy
Rigid	_____	_____	_____	_____	_____	Flexible
Competent	_____	_____	_____	_____	_____	Incompetent
Compassionate	_____	_____	_____	_____	_____	Cold
Attentive	_____	_____	_____	_____	_____	Preoccupied
Friendly	_____	_____	_____	_____	_____	Aloof
Agreeable	_____	_____	_____	_____	_____	Disagreeable
Mature	_____	_____	_____	_____	_____	Immature
Modest	_____	_____	_____	_____	_____	Flamboyant
Pleasant	_____	_____	_____	_____	_____	Abrasive

Technique: *Life-o-gram*

Counseling Intention   To bring the then-and-there into the here-and-now; to identify transgenerational issues and behavior patterns.

Description   Write a one-page autobiography that focuses on the things most important to your life up to the present. Reread it and then write a description of how the places, people, events, or crises shaped who you are today—your values, your beliefs, and your goals.

Technique: *Lifeline*

Counseling Intention   To bring the then-and there into the here-and-now; to identify behavior patterns and significant role models (Howe & Howe, 1975).

Description   Draw a horizontal line on paper. On the far left, place an "X" and indicate date of birth; on the far right, place an "X" for today's date. Divide the line into three parts: childhood, adolescence, and adulthood. Write in significant people and meaningful events along the lifeline. What significant events brought fond memories? Process what significant events brought painful memories. What messages were heard? What values were imparted and assimilated by the significant people and meaningful events?

Technique: *Twenty Questions for the Chair inside the Circle*

Counseling Intention To encourage self-disclosure; to provide an opportunity to focus on deeper levels of understanding (Vriend, 1985).

Description A chair is placed in the middle of the group circle. Any group member may be invited to occupy the chair and assume the risk of answering any question that group members ask the occupant of the chair. Questions can reflect various levels of self-disclosure, such as family or interpersonal relationships, fears, expectations, unfulfilled dreams, or feelings toward other members or the group leader. Both questions that are answered or declined reveal the risk-taking capacity of the group member.

Vriend (1985) found that taking a risk in the controlled context of the group fosters more consequential risk-taking in the client's real world; appropriate risk-taking goals can be targeted in the interval between group sessions. The chair in the middle also can be used in the introductory stage of the group.

Members can be asked to introduce themselves without reference to the roles they enact in their lives by answering the question "What kind of person am I?" while seated in the chair in the middle. Two chairs in the middle can be used for members who are in conflict or to process a psychodrama. All group members can turn outward to the circle (backs toward the center) in order to be less distracted when the leader wants to introduce a guided imagery for the group.

> *Perspective for the Therapist: On success and failure*
>
> *People can alter their lives by altering their attitudes.*
>
> William James

Technique: *Superlatives*

Counseling Intention To bring closure to the group in a positive way.

Description To provide a structured opportunity for group closure, group members are asked to list the names of all participants including themselves and indicate what positive behavior each member is likely to accomplish as the result of the group experience by responding to the superlative "Most likely to . . ." For example, "John is most likely to stop procrastinating." "Susan is most likely to charge less on her credit cards." "Tammy is most likely to finish graduate school." Positive affirmations and collective feedback provide a tremendous opportunity for group closure.

Technique: *Strength Test*

Counseling Intention   To focus on individual strengths.

Description   An index card for each group member is passed around the group. The leader asks each member to write a positive strength for every group member on his or her card. Incomplete sentences can also be used as stimulus statements about likes, dislikes, family, friends, goals, or wishes. Focus topics can help the counselor understand clients, identify problem areas, and establish rapport. Some examples are as follows:

> My greatest fear is _____.
> The thing that creates the most difficulty for me is _____.
> The thing I like to do most is _____.
> The person in my family who helps me most is _____.
> The nicest thing I ever did for anyone was _____.
> The nicest thing anyone ever did for me was _____.
> I used to be _____, but now I'm _____.
> The thing I would like people to admire me for is _____.
> Something I've never told anyone about before is _____.
> The one thing I most want to accomplish is_____.

Technique: *Actualizing Human Strengths*

Counseling Intention   To help actualize positive strengths of people in the group.

Description   Each person writes his or her name on a piece of paper. One member's name is chosen at random. A volunteer is chosen as recorder of the member's strengths. The member who was selected at random expresses to the group all the strengths she sees in herself. She then asks the group to express the barriers they see that he or she must overcome. Engage all participants to process the experience.

Technique: *Confronting Member Resistance*
with a Chair outside the Circle

Counseling Intention   To encourage a greater self-disclosure; to confront resistance (Vriend, 1985).

Description   It is not unusual for a group member to engage the group in circular counseling by either rejecting facts or information, or becoming defensive, excluding any possibility for helpful intervention. Members become frustrated with their attempts to mend a "broken record" (Vriend, 1985). An intervention may resemble the following:

"Bill, I'd like to pause and ask you to look at yourself as a member of the group for a moment. Would you mind some feedback from myself and other members? You seem to be going on and on about your situation and have told us everything you would like us to know. You've also been repeating yourself and objecting to whatever suggestions you receive from anyone.

"Perhaps it would be helpful now if we gave you a reprieve, another chance to hear us and respond to our suggestions. I'm going to ask you to move your chair back out of the circle and turn it around so that you face away from all of us. We'll close you out of the circle for a moment. Then what we're going to do is go over what you have told us and figure out ways to be of help to you. Don't look around and don't respond to anything anyone says. When we're finished, we'll invite you back in. That's when you can tell us if you heard anything you think would work for you in this situation. You'll then get a chance to react, OK?" (Vriend, 1985, p. 217)

When the client is situated outside of the circle, the counselor leads a review and evaluation of what has transpired during the group process. All members are involved in talking about rather than to the outside member and providing information about their perceptions, the member's needs, expectations, and self-defeating behaviors. The member is invited back into the circle and responds to what he or she has heard.

This should resemble a gentle carefrontation (i.e., gently share cares and concerns with the member without hostility) between group members. Process completely with all members.

Technique: *Role Reversal*

Counseling Intention   To facilitate a change in attitude; to experience opposing beliefs, to reevaluate the intentions of another; to become more understanding of another's position or belief.

Description   The client is requested to play a role opposite to her own natural behavior or to examine her attitudes and beliefs about a situation (e.g., "for gun control" vs. "against gun control"). The client may also play the role of another person she knows or switch roles with another person in a dyadic role-playing situation within a group setting. This allows the client to experience rather than talk about a situation.

Members briefly state their position to each other about their beliefs. Members switch roles with each other and present their positions as if they were the other person. When reversing roles, members should be authentic and as accurate as possible in restating the other's position.

Technique: *Journal Writing*

Counseling Intention   To record experiences, feeling, and thoughts.

Description   Journals may be used by the client to record innermost feelings, thoughts, or other events. (Note: Children often respond well to a homework assignment of keeping a diary, and it often provides a feeling of closeness to the counselor between sessions.)

The journal or log provides the counselor and client with a record of feelings, thoughts, and events to be explored. It is also helpful to have group members write logs at the end of every session. Also, a 3 × 5 card entitled "Group Reflections" provides a useful format to use after each group session. The cards can be signed so that the leader can keep in touch with each member. These logs should never be read aloud to the group or referred to in the group by the leader.

Technique: *The Three Most Important People in Your Life*

Counseling Intention To focus on role models and transgenerational issues.

Description Have individual group members identify who were three important people in their lives at ages 5, 10, and 20. Then have them project into the future: "Who will be the most important people in your life?" This technique helps the counselor gain valuable insights into the individual's world at various life stages, particularly in the dimension of psychological dependency.

Technique: *Double Dialogue Technique*

Counseling Intention To provide feedback to other members over issues discussed.

Description After group counseling, a double dialogue technique can be used among group members to provide feedback to other members over issues discussed, or the counselor may have each member close the group experience by writing to the counselor on index cards about their group experience at that particular session. This allows the counselor to keep in touch with each individual group member about significant issues that may be affecting him or her (Powers & Hahn, 1977).

Technique: *Writing a Letter Aloud*

Counseling Intention To focus on unresolved issues or on unfinished business in relationships (Dyer, 1985; Dyer & Vriend, 1977).

Description The leader asks a group member to write an oral letter within the group setting. The recipient of the letter is an individual who is significant in the group member's life, someone to whom the group member is having some difficulty relating, with whom the group member has never resolved a conflict, or someone who is deceased. The letter should contain whatever the group member would like to say that has not been previously said, the reason for any existing bitterness, and how the relationship should change. When the letter has been completed, everyone in the group is requested to react and to say what thoughts and feelings the letter elicited.

This technique is most appropriate when an individual expresses a concern about a significant other who is troublesome, agonizing, bitter, frustrating, and full of upsetting interactional demands and unreasonable behavior. The technique is most appropriately invoked after a member has emitted considerable data about the relationship's difficulties and has expressed obvious frustration about attitudes or abusive actions (Dyer & Vriend, 1977).

Rewriting the letter in the group is very important to demonstrate what the group member can say in a more positive and effective manner. The contrast in letters will actively demonstrate differences in effective and self-defeating thinking patterns. "This is a very powerful tool; not a gimmick or a game" (Dyer & Vriend, 1977).

> *Perspective for the Therapist: On goals and decisions*
>
> *When you have to make a choice and don't make it,*
> *that in itself is a choice.*
>
> William James

Technique: *I Have a Secret*

Counseling Intention   To explore self-disclosure; to confront irrational assumptions.

Description   This exercise can be a method to explore fears, guilt feelings, and catastrophic expectations. Clients are asked to think of some personal secret. They do not actually share the secret with others but imagine themselves revealing the secret. Clients are to explore what fears they have about other people knowing their secret and how they imagine others might respond.

Technique: *Here-and-Now Face*

Counseling Intention   To disclose feelings and emotions (Kranzow, 1973).

Description   The here-and-now face is an activity designed to help group members disclose and discuss their feelings and emotions. Instruct members to draw a face that represents the feelings they are experiencing at the present time. Below the face have them write a verbal description of those feelings and the reasons for them. The discussion should include both "what" the feelings are and "why" they exist in the person at the present time. For example, "I am feeling _____ because _____." This exercise is a means of generating a discussion of the importance of feelings in their lives and brings the group into personal contact.

Technique: *Life-Picture Map*

Counseling Intention   To bring the then-and-there into the here-and-now.

Description   Ask group members to draw an illustrated road map that represents their past, present, and future. The map should pictorially depict experiences the members have had, obstacles they have overcome, what their present lives are like, what their goals are for the future, and what barriers stand in the way of accomplishing those goals. Upon completion of the drawings, have members share their maps with the group, explaining various illustrations. Process the experience.

Technique: *Competitive Thumb Wrestling*

Counseling Intention   To confront aggressive and hostile behaviors among group members.

Description   This exercise is useful when the leader perceives that two members may be experiencing hidden aggression or hostility toward one another. Those involved should select their preferred hand and interlace their fingers, and hook their thumbs. One person then attempts to force the thumb of the other person down for a count of three. The leader then assists in processing the feelings of hostility between members.

Technique: *Strength Bombardment*

Counseling Intention   To explore perceptions held by self versus those held by others (Canfield & Wells, 1976).

Description   One group member volunteers to tell his or her personal strengths; the group responds by telling the strengths they see in him or her. The member continues and asks, "What do you see that is preventing me from using my strengths?" The group responds again. Finally, group members construct a group fantasy in which they imagine what the focus member can be doing in five or more years if he or she uses those strengths to their full potential. The focus member reflects on this experience in the group.

Perspective for the Therapist: On feelings and attitude

Everything can be taken away but one thing . . . to choose one's attitude in any given set of circumstances.

Victor Frankl

Technique: *I Am Becoming a Person Who . . .*

Counseling Intention   To assess personal growth in the group.

Description   Group members are given paper and pencils and are instructed to write their first names in large block letters on the top of the sheets. Then they are asked to complete the following sentence in as many ways as they can: "I am becoming a person who . . ." They silently mill around the room reading each other's sheets, then they leave the group session.

Technique: *Map of Life*

Counseling Intention   To review significant life events.

Description   On sheets of newsprint, members draw maps of their lives, illustrating significant events. In an insert, they draw a map of the current week up to the here-and-now. Each member explains his or her map to the group.

Technique: *Think—Feel*

Counseling Intention   To focus on cognitive-emotional issues.

Description   Members are instructed to write on one side of a 3 × 5 index card a sentence beginning with the phrase "Now I am thinking . . ." and on the other side a sentence beginning with "Now I am feeling . . ." Members are asked to process their thoughts and feelings from both sides of their cards.

Technique: *Here-and-Now Wheel*

Counseling Intention   To identify and focus on feelings.

Description   This can be used as a closure activity to enable people to get in touch with the emotions they are feeling, to put a label on them, and to try to determine why they are feeling them.

1. Have group members draw a circle on a piece of paper and divide the circle into four parts (four quadrants).
2. In each part, they are to write a word that describes a feeling they have at the moment.
3. The leader can ask for five volunteers to share their wheels with the entire group.
4. Process the experience.

Technique: *Value Box*

Counseling Intention   To explore what clients value.

Description   Each group member is to bring in a box containing three to six items. These items are those that hold special meaning or represent something that holds significant meaning for the individual. Group members take turns explaining the content of their boxes, each person revealing and explaining the objects he or she has selected.

Technique: *Who Are You?*

Counseling Intention   To explore dimensions of the self (Simon, Howe, & Kirschenbaum, 1972).

Description   *Who are you?* Have the group members take nine pieces of paper and respond to the question "Who am I?" nine times. Record each answer on one of the sheets. Members may reply with anything that comes to mind as self-identification: age, sex, profession, a symbol, image, or a value. After members have finished, direct them to rank the papers in importance (9 being the highest and 1 the lowest). Direct members to place each piece of paper face down in front of them and turn up number nine and think about what it represents. Have them consider what life would be like without number nine, and proceed through each number to number one.

Process the filtering out of parts that are not essential to oneself. Do members think beyond their activities, titles, or career? Are there aspects of codependency with others regarding their identity and meaning to others?

Perspective for the Therapist: On self-acceptance

The curious paradox is that when I accept myself just as I am,
then I can change.

Carl Rogers

Technique: *Cued Sharing*

Counseling Intention   To promote more open dialogues among group members; to assess locus of control.

Description   Cue the group to share with one another:

1. An episode from childhood or adolescence that was very formative.
2. A personal secret.
3. Feelings about a part of one's body (e.g., proud or ashamed).
4. Feelings about occupation—satisfactions or frustrations.
5. Information on their financial situation.
6. Feelings about their love life, past and present, or marriage.
7. Feelings about other members in the group.

Technique: *Leave the Room*

Counseling Intention   To confront the worst kind of rejection—being completely cast away from the group, ignored, or not taken seriously by others (Lewis & Streitfeld, 1970).

Description   Lewis and Streitfeld (1970) provided the following confrontation strategy for processing the experience of rejection.

Out in the Cold. The group forms a circle. Each member in turn steps out of the circle. Each member wanders around the room exploring how he feels in different locations, focusing on how it feels to step away from the group. For example, he or she may feel intensely rejected, isolated, weak, or meaningless to the group. On the other hand, he or she may be relieved and may feel liberated.

The member then returns to the group and focuses on how he or she feels now. For example, do you feel whole or fragmented? Do you feel awkward or comfortable? Are you happy or sad? Other members should focus on how they felt when someone leaves. Are you sorry? Or do you feel rejected when someone moves away? Some members may feel that the group has annihilated the one who has left and that they can abuse him. Others may feel that the person who has left is freer and stronger than the group.

Technique: *Impressions of Self*

Counseling Intention   To gain a fuller impression of how one sees oneself.

Description   Build a representation of yourself in three dimensions. To do this empty a junk drawer or closet. Dump out a collection of heterogeneous materials such as papers, pictures, matchbooks, strings, scraps of wood, magazines, and any other miscellaneous finds. Gather some of these things from the pile and build a portrait of yourself out of them. Process the experience.

Technique: *Group Reentry Questions*

Counseling Intention   To check in with group members regarding their group experiences (Canfield & Wells, 1976).

Description   Reentry questions help to reestablish the level of group rapport that has been developed as well as positively enhance self-concepts of group members. Questions such as these are useful:

1. What was the most exciting thing that has happened to you in the last week?
2. What was one of the most exciting things that you did?
3. Suppose you had a magic box. In it can be anything you want that will make you happy. What is in your box that makes you extremely happy?
4. If you could teach everyone in the world just one thing—an idea, a skill, a hobby—what would it be?

Technique: *Group Drawings*

Counseling Intention   To enhance group cohesiveness (Brown, 1996).

Description   Doodling and drawing can say a lot about a person. Sitting in groups of four to six people around a large piece of poster board, group members draw with crayons and marker pens. Do not specify if the drawings are to be an individual or a group effort—that's up to the group.

Process by discussing the drawings, how they compare to other groups' drawings and were influenced by each member, and the group dynamics that transpired while creating the drawings. Compare the drawings from the different groups to see if this reveals any similarities and differences in group dynamics.

Technique: *Mood Role Plays*

Counseling Intention   To see how moods and emotions affect group dynamics.

Description   Take the group's pulse by going around the room and having each member state one word that describes how he or she is feeling at that moment. Divide the group into subgroups so that everyone in each subgroup has a similar mood state, such as, anxious/stressed, relaxed/satisfied, happy/feeling good, or angry/annoyed.

Have each group discuss their mood state among themselves and then create a role-play that illustrates that mood. Each group then takes turns improvising their role-play before the group.

Process how a particular mood affects group dynamics. For example, how are communication patterns, body language, group cohesion, task performance, and self-disclosure affected by the emotion in the group?

Technique: *The Group Tell-a-Story*

Counseling Intention   To explore the various facets of a group's personality.

Description   Group members create a story, *one word at a time*. The group sits in a circle and one person is chosen to start the story by offering one word. The person sitting next to that person then offers the second word, and so on around the circle, with each person adding one more word to the story. Periods to end one sentence and start another usually happen spontaneously, but a person may insert one explicitly if she so chooses. Process the following questions to encourage members to think about how the story might reflect underlying group dynamics:

• How does the story start off? Might this say something about how the group started off?

- Are there themes or issues that repeat in the story? Are these important themes in the group itself?
- Is there a pattern to the verbs and adjectives in the story? What does this say about the group?
- Are there symbols in the story?
- What are the feelings and moods in the story? Do they change?
- What are the relationships among the people in the story?
- Where does the story "fall apart" (become chaotic) and where does it flow well? What might that mean?
- Do conflicts or problems arise in the story? Are they resolved?
- What other changes or transitions occur in the story?

Technique: *Group Checkers*

Counseling Intention   To enhance cohesion and collaboration among team members.

Description   Members of the group try to beat the leader in the game of checkers. Members must make the move as a team. That is, the team (group) must decide on what will be the move of choice and who will be moving the checker, prior to the actual move.

Process the experience by discussing issues of teamwork, communication, frustration/anger management, being heard, winning (or losing), problem solving, compromise, and how this activity is like school, work, or home.

Technique: *Family Sociograms*

Counseling Intention   To discover patterns of relationships in the group (Suler, 2003).

Description   Explain to the group how sociograms work. Circles represent people in a group. A solid line with an arrow at the end represents that one person "likes" or feels close to another (there may be arrows at both ends if the feeling is mutual). A broken line represents a person "not liking" or being in conflict with another.

The patterns created by the lines indicate the patterns of relationships and subgroupings within the group, as well as the overall cohesion of the group. So in the illustration above, there is an alliance between B and C; an A–D–E subgroup;

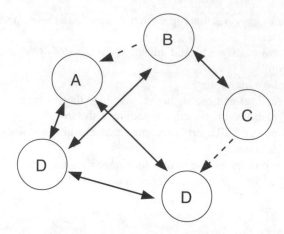

FIGURE 3.1. Family Sociogram. Source: Suler, J. R. (1996). *Teaching clinical psychology: Family sociograms.* (Reprinted with permission)

conflicts between A and B, and C and D; and B serves as a bridge between the dyad and triad groups. The overall cohesion of the group is moderate in strength.

Ask group members to draw a sociogram of their family. Process issues about the sociogram drawing that might be significant in revealing the person's feelings and attitudes about his or her family.

1. What circles did you draw first?
2. How do the sizes of the circles compare to each other?
3. How are the circles placed in relation to each other (close, far away, on top, below, or next to each other)?
4. How complex or simple is the drawing, or parts of it?
5. Was anything erased or changed?

Technique: *Management of Resistance Using the Time-out Technique*

Counseling Intention   To confront group resistance that has occurred over an extended period of time, for one or several sessions.

Description   The therapist says something like the following: "I sense there was so much more going on here than what was expressed. We have about 10 minutes remaining; perhaps we can take time out to reflect upon what could have happened that didn't. Could each of you say something about what you did not express during the session? Even a headline or opening statement would help" (Barbanell, 1997, p. 510).

CONCLUSION

Group psychotherapy has been effective as a treatment for loss and grieving (Piper, McCallum, & Azim, 1992); depression (Free, Oei, & Sanders, 1991); obsessive-compulsive disorder (Fals-Stewart & Lucente, 1994); eating disorders (Mitchell, Pyle, Eckert, Hatsukami, Pomeroy, & Zimmerman, 1990); clients experiencing bipolar disorder (Baur & McBride, 2002) and personality disorders (Tschuschke & Dies, 1994); and substance abuse (Miller, Brown, Simpson, Handmaker, Bien, Luckie, Montgomery, Hester, & Tonigan, 1995). Coping and social skills training (Monti, Rohsenow, Colby, & Abrams, 1995) have demonstrated significant efficacy. Group psychotherapy is suitable for a large variety of problems and difficulties, beginning with people who would like to develop their interpersonal skills and proceeding to people with emotional problems such as anxiety, depression, or panic disorder.

Chapter 4

Classic Gestalt Techniques

Perspective for the Therapist:
On a More Contemporary View of Gestalt Therapy

One of the greatest unsolved mysteries in science is the nature of consciousness and the human mind. The consciousness appears as a volumetric spatial void, containing colored objects and surfaces. This reveals that the representation in the brain takes the form of an explicit volumetrics spatial model of external reality. The world we see around us therefore is not the real world itself, but merely a miniature virtual-reality replica of that world in an internal representation. The phenomena of dreams and hallucinations clearly demonstrate the capacity of the brain to construct complete virtual worlds even in the absence of sensory input. Perception is therefore somewhat like a guided hallucination, based on sensory stimulation.

Steven Lehar, *The World in Your Head: A Gestalt View*
of the Mechanism of Conscious Experience, 2002, p. 2
(Reprinted with permission)

Today, within the realm of more humanistic-existential psychotherapies, Gestalt therapy is perhaps the most prominent. It is parallel to other "third force" approaches (Seltzer, 1986) with its strong conceptual emphasis on self-fulfillment and the development of authenticity and self-responsibility. Gestalt therapy stresses here-and-now awareness and the unity of mind, body, and feelings. "Lose your mind and come to your senses" (Perls, 1969) is a major tenet in this counseling approach. Gestalt therapy, unlike psychoanalysis, has little to add to a dynamic interpretation of psychopathological phenomena. It is a "therapy" more than a theory, an art more than a psychological system.

Inherently, it is an experiential therapy designed to help people experience the present moment more fully and gain awareness of what they are thinking, feeling, and doing. Unfinished business from the past (such as unexpressed feelings of resentment, anger, guilt, or grief) is viewed as needless emotional debris that clutters present-centered awareness. Gestalt therapy uses confrontational techniques as an invitation for the client to become aware of discrepancies between verbal and nonverbal expressions, between feelings and actions, or between thoughts and feelings.

Perls maintained that people often fragment their lives and sabotage their potential by losing touch with their inner selves, and by not coming to terms with unfinished business (i.e., unfulfilled needs, unexpressed feelings, or lack of closure to significant life events such as loss). Individuals often find themselves experiencing a split in their being between what they think they should do and what they want to do. People also tend to flounder at times between existing polarities in their lives such as love/hate, internal/external, or real/unreal. Gestalt techniques are experiential exercises to bring clients in touch with the full range of their experiences. It is concerned with wholeness and the completion of form. A Gestalt includes both the formation and the destruction of the whole (Van De Riet, Korb, & Gorrell, 1980). As a need grows within a person, it comes to the foreground of attention-seeking resolution. The primary focus of attention is referred to as the *figure*, and all else in awareness is known as the *ground* (Polster & Polster, 1973). The process involves many of the following components:

Enhancing awareness. Clients are helped to attend to that which they are presently experiencing.

Changing questions to statements. Clients are encouraged to use statements rather than questions, which leads them to express themselves unambiguously, and to be responsible for their communication.

Assuming responsibility. The client is asked to substitute the use of the word *won't* for *can't.* Experimentation in this substitution often leads individuals to feel that they are in control of their fears.

Asking "how" and "what." Asking *"why"* leads to defensiveness and intellectualization rather than experiencing and understanding. *"How"* and *"what"* enable individuals to get into the experience of their behavior.

Bringing the past into the now. Much of that which is dealt with in counseling is concerned with past events. Rather than rehashing the past, previous experiences or feelings can be brought into the here-and-now.

Verbal and nonverbal congruency. The counselor observes the client's body language and focuses attention on discrepancies and brings them to the client's awareness.

Gestalt therapy alerts us to the interrelationship between awareness and energy. When awareness is scattered and bound up in unknown feelings and thoughts, energy flow is diminished throughout one's personality. A Gestalt counselor by suggesting the practice of structured experiences focuses and amplifies effort to free themselves from mental, emotional and physical block to greater self aware-ness. The Gestalt approach is designed to approach observable behavior rather than merely to lead the person to talk about what he or she is thinking. The aim of Gestalt therapy is to enable the client to act on the basis of all possible informa-tion and to apprehend not only the significant factors in the external field, but also significant information from within. The Gestalt therapist pays close attention to the whole person—to body movement, to emotional congruity, and to the lan-guage that deflects from the client's awareness (Crose, 1990). The client is di-rected to pay attention at any given moment to what he or she is feeling, what he or she wants, and what he or she is doing. The goal is noninterrupted awareness. The process of increasing awareness enables individuals to discover how they interrupt their own functioning.

Basic Tenets of Gestalt Therapy
1. Live now. Be concerned with the present rather than with the past or future.
2. Live here. Deal with what is present than with what is absent.
3. Stop imagining. Experience the real.
4. Stop unnecessary thinking. Rather, taste and see.
5. Express rather than manipulate, explain, justify, or judge.
6. Give in to unpleasantness and pain just as to pleasure. Do not restrict your awareness.
7. Accept no *should* or *ought* other than your own.
8. Take full responsibility for your actions, feelings, and thoughts.
9. Surrender to being as you are. (Fagan & Shepherd, 1970, pp. 49–50)

STAGES IN GESTALT THERAPY

From the Gestalt perspective, every psychological problem can be explored and resolved as a polarized conflict between two aspects in personality. Fiebert (1983) identified four stages in the unfolding of a therapeutic session and the corresponding counselor behaviors that serve to guide a conflict into awareness, expose its rami-fications and internal experience, and aid in its resolution.

Stage 1: Emergence of the Problem

The first stage involves a client bringing into awareness with increasing intensity a major conflict in the here-and-now to a counseling session. Initial interventions guide the client's attention to his or her immediate experience—the "what and how" of behavior—and away from speculations as to causes—the "whys" for

such action. During this process, clients are encouraged to assume increasing responsibility (ability to respond) for individual thoughts, feelings, sensations; and
to experience the intimate, basic connection between verbal and nonverbal behaviors. The focus of the first stage consists of exploring what a client is currently
experiencing in awareness. Clients can be guided to experience greater degrees of
personal responsibility by the simple means of restating and repeating particular
phrases in communication, such as, substituting "want" for "should," "won't" for
"can't," "I" for "it," and presenting all material in the present tense. The end phase
of Stage 1 is marked by a client's ability to readily focus awareness when directed
and express feelings and sensations in the immediate present.

Stage 2: Working with External Polarities

The client is now asked to take the growing tension that is experienced and explore it within the framework of an external dialogue. With an interpersonal problem, there is little difficulty in employing two chairs and having the client change
places as a conversation unfolds. The major thrust of the work at this point is to
bring hidden feelings into awareness by dramatizing the outer manifestation of an
inner conflict. In the closing phase of Stage 2, clients can become quite immersed
in the process of self-discovery and need little overt guidance to shuttle between
chairs, appropriately express feelings, and monitor and modify behavior patterns.
It is useful to have the client sequentially express: (1) what direct issues and feelings are present in the relationship with the significant other, (2) what covert
feelings and hidden agendas are perceived in the relationship, and (3) what the
desired solutions are to the stated issues and conflicts.

Stage 3: Working with Internal Polarities

The central focus of activity in Stage 3 is a growing confrontation between two
significant and opposing aspects within the client's personality. The more fully
each aspect or pole of tension is dramatized and experienced, the more likely it
can be resolved. During a session, one can observe an inner conflict, initially
latent, emerge with increasing power as the thoughts, feelings, sensations, and
bodily responses associated with a historical trauma come into awareness. As
each polarity expands its "territory" into awareness, the tension may painfully
stretch until it becomes unbearable for the client. This phenomenon is indicative
of the "implosive layer" of personality and is a necessary precondition for the
formation of a new Gestalt.

Stage 4: Integration

The integration stage celebrates the triumph of unity over separate factors within the client's personality, signals the emergence of a new Gestalt, and reflects that within the struggle between the yin and the yang is the *tao*. The core element at this stage is a resolution of the internal conflict resulting from a major reorganization and renewed perception of the problem. Integration is a continual, evolutionary, life-sustaining experience—there is no "final" Gestalt. In the process of integration, factors that were opposing each other in consciousness are identified. Encourage clients to express verbally what each opposing aspect can truly appreciate and respect in the other one. Some clients will respond more effectively to the opportunity to express these attitudes in a nonverbal manner, through gesture or movement. A guided fantasy of mutual acceptance can be presented by the therapist, who incorporates the positive qualities of each aspect of each polarity by moving them toward each other and embracing them. Some clients may choose to work with a meditation technique that allows them to harmonize and integrate the polar tension. To facilitate a client's cognitive reorganization, the therapist may present his or her perceptions of the changes observed from the beginning to the end of a session.

Finally, there are a number of different styles of processing, and different general subjects to process. Some of the most used tools are:

Dialoguing—talking back and forth about the issue, seeing it from different angles, trying to zero in on what is going on.

Hunting for illogic—following or challenging illogical statements, trying to get to the underlying meanings.

Reframing—inviting the client to see something from a different perspective.

Unfixing—freeing up fixed ideas, stuck thoughts, and stuck emotions.

Reexperiencing—clearing up kinesthetic reactions by experiencing events differently.

Recursion—repeating the same action or question to exhaust the responses to it.

Polarity integration—bringing opposite personality traits together.

Soul retrieval—bringing back parts of the person that are lost.

Perceptual processing—isolating and changing the perceptions associated with an issue.

Entity processing—addressing perceptual phenomena as a live, independent unit.

Awareness—attending to and observing one's own sensing, thinking, feelings, and actions; paying attention to the flowing nature of one's present-centered experience.

Confluence—creating a disturbance in which the sense of the boundary between self and environment is lost.

Confrontation—inviting the client to become aware of discrepancies between verbal and nonverbal expression, between feelings and actions, or between thoughts and feelings.

Deflection—avoiding contact and awareness by being vague and indirect.

Dichotomy—splitting a person's experiences into opposing forces of a polarity; weak/strong, dependent/independent.

Unfinished business—having unexpressed feelings (e.g., resentment, guilt, anger, grief) going back to childhood that now interfere with effective psychological functioning; needless emotional baggage that clutters present-centered awareness and functioning.

These techniques are unique to Gestalt therapy, providing another lucrative means for exploring the client's world.

Technique: *The Empty Chair Technique*

Counseling Intention   To address conflict or relationship issues for the client; to stimulate thinking and to highlight emotions and attitude (Tillett, 1984).

Description   A role-playing technique involving the client and an imaginary person in the empty chair is presented. The client sits opposite the empty chair when speaking to the imaginary person; the client plays his or her role and the role of an imaginary person or partner.

Technique: *Accept Responsibility for Choices Made*

Counseling Intention   To examine how one denies responsibility for many choices, wants, fears, and weaknesses.

Description   Begin this experience by completing these sentences with several responses:

1. I had to _____,_____,_____
2. I can't _____,_____,_____
3. I need _____,_____,_____
4. I'm afraid to _____,_____,_____
5. I'm unable to _____,_____,_____

Now, go back and try substituting these words for the five beginnings above:
1. "I chose to" instead of "I had to."
2. "I won't" instead of "I can't."
3. "I want" instead of "I need."
4. "I'd like to" instead of "I'm afraid to."
5. "I'm unwilling to work hard enough to" instead of "I'm unable to."

Technique: *Working through Unfinished Business*

Counseling Technique   To understand emotional "leftovers" from previous experiences (Perls, 1969).

Description   When experiencing a strong *unwanted emotion* (e.g., anger, sadness, loneliness, or insecurity), first, let go and feel the emotion full strength, no matter how unreasonable, dangerous, crazy, and unreasonable it may be. Second, go looking for concealed emotions, asking, "Do I also feel something else?"

Classic Examples of Intense Emotions
- Crying hides anger
- Dependency suppresses anger
- Excessive smiles conceal depression
- Physical complaints contradict anxiety
- Anger overshadows fears.

Third, investigate bodily sensations and emotions for more subtle additional feelings. Fourth, ask yourself "What do these current feelings and the situation remind me of in the past?" and "Have I been there before?" Relive the earlier experiences over and over until the strong emotions are drained. The next time there is a feeling of overresponding emotionally, reflect on unfinished business that is brought to the situation. Say to yourself, "It's not the orders from the boss that are irritating me, it is my resentment of my mother's criticism."

Technique: *Centering*

Counseling Intention   To become comfortable in the present; to reach a state of rest mentally, emotionally, and physically when doing something.

Description   Sit down comfortably with closed eyes and do nothing but be aware of what is going on. Don't try to do anything in particular, and don't try to not do anything in particular. Just notice what is happening, what sounds are in the room, how your body feels, and the thoughts going through your head. Don't try to change or stop any of it. Just perceive it all as naturally occurring noise. Simply allow everything to happen and thoughts and feelings will become quiet.

Technique: *Four Magic Questions to Handle Upsets*

Counseling Intention   To uncover something hidden that causes the upset.

Description   These questions are general enough to cover most recent upsets:

1. "What did_____do that wasn't right?"
2. "What did_____fail to do?"
3. "As far as_____is concerned, what did you do that wasn't right?"
4. "As far as_____is concerned, what did you fail to do?'

These questions are general enough to cover most upsets, but the client is most likely to provide the exact keys producing the upset. Another series of questions along similar lines would be:

1. "What should I have known?"
2. "What should_____have known?"
3. "What should you have known?"
4. "What should have been known?"

Fundamentally, the upset is there because somebody did not know what the other person expected and therefore acted differently.

Technique: *Dialoguing*

Counseling Intention   To find something that is in need of resolution; to narrow down an area so that a more specific technique can be used (Perls, 1969).

Description   Dialoguing is a free-form method of assessing or resolving an area and the client's answers. This goes on until either enough information has been compiled or until the area has been resolved. The purpose of the dialoguing process is for the facilitator and the client to both understand the nature of the subject to a point where it is either resolved for the client or the client knows what to do with it. The object is to get a mutual understanding about what it is, and the client to take responsibility for it.

The therapist helps the client resolve the subject by asking the right questions. The therapist will get the client to keep looking and talking about what is there until he or she has progressed. To help the client, the therapist can ask various things concerning the subject:

- Possible causes
- Ideas
- Thoughts
- Considerations
- Data
- Solutions
- Attempted solutions
- Failed solutions
- Feelings
- Remedies
- Improvement
- Attempts to get rid of
- Help toward
- Time, place, form, and event
- Who, what, where, when, and how
- What one could do about it
- Possibly taking responsibility for it
- How things would be without it

Any question is to help the therapist clarify what the client said, and summarize it without judging it.

Technique: *Unblocking*

Counseling Intention To provide a list of meaningful questions that will unblock an area.

Description Unblocking is a list of keys that are useful to use in dialoguing to free up some kind of positive direction. The keys on the list are mostly factors that might inhibit a positive outcome:

- Holding back
- Obstacles
- Resources
- Attempts
- Failures

- Consequences
- Judgments
- Inhibitions
- Obsessions
- Mistakes
- Anxiety
- Suppressed
- Forgotten

Out of each key concept, the therapist constructs a question, such as:

"In regard to _____ is there anything that you are holding back?"
"Has anything been held back about _____?"
"Are you holding yourself back concerning _____?"
"Is someone else holding something back about you _____?"
"What resources are available to use for _____?"
"Do you have any anxiety about _____?"

Technique: *Hot Seat*

Counseling Intention   To confront a group member regarding interpersonal issues or resistance (Perls, 1969).

Description   A technique to focus intensely on one member of the group at a time. The member sits opposite the group leader and dialogues on a life problem with intermittent input from other members upon request by the group leader.

Technique: *Mirror*

Counseling Intention   To provide feedback to the client regarding how he or she is perceived by the group or one member.

Description   A technique employing role-playing: The role-playing group member with the problem is asked to remove himself or herself from the group setting while a volunteer group member comes forth to imitate the role-player and also to provide alternative role-played behavior. The original role-player observes as an objective, nonparticipatory learner.

Technique: *Monotherapy*

Counseling Intention   To facilitate awareness and a therapeutic dialogue (Perls, 1969).

Description   In Gestalt therapy, a technique in which the counselor requests that the client write or create a dramatic scene and role-play all characters involved; the client is encouraged to role-play personal fantasies or repressed wishes.

Technique: *Playing the Projection*

Counseling Intention   To gain a deeper awareness of one's own projections from the perspective of others (Perls, 1969).

Description   The purpose of this exercise is to demonstrate how often we see clearly in others the qualities or traits that we do not want to see or accept within ourselves. Group members are to make a direct statement to each person in their group, and then apply that statement to themselves. For example, one member might say to another member, "I think you are very manipulative" and then say "I am manipulative." Or one member might say to another member, "I don't think you really care about me" and then say "Then I don't care about me." This technique serves to create a deeper awareness of one's own projections.

Technique: *Territoriality and Group Interaction*

Counseling Intention   To reveal a group sociogram of member interaction.

Description   After the group has been in session for a time, ask them to change seats. Process the issues of territoriality—that is, did the group members tend to arrange themselves in the same seating order? How did they feel when they saw someone else sitting in their seat? Ask group members to diagram with arrows the interactions of a given period of group discussion. Discuss cross-currents in the group. Who are isolates? Who are stars? Is there ease of communication, direct eye contact, and equal air time?

Technique: *Think—Feel*

Counseling Intention   To focus on discrepancies between thoughts and feelings.

Description   Members are instructed to write on one side of a 3 × 5 index card a sentence beginning with the phrase "Now I am thinking" and on the other side a sentence beginning with "Now I am feeling." Members are asked to process their thoughts and feelings from both sides of their cards.

Technique: *Making the Rounds*

Counseling Intention   To provide a structured opportunity to relay difficult feelings or thoughts.

Description   In this exercise a person goes around the group and says something that is difficult to say. For example, one member might have mentioned that she does not trust the other group members enough to risk any self-disclosure. She may be given the opportunity to go around the group and say to each member: "I don't trust you because_____" or "If I were to trust you, then_____."

The person making the rounds completes the sentence with a different ending for each group member. The purpose of the exercise is to give participants the experience of confronting a given fear and concretely stating that fear in the group.

Technique: *"I and Thou"*

Counseling Intention   To enhance communication; to get in touch with barriers to communication as it is perceived by others. (Perls, 1969).

Description   Clients often respond as if they are talking either to a blank wall or about a person or persons rather than to another person, as if they did not exist. The client is asked, "To whom are you saying this?" He or she is led to discover the distinction between "talking to" or "talking about" another. The client is led to discover whether or not his or her voice and words are reaching the receiver. Awareness of how voice and verbal behavior may inhibit relating to others also can be explored.

Technique: *The Principle of the Now*

Counseling Intention To relate experience in the here-and-now; to gain greater self-awareness (Perls, 1969).

Description To encourage communication in the present tense, the therapists asks, "What is your present awareness?" "What is happening now?" "How do you feel at this moment?" The client is taught to experience himself or herself in the now to gain awareness. Self-awareness is not a thought about the problem but is itself a creative integration of the problem.

Technique: *Turning "It" Language into "I" Language*

Counseling Intention To empower the client to take responsibility.

Description It is not at all uncommon for individuals to refer to their bodies and their behavior in "it" language (for example, "What are you experiencing in your stomach?" The client answers, "It is upset."). The client is directed to change "it" into "I"—instead of "it is upset," "I am upset," and going a step farther, "I am upsetting myself." The client begins to see himself or herself as an active agent who does something rather than as a passive recipient to whom things somehow happen. The client can see immediately the degree of responsibility and involvement that is experienced.

> *Perspective for the Therapist: On expectations*
>
> *I do my thing and you do your thing. I am not in this world to*
> *live up to your expectations. And you are not in this world to*
> *live up to mine.*
> *You are you and I am I. And if by chance we find each other, it's*
> *beautiful. If not, it can't be helped.*
>
> Fritz Perls

Technique: *Awareness Continuum*

Counseling Intention To guide the client(s) into the present; to diminish the façade of rationalizations, verbalizations, explanations, and interpretations.

Description   The client is diverted away from the emphasis on the *why* of behavior, as in psychoanalytic interpretation, toward the *what* and the *how* of behavior. Questions can include, "What are you aware of at this moment?" "How do you experience this now?" "Can you be your thoughts and your eyes and tell me the dialogue for them?"

Technique: *Parallel Dialogue*

Counseling Intention   To integrate personality and create a greater awareness of conflicting forces (Perls, 1969).

Description   When a dichotomy is manifested in the perceptions or behavior of a client, the client is asked to have an actual dialogue between these two components—for example, aggressive versus passive, secure versus insecure, outgoing versus shy. The dialogue also can be developed between the individual and some significant person. The client simply addresses the person as if he or she was there, imagines the response, or replies to the response. An understanding of more satisfying behaviors can be outlined.

Technique: *No Gossiping*

Counseling Intention   To facilitate direct confrontation of feelings (Fagen & Shepherd, 1970).

Description   The "no gossiping norm" facilitates direct confrontation of feelings. Clients often gossip about others when they have not been able to handle directly the feelings they arouse. Gossiping is defined (Fagen & Shepherd, 1970) as "talking about" individuals who are present rather than "talking to" them. For example, a group member might speak about another group member. Sue comments, "It frustrates me that we cannot begin on time because John is always late." The counselor intervenes and asks Sue to "talk to" John rather than about him. "John, I get frustrated when you come late because the group cannot begin on time."

Technique: *May I Feed You a Sentence?*

Counseling Intention   To confront thematic issues; to clarify perceptions (Fagen & Shepherd, 1970).

Description   By listening and observing the client, the counselor may infer that a particular theme, attitude, or message is implied—a key sentence. He or she may suggest or say, "May I feed you a sentence?" The key sentence is proposed for the client to practice with others in the group or with others in the client's daily interactions.

The counselor proposes the sentence, and the client tests out personal reactions to the sentence. Although this technique may seem highly interpretive, the client is encouraged to make it his or her own experience through active participation. With the counselor's selective framing of the key issue, the client then can provide spontaneous development.

Technique: *Can You Stay with This Feeling?*

Counseling Intention   To confront issues habitually avoided; to encourage self-confidence and autonomy (Fagen & Shepherd, 1970).

Description   This Gestalt technique is most effective when the client refers to a feeling, mood, or state of mind that is unpleasant, coupled with the defense mechanism of denial or avoidance. At a therapeutic junction the client may feel empty, confused, frustrated, or discouraged. The counselor says, "Can you stay with this feeling?"

The counselor asks the client to remain deliberately with his or her present experience. The counselor asks the client to elaborate on the what and the how of his or her feelings, for example, "What are your sensations . . . your perceptions . . . your fantasies . . . your expectations?"

Technique: *Shuttle between Here and There*
(between Reality and Fantasy)

Counseling Intention   To discover what is missing in the now.

Description   Close your eyes, and go away in your imagination to a place where you feel secure and happy. Come back to the here-and-now. Compare the two situations. You may be more aware of this world and have your goals more clearly in mind. Very often the "there" situation was preferable to the "here" situation. How was it preferable? What is it you want? Close your eyes and go away again, wherever you'd like to go. Did you notice any change since your last fantasy?

Come back to the here-and-now, and again compare the two situations. Has any change taken place? Continue to shuttle between the here and there until you feel comfortable in your present situation. Do this in any boring, tense, or uncomfortable situation. Very often, Perls (1969) maintained, the there situation gives you a cue for what is missing in the now. The difference between your "there and here" can show you the directions in which you want to move. As a long-range goal, the client may try making the real life more like his or her fantasy life.

Technique: *Bringing a Dream Back to Life*

Counseling Intention   To use dreams as a way to reveal unfinished business; to understand images in dreams that represent aspects of the client's personality (Fagen & Shepherd, 1970).

Description   Relive your dream as if it were happening now. Act it out in the present. Say the dream aloud, using the present tense. Be aware of what you are feeling when you say it. List all the elements of your dream: the people, animals, objects, colors, and moods. Be particularly aware of any situations, such as dying or falling, which you avoided in the dream by running away or waking up. Act out each of the elements. What does each part have to say? What do you have to say to it? What do the parts say to each other?

If in your dream there were situations you avoided, try to finish the dream by acting through frightening situations in fantasy. In acting out parts of your dream, you turn into a dreamer again and become one with your dreaming self. You may give words to characters whose emotions were unspoken in the dream so that now they engage in a dialogue.

Keeping a "dream diary" may help a client remember dreams. The following guidelines may be helpful:

1. Before going to sleep, repeat aloud, "Tomorrow morning I will remember my dreams." Say it 10 times slowly, like a chant.
2. Keep a paper and pen next to your bed. Upon awakening, record your dream in the greatest detail possible. If you do not remember a dream, lie quietly and see what comes to you. Very often any images or pictures that come to you are pieces of a dream.
3. After accumulating several weeks of notes on dreams, review them. What kinds of situations and which people occur most often? Notice images, sounds, colors, tastes, or smells that occur.

Sort your dreams in any way that seems meaningful to you. A dream is a personal letter to yourself. Dreams are windows to the subconscious.

Perspective for the Therapist: On support

Sickness, playing sick, which is a large part of this getting crazy, is nothing but the quest for environmental support. . . . Regression means a withdrawal to a position where you can provide your own support, where you feel secure.

Fritz Perls

Technique: *Mothers and Fathers/Husbands and Wives*

Counseling Intention   To evoke resentment and resolve conflict.

Description   Perls called resentment "the bite that hangs on." Resentment is eclipsed in guilt. The two always go together. Any time you feel guilty, you resent the person you feel guilty toward. When you feel resentful, you also want the other person to feel guilty. This exercise seeks to destroy symbolically the object of resentment.

Close your eyes and picture your mother (father, husband, or wife) in your mind's eye. Bang on a pillow and scream until you have discharged completely the resentment held toward this individual. Seek to destroy symbolically this oppressive individual. Become so physical with the pillow that you could answer yes to the question, "Is the individual dead'?"

Next, name all things that you hate a person for. "I hate him or her for beating me when I was a kid." "I hate him for embarrassing me in front of my friends." "I hate him for being so abusive toward my mom and for dying before I grew up." Then look at these resentments and forgive the person for it. If you get your feelings out, you will free the self from a demoralizing conflict. In addition, you can no longer go back and blame that individual again, because, symbolically at least, he or she is dead inside you.

Technique: *Reviewing Past Experience in the Here-and-Now*

Counseling Intention   To assist clients who are suffering from post-traumatic stress disorder, unresolved conflicts, or unfinished business; to encourage the client to reenact stories from the past by bringing them in present-tense language (Levitsky & Perls, 1973).

Description   The therapist should encourage reexperiencing the emotion so that the confusion, the fright, and the panic of a past event are experienced again in the present. For example, if a client says, "I was walking down the street and I felt disoriented," the therapist may have the client restate this as though it were happening in the present and in greater detail so that the statement might be, "I am walking down Elm Street. It is 10:00 in the morning. The air is humid and I feel hot and sticky. I am aware that I am lightheaded and confused. I realize that I am lost and I am feeling scared. Now I am feeling a sense of panic" (Crose, 1990, p. 283).

This maneuver allows the client to relive the experience rather than merely report what had occurred. By bringing the incident into the here-and-now, the therapist can facilitate the client's closure on the disturbing past event. Bringing past feelings into present awareness can assist a client in the final development state of ego integration.

Technique: *Dialoguing*

Counseling Intention   To process or articulate feelings of resentment.

Description   Identify someone for whom you have strong feelings of resentment. Sitting in a chair, get in touch with all the emotions, feelings, and behaviors that you resent about the individual. Verbally express your resentful feelings.

Next, switch chairs; think about what behaviors you demand they change. Identify your feelings toward the individual when they change the behaviors you resent. Verbally express your demands to that person. Finally, switch chairs again and think about the things that you appreciate about the individual.

Identify your feelings of appreciation for this individual. Verbally express all your feelings of appreciation to this individual. Shift back-and-forth, switching chairs between resentment, demands, and appreciation. The therapist assists the client in processing the experience.

> *Perspective for the Therapist: On self-actualization*
>
> *From Freud we learned that the past exists now in the person. Now we must learn, from growth theory and self-actualization theory, that the future also now exists in the person in the form of ideals, hopes, goals, unrealized potentials, mission, fate, and destiny. One for whom no future exists is reduced to the concrete, to helplessness, to emptiness. For him, time must be endlessly "filled." Striving, the usual organizer of most activity, when lost, leaves the person unorganized and unintegrated.*
>
> Abraham Maslow

Technique: *I Take Responsibility for . . .*

Counseling Intention   To help a client accept personal responsibility for his or her own feelings (Levitsky & Perls, 1973).

Description   Aloud, have the client make a statement describing personal feelings, and then add, "I take responsibility for it." For example, if the client often feels helpless, he or she might say, "I feel helpless, and I take responsibility for it." Other feelings that can be the objects of this exercise are boredom, isolation, rejection, or feeling unloved.

Technique: *Developing a Personal Vocabulary of Sight, Sound, and Movement*

Counseling Intention   To identify one's personal vocabulary by expressing perceiving sights, sounds, and motions all at once as preverbal language.

Description   With chalk, crayons, pens, brushes, and paints instruct the clients to draw. Make happy lines, tender lines, angry lines. Fill in shapes that express something about the self. Try different colors and various combinations of shapes. Recognize those that have significance. "You learn for yourself your own visual language; in creating your individual way of expression, you discover the messages you give yourself" (Rhyne, 1970, p. 277). Next, begin making sounds to express the form that is emerging from the paper. Let the sounds flow with the lines being drawn; synchronize visual rhythms with vocal ones. Next, stop drawing and direct the clients to express what has been drawn by moving their body: stand up and dance, lie down and roll, sit and rock, crawl, stomp, wiggle, leap, or curl up to convey what is being felt.

Process that movements are part of private sensory language and sounds are a way of saying something without wordiness. Communicating nonverbally, with sights and sounds and movements sending and receiving messages, is one's personal preverbal vocabulary.

Technique: *Creating Yourself with Clay*

Counseling Intention   To accept one's being (Rhyne, 1970).

Description   Ten to 12 people sit on the floor in a large circle facing each other. Each is given lump of clay. Direct them to feel and explore the clay, mold the clay, change its surface, texture, and form. Press, twist, squeeze, stretch, break, gouge, fold, smooth, scratch, and caress the clay, becoming aware of their feelings as this is done. With eyes closed, stay with the feelings.

Play—fantasize as if you were dreaming—play a game with yourself in pretending this lump of clay is you. You can create yourself by what you do to yourself. Do what you feel like doing, and feel what you like doing. Do not try to conceive of any representation of yourself or try to form any image of yourself. Open your eyes and see the form you have created. Be aware of your identity with it and of how much you can accept the clay as being an expression of you. As you look at your clay figure, relax your eyes, letting them become receivers of your image and your perception of yourself. Beginning with your eyes, relax your whole body. Lie down on the floor in a comfortable position and let yourself go on a fantasy trip. For a few minutes, imagine that there is no one in the world but you. What are you? You are not a simple, monumental being. You are a complex structure, with many parts making up the whole. Physically, emotionally and spiritually you are continuously in motion within yourself. Every part of you is affected by every other part—you cannot separate your mind from your body from your soul. Your breathing affects your feeling, your thinking affects your breathing; when you feel fear, you become tense, when you become tense you can't feel—when you don't trust your senses, you think so much you can't know anything that makes sense. All of these complex, interwoven patterns are you. You are a whole, too, functioning as a figure with the world around you as your background. You are a constellation in a galaxy. You are enough to make you dizzy. Allow yourself to be dizzy. Stop analyzing, stop thinking and allow yourself to sense and accept your being as you are—let yourself flow with yourself wherever your fantasies take you. (Rhyne, 1970, pp. 278–279)

Instruct members to come back to the world of the here-and-now. They may speak to others about their experience but also understand that words cannot describe the totality of their experience.

Technique: *Yourself and an Other in Space*

Counseling Intention   To communicate graphically (Rhyne, 1970).

Description   Place a large piece of blank paper and chalks of many colors between partners. Direct the partners to look at each other until they feel they have made contact and on some level know each other. Direct them to look at the paper between them. The paper represents an environment in which partners are being together. Have them draw on the one sheet at the same time. Discover what each feels in sharing his or her relationship with the other within that space. Using lines, shapes, and colors, they must communicate nonverbally. While drawing, partners can demand that space be left alone, push his or her partner into a corner, share some areas or the whole page, go toward or retreat from each other, support, cross out, cover up, or cooperate with each other. Each can oppose, lead, or follow his or her partner. Process how each person graphically communicated and how well each gave and received messages.

Technique: *An* Other *Who Is Also* You

Counseling Intention   To explore and discover awareness with clay (Rhyne, 1970).

Description   Provide clients with a large amount of clay. Direct them to move the mass with their hands and express what they are feeling. Have the clients close their eyes and gradually focus their awareness on some person with whom they have deep emotional ties. With the clay form, have clients form an image of this person as the client perceives that person. Process the following: "How much of your emotional energy is invested in the other?" "Do you know experientially who the other *is* in a part of you?" "Can you separate his 'is-ness' from your own?" "Is this other also you?" "Are you making an image of a disowned part of yourself?"

Technique: *Giving Attention to Another Person*

Counseling Intention   Partners from a group are given handfuls of clay and a clay board on which to work. First, the partners are to sit down back to back on the floor, placing the clay in front of them. Partners touch as much of each other's back, shoulders, head, and arms as can be agreed upon nonverbally. They are to give full attention to sensing each other, as they perceive each other to be. Next, they work the clay into an image representing what impressions they received from each other on making the initial back-to-back contact. Upon completion of the clay image, partners turn and face each other and discuss briefly with each other how the nonverbal responses are reflected in the clay images.

Second, with paper and drawing tools, partners are to sit facing each other and, by making eye contact, discover as much as they can about each other. Then they draw a portrait of the other, using only eyes as senders and receivers of messages. The portrait can be representational, abstract, or symbolic. Upon completion of the portraits, briefly discuss the portrait without going into detailed interpretations or explanations.

Third, partners should try knowing each other through hands. They should touch and explore each other's hands, move each other's hands together, and be aware of feelings, desires, and resistances and what each is trying to convey. Each partner is to draw a representation of how he or she felt they were experienced through the exploration of their hands.

Using the three images as a reference, partners speak to each other using words, touching, drawing, movement, and perhaps silence to reflect on the experience.

Technique: *Creating a World That Is "You"*

Counseling Intentions   To graphically represent on a primitive level one's perception of territoriality and how it affects and is affected by one's relationship with another person (Rhyne, 1970).

Description   Provide a collage and collection of art materials such as paper, wood, wire, leaves, stones, magazines, newspapers, cardboard, or parts of boxes. The client is to create his or her world from the materials provided. The client is to choose any material he or she feels like, and use them in any way he or she has a feeling for doing. The important goal is for the client to see his or her own world and recognize it for what it is. From a Gestalt point of view the client should embrace that "I structured this world with materials I chose; within the limits of what is possible for me, I take responsibility for creating my own personal world" (Rhyne, 1970, p. 283).

Technique: *Accepting and Rejecting What Is Offered*

Counseling Intention   To become aware of feelings and to express them.

Description   Sit in a closed circle of 10 to 12 members with one sheet of paper and felt-tip pens in many colors. The client begins drawing on his or her sheet of paper, starting but not finishing a graphic description of something important to him or her. The members are instructed to pass their drawings to the person on the left, at the same time receiving a drawing from the person on the right. Members are to work on the drawing they received as it were their own, adding and changing it at will. This rotating process continues until the members receive their own original drawings.

Upon receiving their modified drawing, members should be directed to become aware of how they feel on seeing the expressions of others imposed on their drawing. Process the following questions: Is there anything of you left in that composite drawing? Is there anything that is not you, but that you would like to keep? Are there areas you would like to obliterate? What do you want to do with this pattern that is in your hands now? Using art materials, what can you do?

Technique: *Making a World Together*

Counseling Intention   To explore, experience, and express what is not imaginary (Rhyne, 1970).

Description   Members sit around a large paper circle with a pile of assorted stuff such as odd shapes of colored paper, pieces of string, straw, beads, bits of wood, and foam rubber. Members are to pretend that the circle is a space where they as a group can create a world and use the materials to create a Gestalt, a figure on and related to the background of his or her world—the world made here-and-now among them. Each member is to choose what he or she wants to represent himself or herself in the world. They will use scissors, crayons, and glue to create a collage on the circle, representing their interrelationships and how they perceive themselves as being in one limited environment.

Members are encouraged to talk with one another as they work. Instruct them to be aware of each one's personal role in this process and to reflect on feelings of how much they are doing now as well as in their real-world living situation. Process that this is an imagery game that makes concrete and explicit the members' acceptance of self as an active creator of the world of process with many others, and what members are being and doing in an environment that is nothing in itself: *With our capacities for awareness and our abilities for action, we make our own world out of materials available to us.*

> *Perspective for the Therapist: On resistance*
>
> *Resistance is the friend of isolation and the enemy of caring. It is a defense against fear, pain, and rejection.*
>
> Herbert B. Pollack
> Judith B. Slan

REDECISION THERAPY

Redecision therapy has emerged out of an amalgamation of transactional analysis (TA) and Gestalt therapy. The theory of transactional analysis serves as the conceptual core, along with terms developed to describe the processes used in redecision therapy. Impasses, contract, cons, games, early decisions anchoring, injunctions, and scripts are part of the lexicon of this treatment (Gladfelter, 1992, pp. 319–334). See Chapter 10 for an overview of transactional analysis.

Redecison therapy is an approach to group psychotherapy. (See Chapter 3 for group psychotherapy techniques.) It combines the cognitive clarity of TA with the affective engagement of Gestalt therapy. The redecision approach is based on the "transaction" and "scripts." The *adult ego state* is the component of the personality that processes incoming data similar to a computer. The *child ego state* is the part that is young and emotional. The *parent ego state* is wise and rational, the part of people that acts and talks like parents, both serious and nurturing. The *child state* is thought of as having two components: the Free Child, which is little, happy, spontaneous, and fun loving, and the Adapted Child, which focuses on trying to find a way to adapt to a grown-up parental world. *Games* are those interchanges between people that repeatedly result in their feeling bad and blaming others, much like scapegoating. *Transactions* are those communicative interchanges between ego states of two or more persons that may contain both social and psychological messages. A *social message* is the meaning content of the message, and the *psychological message* is the emotion and the value content. A *script* is a life plan chosen early by the child ego state that enables the child to survive and can result in maladaptive behavior for an adult. The early decision of the child ego state is the beginning point of the script (Gladfelter, 1992, p. 320).

Goals of Redecision Therapy

1. Clients reclaim power and responsibility for their own lives.
2. Clients make changes in themselves in a nurturing and therapeutic environment.
3. The therapist models more appropriate ways of living and being.
4. The errors in thinking that the client manifests are consistently confronted.
5. Incongruencies between behavior and thinking are identified and confronted.
6. Modified Gestalt techniques such as the empty chair are used to engage the client's bad feeling.
7. The group operates on the basis of clear rules established by the therapist.

The therapist focuses on the early decisions made from the child ego state. From early on clients made decisions about their feelings, their thinking, and their behavior that may have been dysfunctional. They were influenced by their caregiver and made their choices based on their own interpretation of the world.

   The theoretical concepts of redecision therapy integrate many of the skills and beliefs of the newer psychotherapy approach (Gladfelter, 1990). A variety of therapeutic techniques from other approaches, such as psychodrama, behavior therapy, cognitive therapy, and Gestalt therapy are integrated into redecision therapy. In the group setting, the therapist works one-on-one with members. The group benefits through contagion of affect from the client who is working with the therapist. The group provides supportive positive feedback to the group member who is working on his or her issues. A goal of therapy is to develop a contract for change that is specific, reasonable, and objective, focusing on changes that are both behavioral and emotional.

Technique: *Parent Interview*

Counseling Intention   To help clients discover changes they want to make in themselves.

Description   The therapist invites the client to be the parent who seems most ambiguous or aloof to him or her. The therapist then invites that parent by given name to talk to the therapist about his or her own life feelings and experiences. The client enters the internal parent ego states and discloses information to which the client may not be aware he or she has access. In the parent interview, the client's voice, demeanor, attitude, and vocabulary change and approximate the parent ego state from early life. The values and beliefs of the parent also become clear. The client is often surprised at the information available through the parent interview. Other members in the group corroborate for the client the changes gone through during the process (Gladfelter, 1990, 1992).

CONCLUSION

Gestalt psychology's emergence in 1912 was in part a reaction against structuralism, an influential school of thought in Germany at the time. Obviously, the structuralist's interest in breaking conscious experience into its component parts seemed ill advised in light of the Gestalt theorists' demonstration that the whole can be much greater than the sum of its parts. At its peak, Gestalt therapy was an active combatant in psychology and counseling theoretical wars and was responsible for some major advances in the study of perception, problem solving, and interpersonal behavior.

   Gestalt therapists try to help clients become aware of their feelings through the use of a variety of techniques. One of the unique approaches in Gestalt therapy is telling clients to "own their own feelings" by talking in an active rather than a passive way. For example, " I feel anxious when he's around" instead of "He makes me anxious when he's around." Redecision therapy is a hybrid therapy that employs a lot of techniques from theories such as Gestalt therapy.

Chapter 5

Nonverbal and Metaphorical Techniques

We respond to gestures with an extreme alertness and,
one might almost say, in accordance with an elaborate
and secret code that is written nowhere, known by none,
and understood by all.

Edward Sapir,
Communication, Encylopedia of
the Social Sciences, 1931, pp. 78–81

Nonverbal communication can be defined as all messages other than words that people exchange (DeVito & Hecht, 1990). Nonverbal messages are used to send three primary meanings: immediacy, power, and responsiveness (Mehrabian, 1971). We communicate about 60% of our meaning nonverbally. Many researchers maintain that another person's actual words contribute only 7% to the impression of being liked or disliked, while voice cues contribute 38% and facial cues contribute 55%. Nonverbal messages are usually more believable than verbal messages. When verbal and nonverbal messages contradict, most adults in the United States believe the nonverbal message. Millions of dollars are spent annually to create impressions or special images. Individuals strive to hide negative feelings and disguise bad moods while spending millions of dollars on medication and cosmetic surgery.

In addition, individuals often fake their real attitudes to create the impression that what they feel is appropriate for the situation. For example, many Americans become uncomfortable with periods of silence; in business or social situations, if a gap occurs they will quickly try to fill it with conversation. There are many different channels of nonverbal communication: facial expressions, the clues in our voices (vocal paralanguage), tactile communication (haptics), body movements (kinesics), spatial communication (proxemics and territoriality), and time (chronemics). The American slogans "time is money," "there is no time like the present," "time flies," "time heals all wounds," and "take time to smell the roses" are indicative of how American culture values time, as well as sending mixed messages to hurry up and to slow down. There are also many cultural differences in nonverbal behavior. For example, when shaking hands, Americans use a firm, solid grip; Middle Easterners and Asians prefer a gentle grip—a firm grip to them suggests unnecessary aggressiveness. In making eye contact, Americans are taught to look directly; Japanese and Koreans are taught to avoid direct eye contact— direct eye contact to them is considered a weakness, and may indicate sexual overtones. Further, the gesture of forming a circle with thumb and forefinger to signal OK means "zero" or worthless in France, money in Japan, and calling someone a very bad name in Germany. Finally, putting feet on a table is found offensive in nearly every other country around the globe except the United States.

Perspective for the Therapist: On body language

The truest expression of a people is its dances and its music. Bodies never lie.

Agnes de Mille

NONVERBAL COMMUNICATION

Look into a person's pupils; he cannot hide himself.

Confucius

Nonverbal behavior can offer a greater understanding of communication. Table 5.1 illustrates Mole's (2002) four basic modes of body language in business.

Eye Contact

The eyes serve as a scanning mechanism, and their input is subject to a variety of secondary perceptual responses, as significant stimuli are differentiated from less important ones. A highly emotional link established as two people simultaneously observe each other's eyes. Gazing at another's eyes arouses strong emotions. Thus, eye contact rarely lasts longer than three seconds before one or both viewers experience a powerful urge to glance away. Breaking eye contact lowers stress levels (as measured by breathing rate, heart rate, and sweaty palms). Visual perception is capable of overriding all other information should any of it conflict with the visual sense (DeVito & Hecht, 1990).

In addition, culturally prescribed norms of visual engagement exert a profound impact on gazing patterns (Hall, 1963). For example, certain cultural groups such as Americans, Japanese, and Navaho Indians are taught not to stare at others, whereas Arabs, Greeks, and South Americans emphasize intense eye contact as evidence of sincerity, intent, and interest (DeVito & Hecht, 1990). In both social and business situations, direct eye contact is very important, and avoiding it implies boredom or disinterest. Winking in America can signal diverse messages: flirtation, friendliness, amusement, or "I am just kidding." Many people stop using eye contact when they are speaking about their successes due to fear of embarrassment. Others stop using eye contact when they are talking about painful things.

People who consistently look upward tend to think mainly in pictures, making visual images of their thoughts. When talking to these people, communication is enhanced if the speaker uses "visual" vocabulary—words and phrases such as "insight," "vision," "picture this," "in my view," "let's take a look." People who tend to look sideways think mainly about what they hear in verbal/analytical terms. When speaking to these people pay attention to order, logic, chronology, and provide a multimedia presentation.

Blank Face

Though expressionless, the blank face sends a strong emotional message: "Do Not Disturb." In shopping malls, in elevators, or on subways, we adopt neutral faces to distance ourselves from strangers. The blank face is a subtle sign used to keep others at a polite distance away.

Looking Down

Averting gaze serves to assure the other person that he or she is not an object of prying or attention. It might be considered "social inattention." Looking down may convey a defeated attitude. It may also reflect guilt, shame, or submissiveness, as when distorting the truth or telling a lie. For example, gazing down while— or shortly after—stating "I am innocent" shows that a speaker may not believe his or her own remarks. True statements are normally given with a confident, face-to-face or level gaze, which may be held longer than three seconds.

Lowering the Eyebrow

Lowering the eyebrows is a sensitive indicator of disagreement, doubt, or uncertainty. Slightly lowered eyebrows may telegraph unvoiced disagreement among colleagues, as comments are presented at a conference table. Ekman (1980) revealed that anger is expressed by eyebrows that are lowered and drawn together, a hard stare and lips tightly pressed together. Further, anger is ambiguous unless expressed in all parts of the face.

Raising the Eyebrow

Raising the eyebrows adds intensity to a facial expression. Eyebrow raising can strengthen a dominant stare, exaggerate a submissive pout, or boost the energy of a smile. Also, a raised eyebrow with forehead wrinkles often indicates skepticism or sadness.

Exhibiting Dominance

Dominance is the influence of power, or control over another. Power labels generally reference the same domain of communication: assertiveness, authority, control, coercion, compliance, dominance, power, social influence, and status (Berger, 1985). Dominance shows in such nonverbal signals such as the business suit, the eyebrow raise, the hands-on-hips posture, and a lower tone of voice. Formal dress has been found to be an indicator of increased power and control. Dominance cues may also be used to express a confident mood. When confronting someone in a close relationship, the person may reach out and take both of the others' hands.

Arms Crossed

Many people claim that they cross their arms not because they are defensive, but because they are cold. Though often decoded as a *defensive* barrier sign, the arm-cross represents a comfortable position for relaxing the arms while speaking. With arms and elbows pulled tightly into the body, the gesture may reveal *acute nervousness* or *chronic anxiety*.

Held less tightly against the chest, with elbows elevated and projecting outward away from the body, the arm-cross presents a guard-like stance, suggestive of arrogance, dislike, or disagreement. This kind of gesture will communicate that you want the difficult words that you are sharing to increase your intimacy rather than to put a wedge in it. A caring gesture during a confrontation can assist the other person in hearing you instead of defending themselves.

Hand behind Head

The hands-behind-head gesture signals feelings of superiority, dominance, and a know-it-all attitude. In a conversation, hand-behind-head may be read as a potential sign of uncertainty, conflict, disagreement, frustration, anger, or disliking (i.e., social aversion). It usually reflects *negative* thoughts, feelings, and moods. In counseling, interviewing, and cross-examining, the gesture telegraphs a probing point—an unresolved issue to be verbalized and explored. In the United States, leaning back and placing *both hands* behind the neck in the bilateral *head clamp*

TABLE 5.1
Decoding Body Language

Responsive	Reflective	Fugitive	Combative
Engaged	**Listening**	**Bored**	**Let me speak**
Leaning forward	Head tilted	Staring into space	Finger tapping
Open body	Lots of eye contact	Slumped posture	Foot tapping
Open arms	Nodding	Doodling	Staring
Open hands	High blink rate	Foot tapping	
Eager	**Evaluating**	**Let me go**	**Aggresive**
(Sprint position)	Sucks on glasses	Feet toward door	Leaning forward
Open legs	or pencil	Looking around	Finger pointing
Feet under chair	Strokes chin	Buttoning jacket	Fists clenched
On toes	Looks up and right		
Leaning forward	Legs crossed		
	(Ankle on knee)		
Ready to agree	**Attentive**	**Rejection**	**Defiant**
Closes papers	(Standing)	Sitting/moving back	(Standing)
Pen down	Arms behind back	Arms folded	Hands on hips
Hands flat on table	Smile	Legs crossed	Frown
	Open feet	(Thigh on knee)	
		Head down	
		Frown	
		Defensive	**Lying**
		(Standing)	Touches face
		Feet pointing in	Hand over mouth
		Hands clenched	Pulls ear
			Eyes down
			Glances at you
			Shifts in seat
			Looks down and
			to the left

Source: Decoding Body Language: The Four Basic Modes in Business. John Mole *www.johnmole.com* articles. 18htm©John Mole. Reprinted by permission.

posture is a nonverbal sign of dominance. "This display reveals that someone feels no need to show eagerness or attention" (Morris 1994, p. 142).

Hands-on-Hips

Hands-on-hips is an aggressive pose, especially if the heart and throat are exposed in a nonverbal display of fearlessness. Critical evaluation gestures are often seen with the hands-on-hips. Hands-on-hips shows that the body is prepared to "take steps" to perform, to take part in, or to take charge of an event, activity, or work assignment. As a nonverbal cue, the posture shows that the body is poised to "step forward" (e.g., to carry out a superior's order, to discipline or threaten a subordinate, or to defend against those who "overstep their bounds").

Drop of the Jaw

The jaw drop is a reliable sign of surprise, puzzlement, or uncertainty. The expression is often seen in adults and children who have lost their way (e.g., in airports), or are entering or walking through unfamiliar, crowded, or potentially threatening places (e.g., darkened restaurants, taverns, and bars).

PROXEMICS

Hall (1968) maintained that proxemics is the study of humankind's "perception and use of space." Informal space is characterized by a personal zone or "bubble" that varies for individuals and circumstances. The use of each of these spatial relationships can impede or promote the act of communication, but the area that humans control and use most often is their informal space. This zone constitutes an area that humans protect from the intrusion of outsiders. The study of spatial territory for the purpose of communication uses four categories for informal space: the intimate distance for embracing or whispering (6 to 18 inches), the personal distance for conversations among good friends (1.5 to 4 feet), social distance for conversations among acquaintances (4 to 12 feet), and public distance used for public speaking (12 feet or more).

Territoriality is established so rapidly that even the second session in a series of lectures is sufficient to find most of the audience returning to their same seats. Further, in business offices territoriality is related to status. An extra chair to a secretarial pool employee, for example, can easily become a symbol of status—a professional reason for having visitors. The proxemic key resides in where the chair is placed, and in what relation to the desk. There are several basic arrangements for the desk:

- Occupant is enthroned and protected from intrusion on three sides (corner)
- Occupant's back faces the entryway (in order to look out the window?)
- Occupant allows entry and space at front and one side of desk.

Business territory is culturally related as well. For example, German business personnel visiting the United States see open doors in offices and businesses as indicative of an unusually relaxed and unbusinesslike attitude. Americans get the feeling that the Germans' closed doors conceal a secretive or conspiratorial operation (Vargas, 1986).

Perspective for the Therapist: On space

Space flights are merely an escape, a fleeing away from oneself, because it is easier to go to Mars or to the moon than it is to penetrate one's own being.

Carl Gustav Jung

Body Space

Americans have a pattern that discourages physical contact, except in moments of intimacy. When riding on a subway or crowded elevator, people have a tendency to "hold themselves in," having been taught from early childhood to avoid bodily contact with strangers. Research has indicated that Americans are especially conscious of their personal space and allow much less intrusion than do other nationalities, even with those people considered to be friends. From a meta-analysis of various studies, Vrugt and Kerkstra (1984) concluded that, "In interaction between strangers the interpersonal distance between women is smaller than between men and women."

Changing the distance between two people can convey a desire for intimacy, declare a lack of interest, or increase/decrease domination. Police interrogators have been taught that this violation of personal space can nonverbally convey a message; they often use the strategy of sitting close and crowding a suspect. This theory of interrogation assumes that invasion of the suspect's personal space (with no chance for defense) will give the officer a psychological advantage.

Public Spaces

ELEVATOR SPACE

"In choosing to approach someone in order to push the [button on the control] panel, men and women reacted to different signals" (Knapp & Hall, 1992). "Men prefer to approach people who stand with eyes averted over people who look at them and smile. Women, however, prefer to approach people who look at them and smile" (Vrugt & Kerkstra, 1984).

ESCALATOR SPACE

"Men will react more to a person standing immediately behind them, just one step behind, with the hands reaching forward on the rail so as to be visible" (Vrugt & Kerkstra, 1984). "Women seem to prefer to act as if they do not notice anything, so that unwanted contact can be avoided. Men make it clear in their reactions that they do not appreciate such a rapprochement" (Vrugt & Kerkstra, 1984).

LIBRARY SPACE

Regardless of the "invader's sex," men who are already seated at an otherwise occupied table will view someone sitting of the opposite sex negatively. Already seated women view other women most negatively (Fisher & Byrne, 1975).

RESTAURANT SPACE

Corner and wall tables are always occupied first (Eibl-Eibesfeldt, 1970).

Neighborhood Space

The prime directive of neighborhood space is, "Stay in your own yard." That we are terribly territorial is reflected by the barriers defined in fencing. According to the American Fencing Association, 38,880 miles of chain link, 31,680 miles of wooden, and 1,440 miles of ornamental fencing are bought annually in the United States. Each year Americans buy enough residential fencing to encircle the earth nearly three times (Givens, 2002).

City Space

The home range spreads outward 15 to 30 miles in all directions from a central *home base*. The home range of those dwelling in the city includes a home base (an apartment or a house) as well, along with favored foraging territories (e.g., a shopping mall and supermarket), child care (i.e., a school), a sporting area (e.g., a golf course), a work space (an office building), and from 5 to 9 nocturnal drinking-and-dining spots. Life is spent occupying these favorite spaces, and orbiting among them on habitually traveled pathways, sidewalks, and roads. "Trip chaining" is the contemporary term for families who combine a series of routine errands with long-distance commutes from home to work.

Initiatives such as New York City's zero-tolerance policy toward abandoned cars, abandoned buildings, and even graffiti have been enacted because even small signs of crime and decay in a neighborhood, such as broken windows, encourage crime by signaling that such behavior is tolerated (Bayles, 2000).

Home Space

There are social zones within a personal environment. Some rooms are acceptable for public gatherings, others for close friends and relatives, some are even considered off-limits to certain family members (e.g., children and pets), and some are left untouched, preserved, and ready for only occasional occupancy (formal dining room). The seating arrangement in a living room presents more difficult proxemics when it revolves around a television set. Rooms with a linear or curved seating alignment are not conducive to small, intimate gatherings, because people like to face each other while talking. If forced to sit side by side, individuals will try to compensate for this lack of eye-to-eye contact by leaning in shoulder to shoulder. The most common space for such direct contact is usually the kitchen or dining room table. The proxemics of the furniture itself and how it defines our use of distance establishes a key factor in what we consider to be a cozy, comfortable, family atmosphere.

Technique: *Actions Speak Louder Than Words*

Counseling Intention   To facilitate awareness and self-understanding of perceptions.

Description   The counselor interprets the nonverbal communication of the client. If the client nonverbally shows anger and hostility while telling about the need to provide for his ailing mother-in-law, the counselor points out the discrepancy.

Technique: *Nonverbal Exaggeration or Verbal Repetition*

Counseling Intention   To confront verbal or nonverbal communication more directly and assertively.

Description   Often a client's verbal or nonverbal communication may become fragmented or incomplete. Gestures may be undeveloped or a sentence may be incomplete. The client could be asked to exaggerate the movement repeatedly to make the inner meaning more apparent. A complementary technique is repeating a statement that has been glossed over. Have the client say the words over and louder to absorb fully the impact of repressed communication.

Technique: *Breaking In*

Counseling Intention   To explore issues of inclusion and exclusion.

Description   Members are asked to stand in a tight circle and one person is left outside the circle. He or she attempts to penetrate the group in any way possible. Break In can be used as a springboard for members to explore their feelings of being rejected, isolated, or made an outsider by the current group, or as experienced in his or her own life at the present. The use of "territoriality" to define in-group and out-group expectations also can be processed.

Technique: *Meeting Someone Halfway*

Counseling Intention   To communicate nonverbally.

Description   Divide the group into two sections at opposite sides of the room, facing each other. Members are instructed that when they choose (or if they choose), they may walk out to the center of the room and wait for someone on the other side to join them. When the two meet, whatever communication the two desire can take place, but communication is to be nonverbal. Members should process their reactions to the experience and explore their relationship with the person who met them and those who did not.

Technique: *Group Sociogram*

Counseling Intention   To focus on communication, relationships, and attachments.

Description   Group members participate to form a living sociogram by placing and moving themselves and each other around the room in ways that are meaningful to them. The final form of the sociogram could be drawn on a flipchart for processing and discussion.

Technique: *Sticks and Stones*

Counseling Intention   To focus on issues of power, dominance, influence, and aggression.

Description   Yardsticks and large stones are placed in the center of the group. The leader instructs the members to use them without talking to express their reactions to each other.

Technique: *Feedback through Posture*

Counseling Intention   To focus on first impressions and perceptions versus reality

Description   Group members focus on each other, one at a time, to receive feedback from other members in the group. Each member assumes a body posture that indicate his or her impressions of the individual. After all members posture for one individual, the exercise is processed before the next member is focused on.

Technique: *Beating Drums*

Counseling Intention   To communicate emotions and feelings; to develop trust.

Description   The leader plays a recording of drum music and instructs group members to dance freely along with the music. The leader stops the music and instructs the members to freeze. Members observe each other's figure and choose a partner to process the experience.

Technique: *Nature Walk/City Streets*

Counseling Intention   To increase sensory awareness; to discuss environmental stress.

Description   Group members take a walk in the park or on the city streets. Members are instructed to explore, in as much detail as they can, their environment and to communicate their feelings to each other without talking.

Technique: *The Eyes Have It*

Counseling Intention   To increase comfort levels, openness, and self-disclosure.

Description   The group stands in a circle. A group member rotates clockwise around in the circle, establishing eye contact and communicating nonverbally with each of the other members. At the conclusion, the member returns to his or her spot in the circle. The next member follows the same procedure of eye contact and nonverbal expression until all members have contacted all others.

Technique: *Talking with Your Hands*

Counseling Intention   To identify and communicate feelings.

Description   Group members get a partner and move a comfortable distance from the other members. The leader instructs partners to communicate nonverbally feelings such as anger, frustration, hate, euphoria, love, grief, joy, contentment, and fear. Each feeling should be announced independently of the others with approximately one minute for the pairs to process each experience.

Technique: *Unwrapping the Problem*

Counseling Intention To provide an opportunity to convey resistance or conflict.

Description A group member who may be experiencing resistance or interpersonal conflict is asked to curl into a tight ball. He or she may choose another member (or ask a member to assume another significant person in his or her life) to unwrap or open him or her up completely. The member may succumb or resist.

Technique: *Touch-Talk Blind Milling*

Counseling Intention To communicate nonverbally.

Description Mill around the room with your eyes closed. As you come in contact with someone, explore that person with your eyes and hands. Touch his or her face, shoulders, hair, and hands. Communicate only through use of touch and try to convey a message about how you feel about the person, allowing time for your partner to communicate back to you. Move on to another person in the group and repeat the process.

Technique: *Eyes as Windows to the Soul*

Counseling Intention To dismantle first encounter facades; to encourage genuine contact.

Description Sit facing a partner, and stare directly into each other's eyes for five minutes. Tell your partner something important with your eyes. See what your partner has to say to you. Follow-up with five minutes of talking to learn as much as possible about each other.

Technique: *Pantomimes*

Counseling Intention To express feelings toward oneself and others that may not be ordinarily verbalized.

Description　Sit with your partner. Stand and pantomime your impression of that person. Show your feelings with gestures and facial expressions. Then pantomime how you feel your partner feels about you. Reverse the process, then discuss revelations about individual impressions.

Technique: *Multiple Body Language Exercises*

Counseling Intention　Understanding body language.

Description　These exercises are designed to help students tune in to the subtleties of body language and what they might mean about interpersonal behavior.

Warm-Up 1: Hand Gestures
Ask clients to demonstrate and describe the meaning of various hand gestures. Discuss how facial expressions and other body movements influence the meaning of a hand gesture. What do hand gestures mean in different cultures?

Warm-Up 2: Bar Body Behavior
Discuss body language in a bar or club. What personality types can you detect just by looking at how people use their bodies? What are the obvious and subtle behaviors of the braggart, the flirt, the wallflower, or the drunk? Consider such factors as personal space, posture, eye contact, and speed and angle of movement.

Warm-Up 3: The Tell
Gamblers and con artists long have known that people reveal their inner thoughts through body language without even knowing it. For example, if one places a coin in one hand behind the back and then presents both fists to a body-savvy person, that person may be able to detect where the coin is. One's "tell" will indicate which hand holds it. A person may lean his or her body to one side, hold one hand higher than the other, point his or her nose toward the object, or unintentionally leak some other behavior that gives away the "secret."

　　Have clients form pairs to try this coin experiment. Some people are much more adept at it than others. This exercise works best if the person with the coin is not told (initially) about the concept of the "tell."

Warm-Up 4: Mirroring
This exercise also works well as a warm-down to improvised role-plays. Have clients pair off. Either sitting or standing, one person in each pair takes the lead and begins to move in any way he or she wishes (tell them to avoid talking, since it's distracting). The task for the other client is to follow or mimic everything that the leader does. Encourage people to use both obvious and subtle behaviors. Do

this for a minute or two, then switch roles of who is leading and who is following. Finally, tell the dyads to do the exercise one last time except that *no one* is the leader or the follower. Both people in the pair should try to move in unison, as if they are mirroring each other simultaneously in a body language "dance." This is somewhat hard to do and takes a bit of practice before a pair gets the hang of it. If the pair is successful, what usually happens is that there are rapid, minute shifts between leading and following. Also, have everyone switch partners several times and repeat the above steps.

This mirroring can be done with body language alone, facial expressions alone, or body language with facial expressions. This last one is considerably more difficult to do than the first two.

This simple exercise sensitizes the client to the details of body movement and expression. It also may say something about interpersonal styles. Some clients prefer to "lead" while others prefer to "follow." In particular, some people are very empathically in tune with the others' movements, while some people cannot focus on this. Also, moving in unison is easy for some people, but not for others, which says something about how "in sync" a dyad is.

IMPROVISED ROLE PLAYS IN GROUPS

Ask the groups to create a role-play that involves only body language and no talking. The group can pick any scene and characters it wants. Encourage the group not to overplan the role-play. Instead, suggest that they pick a scene, define the characters in the scene, and think of a few possibilities for events that might occur in the scene. Then improvise within that general structure. This makes for a much more spontaneous and interesting role-play than the more rigid alternative of carefully scripting all the action.

Each group takes its turn at improvising its scene in front of the group. A group may set up the role-play by telling the members where the scene is taking place and who is in the scene. Another interesting and fun alternative is for the group to provide no introduction to the role-play. The group can then guess what is happening in the scene.

Rather than having clients come up with the ideas for the improvisations, the therapist can provide them. Give each group a card with a scene on it that they will role-play—a scene that involves no talking. For example:

- It's 11:30 on New Year's Eve. The bus is late.
- It's the end of a party. You are the last people left.
- You are all friends at a funeral.
- You are family members on the way back from a vacation. A few minutes ago you had a big fight.

Each group takes its turn performing its role-play in front of the group. Before each group starts, the therapist can read to the group the scene descriptions from the cards, or not read the descriptions and let the group guess what the scene is about. After each role-play, the group discusses what they believe was happening in the scene based on what they saw in the body language. What are the personalities of the people, their relationships with each other, or the issues affecting the group?

CONTEMPORARY THEORY ON THE USE OF METAPHOR IN COUNSELING

Metaphorical communication has been used in the form of stories, myths, parables, fairy tales, allegories, and anecdotes. In counseling and psychotherapy, it can serve as a technique to access resources within the client that may not be recognized or utilized. Towers, Wollum, Dow, Senese, Ames, Berg, & McDonald (1987) found that metaphors arouse client interest in the counseling process and increase the client's view of the counselor as a trustworthy person. Metaphors also can be used to illustrate specific interpersonal issues, suggest solutions, help clients recognize themselves or clarify their circumstances, and reframe problems (Barker, 1985).

Metaphor is an indispensable dimension of human understanding and experience and is essential to understanding the way individuals think, reason, perceive, imagine, communicate, believe, and relate. Adopting language that is more consistent with the client's way of thinking increases a therapist's effectiveness (Wickman, 1999). Much of client's self-understanding is the product of the search for appropriate personal metaphors that give meaning to their lives. Understanding conceptual metaphors allows counselors to join with clients through increased rapport and empathy, and to structure therapeutic interventions that are more consistent frameworks (Wickman, Daniels, White, & Fesmire, 1999, p. 393). Contemporary theory of metaphor provides counselors with more complete and rapid access to the client's conceptual world. The therapist attempts to gain an understanding of the client's experience where abstract ideas (like relationships) are understood in terms of more concrete experiences (like journeys). Hence, when a couple in therapy says, "It feels like we're just spinning our wheels," or when a client in therapy says, "It feels like I'm on an emotional roller coaster," both are giving information about how they conceptualize their relationships or themselves in relation to their environment.

Technique: *Self-metaphors*

Counseling Intention   To evoke a more creative perspective on one's self (Goodman, 1985).

Description   Metaphors are powerful tools that people can use to enjoy new and creative perspectives on themselves, their values, and their world. This exercise provides an opportunity for validation from self and others, focusing on what they prize or value for themselves. The leader suggests that this activity will be an opportunity for each member to reinforce feelings of "I like me" by completing the statement "I am like *X* because *Y*," thereby creating a positive self-metaphor. Members should be directed to write in first person (i.e., "What do I like about myself and what from my environment is most like me?"). Read the examples below to the group:

> *"I am like a snowman. People think of me as a really cool guy, but I have an emotional side that people don't always see. When someone else gets all hot and bothered, I can melt quickly. I really do feel for someone who is upset."*

> — —

> *"I am a stream. I have a surface that everyone can see. But there are many things going on underneath that surface. I am one stream; within that stream are many different currents that flow at different speeds and in different directions. I hope to get in touch with my flow."*

> — —

> *"I am like the wind. I can be as noticeable as a hurricane or as unassuming as a light breeze. I can go anywhere. It's my choice. People are concerned about me and like to hear the daily forecast. Yet I'm unpredictable and like myself that way."*

After each person has completed a metaphor, place all the papers together in a pile. Shuffle them, and then redistribute them to people at random. Each person then writes a validating response to the self-metaphor he or she has received. This validation should reflect empathic listening—expressing ways that person supports, identifies with, and/or appreciates the individual who wrote the self-metaphor. The response should speak directly to the metaphor itself, as in the samples below:

> *"Hello Snowman! You are a very refreshing person! I always have enjoyed being around you. You are so versatile. I admire your ability to stand your ground when it's rough outside; and I appreciate how you can 'flow' with the situation when things heat up. Your quiet presence is reassuring. The delight you bring to young people is wonderful to watch. Take care, be cool, The House."*

--

"Dear Stream: It must be exciting to be a stream, to have the different speeds and directions to pick from. To choose what fills your needs, when you are needing. Getting in touch with your flow probably will make you more aware of what choices you have—smooth flowing! Yours truly, The Bee."

--

"Hi Wind! I enjoy the feeling your description of yourself imparts to me. I can feel your looseness and freedom and feeling about yourself. You seem spontaneous and open and happy and have a clear understanding of yourself and your relationship to others. I like you, too. Sincerely, The Leaf"

When everyone has finished, put the papers back into one big pile. Each person can then fish out his or her original metaphor with the response written below it. Volunteers can read their metaphors or response papers aloud to the whole group (Goodman, 1985).

Technique: *Friends as Metaphors*

Counseling Intention   Describing friends at a deeper level.

Description   Images are more experiential than other forms of communication, as they move the client closer to his or her feelings. Use metaphors to describe friends and family members.

Technique: *"Which Train Should I Choose?"*

Counseling Intention   To present important ideas metaphorically (Jacobs, 1988).

Description   Using paper and felt-tipped pen, draw simple lines, rectangles, and circles to represent a train headed to a fork in the track; one direction leads to trouble on a track labeled "OD" (overdone choices); and the other leads to positive outcomes on a track labeled "OK." Process with the client, decision-making and offering productive options.

Technique: *"The Face I Show"*

Counseling Intention   To help the client see that he or she is choosing a feeling response in a given situation (Nelson, 1992, p. 217).

Description   Draw a series of three ovals and mouths that represent a smiling face, a neutral face, and a scowling face. Ask the client to choose the one that represents him or her and label it.

Technique: *"Who Holds the Power?'*

Counseling Intention   To show how a client may be exaggerating someone else's power in his or her life, be it a boss, spouse, parent, or significant other.

Description   Draw a huge stick figure towering over a cringing, smaller figure, and label it.

Technique: *"Which Way to Go?"*

Counseling Intention   To illustrate the frustration a client may feel when caught between two people (e.g., parents, or between boyfriend and girlfriend).

Description   Sketch two people pulling on the client with both of them saying "You've got to choose between us!" and label it.

Technique: *"When I Feel Like Fighting"*

Counseling Technique   To provide a client with an alternative behavior to fighting and aggression.

Description   Cooperatively, the therapist and the client can develop a list of alternatives to fighting. For example, walk away, talk to some one, or excuse yourself and walk away.

Technique: *Styrofoam and Self-Esteem*

Counseling Intention   To help the client see that he or she can assume control of their self-esteem.

Description   Take a Styrofoam cup and have the client put his or her name on it to represent his or her self-esteem (e.g., "Sue's self-esteem"). Have the client hold it for a moment and then put it on a table. The action of putting the cup on the table represents the client giving his or her self-esteem to his or her boss, parent, spouse, sibling, friend, and so on. Help the client see that he or she can give away control or can assume control, and thus can take back control when he or she chooses to take back the cup.

Technique: *Rubber Band Relationship*

Counseling Intention   To symbolize the tense relationship that also bothers the client.

Description   The therapist takes one side of a rubber band, and client has the other end of the rubber band and should pull. After a moment relax. Ask the client, "What would happen if you choose to relax and accept [the other person] rather than spending an enormous amount of energy trying to change [him or her]?"

A variation of this strategy is to have both people who have a conflict present, and ask both to suggest how they might reduce the tension in the relationship.

Technique: *Turning into the Positive Rather Than the Negative*

Counseling Intention   To replace negative self-messages that interfere with progress.

Description   Using a tape recorder, have clients record negative self-messages that interfere with their progress (e.g., "I'm worthless," "I'm stupid," " I'm never going to amount to anything") and play those messages over and over. After a time, suggest, "You won't make progress if you choose to listen to this all day." Help the client develop a series of positive self-statements and tape them over the negative self-images. Encourage the client to listen to those messages regularly.

Technique: *Diminishing the Effects of a Previous Traumatic Event*

Counseling Intention   To temper a previous life event.

Description   If a previous life event continues to trouble a client, have the client tape the date of the event or a descriptive phrase ("mother's death") to a chair so that it remains in view constantly. Help the client see that he or she chooses to allow the event to dominate his or her life, but that he or she doesn't have to.

Technique: *Getting It Together*

Counseling Intention   To help the client see how he or she continues to be self-critical.

Description   The lump of clay the therapist holds represents the client. Pull off one piece after another, suggesting to the client that the first piece represents how he tears himself up over his mother's criticism, the second stands for his problems with his boss, and the third piece simulates his own negative feelings about himself. After some discussion, put the lumps together and reform the whole. Help the client see that he can make the choice to get himself together.

CONCLUSION

There is no better tool for developing self-awareness than to learn the interpretation of body language. The human form is constantly giving nonverbal signals of the present condition of its inner self. We can read thousands of messages from the expressions of the face alone. The positions and actions of the rest of the body also can accurately reflect what the face has learned to conceal. For example, empathy depends on one's ability to identify someone else's emotions, to put oneself in the other person's shoes, and to experience an appropriate emotional response—a critical component in the helping relationship.

Metaphor is an indispensable dimension of human understanding and experience and is essential for understanding the way individuals think, reason, perceive, imagine, communicate, believe, and relate. Assessing the client's experience from a projected, less threatening perspective provides a watershed for understanding emotion and feeling, as well as behavior.

Chapter 6

Expressive Techniques

ART THERAPY, DANCE/MOVEMENT THERAPY, DRAMA THERAPY, MUSIC THERAPY, PSYCHODRAMA, AND WRITING AS THERAPY

September 11, 2001
Too stunned
to speak,
too numbed
to think,
images instead crowd the mind—
smoke billowing,
plane colliding,
suiciding,
crashing through glass and steel,
flesh and bone,
delusion and hope,
the present,
the future unraveled and rewoven

as flames plume,
bodies plummet,
people choose
to fall into death
rather than be crushed
by it as towers of power implode,
and lives cry
good-bye into a blackened sky.

Cathleen Callahan, Educator, Bridgeport, Missouri
National Association for Poetry Therapy
(2003, reprinted with permission)

The expressive or creative arts therapies include art therapy, dance therapy, drama therapy, music therapy, psychodrama, phototherapy, writing as therapy, and poetry therapy. These therapies use arts modalities and creative processes during intentional intervention in therapeutic, rehabilitative, community, or educational settings to foster health, communication, and expression; to promote the integration of physical, emotional, cognitive, and social functioning; to enhance self-awareness; and to facilitate change. Although unique and distinct from one another, the creative arts therapies share related processes and goals, providing meaningful therapeutic opportunities for awareness and self-expression that may not be possible through more traditional therapies. Brown (1996) maintained that "both the counselor and members can expect to realize benefits from using the expressive process. The counselor will find the counseling process to be enhanced and expanded, and group members can expect progress toward their individual therapeutic goals" (p. 19).

ART THERAPY

Art therapy is a human service profession that uses art media, images, the creative process, and patient/client responses to their created products as tangible products that symbolize the client's inner world—reflections of an individual's development, abilities, personality, interests, concerns, and conflicts. Art therapy is reaching and touching emotions through artwork to promote the recognition and identification of feelings about oneself and others. This nonverbal process allows clients to work through concerns, conflicts, and unresolved issues in a therapeutic setting. The goals of art therapy are to move toward healing and growth. The therapeutic outcome can be enlightening, empowering the client with a stronger sense of awareness, identity, accomplishment, and self-knowledge.

Using art materials in a psychotherapeutic environment for the purpose of self-disclosure allows the client to connect with the symbolic language of the unconscious. Art therapy practice is based on human developmental and psychological theories, and can be used for diagnostic purposes as well as therapeutic understanding. It is implemented in the full spectrum of models of assessment and treatment, including educational, psychodynamic, cognitive, transpersonal, and other therapeutic means of reconciling emotional conflicts, fostering self-awareness, developing social skills, managing behavior, solving problems, reducing anxiety, and increasing self-esteem. It is especially conducive for populations who tend to be nonverbal (such as children) or for clients who overintellectualize and have difficulty in reading other parts of their psyche. Art therapy is an effective treatment for the developmentally, medically, educationally, socially, or psychologically impaired, and it has been practiced in mental health, rehabilitation, medical, educational, and forensic institutions. Art therapists work with individuals, couples, family, and groups and serve populations of all ages, races, and ethnic backgrounds. Research in art therapy has included studying the influence of depression on the content of drawings, using art to assess cognitive skills, the correlating psychiatric diagnosis and formal variables in art, and the effect of art therapy interventions as measured by single-case designs.

Technique: *Melting Mirror*

Counseling Intention   To identify early memories that made deep impressions.

Description   Reach back to childhood imaginatively. As you look at yourself in a mirror, it seems to melt and the image wavers. When it settles it reveals you as a child in a room in your house. Imagine the room and a conversation between you and your child-self. What does the child say to you? What do you reply? Paint the situation and see if there are any messages in it for you now (Liebman, 1986. p. 145).

Technique: *Life Priorities Collage*

Counseling Intention   To reassess priorities.

Description   On a large piece of paper, paint three horizontal bands of color to represent far, middle, and near distances. Then cut out or draw pictures to represent different aspects of your work, family, and social life. Glue or tape these pictures on the appropriate band of color. When you have finished, reflect on the results and move pictures around until the whole feels comfortable (Liebman, 1986, p. 144).

DANCE/MOVEMENT THERAPY

Dance therapy, also referred to as movement therapy, is the psychotherapeutic use of movement as a process to integrate the emotional, cognitive, social, and physical processes of the client. Dance is the most fundamental of the expressive arts, involving direct expression through physical movement of the body. Based on the assumption that body and mind are interrelated, dance therapy is defined as "the psychotherapeutic use of movement as a process which furthers the emotional, cognitive and physical integration of the individual." Dance therapy effects changes in feelings, cognition, physical functioning, behavior, and attitude, helping clients to:

- Reduce stress.
- Tap emotions and sensations that people ordinarily avoid.
- Build self-confidence.
- Define boundaries personally and somatically without having to do so in relation to others.
- Be assertive or intimate without losing sense of self.
- Experience and honor the present no matter what stage of healing.
- Express themselves authentically through dance, movement, music, writing, and art making.

In addition to those with severe emotional disorders, people of all ages and medical conditions receive dance/movement therapy. Examples of these are individuals with eating disorders, adult survivors of violence, sexually and physically abused children, dysfunctional families, the homeless, autistic children, the frail elderly, and substance abusers. An emerging area of specialization is using dance/movement therapy in disease prevention and health promotion programs and with those who have chronic medical conditions. Many innovative programs provide dance/movement therapy for people with cardiovascular disease, hypertension, chronic pain, or breast cancer.

PHOTOTHERAPY

Phototherapy is an interactive system of techniques that makes use of people's personal snapshots and family albums to access feelings and memories not easily available in more directive approaches in counseling and psychotherapy. The therapeutic assumption is that every photograph taken or kept is in many ways a self-portrait or interpersonal story. What a snapshot is about is often more important emotionally and therapeutically than what a snapshot attempts to capture. Ordinary personal snapshots serve as "mirrors with memory," visual footprints marking where a client's life has been or where it may be going. As representational objects, photos represent symbolic self-constructs, or metaphoric transitional objects; a much deeper form of "insight" can emerge to help bridge into the emotional life of the unconscious in ways that words alone cannot fully reflect.

The embedded feelings captured in personal photos become "bridges" for accessing, exploring, and communicating feelings and memories (including unconscious ones), as well as related psychotherapeutic issues these suggest. Clients interacting with the therapist about their own personal and family photos begin discussing what their own personally meaningful snapshots are about. Many associated thoughts and feelings will spontaneously emerge and thus be more available for conscious and cognitive exploration and integration. It is not what is shown on the surface of a photo that is so significant, but rather what the visual contents mean; the stories photos tell along with related feelings will be quite different for every individual who takes them, poses for them, or views the results later.

DRAMA THERAPY

Drama therapy is the systematic and intentional use of drama/theater processes, products, and associations to achieve the therapeutic goals of symptom relief, emotional and physical integration, and personal growth. Drama therapy is an active approach that helps the client tell his or her story to solve a problem, achieve a catharsis, extend the depth and breadth of inner experience, understand the meaning of images, and strengthen the ability to observe interpersonal roles and intrapersonal feelings. The balanced verbal and nonverbal components of drama therapy, with its language of metaphor, allow clients to work productively within a therapeutic alliance.

Drama therapy benefits many client populations and is used in a variety of settings. Drama addresses the needs of people from young children to the elderly. It can be used in the assessment and treatment of individuals, couples, families, and groups, and in settings such as psychiatric hospitals, mental health facilities, day treatment centers, nursing homes, centers for the physically/developmentally/ learning disabled, substance abuse programs, schools, businesses, and correctional facilities. Some populations served include children with learning and social difficulties, the developmentally delayed, psychiatric patients, the disabled, substance abusers, HIV/AIDS patients, and those with disorders associated with aging.

Benefits associated with drama therapy are reducing feelings of isolation, developing new coping skills and patterns, broadening the range of expression of feelings, experiencing positive interactions, and developing relationships. Drama therapy is firmly rooted in a belief in the healing power of drama. Drama therapy is dynamic, active, and experiential. This approach can provide the context for participants to tell their stories, set goals, solve problems, express feelings, or achieve catharsis. Through drama, the depth and breadth of inner experience can be actively explored and interpersonal relationship skills can be enhanced. Participants can expand their repertoire of dramatic roles to find that their own life roles have been strengthened. Behavior change, skill-building, emotional and physical integration, and personal growth can be achieved through drama therapy in prevention, intervention, and treatment settings.

PSYCHODRAMA

As conceived and developed by Moreno (1975), psychodrama employs guided dramatic action to examine problems or issues raised by an individual client (psychodrama) or by a group (sociodrama). Psychodrama is more of a systematic therapeutic procedure than a counseling technique. Using experiential methods such as sociometry, role theory, and group dynamics, psychodrama serves to promote insight, personal growth, and the integration of cognitive, affective, and behavioral domains. It clarifies issues, increases physical and emotional well-being, enhances learning, and develops new skills by concentrating on the private components of roles. The therapeutic "team" in psychodrama has five elements: the director, the protagonist, the auxiliaries, the group, and the action space.

- *Protagonist:* Person(s) selected to "represent the theme" of group in the drama.
- *Auxiliary egos:* Group members who assume the roles of significant others in the drama.
- *Audience:* Group members who witness the drama and represent the world at large.
- *Stage:* The physical space in which the drama is conducted.
- *Director:* The trained psychodramatist who guides participants through each phase of the session.

In a classically structured psychodrama session, there are three distinct stages (structural components) of group interaction:

1. *Warm-up:* The group theme is identified and a protagonist is selected. The primary objective is to increase the level of readiness.
2. *Action:* The problem is dramatized and the protagonist explores new methods of resolving it. This includes three fluid connected segments:
   A. The first segment outlines the role playing of "the complaint"—the present difficulty.
   B. The second segment is "explorations" and "clarifications," which include a number of scenes to investigate the difficulty.
   C. The last segment is "rehearsing and searching for alternatives" by presenting an enactment of solutions for the conflicts.
      "It is the shift from one scene to another that produces the therapeutic effect not excessive exploration of the scene" (Kipper, 1992). The action stage typically lasts for 60% of the session.
3. *Sharing:* Group members are invited to express their connection with the protagonist's work. The auxiliaries and group members share their common or similar experiences with the protagonist so that he or she is not left feeling alone with the difficulty (Kipper, 1992).

Psychodrama affords participants a safe, supportive environment in which to practice new and more effective roles and behaviors. A classic psychodrama session follows a unique structure. Following a contractual agreement between the protagonist and director, the presenting scenes or issues—usually recent events or here-and-now feelings—are enacted. Following scenes move closer toward origins or core issues of the presenting problem. From insights gained, it then becomes possible to return to the presenting issues; role training and a review of the contract may precede sharing and closure.

Psychodrama is a therapeutic approach that uses action methods, sociometry, role playing, and group dynamics to facilitate constructive change in the lives of psychodrama participants. By closely approximating life situations in a structured therapeutic environment, the client can re-create and enact scenes in a way that promotes awareness, insight, and an opportunity to practice new life skills. In psychodrama, the client (or protagonist) focuses on a specific situation to be enacted. Other members of the group act as auxiliaries, supporting the protagonist's work by taking the parts or roles of significant others in the scene. This encourages the group as a whole to partake in the therapeutic power of the drama. Because the therapist helps to recreate scenes that might otherwise not be possible in real life, the psychodrama then becomes an opportunity to practice new and more appropriate behaviors, and evaluate their effectiveness within the supportive atmosphere of the group. The dimension of action is present, so psychodrama is often empowering in a way that exceeds the more traditional verbal therapies (Blatner, 1988; Leveton, 1992).

There are two additional branches of psychodrama: sociometry and sociodrama. Sociometry, the study and measure of social choices within a group, helps to bring to the surface patterns of acceptance or rejection and fosters increased group cohesion. This surfacing of value systems and norms of a group allows for restructuring that will lower conflicts and foster relationships. Sociometry has been used in schools and corporations as well as within the mental health field. Sociometry had several goals (Treadwell, Kumar, & Collins, 1997; Treadwell, Kumar, Stein, & Prosnick, 1997, 1998):

- Facilitate constructive change in individuals and groups.
- Increase awareness, empathy, and reciprocity in social interactions.
- Explore social choice patterns and reduce conflicts.
- Clarify roles, interpersonal relations, and values.
- Reveal overt and covert group dynamics.
- Increase group cohesion and productivity.

Sociodrama is a form of psychodrama that addresses the group's perceptions of social issues. Rather than being the drama of a single protagonist, this process allows the group as a whole to safely explore its perceptions. Members might address problems such as teenage pregnancy or drug abuse, and together arrive at understanding and innovative responses to these difficult issues.

Psychodrama seeks to use a person's creativity and spontaneity to reach his or her highest human potential. With its focus on the social network in which an individual lives, it promotes mutual support and understanding. Moreno (1975) explained psychodrama's goal as making it possible for every person to take part in creating the structure of the universe, which "cannot have less an objective than the whole of mankind."

Technique: *Psychodrama Techniques*

Counseling Intention   Improvising an encounter in the here-and-now to circumvent habitual defensive patterns.

Description   Physical enactment provides an immediacy and vividness that leads to a more emotionally anchored "action insight." The following represent typical techniques used in psychodrama:

> *Aside:* The actor speaks to the audience while indicating through gesture that the others in the scene cannot hear, thus bringing ideas and feelings at the edge of awareness out into the open.
> *Soliloquy and speaking behind the back:* The client says things regarding another person as if that other person were not present; this is particularly helpful in promoting disclosure in family therapy (Blatner, 1988, 2000).
> *Role reversal:* The therapist suggests that the client imagine what it is like to be in the role of a significant other, and then helps the client foster a more mature level of understanding and empathy.
> *Active empathy:* Working through the client's self-system, the therapist expresses what might be the client's inner thoughts or feelings. Then the therapist checks out the performance and invites the client to correct it so that the therapist can be more understanding of the client's point of view.

MUSIC THERAPY

Music therapy unites the fields of music and therapy to provide a creative treatment and medium. It combines music modalities with humanistic, psychodynamic, behavioral, and biomedical approaches to help clients attain therapeutic goals that are usually mental, physical, emotional, social, and/or spiritual in nature. Problems or needs are addressed through the therapeutic relationship between the client and music therapist, as well as directly through the music itself. Music is one of the most social art forms in that it creates communication between people in many different ways. Many studies have been done on the beneficial physiological changes promoted by music on mood, blood pressure, breathing, pulse rate, respiration, cardiac output, heart rate, muscle tension, pain, and relaxation. Music therapeutically addresses physical, psychological, cognitive, behavioral, and/or social functioning.

Music therapists work in a wide variety of settings with the emotionally disturbed, the learning disabled, the mentally handicapped, and the physically challenged. They also work with clients with psychiatric disorders, alcohol and drug problems, and neurological disorders, and those who are terminally ill. Music therapists offer services in skilled and intermediate care facilities, adult foster care homes, rehabilitation hospitals, residential care facilities, hospitals, adult day care centers, retirement facilities, senior centers, hospices, senior evaluation programs, psychiatric treatment centers, and other facilities. Music therapists also work for agencies that provide in-home care. Music therapy is also used with healthy individuals to assist in stress reduction, childbirth, and biofeedback. Advanced opportunities in education and private practice are possible.

Music Therapy for Families and Children

- Provides a forum to share common experiences and enjoyment as a couple or family.
- Gives meaningful time spent together in a positive, creative way.
- Achieves unity and intimacy for families through verbal and nonverbal interaction therapy.
- Stimulates all of the senses and involves the child at many levels. This "multimodal approach" promotes developmental skills.
- Allows play to occur naturally and frequently.
- Resolves conflicts, leading to stronger family and peer relationships as well as positive changes in mood and emotional states.
- Can help a child manage stressful situations.
- Encourages socialization, self-expression, communication, and motor development as well as helps explore personal feelings and therapeutic issues such as self-esteem or personal insight.
- Improves reality testing, problem solving, concentration, attention span, as well as develops independence and decision-making skills.
- Because the brain processes music in both hemispheres, can stimulate cognitive functioning and may be used for remediation of some speech/language skills (Bartlet, Kaufman, & Smeltekop, 1993; Boldt, 1996).

Music therapy may serve as a positive outlet for interaction, providing fun activities that can include parents, siblings, and extended family. Often music therapy allows a family to see a child in a new light as the child's strengths are manifested in the music therapy environment. Music therapy can be an eclectic one that encompasses concepts found in Rogerian psychotherapy (humanistic), cognitive behaviorism (e.g., positive self talk), and Jungian psychotherapy (analytical) to help clients attain their therapeutic goals.

Music therapists have been successful in a wide variety of settings with the emotionally disturbed, the learning disabled, the mentally handicapped, and the physically challenged. They also work with clients with psychiatric disorders, alcohol and drug problems, neurological disorders, and those who are terminally ill. Music therapy is also used with healthy individuals to assist in stress reduction, childbirth, and biofeedback (Bartlett, Kaufman & Smeltekop, 1993; Boldt, 1996).

Poetry Therapy and Bibliotherapy

> *Poetry is the response of our inner most being to the ecstasy, the*
> *agony and the all-embracing mystery of life. It is a song, or a sigh,*
> *or a cry, often all of them together.*

Charles Angoff

Poetry therapy and bibliotherapy are terms used synonymously to describe the intentional use of poetry and other forms of literature for healing and personal growth. Inherently, bibliotherapy is the use of literature to promote health and well-being. Moreover, bibliotherapy can be divided into developmental interactive or clinical interactive. Developmental interactive bibliotherapy refers to the use of literature, discussion, and creative writing with children in schools and hospitals, with adults in growth and support groups, and with older persons in senior centers and nursing homes. In these community settings, bibliotherapy is used not only to foster growth and development, but also as a preventive tool in mental health. Clinical interactive bibliotherapy refers to the use of literature, discussion, and creative writing to promote healing and growth in psychiatric units, community mental health centers, and chemical dependency units.

Bibliotherapy has a broad range of applications with people of all ages and is used for health and maintenance, as well as with individuals undergoing treatment for such conditions as heart disease, cancer, and addiction. Bibliotherapy has been effective with veterans of the armed services, substance abusers, adolescents, the learning disabled, dysfunctional families, prisoners in rehabilitation, the elderly, the physically challenged, and survivors of violence, abuse, and incest. The literature and case studies provide evidence that poetry therapy is an effective and powerful tool with many different populations.

The Goals of Poetry Therapy
- To develop accuracy and understanding in perceiving self and others.
- To develop creativity, self-expression, and greater self-esteem.
- To strengthen interpersonal skills and communication skills.
- To ventilate overpowering emotions and release tension.
- To find new meaning through new ideas, insights, and information.
- To promote change and increase coping skills and adaptive functions.

The therapy is an interactive process with three essential components: the literature, the therapist, and the client(s). The therapist selects a poem or other form of written or spoken media to serve as a catalyst and to evoke emotion, feelings, and the identification of certain themes for discussion. The interactive process helps the client to develop and grow on emotional, cognitive, and social levels. The focus on the client's reaction to the literature promotes psychological health and well-being. The therapist creates a gentle, nonthreatening atmosphere where clients feel safe and are invited to share feelings openly and honestly. The therapist chooses literature that will be effective therapeutically. Four stages emerge with the interactive process of working with poetry and other forms of literature (Hynes & Wedl, 1990):

1. *Recognition:* Clients must be able to recognize and identify with the selection.
2. *Examination:* Clients explore specific details with the assistance of the therapist.
3. *Juxtaposition:* This process explores the significant interplay between contrasts and comparisons in poetry and literature. Comparing or looking at an experience from a directly opposite point of view can provide an awareness that may become the basis for wise choices in attitude, behavior, and decision-making.
4. *Application to self:* Clients make the connection between the individual and the literature, and apply the new knowledge to themselves in the real world. At the end of the session, the therapist provides closure to deal with unfinished business, and help participants to integrate what has been learned. The process of reading and writing serves as a significant catalyst for self-integration.

The indispensable function of writing is that its structure provides a tangible equivalent of the inner space in which one's life can evolve until an appropriate level of self-integration can be found. This method serves as a vehicle of individual initiation into the larger process of existence. Poetry therapy and bibliotherapy intentionally use of the written word to further therapeutic goals and enhance the well-being of individuals and groups through the integration of emotional, cognitive, and social aspects of self. Poetry therapy is a recognized modality employing poetry and other forms of literature to achieve therapeutic goals and personal growth. The goals are to promote understanding of the self and the individual in society, to accept and change feelings and behavior, and to enhance mental and social wellness. The focus of poetry as art is the poem itself, but the focus of poetry for healing is self-expression and growth of the individual. Both art and healing use the same tools and techniques—language, rhythm, metaphor, sound, and image—and the end result often is the same.

Technique: *The Meaning of Poetry*

Counseling Intention   To share in clients' despair (Leedy, 1985).

Description   The therapist can present a reason for the poem choice for that day, or wait until someone reads it, and let the group decide if it has anything to do with them. One or two of the members may read the poem so that the rhythm, the music of the poem will enter their minds to help them focus, replacing the chaos of thought. Usually there will be a silence after the reading, as members survey the field of words as if it is a lake or meadow or scene to absorb. The silence gives way to meaningful dialogue, as members begin to discuss lines or images that appeal to them.

Technique: *Writing Poetry*

Counseling Intention   To have clients express themselves and reveal inner feelings through poetry.

Description   Poetry is a popular form of written expression used in counseling (Blades & Girualt, 1982; Mazza, 1981). Developmental tasks and interpersonal struggles often project the angst of the universality of life's struggles. The following poem is an example.

Winter Storms

Silently
  I watch the snow drift up into little piles
    on my office window.
Suddenly winter storms, like anger,
  sometimes frighten me.
Yet, with the wind and fury of outbursts,
  there is also a calm.
Nature has a way of balancing.

In the midst of our session
  I wanted to quiet your rage,
    settle you down and send you home.

Instead, I waited.
Restlessly, your words came out
  falling on my ears like heavy snow.

I both absorbed the thoughts
and helped you shape them into forms you could handle.
Carefully now, I walk down clear iced paths
sliding occasionally, as I make my way
toward the train to New Haven.
Spring is only two months away,
but time, like adolescence,
travels slowly in the process of change.

Samuel T. Gladding
(Reprinted with permission)

Bibliotherapy

Bibliotherapy is a discussion process, guided by a therapist, using literature as the catalyst to promote insight, normal development, or rehabilitation. Bibliotherapy has three fundamental processes: identification, catharsis, and insight. The therapist helps the client use facts to identify with and analyze book characters or situations. A person achieves an awareness of the problem vicariously by experience and catharsis, thus gaining the ability to develop a solution to the problem. Bibliotherapy and poetry therapy are therapeutic adjuncts similar to art or music therapy, except all literary genres are applied to the therapeutic process.

Writing Therapy

Perspective for the Therapist: On feelings

Denying one's feelings doesn't make them go away. Nor can one
overcome a feeling which is really an aspect of the self.

Alexander Lowen

"Writing as therapy" is in itself an active means of confronting interpersonal issues. Writing breaks through the human reluctance to face inner conflict and evasive self-deception. In narrative therapy, the therapist observes the client's story to effect a more constructive interpretation of sensitive events. The client engaged in writing as therapy not only creates data but also is the observer of that creation. Clients learn how to recognize intricacies that contribute to their situation, by recording on paper the emotional habitats nurtured by those inner forces. In writing as therapy, the therapist addresses *the writer* as personal confidence grows regarding the expression of feelings on paper. Reluctance to communicate feelings on paper dissipates when the writer feels confident that his tentative words will not be judged or reshaped to fit somebody else's expectations.

The therapist refrains from editing or probing the content of the writings, especially while the writer is first becoming acquainted with this therapeutic process. Comments can be made in response to these passages, but more as positive reinforcement; for example, "This passage seems particularly vivid. It captures how you feel sometimes. Yet, I'm a little confused by this phrase. Is there a way you can make it clearer or more direct?"

Writing information down provides a clear means to express emotions, vent on paper, and examine feelings. It is a good form of therapy in and of itself, and is recommended for victims, although it is usually done in the form of letters to the victimizer and the letter is usually destroyed as part of the method of ridding oneself of negative emotions. Writing is a powerful tool for therapy, an excellent method for self-examination and reflection especially for spiritual direction or development of self-esteem and better self-image. Writing helps clients see the thread of their thoughts and get insight into problems. Writing is a long process of introspection; a voyage toward the darkest caverns of consciousness. Writing is largely a process of choosing among alternatives from the images and thoughts of endless flow, and this choosing is a matter of making up one's mind—and this making up one's mind becomes, in effect, the making up of one's self.

Technique: *Writing as Reality Therapy*

Counseling Intention   To provide a daily record for tracking goals and accomplishments, as well as providing a real look at what the client is doing in life.

Description   Reality therapy asks four basic questions:

1. What do you want to do [stated goal]?
2. What did you do today about it?
3. What stopped you from accomplishing your goal?
4. What are you going to do about it now?

By tracking goals and objectives and asking reality-based questions, the client can not only see what some of the stumbling blocks are in life but also try to work out problem-solving strategies and solutions. The client can look at behavior and determine if he or she keeps putting themselves in the same situations, and if so why? The client can start to move forward instead of being doomed to repeat failures or mistakes. Reality therapy allows the client to do a reality check daily and move toward personal growth.

Technique: *Writing for Introspection*

Counseling Intention   To help the client explore more deeply thoughts and feelings through use of writing.

Description   Writing can be a powerful therapeutic tool in counseling because it can generate a profound network of thoughts, feelings, emotions, and images. It also refines cognition. On an even deeper level, writing enhances awareness by (1) helping individuals organize their inner selves, (2) contributing to personal integration and self-validation, and (3) providing a cathartic emotional release (Brand, 1987, p. 266).

Expressive writing can be psychologically liberating, having intrinsic worth because it explores an entire range of inner satisfactions and deeper regions of personality development. Psychoanalytic, humanistic, and cognitive therapeutic models have made a significant impact on current therapeutic writing practices. Approaches to writing can be open-ended, loosely structured, expressive, or directed.

Brand (1987) maintained that although therapeutic writing practices are not necessarily organized around a particular psychological premise, they tend to be linked to certain theoretical premises (p. 267). Below is a compendium of descriptors of therapeutic writing practices.

Writing in Individual or Group Writing Sessions   A counselor may take notes during an individual counseling session for a client to review between sessions. As homework, the client can process insights gained during the counseling session, work on behavior change, and preface the next counseling session with significant learning or personal triumphs.

Long-distance Writing   Long-distance writing may be used when counseling is interrupted by illness or professional obligations. The Internet and electronic mail (e-mail) are additional options, as are bulletin boards and computer linkups (Hofling, 1979; Oberkirch, 1983).

Structured Journal Logs   Structured journal logs or journal keeping as described by Progoff (1975) and Hughes (1991) have particular value in the counseling process. Progoff introduced the structured journal that divides life experiences into several categories that guide personal, written responses. The intensive journal process enables all individuals regardless of age, social, or educational background to begin wherever they are and to draw their lives progressively into focus.

Client could begin with a "period log" placing themselves between the past and the future in particular situations that are issues in their life. The client is encouraged to feel the implications of the question, "Where am I now in my life?"

"What is this present period in my life?" "What marks it off?" "How far does it reach?" "What have been the main characteristics of this recent period?" The exercise is intended for clients to position themselves in the moment of their life (e.g., "This period in my life has been like a . . ."). The goal of the intensive journal process is to teach clients how to make more contact with themselves and gain deeper meaning from their life experiences.

Keeping a Daily Log   A daily log can reinforce the clients dialogue with whatever is taking place inside themselves (i.e., examining the strong-flowing stream of inner experience). The individual's entries must be a succinct reflection of his or her own inner mental and emotional imagery.

The Period Log   Clients are encouraged to define a recent period in their lives, and reflect on their experiences and life events during that period. They should record their feelings, impressions, and descriptions. Listing the stepping-stones of significant periods can represent important life transitions (Progoff, 1975).

Technique: *Book of Self*

Counseling Intention   To get in touch with experienced grief, loss, loneliness, success, triumph, and stability.

Description   The *"Book of Self"* begins with a brief biological sketch limited to one to three pages. Next, include some photographs of the person at various stages of life. Awards, certificates, and other forms of appreciation and recognition are collected for the next section. Hobbies and recreation activities can be included. A summary statement or a collage of self as the person is today forms the final part (Brown, 1996).

Technique: *Creative Writing*

Counseling Intention   To encourage clients to project inner thoughts and feelings through writing.

Description   Creative writing is another written format through which clients can clarify projections and in which problems are explored and therapeutic dialogue interchanged. Troubling issues and concerns can have a therapeutic outlet, especially among adolescents (Dehouske, 1979).

Technique: *Structured Writing and Therapeutic Homework*

Counseling Intention   To encourage clients to keep records of their ideas and questions so that counseling time can become more structured.

Description   Therapeutic homework originated from behavioral and cognitive models, which traditionally have favored briefer forms of therapy. This method tends to reduce the need for repeated counseling and is applicable to both individuals and small groups. Clients who seek help for personal or academic problems may keep structured notebooks about their concerns and receive highly organized answers and instructions from counselors. They may complete inventory questionnaires, writing contracts, or document behavior modification procedures systematically (Corbishley & Yost, 1985; Klier, Fein, & Genero, 1984).

Technique: *Fix Your Attention on Each of Your Five Senses*

Counseling Intention   To be in the moment, the here-and-now (Hughes, 1991, pp. 70–71).

Description   Think for a moment about each of the five senses and the organs primarily responsible for that sense.

> *Eyes*—sight: "What do you see?"
> *Ears*—hearing: "What do you hear?'
> *Nose*—smell: "What do you smell?'
> *Mouth*—taste: "What do you taste?"
> *Skin*—touch: "What do you feel?"

- Write three to five separate sentences for each of the five senses.
- Write the sentences in the present tense, as if the experience is happening now.
- Locate the experience in time and space.
- Use comparisons if they strike you.

Technique: *Early Rejection*

Counseling Intention   To reexperience an early feeling of rejection and discover how it has affected the client (Hughes, 1991, pp. 55–59).

Description   Using one of the meditation techniques in this book, take yourself gradually back to your childhood. Try to recapture the feelings you had at that particular stage of life.

1. *Replay the incident in your imagination.*
   - How old were you?
   - Where are you?
   - Who is with you?

2. *Focus on the moment of rejection.*
   - Expand and amplify that moment as fully as you can.
   - What happened specifically that caused you to feel rejected?

3. *Locate in your body where you still feel this rejection. Scan your body and find out exactly where you still feel rejection.*
   - Is this feeling rejection? Could it be something else?
   - Does focusing on this spot recall other experiences with rejection?

4. *Contemplate your relationship with rejection.*
   - How would I describe rejection? What is it?
   - What is most difficult for me about feeling rejection?
   - What have I learned from and about rejection?

5. *Return briefly to your early rejection incident.*
   - What did I decide as a result of this early rejection?
   - How did the incident shape my future?
   - In what way is this experience still affecting my life?

Write down a detailed, almost analytical account of your early experience with rejection, and then bring it into the present. Include a description of what you think rejection is. Is it one of the basic feelings? A cluster of feelings? Also, reflect on what underlies the *idea* of being rejected.

Technique: *Someone You Love*

Counseling Intention   To look at someone we love objectively (Hughes, 1991).

Description   Form an image of someone you love and put his or her image on your mental screen.

1. *Slowly look them over from head to foot.*
   - See them in a full-body shot, then zoom in for a close-up of particular body parts, and finally have a close-up of their face.
   - Look for any unusual physical characteristics; especially features that distinguish them from others. Take time to look closely at these unusual physical features.

2. *Move in for a close-up of their face. Look directly in their eyes for a while and study them in detail.*
   - What do you see in those eyes? What are the real feelings behind them?
   - Do you see anything you've never seen before?

3. *Observe them with other people. While you are watching them with others, think about these additional aspects and characteristics of the person:*
   - Physical mannerisms
   - Habits of thought
   - Speech patterns
   - Temperament
   - Attitudes

As you begin to write, keep the person you love in front of you, either mentally or by using a photograph, to help keep your focus. Describe the person fully, as if you're explaining what they're like to a perfect stranger.

CONCLUSION

Expressive techniques and the creative arts therapies use arts modalities and creative processes during intentional intervention in therapeutic, rehabilitative, community, or educational settings to foster health, communication, and expression; to promote the integration of physical, emotional, cognitive, and social functioning; to enhance self-awareness; and to facilitate change. Although unique and distinct from one another, the creative arts therapies share related processes and goals, providing meaningful therapeutic opportunities for awareness and self-expression that may not be possible through more traditional psychotherapies.

Chapter 7

Cognitive-Behavioral Therapy, Dialectical Behavior Therapy, Scheme-Focused Cognitive Therapy, and Paradoxical Techniques

Perspective for the Therapist: On attachment

Intimate attachments to other human beings are the hub around which a person's life revolves, not only when he is an infant or a toddler or a school-child but throughout his adolescence and his years of maturity as well, and on into old age.

John Bowlby, *Attachment,* 2nd edition, 1982, p. 11

COGNITIVE THERAPY

Cognitive therapy is a focused, problem-solving approach to psychological treatment that was developed by Aaron T. Beck in the 1970s. Earlier in his career as a psychiatrist, Beck practiced from a psychoanalytic tradition and found himself frustrated by the painfully slow progress of his patients. He strove to develop a more direct and potent approach to therapy; his ideas have become widely known as cognitive therapy (also known as cognitive-behavioral therapy or CBT).

Cognitive therapy is essentially a method that identifies thoughts that produce negative or painful feelings, as well as result in maladaptive behavior or reactions. Beck discovered that the primary point of intervention was at the level of a person's thoughts; if changes are made in thinking (automatic thoughts, assumptions, and core beliefs), changes in emotions and behavior will follow. Behavioral techniques and strategies are employed as needed to enhance the treatment outcome (i.e., anger management, relaxation training, graduated exposure to feared situations, assertiveness training). The course of treatment is typically brief, and people usually experience relatively rapid relief and enduring progress.

A Meta-Analysis on the Effectiveness of Cognitive Therapy

How effective is cognitive therapy, for which disorders, and compared to what? Butler and Beck (2000) reviewed 14 meta-analyses that investigated the efficacy of cognitive therapy with a total of 9,138 subjects in 325 studies involving 465 specific comparisons. Meta-analysis is a statistical approach that allows researchers to aggregate the results of multiple studies and describe these results in a standard unit known as an effect size. In their review, they examined how cognitive therapy outcomes compared to the outcomes of various control groups in terms of their effect sizes (Table 7.1).

Features of Cognitive Therapy
- **Empirically based.** Cognitive-behavioral methods have been shown in controlled studies to provide effective treatment for numerous clinical problems. Cognitive-behavioral therapy has been shown to be as effective as drug treatment for depression and anxiety disorders.
- **Goal-oriented.** The cognitive-behavioral therapist works with his or her patient

TABLE 7.1
Summary of Meta-Analytical Findings on the Effectiveness of Cognitive Therapy: Comparisons of Cognitive Therapy to No-Treatment, Wait List, and Placebo Controls

Disorder	Average effect size	Cognitive therapy patients superior to controls (%)
Adult unipolar depression	0.82	79
Adolescent unipolar depression	1.11	87
Generalized anxiety disorder	1.04	85
Panic disorder with or without agoraphobia	0.91	82
Social phobia	0.93	82
Childhood depression and anxiety disorders	0.90	82
Marital distress	0.71	76
Anger	0.70	76
Childhood somatic disorders	0.47	68
Chronic pain (not headache)	0.46	68

Source: Butler, A. C., & Beck, J. S. (2000). Cognitive therapy outcomes: A review of meta-analyses. *Journal of the Norwegian Psychological Association, 37,* 1–9. (Reprinted with permission)

to set goals for therapy and to monitor progress periodically to assess whether the goals are being met.

- *Practical and concrete.* Therapeutic goals focus on solving concrete problems. Typical goals include reducing depressive symptoms, eliminating panic attacks, reducing or eliminating compulsive rituals, reducing hair-pulling, decreasing procrastination at work, improving relationships with others, or decreasing social isolation.
- *Active.* Both patient and therapist play an active role in therapy. The therapist serves as teacher and coach, teaching the client about what is known about his or her problems and solutions to those problems. The client works outside of the therapy session to practice the strategies learned in therapy.
- *Collaborative.* Client and therapist work together to understand and develop strategies to address the patient's difficulties.
- *Short term.* Cognitive-behavioral therapy is short term whenever possible.

To date, this approach to therapy has produced the empirical data to demonstrate therapeutic outcomes. When compared with other treatment approaches, cognitive therapy has demonstrated the following aspects of effectiveness and efficiency.

COMPARISONS OF COGNITIVE THERAPY WITH ALTERNATIVE TREATMENTS

Cognitive Therapy versus Antidepressant Medication
- Cognitive therapy was somewhat superior to antidepressant medications in the treatment of adult unipolar depression (average effect size = 0.38).
- One year after treatment discontinuation, depressed patients who had been treated with cognitive therapy had half the relapse rate of depressed patients who had been treated with antidepressant medication (30% versus 60%).

Cognitive Therapy versus Supportive/Nondirective Therapies
- In the small number of direct study comparisons—two for adolescent depression and two for generalized anxiety disorder—cognitive therapy was moderately superior (average effect size = 0.77).

Cognitive Therapy versus Behavior Therapy
- Cognitive therapy was equally effective as behavior therapy in the treatment of adult depression and obsessive-compulsive disorder (effect size = 0.05 and 0.19, respectively).

Other Comparisons
- Cognitive therapy was somewhat superior to a group of miscellaneous psychosocial treatments for sex offenders (effect size = 0.35). There is no treatment

(including hormonal therapy) that is superior to cognitive therapy for reducing recidivism in this population.
• Large effect sizes have been found for pre- to post-treatment improvement of bulimia nervosa symptoms using cognitive therapy.

There has been a trend since the 1970s to apply cognitive therapy to an increasingly wider spectrum of disorders. Substance abuse, post-traumatic stress disorder, bipolar disorder, personality disorders, anorexia nervosa, and schizophrenia are among the disorders receiving recent empirical attention (Butler & Beck, 2000).

Cognitive-Behavioral Techniques

Millions of individuals suffer from a wide range of emotional distresses because they hold harmful, mistaken beliefs about themselves and the world around them. This directly or indirectly impacts their relationships with others. Cognitive-behavioral therapy (CBT) and cognitive restructuring therapy (CRT) are the most contemporary approaches used in counseling and psychotherapy today. Cognitive-behavioral therapy (Beck, 1976; Burns, 1989; Ellis & Harper, 1975; McMullin, 1986; McMullin & Giles, 1981; Meichenbaum, 1977) is a model for client reeducation. It is built on the premise that all behavior is learned and that new behaviors can be learned to replace faulty patterns of functioning.

Inherently, individuals' thoughts mediate between feelings and behaviors. Thoughts always come before our emotional reactions to situations. Individuals experience emotional distress because of distorted thinking and faulty learning experiences. This approach emphasizes individuals' capacity for creating their emotions, their ability to change and overcome the past by focusing on the present, and their power to choose and implement satisfying alternatives to current patterns.

Cognitive Therapy Approach to Loneliness

From a person-centered approach, individuals can learn better ways of communicating and listening to others. Many of the problems individuals experience today originate in fragile relationships. Lonely people make two big mistakes: (1) When socializing they feel they are being evaluated (and thus, they start to worry about the impression they are making, and are uptight instead of relaxed and fun to be with); (2) because they think they have been evaluated, when someone rejects them it becomes "proof" that they haven't measured up—that they have failed and are unattractive or no good. These wrong conclusions must be corrected.

Loneliness is an unavoidable human condition to be confronted and resolved, The first task is to identify the automatic self-defeating thoughts in each phase.

Phase 1: Being alone. "Being alone is terrible." "There's something wrong with me." "It's better to be at home alone than go out alone."

Phase 2: With casual friends. "I'll make a fool of myself." "People will laugh at me." "No one likes me." "No one cares about someone like me."

Phase 3: In a situation for mutual self-disclosure. "I'm different; they wouldn't understand me." "If I were honest, people would hate me."

Phase 4: Meeting a potential boy/girlfriend. "He won't like me." "I can't approach women." "It would crush me to be turned down; I'd rather not approach anyone."

Phase 5: Getting intimate. "I always screw it up." "I can't stand to be dumped again." "If you're dumped, there's something wrong with you." "If people really care, they have no right to leave."

Phase 6: Making an emotional commitment. "I can't meet all her needs." "I'll lose my real self if I fall in love." "I should meet all his needs." "It would be terrible if we didn't love each other equally."

Social and dating skills training for meeting people includes assertiveness training for improving relationships, empathy and self-disclosure training for deepening relationships, and decision-making and problem-solving training for planning the future with others and alone. Poor conversationalists benefit most from learning empathy responding. It provides a different (but easy), highly effective, caring, genuine way of responding one to one. If you frequently don't know what to say, be sure to learn to empathize.

Technique: *Cognitive Restructuring*

Counseling Intention   To recognize and stop self-defeating thoughts; to substitute self-defeating thoughts with positive, self-enhancing, or coping thoughts.

Description   Clients are instructed to note what they tell themselves before, during, and after a problem situation or setting. Further, clients are instructed to note and record their negative thoughts before, during, and after stressful or depressing situations for one or two weeks. A client's log should be analyzed for self-defeating and illogical thoughts and the location of negative thoughts (i.e., before, during, or after the experience).

The therapist helps the client work toward identifying more positive coping thoughts that can replace the negative ones. Coping thoughts should be incompatible with self-defeating thoughts. Coping thoughts can be practiced and applied using imagery and role-playing exercises.

Perspective for the Therapist: On reality

Tragedy occurs when, out of a misguided notion of control, we attempt to "adjust" reality to our beliefs, rather than to adjust our beliefs to reality. Tragedy occurs when we cling to our beliefs blindly and manipulate events without awareness of doing so, insensitive to the fact that alternative possibilities exist. Tragedy occurs when we would rather be "right" than happy, when we would rather sustain the illusion that we are "in control" than notice that reality is not the way we have told ourselves it is.

Nathaniel Branden
(Reprinted with permission)

Technique: *The Cognitive Therapy Process*

Counseling Intention   To introduce the client to specific steps in resolving problems using cognitive therapy.

Description   Guide the client through the following steps:

1. Help clients become aware of precisely what they think when they feel anxious.
2. Write or record in some way those thoughts so that the client can read them, and study the exact words used.
3. Analyze thoughts for errors in thinking. For example, is the client using all-or-nothing thinking, comparative thinking ("I'm not as good as"), perfectionism, or overgeneralizing?
4. Brainstorm goals to change the client's unwanted behavior.

SMART Goals
- *S—Specific.* Clarify and identify steps.
- *M—Motivating.* Self-motivating begins with stating the goal as "I will."
- *A—Achievable.* It has a time frame and it is realistic.
- *R—Realistic.* The client can succeed.
- *T—Trackable.* Change can be measured and progress can be monitored.

5. Break the problem down to workable parts.
6. Analyze possible courses of action by making separate lists of the advantages and disadvantages of pursuing or not pursuing each one.
7. Prepare a backup plan ("Plan B") by going through the same steps as required for the first plan. Have the client take action. (Freeman & DeWolf, 1989, pp. 18–19)

Technique: *Turning Negative Thoughts about Studying into Positive Thoughts*

Counseling Intention   To reduce anxiety by turning negative thoughts around, or replacing them with positive thoughts.

Description   Three steps:
1. Identify your goals.
2. Try to figure out the negative messages you are giving yourself.
3. Rephrase the message in positive terms (e.g., My goal is to get a "B" in geometry).

- Ask for clients share a goal and go through the process with them.
- Have each client practice writing affirmations.
- Lead a "go around" so that all members can practice saying their affirmations aloud.
- Have clients pick the affirmation they like best.
- Tell them to write it 10 times and think it to themselves as they write it.
- Have them practice it every night and at the beginning of every session.

Negative thoughts	Affirmations
The work is too hard.	I am bright and capable.
I'm dumber than anyone else.	Teachers and friends like me.
I don't know how to begin.	I know how to ask questions and get started.
I'm tired.	I'm ready for action.

Technique: *Reducing Test Anxiety*

Counseling Intention   To provide strategies to reduce test anxiety.

Description   Everyone at some time experiences test anxiety. There are strategies to reduce this vague feeling of uneasiness that frequently looms before tests and examinations. The following strategies and techniques can help clients cope:

- Engage in deep breathing exercises for two- to five-minute intervals. Instruct the client to close his or her eyes and concentrate on the air going in and out of the lungs. Take long deep breaths, fill the lungs and abdomen, hold the breath, and then exhale.

- Tense and relax muscle groups such as your neck and shoulders. This will help you to be aware of the relaxation of muscles and help you relax more. You will feel more in control of your anxiety.
- Engage in positive self-talk by thinking about (1) rational responses to counter negative thoughts, (2) thoughts that help one cope with stress, and (3) thoughts that keep one on task. Example: "I have the ability to do this." "A little bit of anxiety is helpful." "I can answer this question if I break it down into parts."
- Visualize doing well.
- Do not fall into the trap of comparing self to others.
- Reward self for doing well.

Technique: *Gaining Confidence and Motivation to Study*

Counseling Intention   To think more confidently.

Description   Self-discipline, confidence in abilities, and motivation to continue studies can be accomplished with the following self-statements:

1. Self-statement: *"I am responsible."* Compare study time with grades achieved. Prove to yourself that you are in control of your grades—not luck, fate, or someone else.
2. Self-statement: *"I can be in control."* Schedule study time and reward your efforts. Take pride in your self-control.
3. Self-statement: *"I have ability."* Develop ability in study skills, reading and test taking, time management, and efficiency. Make an effort to gain control of your aptitude and achievement.
4. Self-statement: *"I value learning." (The greater the island of knowledge, the longer the shoreline of wonder.)* Remind yourself that each successful step in school means four things: good grades, a better career, greater income, and a feeling of self-fulfillment.

Technique: *Creative Problem-Solving*

Counseling Intention   To look at problem-solving more creatively.

Description
Sensing Problems
Recognize situations that need improvement and choose one area of concern to explore.

- What needs to be improved?
- What really bothers me?
- What is not working?

Think, brainstorm, seek information, and list alternatives.

Fact-Finding
Identify attributes, aspects, and facts related to the area of concern.

- Why am I concerned?
- Who is involved? What is involved? Where? How? When?
- How does the situation affect others?

Observe, ask questions, and list alternatives.

Problem-Finding
Examine the facts and analyze the situation. Look at the various aspects of the situation from different points of view. Restate the problem as questions until one that best describes the situation is found.

- Who is involved? What is involved? Where? When?
- How many ways can I state the problem? (i.e., flexibility)
- How can I review, analyze, brainstorm, list alternatives?

Idea-Finding
Explore and generate alternative ways of improving or solving the problem (i.e., fluency). What are all the possible solutions to this problem? What could be done to improve the situation? Brainstorm, graphically organize information, and develop lists, charts, or other cognitive maps.

Solution-Finding
Examine all ideas and select five ideas that seem most appropriate. Develop criteria for analyzing and evaluating ideas to improve the situation or to solve the problem. Select the best idea to implement and try it.

Acceptance-Finding
Develop a plan of action by describing what needs to be done and how to accomplish it.

- Ask questions.
- Construct an idea web.
- Put plan into action and evaluate results.

Technique: *Strategies and Attitudes in Problem-Solving*

Counseling Intention   To reach the best possible solution.

Description
1. Do not settle for the first plan presented.
2. Search vigorously for alternatives.
3. Examine how the problem is perceived. Are there unnecessary assumptions? How else could the problem be conceived?
4. List possible solutions uncritically, then sift them.
5. Carefully make a comparative evaluation of alternatives (consider consequences and costs).
6. Maintain attitudes of perseverance and playful exploration.
7. Apply subskills of creative thinking.

Technique: *Cognitive Focusing*

Counseling Intention   To help clients crystallize their emotional reactions to certain stimuli; to help clients clearly identify the causes of their personal unhappiness; to shift core beliefs that are irrational and replace them with a more rational belief (McMullin, 1986).

Description
1. Ask the client to relax briefly, clearing the mind and focusing inwardly for the next few minutes. Changing the focus from an external to internal focus narrows attention, increasing the likelihood that images will form.
2. Present the client with an analogy to help uncover the major sources of discomfort. McMullin (1986, pp. 144–145) provided the "storeroom analogy" as follows: Imagine sitting in a storeroom cluttered with boxes. In each box is the client's problems. Each problem has a different box, and the largest boxes contain the largest problems.
3. Now picture that the boxes move, one at a time, into the corners of the room, so that there is space to sit down. From a relatively comfortable perch in the middle of the room, survey the boxes around carefully. Pull out the box that the client most wants to open, and open it.
4. Lift the problem out of the box and look at it. Turn it from side to side so that every aspect of it can be seen. Try to step outside yourself and watch your reactions to it.
5. Once that client has selected a problem from his or her "storeroom," ask the person to focus upon how he or she feels about the problem.

6. Instruct the client to focus on the overall emotion that best captures how he or she feels about the problem.
7. Once the overall emotion has been defined, involve the client in a careful analysis of various aspects and components of that feeling.
8. Have the client recall, in detail, other similar situations in which he or she has felt that same emotion.
9. Have the client resonate those situations with the feelings so that you can confirm that an association has been made between the anxiety and the situations (past or present).
10. Probe to determine what thoughts sparked the same emotion in each of these similar situations. In each setting, determine what the client has been saying to himself or herself. What meaning does the client assign to these situations?
11. Try to help the client switch the emotion. First, ask the client to focus on similar situations that did not incite the negative emotion. Remind him or her to not simply recall what was experienced but to try to recreate the same feelings.
12. Instruct the client to focus on his or her thoughts, beliefs, or what self-talk occurred during similar situations when the overall emotion was different. Guide the client through an analysis of these feelings.
13. Have the client practice replacing those initial feelings (Steps 4 and 5) with those feelings in the other situations (Step 8). McMullin (1986) maintained the key to switching the emotions is switching the thoughts. Have the client imagine those thoughts when he or she was not anxious (Step 9, rather than Step 7). Teach the client how to practice this shifting technique at home, using a variety of concrete examples from the client's own experiential repertoire. Continuous rehearsal of shifting from negative to positive emotions is necessary to assimilate the new behavior.

Perspective for the Therapist: On perceptions

It all depends on how we look at things,
and not on how they are in themselves.

Carl Jung
On the Psychology of the Unconscious, 1917, p. 48

Technique: *Alternative Interpretation*

Counseling Intention   To encourage the client to suspend judgment until he or she has obtained more information and to perceive the situation more objectively.

Description   A client's first impression of an event is usually not the best; later judgments are often more rational. The intent of this exercise is to get the client to suspend judgment until he or she obtains more information and perceives situations more objectively. Between counseling sessions, have the client keep a written log of the worst emotions experienced during a one-week period identifying (1) the activating event and the initial interpretation of this event and (2) thinking about the event.

After the next session, for the next week have the client continue the log, finding at least four interpretations for each event. At the next counseling session, help the client rationally decide which of the four interpretations has the most objective evidence to support the belief. The client should then be instructed to continue to find alternative interpretations and to actively suspend judgment until some time and distance provide a more objective assessment. This process should be continued for a month until the client can assimilate the procedure automatically (McMullin, 1986, p. 11).

Technique: *Anti-catastrophic Reappraisals*

Counseling Intention   To overcome the negative emotion caused by catastrophizing (thinking the worst) about situations and events.

Description   Clients often distort reality; their exaggerations become habitual, causing chronic anxiety and chronic dread of unpleasant situations. The therapist frames a new interpretation to overcorrect the negative emotion caused by catastrophizing. List the situations the client catastrophizes. Record the damage the client anticipates for each situation on a continuum from 1 to 10. Discuss counter-catastrophizing with the client and record the best possible thing that could happen in each of the situations. Mark the extent of the damage for this outcome. Have the client decide, based on past experience, whether the catastrophic or best possible outcome is most likely to occur. Have the client use the continuum to predict danger in upcoming situations that are feared. After the event actually occurs, have the client check the scale to see whether the anticipated level of damage occurred. The client should practice counter-catastrophizing regularly until he or she can more realistically assess anticipated damage.

Technique: *Changing Thinking Patterns and "Internal Conversations"*

Counseling Intention   To change distorted thinking and negative self-talk.

Description   Emery (1981) outlines the following procedures for changing dysfunctional thinking patterns:

- Maintain a continuing quest for greater self-awareness—assess your goals, dreams, feelings, attitudes, beliefs, and limitations. Recognize, keep track, and challenge your "automatic thoughts," that is, the involuntary inner dialogue that occurs especially in stressful situations. Use critical thinking skills to clarify emotional reactions to an event (e.g., "Is my reaction logical, based on evidence?").
- When looking at a situation, consider alternative explanations and another perspective. Try to substitute positive images for negative ones, and view challenges or criticism as opportunities for change rather than condemnation. Do something specific to change negative thoughts, keep a journal, make a plan, and monitor your progress.

Technique: The Anxiety Formula: "Knowness" versus Importance

Counseling Intention   To reduce the level of anxiety.

Description   With the anxiety formula, anxiety is the degree of known multiplied by the importance of loss. Have the client think about an anxiety-provoking situation. (1) Rate its degree of "knowness" and importance from 0 to 10 to find the anxiety score. (2) Generate ideas that would help lower the unknown aspect of the situation. (3) Generate ideas that would make the event less important, then go back and redo Step 2 (Emery & Campbell, 1986). An example is as follows:

Situation: Airplane Flight
Rate degree of knowness and importance: Unknown × Importance = Level
of Anxiety
$9 \times 10 = 90\%$ Anxiety
What would make the event less important? Course on fear of flying
Rate knowness and importance again: $4 \times 10 = 40\%$ Anxiety

Technique: *The ACT Formula: Accept, Choose, Take Action*

Counseling Intention   To help the client focus on personal choice (Emery & Campbell, 1986).

Description   If a client is experiencing painful, overwhelming anxiety, introduce the ACT formula:

A—*Accept* your current reality.
C—*Choose* to create your own vision, that is, your picture of what you want
in life.
T—*Take* action to create it.

Technique: *Create What You Want*

Counseling Intention   To assist the client in planning for his or her vision for the future

Description   The client should be instructed to keep a journal and to write in it 10 experiences he or she wants to create. Make each item specific and measurable (for example, "I will walk 2 miles a day for the next month.") Put an "I choose to have" in front of each vision and say the sentence aloud (for example, "I choose to walk 2 miles a day for the next month.") Have the client update the list as he or she reaches each desired vision (Emery & Campbell, 1986).

> *Perspective for the Therapist: On failure*
>
> *What is failure?*
>
> *It is a word used to define a stage.*
> *It is not a condemnation of character.*
> *It is not a permanent condition.*
> *It is not a fatal flaw.*
> *It is not a contagious social disease.*
>
> *It is a judgment about an event. How well you cope with that event in large part determines what kind of person you become. The point is to remember that it is the way you cope with failure that shapes you, not the failure itself.*
>
> Carole Hyatt & Linda Gottlieb
> *When Smart People Fail,* 1993, p. 46

Technique: *Alternative Solutions*

Counseling Intention   To assist the client in understanding that alternatives are usually unending.

Description   A client is asked to list all of the possible alternatives to a situation without any initial judgments of these alternatives. Then the counselor can assist the person in placing various value judgments on the most reasonable possible solutions. From this more limited list, the individual then can begin to weigh and select an ultimate choice.

Technique: *Changing Inner Beliefs*

Counseling Intention   To enhance positive inner beliefs.

Description   Decide what behavior you would like to change about yourself. Think positively. Develop your own positive inner belief.

- Write down your negative inner belief and change it to positive. State it in the present tense ("I believe this about myself").
- Repeat your positive inner belief at least 10 times a day. Write your positive inner belief on a card that you can see frequently.
- Visualize your positive inner belief as if it was already happening. See and feel what it would be like to let go of your negative inner beliefs. Picture yourself being successful.
- Act as if the positive inner belief is already true.

Technique: *Nine Ways to Handle Stress Effectively*

Counseling Intention   To enhance inner well-being.

Description   To reduce stress, acknowledge your feelings, identify them, and allow yourself to experience them.

1. *Work it off.* Hard physical activity—running, tennis, working in the garden— is a good outlet.
2. *Talk it out.* Share your feelings with someone you trust so you do not become overwhelmed. Share your sense of stress. Sometimes another person can help you get a new perspective on your problem.
3. *Learn to accept what you cannot change.* Spinning your wheels gets you nowhere. Don't overcommit. Save time for yourself. Acknowledge that you are not perfect, and are not supposed to be.
4. *Avoid self-medication such as alcohol.* The ability to cope with stress comes from within, not from a bottle.

5. *Get enough rest.* Give yourself an occasional break. Schedule recreational activities that require you to give your mind a vacation, even a brief one.
6. *Do something for others.* Another way of getting your mind off your own problems is to help solve someone else's problems.
7. *Take one thing at a time.* Don't deliberately put yourself in a loser's position by biting off more than you can chew.
8. *Give in once in a while.* Don't insist on being right all the time. It's relaxing to admit you're wrong from time to time.
9. *Make yourself available to others.* Don't feel sorry for yourself.

Technique: *Coping with the Feeling of Being Overwhelmed*

Counseling Intention   To maintain manageable frustration levels.

Description   In today's information age, there are many times when clients may feel overwhelmed. The stress and anxiety associated with this feeling can have long-range implications for one's own mental well-being.

- With the first signs of anxiety, just pause.
- Keep the focus on the present; what is it you have to do?
- Label your fear from 0 to 10 and watch it change.
- You should expect your fear to rise.
- Don't try to eliminate fear totally; just keep it manageable.
- You can convince yourself to do it. You can reason your fear away.
- It will be over shortly.
- It's not the worst thing that can happen.
- Just think about something else.
- Do something that will prevent you from thinking about fear.

Technique: *Self-Talk to Maintain Composure*

Counseling Intention   To gain self-control.

Description   Self-talk statements should be generated that would be useful *before, during,* and *after* the situation.

Before   Take a minute to become more centered. "What is it that I want to do?"

During   Take a moment to exhale. Take things one step at a time.

1. People get irritated. It's nothing more than that.
2. Clearly say what you want. Don't raise your voice.

After: Rate yourself. On a scale of 1 to 10, you handled that with a 9. "I'm getting better at this every time I try."

Technique: *Using Self-Control Techniques*

Counseling Intention   To maintain calm and composure.

Description   Maintaining self-control is a skill that may take some time and practice to learn. It is not easy maintaining grace under fire. Listed below are some self-control techniques.

• Avoid frustrating situations by noting where you have become angry in the past.
• Reduce your anger by consciously taking time to focus on other emotions that are more passive, avoiding the weapons of aggression.
• Respond calmly to an aggressor with empathy or unprovocative comments, or make no response at all.
• If angry, concentrate on the undesirable consequences of becoming aggressive. Tell yourself that you are not going to give them the satisfaction of seeing you get upset.
• Review your present circumstances and try to understand the motives or point of view of the other person.
• Learn to become empathetic and forgiving of others and to tolerate individual differences.

Technique: *Aggression Control Methods*

Counseling Intention   To gain control over anger.

Description   Methods for preventing and controlling anger can be learned.

• **Reduce your frustrations.** Try to avoid topics of conversation, personal opinions, or situations that *grate on you*.
• **Reduce the environmental settings** that encourage an aggressive response. Avoid aggressive subcultures, gangs, hostile friends, television violence, or violence in other forms of media such as the movies or music.

- **Cultivate new friends** who are not quick tempered, hostile, prejudiced, or agitators.
- **Disclose some of your own anxiety** prior to being abrasive or rude. Comments such as "I'm having a bad day," "I'm stressed out," or "I'm upset" change the context and soften your remarks.
- **Control anger through stress management,** problem-solving methods, using I-messages, or positive self-talk.
- **Stop hostile fantasy building.** Preoccupation with frustrating situations increases anger. Move out of the situation or use thought-stopping techniques.

Technique: *Writing a Learning History of Angry Reactions*

Counseling Intention   To assess the extent of angry reactions.

Description   Take two weeks and carefully and systematically record anger-causing thoughts to become aware of the common but subtle triggers for your emotional reactions and how to avoid future conflict. A learning history of the behavior or angry reactions should include the following:

- Record the specific situations that triggered the reaction.
- Record the nature and intensity of your anger.
- Note your thoughts and feelings of the situation immediately before and during the anger.
- List what self-control methods you used and how well they worked.
- Record the consequences and how others responded following your emotional reaction.

Evaluate the payoffs you get from your anger, clarify to yourself the purpose of your aggression; and give up some of your unhealthy payoffs.

Technique: *Psychological Forces That Block Intelligent Decision-Making*

Counseling Intention   To understand the forces that block decision-making.

Description   There are numerous conscious and unconscious barriers that block decision-making.

- You may block clear thinking because you may be *out of touch with painful or stressful feelings.*

- You may be experiencing *anxiety, depression, self doubt, or lack of hope,* which may lead to self-defeating behaviors or lack of action.
- You may feel *overly dependent on someone or something,* which may get in the way of logical thinking.
- You may have an *unrealistic image about yourself and what you are capable of achieving,* which may lead to a poor decision.
- You may be experiencing *wishful thinking* such as perfectionism and all-or-nothing thinking that gets in the way of making a realistic decision.
- You may *procrastinate and drag things along to avoid making decisions* because of failures in the past.
- You may become *emotionally overwhelmed and rush decisions,* which may ultimately lead to a bad choice.

Technique: *Confronting Irrational Thoughts*

Counseling Intention   To overcome depression, stress, and panic attacks.

Description   It's important to confront irrational thought and related anxiety; to counteract depression, stress, and panic attacks. Irrational beliefs can be classified into one of five categories:

- *Self-defeating beliefs* that interfere with basic goals and drives.
- *Dogmatic, highly rigid beliefs* that lead to unrealistic preferences and wishes.
- *Antisocial beliefs* that cause people to destroy their social groups.
- *Unrealistic beliefs* that falsely describe reality.
- *Contradictory beliefs* that originate from false premises.

Technique: *Changing Thinking Patterns and "Internal Conversations"*

Counseling Intention   To change distorted thinking and negative self-talk.

Description   Follow these procedures for changing dysfunctional thinking patterns.

1. Maintain a continuing quest for greater self-awareness. Assess your goals, dreams, feelings, attitudes, beliefs, and limitations.
2. Recognize, keep track, and challenge your "automatic thoughts"—the involuntary inner dialogue that occurs especially in stressful situations.
3. Use critical thinking skills to clarify emotional reactions to an event. "Is my reaction logical, based on evidence?"

4. When looking at a situation, consider alternative explanations and another perspective.
5. Try to substitute positive images for negative ones; view challenges or criticism as opportunities for change rather than condemnation.
6. Do something specific to change negative thoughts; keep a journal, make a plan, and monitor your progress.

Technique: *The ABCs of Stopping Unhappy Thoughts*

Counseling Intention   To identify how many times negative thoughts and feelings occur.

Description   *Keep a journal on negative thoughts and feelings.* Record in your journal when you notice being upset following a situation or an event:
  A: *Facts and events:* Record the facts about the unhappy event.
  B: *Self-talk:* Record the things you tell yourself about the event.
  C: *How you felt:* Record how you felt.
  D: *Debate:* Debate or dispute any statement that is not logical or objective.
  E: *Examine the future:* State how you want to feel in the future in this kind of situation.

Technique: *Giving Constructive Criticism*

Counseling Intention   To resolve conflict in a more positive way.

Description   A formula for giving someone constructive criticism involves six steps:
  Step 1. Give the person two compliments. Be honest, sincere, and specific.
  Step 2. Address the person using his or her name.
  Step 3. In a pleasant tone of voice, and with a pleasant look on your face, state your criticism in one or two short, clear sentences.
  Step 4. Tell the person what you would like him or her to do. Keep it simple. Set a time limit if it is appropriate to do so.
  Step 5. Offer your help, encouragement, and support.
  Step 6. Thank the person for their time and for listening.

In reality, when confronting another individual, the client should be cautioned that they may be interrupted. He or she should be encouraged to listen and acknowledge the other person and adhere to the formula. A helpful procedure is to role-play or practice the formula ahead of time.

Technique: *The ABCs of Stopping Unhappy Thoughts*

Counseling Intention To keep a journal on negative thoughts and feelings (Maultsby, 1975).

Description The client is directed to record the following in a journal when he or she notices being upset following a situation or an event:

A: *Facts and events.* Record the facts about the unhappy event.
B: *Self-talk.* Record the things you tell yourself about the event.
C: *How you felt.* Record how you felt.
D: *Debate.* Debate or dispute any statement in "A" that is not logical or objective.
E: *Examine the future.* This is how I want to feel in the future in this kind of situation.

Technique: *Mood-Monitoring Chart*

Counseling Intention To record sensations of anxiety or panic.

Description The following information is charted: Date/Time; Situation (where the client was and who was there); what happened (preceding anxiety or panic); thoughts (before and during the attack); feelings experienced (include label used and possible alternative labels); degree of discomfort (from 0 to 10, low to extreme discomfort) (Belfer, Munoz, Schacter, & Levendusky, 1995).

Technique: *Staying with Anxiety*

Counseling Intention To stay in the situation; to not flee or panic when anxiety is present or impending (Belfer et al., 1995).

Description For anxiety-provoking situations, the client should write the following self-instruction statements on an index card and refer to them as needed:

1. Face the situation. Don't avoid.
2. Accept the feelings. Don't fight them.
3. Float through the experience. What will happen will happen. There is no need to offer resistance.
4. Let time pass. The experience will have an end. The feelings of anxiety will pass (Belfer et al., 1995).

Technique: *Counterargument to Avert a Panic Attack*

Counseling Intention　To replace anxious thoughts with self-statements in the form of counterarguments (Belfer et al., 1995).

Description　Counterarguments prevent feelings of anxiety from spiraling and averting a panic attack.

Catastrophic thought → Counterarguments → Anxiety reduction

Instruct the client about a three-step procedure:

1. Recognize anxiety: "I feel anxious,"
2. Specify fears: "I'm afraid that . . ."
3. Counterargue: "My counterarguments are . . . "

Cognitive Behavioral Techniques for Stress and Anxiety

Technique: *Stress Inoculation*

Counseling Intention　To reduce the effects of stress and anxiety.

Description　Stress inoculation is basically learning to "talk yourself down" or facing a stress and finding ways to handle it. For others, "stress inoculation training" is a complex therapeutic process. It is a major part of cognitive behavioral therapy and involves (1) helping the patient become a better observer and a more accurate interpreter of incoming information; (2) teaching stress management skills, such as social interaction, problem solving, and how to use self-instructions for relaxation, self-control, and praise; (3) help in applying the various self-help skills in life.

- *Use "nervous energy."* Channel the anxiety created by stress into constructive, beneficial activities, such as taking a course, preparing for a promotion, or helping others. Good stress keeps us motivated and enthusiastic about life.
- *Develop psychological toughness.* Physical demands must be made on the body to develop strength, and we must be exposed to bacteria and diseases to develop an immunity to them. Similarly, humans may need to be exposed to stresses and emotions before we develop coping mechanisms and toughness. Clients can develop toughness by being repeatedly exposed to demanding situations while having the skills, power, courage, and confidence to deal with the challenges. We increase toughness by being committed to work, having a sense of control over what happens in life, embracing challenges, feeling we will learn from experiences, problem solving to reduce stress, and focusing on self-improvement.
- *Acquire skills training.* Reduce stress by acquiring helpful skills such as problem-solving ability, decision-making skills, social skills, assertiveness skills, empathic response skills, and time-management skills. To reduce fears, change self-talk and thinking by substituting constructive, positive self-statements for self-defeating statements.
- *Correct faulty perceptions.* Change automatic assumptions from "I will fail" to "I can handle it." Validating or having our perceptions confirmed by others is sometimes a critical step. Learn to recognize tendencies to distort, such as exaggerating our importance, denying our responsibility, expecting the worst, being overly optimistic, blaming ourselves, or distrusting others. Be aware of perceptual biases, and constantly check impressions or views in that area with others. Replace the catastrophic thinking with rational, reassuring thoughts: "I can prevent this panic attack" or "My heart is beating fast but that is okay."

Technique: *Overcoming Depression*

Counseling Intention To eliminate loneliness, anxiety, and despair. Change in thinking, feeling, and acting is a key feature in depression. A depressed client can be helped by changing his or her errors in thinking, rather than by concentrating on his or her depressed mood.

Description Self-Talk That Manifests as Depression:

- "My wife left me because I wasn't good enough for her. I will never be able to get along without her."
- "My hair is thinning. I'm losing my looks. No one will care about me anymore."
- "I just can't get myself to do any work around the house. My marriage is falling apart."

It is important to (1) recognize negative thoughts, and (2) correct them and substituting more realistic thoughts.

Technique: *Checklist of Negative Thoughts*

Counseling Intention   To counter depressive feelings.

Description   Whenever depressing feelings occur, think back and try to recall what thought either triggered or increased the feeling of sadness. This thought may be a reaction to something that happened quite recently, perhaps within the last hour or the last few minutes, or it may be a recollection of a past event. The thought may contain one or more of the following themes.

- *Negative opinion of yourself.*   This notion is often brought about by comparing oneself with other people who seem to be more attractive or more successful or more capable or intelligent: "I am a much worse student than Mike," "I have failed as a parent," "I am totally lacking in judgment or wit."
- *Self-criticism and self-blame.*   The depressed person feels sad because he focuses his attention on his presumed shortcomings, he blames himself for not doing a job as well as he thinks he should, for saying the wrong thing or causing misfortune to others. When things go badly, the depressed person is likely to decide it's his own fault. Even happy events may make you feel worse if you think, "I don't deserve this—I am unworthy."
- *Negative interpretations of events.*   Depressed people often respond in negative ways to situations that are not a concern to them when they are not depressed.
- *Negative expectations of the future.*   People can fall into the habit of thinking that feelings of distress or problems will last forever. The depressed person tends to accept future failure and unhappiness as inevitable and may tell herself it is futile to try to make her life go well.
- *"My responsibilities are overwhelming."*   People may feel unable to do tasks or feel that it will take weeks or months before they are completed. Some depressed clients deny themselves rest or time to devote to personal interests because of what they see as pressing obligations coming at them from all sides. They may even experience physical feelings that can accompany such thoughts—sensations of breathlessness, nausea, or headaches.

Technique: *Changing Negative, Depressive Thoughts*

Counseling Intention To gain control over negative thoughts and to focus on the positive.

- *Daily Schedule.* Try to schedule activities to fill up every hour of the day. Do not ruminate about negative thoughts.
- *"Mastery and Pleasure" Method.* Write down all of the events of the day and then label those that involve some mastery of the situation with the letter "M" and those that bring some pleasure with the letter "P."
- *The ABC of Changing Feelings.* Feelings are derived from thinking. Sort out three parts of a problem:
  1. The event
  2. Your thoughts
  3. Your feelings
- *The Double-Column Technique.* Write down unreasonable automatic thoughts in one column and answers to the automatic thoughts opposite these. (*Example:* John has not called. He doesn't love me. *Answer:* He is very busy and thinks I am doing better than last week—so he doesn't need to worry about me.)
- *Solving Difficult Problems.* Write down each of the steps that you have to take to accomplish the job and then do just one step at a time. Problems that seem unsolvable can be mastered by breaking them up into smaller manageable units.

Techniques for Depressed Clients

> All of us succumb at times to feelings of doubt and despair. These
> vulnerabilities are universal, and are part of what makes us
> uniquely human . . . I want you to learn to accept your strengths
> as well as your weaknesses without a sense of shame
> or embarrassment.
>
> David D. Burns, *The Feeling Good Handbook: Using the New
> Mood Therapy in Everyday Life,* 1989, p. xviii

Downing (1988) provided a multidimensional intervention system based on a learning theory approach for countering depression. Learning life skills to change debilitating behavior is much more productive than merely a lot of rhetoric about the problem. Clients can be taught depression-coping and control techniques such as recognizing depressive feelings, ways to increase activity level, the use of daydreams, ways to relax, and positive self-talk. The desired outcome of coping and control techniques is an improvement of the level of functioning in all aspects of a child's, adolescent's, or adult's life. Changes are best achieved through a multifaceted support system involving an intervention team who maintain consistent, frequent, and regular monitoring of the helping process. Skilled therapists can work with depressed individuals to:

1. Pinpoint the life problems that contribute to their depression, and help them understand which aspects of those problems they may be able to solve or improve. A trained therapist can help depressed patients identify options for the future and set realistic goals that enable these individuals to enhance their mental and emotional well-being. Therapists also help individuals identify how they have successfully dealt with similar feelings, if they have been depressed in the past.
2. Identify negative or distorted thinking patterns that contribute to feelings of hopelessness and helplessness that accompany depression. For example, depressed individuals may tend to overgeneralize—that is, to think of circumstances in terms of *always* or *never*. They may also take events personally. A trained and competent therapist can help nurture a more positive outlook on life.
3. Explore other learned thoughts and behaviors that create problems and contribute to depression. For example, therapists can help depressed individuals understand and improve patterns of interacting with other people that contribute to their depression.
4. Help them regain a sense of control and pleasure in life. Psychotherapy helps people see choices as well as gradually incorporate enjoyable, fulfilling activities back into their lives.

Technique: *Strategies for Overcoming Depression*

Counseling Intention   To eliminate anxiety, guilt, sadness, hopelessness, loss, low self-regard, loneliness, guilt, and shame, which are complex conditions or processes.

Description   The focus is on behavior, emotion, cognition, and unconscious factors.

> *Behavior.* Increase pleasant activities, avoid upsetting situations, get more rest and exercise, use thought-stopping, reduce your worries, atone for wrong-doings, seek support, and use other behavioral changes.

Emotions. Desensitize sadness to specific situations and memories, vent anger and sadness, and try elation or relaxation training.

Skills. Learn social skills and decision-making, and self-control techniques to reduce helplessness.

Cognition. Acquire more optimistic perceptions and attributions, challenge depressing irrational ideas, seek a positive self-concept, become more accepting and tolerant, and select good values and live them.

Unconscious factors. Read about depression, learn to recognize repressed feelings and urges that may cause guilt, explore sources of shame (perhaps even going back to childhood).

Positive events or activities lead to positive moods; negative events to depression. The depressed person must become aware that this is true in everyone's life. Have clients rate their mood on a 1 to 10 scale and keep a daily log or a diary of positive events and activities. It is likely that mood reflects what is happening in the client's life. After about a week, have the clients plot their daily mood rating and the number of pleasant events for that same day on a graph. Ascertain if the client's mood doesn't go up and down according to how many pleasant events occurred that day. If so, this is a powerful argument to *increase the number of pleasant events* in the client's life and to help the client appreciate the nice things that happen.

Technique: *Focus on Positive Events*

Counseling Intention   To help the client realize contributions to success and reduce the responsibility for failure.

Description   Think of an important recent event and describe it.

- In what ways were other people, chance, luck (good or bad), or fate responsible for this event?
- In what ways were you (your efforts, skills, abilities, experience, appearance—or lack thereof) responsible for this event?
- What percentage of the responsibility for this event was attributable to you?

Do this for several events, including both positive and negative events. Work toward positive events and against depressing events. So if clients do not think they are truly responsible for more than 50% of the pleasant events, have them reconsider their explanation of those events and see if they aren't causing more positive things than they thought. Factually based confidence in self-control is a powerful antidote to pessimism and helplessness. (Remember that depressed people underestimate their problem-solving ability.)

Technique: *Reversing the Downward Depression Spiral*

Counseling Intention   To provide a number of strategies to assist the client.

Description

- *Use self-reinforcement.*   Make a list of assets—true positive traits. Read it frequently and add accomplishments to it. Make another list of possible rewards, and use them in self-help projects. Depressed people need more good things in their lives.
- *Get active.*   Undertake profitable, beneficial activities that solve problems, improve the current situation or the future, and replace sad thoughts. Start with easier tasks, work up to harder ones. Reward progress.
- *Avoid unpleasant, depressing situations.*   Interpersonal situations powerfully influence happiness. Depression, introversion, loneliness, dependency, and marital problems often precede the onset of depression. Avoid losses and these conditions if possible.
- *Change the environment.*   Try to change depressing environments—working conditions, family interactions, stressful relationships, and so on. Mood reflects one's surroundings.
- *Reduce negative thoughts.*   Reduce the negative thoughts that characterize depressed people: self-criticism ("I'm really messing up"), pessimistic expectations ("It won't get any better"), low self-esteem ("I'm a failure"), and hopelessness ("There's nothing I can do"). How does the client stop or limit these depressing thoughts, memories, or fantasies? Try using *thought-stopping*, *paradoxical intention* (massed practice), or *punishment.*
- *Have more positive thoughts.*   Make an effort to have a lot more positive thoughts: satisfaction with life ("Living is a wonderful experience"), self-praise ("I am thoughtful—my friends like that"), optimism ("Things will get better"), self-confidence ("I can handle this situation"), and respect from others ("They think I should be the boss").
- *Avoid self-put-downs.*   Become aware of any payoffs for depression or self-put-downs. A therapist shoudl reduce these reinforcements: Don't complain or display sadness, and ask others to ignore the client's sadness as well (but interact with him or her more during good times). Remember excessive talking about depression may sometimes increase depressed feelings. (But clients should not use this as an excuse for not seeking help.)

- *Pursue happiness.*

  1. Focus on achieving *emotional closeness with loved ones.*
  2. Find things about *work* that are enjoyable work hard on them.
  3. *Help others.*
  4. *Exercise* and doing something enjoyable.
  5. Plan to do *new* fun things too.
  6. Have lots of nice "moments," not just big highs.

- *Practice desensitization and stress inoculation.*   If the depressing event is anticipated, use desensitization and stress inoculation could be used in advance to reduce the impact.
- *Challenge faulty perceptions.*   Question any irrational ideas, automatic ideas, faulty conclusions, or excessive guilt. If "automatic negative thoughts" slip by too quickly to notice (but they still cause sadness), try starting the search for the negative thoughts at the moment the emotions occur. Write down thoughts, and then objectively ask:

  1. What is the evidence for this idea that may be causing me to feel bad? Is it true?
  2. Is there another way of looking at the situation?
  3. Even if my first thought were correct, is it really as awful as I feel it is? Or is the situation just "awful" reality?

- *Use tolerance training (challenge irrational demands).*   Help the client learn that he or she can't always avoid unwanted outcomes.
- *Challenge false conclusions.*   The depressed person has been preprogrammed to think negatively and irrationally. This is not a conscious, intentional effort to come to negative conclusions; it is an automatic process. Challenge the client's negative thinking (Table 7.2).
- *Attribution retraining.*   An old adage says everyone fas three characteristics:

  1. That which he or she has.
  2. That which he or she thinks he or she has.
  3. That which others think he or she has.

The depressed person is prone to believe "this bad situation will never get better," "it will ruin my whole life," and "it's all my fault." If those views of the situation were accurate, the person would have a right to be depressed. Shift attributions to show clients they are less responsible for an unfortunate happening (divorce, failure, accident, thoughtless inconsiderate act) to make them feel less guilty or depressed. Changing attributions can provide more hope of improving the situation in the future.

TABLE 7.2
Challenging Negative Thinking

	False Conclusion	More Reasonable Idea
Self-blaming	I forgot the assignment, I'm irresponsible.	A mistake, I'll not do that again.
Overgeneralization	John snubbed me, nobody likes me.	I'd better talk to John; others like me because I'm so good to them.
Absolutism	It's terrible if I can't be a doctor.	What a downer. What is my next choice?
	I'm a nerd, always will be.	I need some better social skills.
Irreversibility	I failed once, I'll always fail.	I'll learn and practice more next time.
Personalization	The teacher is mad because I forgot to do the paper.	Half the class is doing poorly, not just me.
Overreaction	After my accident, they'll never trust me.	One mistake doesn't destroy trust.

Technique: *Success Experiences*

Counseling Intention   To systematically manipulate success and positive feedback for the client by ensuring daily successful experiences.

Description   Determine appropriate and reasonable success objectives by establishing small attainable goals.

Technique: *Increased Activity Levels*

Counseling Intention   To control depression by increasing the client's activity level.

Description   Cantwell and Carlson (1983) found that depression could begin to be controlled by increasing the client's activity level. Client involvement in selecting and planning the activities will improve the likelihood of a more successful intervention. When the activities are fun, the probability of a positive response will be enhanced.

The major obligation for adolescents, for example, is one of attending school and should be a priority. Parents should insist gently that the child do chores and participate in family activities as well as think small and accept small gains (Downing, 1988). With the child's involvement in the intervention process, he or she may assimilate the system of skills without adult assistance in the future. The more commitments or obligations the youth meets, the more he or she maintains a self-perception of normalcy and confidence.

Technique: *Limit Inappropriate Attention*

Counseling Intention   To reinforce behaviors that gain attention in positive ways.

Description   Sometimes family relationships become co-dependent, where individuals take responsibility for another's behavior and consequences. Members of the intervention team should not feel that they need to ask continually how the child is feeling. Response efforts should be focused on behaviors that gain attention in positive ways.

Technique: *Teaching Coping and Changing Skills*

Counseling Intention   To learn ways to avoid feelings or ideas that may provoke depression.

Description   Clients can be taught to be aware of depressive feelings and thoughts when they occur. The client should be helped to develop a repertoire of activities to implement when feeling depressed such as (1) increasing their activity level, (2) redirecting thoughts to pleasant experiences, (3) using deliberate internal affirmations, (4) using productive fantasies or daydreams, or (5) using biofeedback either to increase or to decrease their pulse rate to control their body. All strategies have one common denominator—they empower the client with strategies that put him or her in control to actualize change (Cantwell & Carlson, 1983; Downing, 1988).

DIALECTICAL BEHAVIOR THERAPY

Dialectical behavior therapy (DBT) is a comprehensive cognitive-behavioral treatment for complex, difficult-to-treat mental disorders. Marsha M. Linehan (1991) pioneered this treatment originally to treat chronically suicidal individuals. DBT has since evolved into a treatment for individuals with borderline personality disorder (BPD); it has since been adapted for seemingly intractable behavioral disorders among the BPD population involving emotion dysregulation, including substance dependence and binge eating. It has been employed in other clinical populations (e.g., depressed, suicidal adolescents) and in a variety of settings (e.g., inpatient, partial hospitalization, forensic).

As a comprehensive treatment, DBT serves five functions:

1. Enhances behavioral capabilities.
2. Improves motivation to change (by modifying inhibitions and reinforcement contingencies).
3. Ensures that new capabilities generalize to the natural environment.
4. Structures the treatment environment in the ways essential to support patient and therapist capabilities.
5. Enhances therapist capabilities and motivation to treat patients effectively.

In standard DBT, these functions are divided among modes of service delivery, including individual psychotherapy, group skills training, phone consultation, and therapist consultation team. The fundamental dialectic in DBT is between validation and acceptance of clients as they are within the context of simultaneously helping them change. Change strategies in DBT include behavioral analysis of maladaptive behaviors and problem-solving techniques, including skills training, contingency management (i.e., reinforcers, punishment), cognitive modification, and exposure-based strategies.

DBT is designed to treat individuals with BPD at all levels of severity and complexity and is conceptualized as occurring in stages. In Stage 1, the primary focus is on stabilizing the client and achieving behavioral control. Behavioral targets in this initial stage of treatment include decreasing life-threatening, suicidal behaviors. DBT targets behaviors in a descending hierarchy:

1. Decreasing high-risk suicidal behaviors—parasuicide acts, including suicide attempts, high-risk suicidal ideation, plans and threats.
2. Decreasing responses or behaviors (by either therapist or patient) that interfere with therapy—missing or coming late to session, phoning at unreasonable hours, not returning phone calls.
3. Decreasing behaviors that interfere with/reduce quality of life—depression, substance dependence, homelessness, chronic unemployment.
4. Decreasing and dealing with post-traumatic stress responses.
5. Enhancing respect for self.
6. Acquisition of the behavioral skills taught in group—skills in emotion regulation, interpersonal effectiveness, distress tolerance, mindfulness, and self-management.
7. Additional goals set by patient.

In the subsequent stages, the treatment goals are to replace "quiet desperation" with nontraumatic emotional experiencing, to achieve "ordinary" happiness and unhappiness and reduce ongoing disorders and problems in living, and to resolve a sense of incompleteness and achieve joy.

In summary, the orientation of the treatment is to first get action under control, then to help the patient to feel better, to resolve problems in living and residual disorders, and to find joy and, for some, a sense of transcendence. Research has shown DBT to effectively reduce suicidal behavior, dropout from treatment, psychiatric hospitalization, substance abuse, anger, and interpersonal difficulties. DBT skills training has also been successfully used to treat bulimia and binge eating.

SCHEMA-FOCUSED COGNITIVE THERAPY

Schema-focused cognitive therapy is the approach developed by Jeffrey E. Young, a protégée of Beck. Prior to his founding the Cognitive Therapy Centers of New York and Connecticut, as well as the Schema Therapy Institute, Young served as the Director of Research and Training at the Center for Cognitive Therapy at the University of Pennsylvania with Beck, where he trained many clinicians in the application of CBT. In working with clients, however, Young and his colleagues found a significant segment of people who came for treatment but had perplexing difficulty in benefiting from the standard approach. He discovered that these people typically had long-standing patterns or themes in thinking and feeling that required a different means of intervention. Young's attention turned to ways of helping patients to address and modify these deeper patterns or themes, which he called "schemas" or "lifetraps."

The schemas or lifetraps that are targeted in treatment are enduring and self-defeating patterns that typically begin early in life, get repeated and elaborated upon, cause negative/dysfunctional thoughts and feelings, and pose obstacles for accomplishing one's goals and getting one's needs met. Although schemas are usually developed early in life (during childhood or adolescence), they can also form in adulthood. These schemas are perpetuated behaviorally through the coping styles of schema maintenance, schema avoidance, and schema compensation. Young's model centers on helping clients break their patterns of thinking, feeling, and behaving, which are often very tenacious.

A Comparison of Schema-Focused Therapy with Cognitive Therapy
- Greater emphasis on the therapeutic relationship
- More emphasis on affect through exercises such as imagery and role-playing
- More discussion on childhood origins and developmental processes
- More emphasis on lifelong coping styles (e.g., avoidance and compensation)
- More emphasis on entrenched core themes (i.e., schemas)

Schema Theory

The four main concepts in the Schema Therapy model are: Early Maladaptive Schemas, Schema Domains, Coping Styles, and Schema Modes. The 18 Early Maladaptive Schemas are self-defeating core themes or patterns that we keep repeating throughout our lives. The 5 Schema Domains relate to the basic emotional needs of a child. When these needs are not met in childhood, schemas develop that lead to unhealthy life patterns. The 18 schemas are grouped into 5 broad schema domains, on the basis of which core needs the schema is related to.

Coping Styles are the ways the child adapts to schemas and to damaging childhood experiences. For example, some children surrender to their schemas; some find ways to block out or escape from pain; while other children fight back or overcompensate.

Schema Modes are the moment-to-moment emotional states and coping responses that we all experience. Often our schema modes are triggered by life situations that we are oversensitive to (our "emotional buttons"). Many schema modes lead us to overreact to situations, or to act in ways that end up hurting us.

The goals of Schema Therapy are: to help patients to stop using maladaptive coping styles and thus get back in touch with their core feelings; to heal their early schemas; to learn how to flip out of self-defeating schema modes as quickly as possible; and eventually to get their emotional needs met in everyday life.

Schema Therapy Treatment Strategies Include the Following:

Phase I: Assessment and Education
• Identify and educate about client's schemas.
• Link schemas to presenting problems and life.
• Bring client in touch with emotions surrounding schemas.
• Identify dysfunctional patterns of maintenance, avoidance, and compensatory behaviors.

Phase II: Change Strategies
• Restruture thinking related to schemas; develop a healthy voice to create distance.
• Practice experiential exercises to grieve for early pain, express anger, and empower the client.
• Initiate behavioral and interpersonal change related to presenting problem.
• Utilize therapy relationship to understand schemas and for limited reparenting.

Techniques Used Include the Following:
• Cognitive Interventions to examine schemas empirically such as using dialogues or self-talk between schemas and "healthy self" and to test the validity of schemas and reframe the past.

- Experiential Techniques include inner-child work, imagery, role-playing and ventilation.
- Behavior Pattern-Breaking to change self-defeating behavior patterns such as graded tasks to change schema-driven behaviors, especially interpersonal patterns outside of therapy.
- Utilize the therapy relationship as an antidote to earlier life experiences.
- Abandonment Assessment and attachment disorders of the past through early imagery of episodes with primary caregiver and current dysfunctional relationship patterns.

In formulating the schema-focused approach, Young combined the best aspects of cognitive-behavioral, experiential, interpersonal, and psychoanalytic therapies into one unified model of treatment. Through Young's work and the efforts of those trained by him, schema-focused therapy has shown remarkable results in helping people to change patterns they have lived with for a long time, even when other methods and efforts they have tried before have been largely unsuccessful. This is a relatively new therapeutic approach that targets specific self-defeating or self-destructive behaviors.

PARADOXICAL STRATEGIES

Paradoxical interventions (techniques that seem self-contradictory or absurd, and yet explicably express the truth) have been described as capable of effecting dramatic change in even the most difficult clients. The popularity and acceptance of these unorthodox methods seem to increase almost yearly; approximately two-thirds of the burgeoning literature on the therapeutic paradox has appeared since the mid-1970s (Seltzer, 1986).

Paradoxical strategies have been effectively employed to deal with a full spectrum of dysfunctional behaviors. The literature reflects the following topics: academic problems, addictive behaviors, adolescent problems, aggression, agoraphobia, anorexia nervosa, anxiety, bulimia, compulsive behaviors, depression, insomnia, marital conflict, obsessive-compulsive disorders, phobias, psychosomatic symptoms, school problems, sexual problems and dysfunctions, and suicidal ideation.

Sometimes using seemingly irrational (paradoxical) strategies in psychotherapy has value. From the theoretical perspectives of psychoanalysis, behavior therapy, humanistic psychotherapy, interpersonal communications and systems theory, paradoxical interventions have been touted as capable of effecting dramatic change in even the most difficult clients. The initial introduction of paradox in psychotherapy is perhaps most accurately associated with systems-oriented therapists working primarily within a family context.

Stanton (1981) delineated an almost unlimited applicability of therapeutic paradox by cataloging the disorders successfully treated from a strategic viewpoint. Stanton's categories include adolescent problems, aging, alcoholism, anorexia and eating disorders, anxiety, asthma, behavioral problems, delinquency, childhood "emotional" problems, crying, depression, dizziness, drug abuse and addiction, encopresis, enuresis, fire setting, homosexuality, hysterical blindness, identity crises, insomnia, leaving home, marital conflict, obesity, obsessive-compulsive behavior, obsessive thoughts, chronic pain, paranoia, phobias, postpartum depression and psychosis, public speaking anxiety, schizophrenia, school problems and truancy, sexual problems, sleep disturbances, stammering, suicidal gestures, excessive sweating, temper tantrums, thumb-sucking, vomiting, stomach aches, and work problems (pp. 368–369).

Strategic family therapists have been most identified with the use of paradoxical interventions. The basic tenet of strategic therapy is that therapeutic change comes about through the "interactional processes set off when a therapist intervenes actively and directly" in a family or marital system (Haley, 1973, p. 7). The goal is to change the dysfunctional sequence of behaviors manifested by couples and families. The therapist works to substitute new behavior patterns or sequences for the vicious, positive feedback circles already existing (Weakland, Fisch, Watzlawick, & Bodin, 1974).

The use of paradoxical intervention techniques has been described by a number of researchers (Anderson & Russell, 1982; Aponte & Van Deusen, 1981; de Shazer, 1978, 1979; Frankl, 1960; Haley, 1967, 1973, 1976; Jacobson & Margolin, 1979; L'Abate & Weeks, 1978; Rimm & Masters, 1979; Watzlawick, Beavin, & Jackson, 1967; Weeks & L'Abate, 1982). Watzlawick et al. (1967) defined paradox as a "contradiction that follows correct deduction from consistent premises" (p. 188). Hare-Mustin (1976) characterized paradoxical interventions as "those which appear absurd because they exhibit an apparently contradictory nature, such as requiring clients to do what in fact they have been doing, rather than requiring that they change, which is what everyone else is demanding" (p. 128). Rohrbaugh, Tennen, and Eron (1982) more precisely described paradoxical interventions as "strategies and tactics in apparent opposition to the acknowledged goals of therapy, but actually designed to achieve them" (pp. 84–124). Seltzer (1986) agreed in this working definition of paradoxical intervention: "A paradoxical strategy refers to a therapist's directive or attitude that is perceived by the client, at least initially, as contrary to therapeutic goals, but which is yet rationally understandable and specifically devised by the therapist to achieve these goals" (p. 10).

Seltzer (1986) also outlined the employment of paradox by various schools: From the psychoanalytic perspective, which includes the work of paradigmatic psychotherapists, we have inherited the descriptors "antisuggestion," "going with the resistance," "joining the resistance," "reflecting (or mirroring) the resistance," "siding with resistance," "paradigmatic exaggeration," "supporting the defenses," "reduction act absurdum," "re-enacting an aspect of the psychosis," "mirroring the patient's distortions," "participating in the patient's fantasies," "out crazing the patient," and "the use of the patient as consultant."

From the perspective of behavior therapy, paradoxical elements are in such procedures as "blow-up," "implosion," "flooding," "negative practice," "paradoxical intention," "stimulus satiation," and "symptom scheduling." Furthermore, from a systems approach to therapy or strategic therapy especially applicable to family systems, the strategic paradoxical strategies include "the confusion technique," "declaring hopelessness," "exaggerating the position," "paradoxical injunction," "paradoxical instructions," "paradoxical rituals and tasks," "paradoxical written messages," "restraining (or "inhibiting") change," "predicting a relapse," "redefinition," "relabeling," "symptom prescription" (or "prescribing the resistance, symptom, or system"), "therapeutic paradox," and the "therapeutic double bind" (Seltzer, 1986, p. 20).

> *Perspective for the Therapist: On genuineness*
>
> *Today we come across an individual who behaves like an automaton, who does not know or understand himself, and the only person that he knows is the person that he is supposed to be, whose meaningless chatter has replaced communicative speech, whose synthetic smile has replaced genuine laughter, and whose sense of dull despair has taken the place of genuine pain. Two statements may be said concerning this individual. One is that he suffers from defects of spontaneity and individuality which may seem to be incurable. At the same time it may be said of him he does not differ essentially from the millions of the rest of us who walk upon this earth.*
>
> Erich Fromm

Technique: *Negative Practice*

Counseling Intention   To break a compulsive habit.

Description   Negative practice is a corrective learning procedure defined as "the practice of a response for the purpose of breaking the habit of making the response." This approach could be applicable to such problems as habitual spelling and typing mistakes, muscular tensions, stage fright, obsessions, compulsions, hypochondria, social anxieties, chronic worry, tics, nail biting, and stammering.

Technique: *Stimulus Satiation*

Counseling Intention   To overdo a particular habit that is satisfying yet dangerous.

Description   "Stimulus satiation refers to the repeated presentation of a positive stimulus to the satiety, in order to lessen or eliminate its abnormally high positive valence" (Seltzer, 1986, p. 50). This technique could be useful when dealing with difficult smoking or eating behaviors. For example, a client may need to chain smoke for extended periods of time in order to finally break the habit. It also could be used with an adolescent who begins to experiment with cigarettes by having the client smoke a pack until smoking becomes undesirable.

Technique: *Implosion and Flooding or "Forced Reality Testing"*

Counseling Intention   To overcome habitual responses of avoidance.

Description   Implosion or flooding focuses on the repeated presentation of an intense phobic stimuli to eradicate the problematic responses connected to them. The technique involves exposing individuals to increasingly intense phobic stimuli while preventing their habitual response of avoidance. Both implosion and flooding concentrate on the presentation of highly anxiety provoking scenes (arranged in a hierarchy).

The client is confronted with the stimulus (imagined or in vivo) without relaxation or pause so as to elicit the maximum sustained emotional response possible and ultimately to "exhaust" the response. Seltzer (1986) pointed out that "overexposure to highly charged stimuli leads, at least theoretically, to an ever-decreasing emotional response, so that self-control is regained through the very process of the individual's agreeing to allow himself to be put 'out of control'" (p. 52). This is most applicable to individuals with poor impulse control, stress, insomnia, fear of rejection, depression, grief, or guilt. It has also been used with such anxiety-provoking fears as speaking in public, receiving injections, being in a elevator, spiders, and snakes.

Marshall, Gauthier, Christie, Currie, and Gordon (1977) and Redd, Porterfield, and Anderson (1979) have suggested, however, that imaginal exposure to horrifying situations may, under certain conditions, strengthen a client's fear. The therapist should be very familiar with (1) identifying anxiety cues, (2) formulating highly anxiety-provoking scenes, and (2) alternative therapeutic approaches for individuals who have a very negative experience.

Technique: *Paradoxical Intention*

Counseling Intention   To challenge and immerse clients in their symptomatic behavior.

Description   Frankl (1960) introduced paradoxical intention as a therapeutic technique. Paradoxical intention advises clients to experience their symptoms freely, frequently, and to the extreme. Deliberately practicing the behaviors adamantly avoided opens clients up to their anxiety directly.

Technique: *Prescribing, Restraining, and Positioning*

Counseling Intention   To modify the problematic behavior.

Description   "Prescribing" tactics encourage or direct clients to engage in the behavior targeted for elimination. "Restraining" methods discourage changes or suggest that change is not even possible. "Positioning" techniques involve altering a problematic stance by accepting and exaggerating it.

Technique: *Reframing, Relabeling, and Redefinition*

Counseling Intention   To modify the problematic behavior.

Description   "Reframing," relabeling, and redefinition are treated synonymously by Seltzer (1986). Treatment involves altering the meaning attributed to a situation by changing the cognitive or emotional context (the frame) in which the situation is experienced. Because the problem is the result of the prevailing cognitive-emotional situation, to modify that situation is inevitably to modify the problem as well (p. 106).

Technique: *Positive Interpretation*

Counseling Intention   To reframe the problem.

Description   In this technique, the therapist prescribes positive motives to clients. The therapist might relabel "hostile" behavior as "concerned interest"

(Weakland, Finch, Watzlawick, & Boden, 1974) or perhaps as a desire to "get the best care possible" for the identified client. Rationale: Blaming, criticism, and negative terms tend to mobilize resistance, rendering the therapist as incapable.

Technique: *Positive Connotation*

Counseling Intention   To re-label the problem from a positive perspective.

Description   Positive connotation is the hallmark of therapy with Selvini-Palazzoli, Boscolo, Cecchin, & Prata (1974) and associates in the Milano group. By describing relationships in a positive way—that is, positively addressing the homeostatic tendency of the family system rather than individual members—greater access to the family system is achieved. Selvini-Palazzoli et al. (1974) maintained that, through positive connotation,

> *We implicitly declare ourselves as allies of the family's striving for homeostasis, and we do this at the moment that the family feels it is most threatened. By strengthening the homeostatic tendency, we gain influence over the ability to change. Total acceptance of the marital or family system by the therapists enables them to be accepted in the family game, a necessary step toward changing the game through paradox.* (p. 441)

Dell (1981) suggested that the therapist's stance is paradoxical in its being at once "benevolent" and "toxic": benevolent because of the loving and charitable motives it ascribes to the family and its symptom bearer (dysfunctional member), and toxic because it radically contradicts family members' perceptions of what is actually happening in the family. In such a context, Dell perceived the family members as changing "in the process of trying to rid themselves of the toxic and stupefying reframing of their family game" (pp. 37–42).

Technique: *Symptom Exaggeration*

Counseling Intention   To magnify or enlarge the problem.

Description   Symptom exaggeration is an amplification technique where the client is instructed to magnify or enlarge upon the problem. Again, the deliberate intensification of behavior previously regarded as involuntary serves to demonstrate to the client that he or she can control the behavior, hopefully in a more positive direction. Aponte and Van Deusen (1981) concluded that symptom exaggeration can increase the magnitude of the symptom beyond the point that it can continue to serve a compensatory function, with the result that it must eventually be abandoned.

Technique: *System Prescription*

Counseling Intention   To make covert family rules more overt.

Description   System prescription is another benchmark of Selvini-Palazzoli et al. The very rules that have resulted in a symptomatic family member are prescribed. The therapist prescribes the various interpersonal components of problem-perpetuating behavior. This maneuver serves to make more overt the covert rules that control the family's interaction. Once members become aware of how the "roles" dictated by their self-defeating rules contribute to their problems, it becomes increasingly difficult to follow them.

Technique: *Paradoxical Written Messages*

Counseling Intention   To obtain greater client involvement by being ambiguous or obscure.

Description   Paradoxical written messages are unexpected mail. L'Abate and his colleagues at the Family Study Center at Georgia State University are perhaps the major proponents of the paradoxical written message. Weeks and L'Abate (1982) found that paradoxical letters are almost always reacted to as "cryptic, obscure, confusing, perplexing, or noncommonsensical and it helps to secure the client's involvement, since the person or system receiving the letter must work on deciphering its meaning" (p. 156).

Reframing positively can be used in families when they are acting out to protect the parental relationship. The defeating pattern can be reframed in order to tie it to success, enjoyment, caring, protectiveness, closeness, or intimacy (Seltzer, p. 36). Below is a list of rules for this assignment followed by a typical letter, much like the ritualized prescriptions used by Selvini-Palazzoli et al. (1974).

1. The father will read this letter to other members of the family.
2. The letter will be read after dinner on Monday, Wednesday, and Friday evenings.

3. The mother will remind the father to read the letter.
4. The content of this letter cannot be discussed with anyone outside of counseling.

Dear_____,

We (the parents) are appreciative of your protecting us because as long as you act up neither Mother nor I will need to look at ourselves and deal with our middle age. You will also help your brother to stay the way he is. Consequently, we will understand that anytime you blow up, it will be to protect your brother and us. We hope, therefore, that you will continue protecting us, because we need it.

Technique: *Prescribing the Defeat*

Counseling Intention   To escalate the behavior that family members are using to defeat each other.

Description   After reframing a behavior, the next step is to prescribe the behavior. Because the defeat is now a positive expression, it follows that the family should assist, continue, and even escalate and increase whatever they are doing to defeat each other. To make sure that the reframing and prescription are not going to be ignored or forgotten, it is helpful to put them in writing and to ritualize them (i.e., "Read this letter after supper on alternating days, either Monday, Wednesday, and Fridays, or Tuesdays, Thursdays, and Saturdays" as the Milano group recommends) (Selvini-Palazzoli et al., 1978). This letter can be given to the child (from the last example) to read to his parents:

1. To be read by son to other members of the family.
2. Please read on Mondays, Wednesdays, and Fridays after dinner.
3. Mother is to remind son to read and, if she forgets, father and daughter are to remind.
4. Do not discuss contents outside of counseling.

Dear_____,

I [the therapist] am impressed with the way in which you show how much you care about this family and especially your mother. I feel you need to be congratulated for having violent temper tantrums, because these tantrums serve as a safety valve for what your father and mother cannot do. I admire you for the way in which you show your loyalty to your mother.

If this is the way you want to protect your parents from each other and continue keeping them apart, you should continue to blow up, but do this on Monday, Wednesday, and Friday of each week. Be sure to break some inexpensive item in your home and continue these outbursts because if you stop, they might get back together.

The prescription of the behavior usually helps the child control the behavior that is problematic. This type of letter may help the parents see their part in the problem so that they begin to change spontaneously (Seltzer, 1986, pp. 266–267). The paradoxical written message has many advantages. First, it commands the attention of all parties involved. Second, communication that is in writing is much less likely to be ignored, repressed, distorted, or manipulated. Third, written communication has a bonding quality, which encourages repeated review outside the therapy session and lends itself to a cumulative effect beyond even the most intense therapy session.

Technique: *Restraining Change*

Counseling Intention   To encourage therapeutic change.

Description   The therapist actively discourages the individual, couple, or family from changing dysfunctional behavior by suggesting that such behavior change is futile. This paradoxical maneuver is particularly effective when therapeutic change is noticeably slow or at an impasse. This often is received as a challenge by recipients, empowering them to demonstrate that the therapist is incorrect in his or her observation.

Technique: *Relapse Prediction*

Counseling Intention   To empower the client to change.

Description   Informing the client that he or she may experience a relapse—that the problem will reappear—creates a therapeutic double bind (Seltzer, 1986). If the symptoms recur as predicted by the therapist, it places the therapist in control. If it does not recur, it comes under the client's control, thus empowering his or her ability to change behavior—a fundamental therapeutic intention. Seltzer (1986) maintained that "when the client's relationship to the therapist is predominantly oppositional, the relapse prediction will be regarded as a challenge to continue to be asymptomatic, so as to deny the validity of (and external control implied by) the therapist's pessimistic forecast" (p. 125). Relapse prescription is a logical extension of relapse prediction. Watzlawick, Weakland, and Fisch (1974) concluded that prescribing a relapse is appropriate when a client has overcome a substantial obstacle so the behavior change is very fragile. Seltzer (1986, p. 126) outlined the therapeutic double bind generated through prescription relapse:

1. Should the client experience a relapse, such an event can be seen as proof that he now has sufficient control over his problem to produce it deliberately.
2. Should he fail to produce a relapse, such nonreoccurrence demonstrates that he now has sufficient control to avoid this problem deliberately.

Technique: *Declaring Helplessness*

Counseling Intention   To gain control during a power struggle between family and therapist.

Description   When there are power struggles between the therapist and the individual or family, it is sometimes advantageous for the therapist to admit defeat. Paradoxically, the therapist must honestly and humbly admit inadequacy to effect changes. The family often moves in this direction of proving that treatment is indeed working. As the therapist proceeds to the door, he or she is invited back by the family and paradoxically gains even greater control in the therapeutic arena.

Technique: *Confusion Technique*

Counseling Intention   To overcome resistance and focus on the primary problem.

Description   The confusion technique is another version of restraining change. The therapist accepts every topic or lists of problems a couple or family may present. He also identifies problem areas of his or her own, which may stimulate the need for change in other areas as a ploy to better understand their relationship. The therapist continues with the confusion tactic until the couple becomes more explicit about their primary problem and goals so that therapy can begin and resistance can end. Essentially, the frustration of identifying so many problems sets the stage for the couple to rebel against what initially began as their own resistance toward articulating essential problems and using treatment productively.

CONCLUSION

Cognitive therapy's concise simple model has proven to be the most powerful and effective type of psychological treatment in outcome studies conducted over the past several decades. Due to the availability of literature and training of professionals in CBT, cognitive behavior therapy currently enjoys widespread popularity, and is practiced by many qualified professionals throughout the United States and internationally. Cognitive therapists believe in the importance of cognitions: "cognition" referring to conceptions, ideas, meanings, beliefs, thoughts, inferences, expectations, predictions, and attributions (Davis & Fallowfield, 1991). These cognitions mediate client problems and are available for scrutiny and subsequent change by the client. These cognitions are the primary target for change in attempting to address the client's cognitive, affective, and behavioral difficulties. Spinelli (1994) suggested that those with a cognitive perspective share the common philosophical viewpoint that humans are disturbed by the views they hold about events rather than the events themselves.

Chapter 8

Rational Emotive Behavior Therapy, Reality Therapy, and Transactional Analysis

BEAUTIFUL HANGUP
(Tune, Stephan Foster, *Beautiful Dreamer*)

Beautiful hangup, why should we part
When we have shared our whole lives from the start?
We are so used to taking one course
Oh, what a crime it would be to divorce!
Beautiful hangup, don't go away!
Who will befriend me if you do not stay?
Though you still make me look like a jerk,
Living without you would take so much work!
Living without you would take so much work!

Albert Ellis,
How to Stubbornly Refuse to Make Yourself Miserable about
Anything, Yes Anything, 1988, p. 45 (Reprinted with permission)

RATIONAL EMOTIVE BEHAVIOR THERAPY

Rational emotive behavior therapy (REBT) is a humanistic, action-oriented approach to emotional growth, which emphasizes (1) the individuals' capacity for creating their emotions; (2) the ability to change and overcome the past by focusing on the present; and (3) the power to choose and implement satisfying alternatives to current patterns. REBT is a comprehensive approach to psychological treatment that deals not only with the emotional and behavioral aspects of human disturbance, but emphasizes its cognitive component: "Nothing is good or bad, but thinking makes it so."

Rational emotive therapy assumes that people do not get disturbed by their early or present life experiences but rather they have a strong innate predisposition to disturb themselves consciously and unconsciously. Clients assimilate their preferential goals, standards, and values from their families and culture and change them into explicit and tacit "shoulds," "oughts," and "musts" that become imposed on their expectations on themselves and other people. Ellis (1992) maintained that when people needlessly disturb themselves they produce dysfunctional thoughts (e.g., obsessions), feelings (e.g., panic disorders, depression, anxiety, self-criticism, self-hatred), and dysfunctional behaviors (e.g., phobias, obsessions, compulsions, mood disorders, and depression). The role of the therapist is to focus on the elimination of emotional responses to irrational thinking by rationally challenging beliefs and providing clients with more accurate and realistic appraisals of themselves and their life experiences. The therapist challenges the client to work to change his or her powerful *"mustabatory"* thinking, emoting, and acting.

REBT is promulgated on a few basic principles, which have profound theoretical implications:

1. A client is responsible for his or her own emotions and actions.
2. A client's harmful emotions and dysfunctional behaviors are the product of the client's irrational thinking.
3. A client can learn more realistic views and, with practice, make them a part of their emotional repertoire.
4. The client will experience a deeper acceptance of self and greater satisfactions in life by developing a reality-based perspective.

REBT distinguishes clearly between two distinct types of problematic difficulties: *practical* problems and *emotional* problems. Flawed behavior, unfair treatment by others, and undesirable situations represent *practical* problems. Universally, clients have the tendency to become upset, serving as a catalyst for creating a second order of problems—*emotional* suffering. REBT addresses emotional suffering with the following four tenets.

First, clients need to take responsibility for their own distress. Only the client can upset himself or herself about current events. Yet the events themselves, no matter how difficult, do not have absolute power to upset the client. Inherently, the client must recognize that neither an individual, nor an adverse circumstance, can ever disturb the client. Essentially, arbitrary emotional disturbance is self-inflicted. The client invariably creates his or her own emotional suffering or self-defeating behavioral patterns as the result of what others say or do.

Second, the client needs to identify his or her inner dialogue of "musts."

Essentially, there are three core distortions that focus on the client's self-defeating "must" dialogue:

- *"Must" 1,* an unrealistic expectation of one's self: "I must do well and get approval, or else I'm worthless." This irrational self-imposed demand causes anxiety, depression, and emotional distress.
- *"Must" 2,* an unrealistic expectation about others: "You must treat me reasonably, considerately, and lovingly, or else you're no good." This "must" leads to resentment, hostility, alienation, conflict, self-destructive behavior, and even violence.
- *"Must" 3,* an unrealistic expectation of situations or circumstances: "Life must be fair, easy, and hassle-free, or else it's awful." This distorted thinking fosters hopelessness, helplessness, procrastination, depression, anxiety, and addictions to self-medicate.

Third, it becomes paramount that therapists teach the client to dispute his or her irrational, self-imposed musts. What is the evidence for his or her "musts"? How are they true? If there's *no* evidence, the client's "musts" are entirely false.

Fourth, the therapist needs to teach the client to reinforce his or her preferences:

Preference 1: "I strongly prefer to do well and get approval; but even if I fail, I will accept myself unconditionally and fully."

Preference 2: "I strongly prefer that others treat me reasonably, kindly, and lovingly, but since I don't run the universe and it's a part of human nature to err, I cannot control others."

Preference 3: "I strongly prefer that life be fair, easy, and hassle-free, and it's very frustrating that it isn't; but I can bear frustration and still enjoy life without self-imposed expectations."

REBT is based on the assumption that clients label "emotional" reactions, which are largely caused by conscious and unconscious irrational and self-defeating evaluations, interpretations, expectations, and philosophies. Thus, clients feel anxious or depressed because their belief system strongly convinces them that it is *terrible* when they fail at something or that they *can't stand* the pain of being rejected, unloved, or excluded. Ellis (1992, p. 63–80) identified 12 irrational ideas that cause and sustain neurosis among clients. Rational therapy holds that certain core irrational ideas, which have been clinically observed, are at the root of most neurotic disturbance. They are:

1. The idea that it is a dire necessity for adults to be loved by significant others for almost everything they do.

2. The idea that certain acts are awful or wicked, and that people who perform such acts should be severely condemned.
3. The idea that it is horrible when things are not the way people like them to be.
4. The idea that human misery is invariably externally caused and is forced on us by outside people and events.
5. The idea that if something is or may be dangerous or fearsome people should be terribly upset and endlessly obsess about it.
6. The idea that it is easier to avoid than to face life difficulties and self-responsibilities.
7. The idea that people absolutely need something other or stronger or greater than ourselves on which to rely.
8. The idea that people should be thoroughly competent, intelligent, and achieving in all possible respects.
9. The idea that, because something once strongly affected our life, it should indefinitely affect it, as well as the idea that people must have certain and perfect control over things.
10. The idea that human happiness can be achieved by inertia and inaction.
11. The idea that people have virtually no control over our emotions and that we cannot help feeling disturbed about things.

Further, Walen, DiGuiseppe, and Wessler (1980, pp. 72–73) have defined the somewhat elusive concepts of rational and irrational beliefs as follows:

1. *A rational belief is true.* The belief is consistent with reality in kind and degree; it can be supported by evidence; and it is empirically verified. Also, it is logical, internally consistent, and consistent with realities.
2. *A rational belief is not absolute but is conditional or relative.* A rational belief is usually stated as a desire, hope, want, wish, or preference. It reflects a desire rather than a demand.
3. *A rational belief results in moderate emotion.* Rational beliefs lead to feelings that range from mild to strong but that are not upsetting to the client.
4. *A rational belief helps you attain your goals.* Rational beliefs are congruent with satisfaction in living, minimizing intrapersonal conflict, minimizing conflict with the environment, enabling affiliation and involvement with others, and personal growth.

Irrational beliefs are defined in terms of a set of opposite constructs (Walen, DiGuiseppe, & Nessler, 1980, pp. 73–74):

1. *An irrational belief is not true.* It does not reflect reality; it often begins with an inaccurate premise and leads to inaccurate deductions. It is not supported by evidence, and it often represents an overgeneralization.

2. *An irrational belief is an intrapersonal command.* It represents an absolute rather than a problem-solving philosophy, and it is expressed as "demands" or "shoulds" rather than "wishes" and "preferences."
3. *An irrational belief promotes disturbed emotions.* Apathy or anxiety is debilitating and nonproductive.
4. *An irrational belief does not help to attain personal goals.* When one is consumed with absolute edicts and paralyzed by upsetting emotions, it becomes increasingly difficult to maximize pleasure and minimize discomfort in order to feel competent in everyday life.

Adolescence is a period that is often characterized by "storm and stress" as well as the developmental task of identity formation. Because this is a very self-conscious period for many teenagers, they may manifest the following irrational beliefs identified by Walters (1981, pp. 136–144):

- It would be awful if peers didn't like me. It would be awful to be a social loser.
- I shouldn't make mistakes, especially social mistakes.
- It's my parents fault I'm so miserable.
- I can't help it, that's just the way I am and I guess I'll always be that way.
- The world should be fair and just.
- It's awful when things do not go my way.
- It's better to avoid challenges than to risk failure.
- I must conform to my peers.
- I can't stand to be criticized.
- Others should always be responsible.

Differences between REBT and Other Schools of Psychotherapy

REBT differentiates itself from other schools of therapy in three areas: (1) it deemphasizes early childhood experience, (2) it applies scientific thinking to irrational thinking and attempts to shift the clients' point of view, and (3) it uses homework to reinforce what was learned in the therapeutic setting. The therapist inherently believes that no matter what the clients' basic irrational philosophy of life, he or she is presently disturbed because he or she *still* believe this self-defeating perception of themselves and the world. If the client will identify exactly what he or she is irrationally thinking in the present and begin to challenge and question these self-statements, the client has the opportunity to improve significantly.

REBT strives to reconfigure the client's outlook on life. It teaches the client that adults do not *need* to be accepted or loved, even though it is highly *desirable*. Clients are shown how to question: (1) the scientifically ambiguous hypotheses that they construct, as well as (2) preconceived notions about themselves and their relationships. Clients are shown how to ask themselves, "Granted that my *acts* may be mistaken, why am *I* a totally *bad* person for performing them? Where is the evidence that I must always be right in order to consider myself worthy? Assuming that it is preferable for me to act well rather than badly, why do I *have* to do what is preferable?" REBT maintains that in reality to be human is to be fallible. This reality can be accepted if one works hard to become a little less fallible and do so without creating undue discomfort and distress.

In REBT, actual homework (or *ownwork*) assignments are frequently given to practice new learnings outside the therapeutic setting. Assignments may include becoming more assertive by asking someone out on a date, or looking for a new job or career, or resolving a relationship that was previously conflicted. The therapist actively encourages the client to undertake such assignments as an integral part of the therapeutic process as well as rate their level of satisfaction at accomplishing assignments by rating them on a scale from 1 to 10 (1 = low, 10 = high).

The REBT practitioner provides clients unconditional rather than conditional positive regard, because the REBT philosophy maintains that no one should be condemned for anything, no matter how deplorable their behavior may be. The therapist's intentions are unconditional acceptance while actively teaching the client how to fully accept themselves, to express their feelings, and to stop berating themselves. Rational emotive behavior therapy uses expressive-experimental methods and behavioral techniques. It is not, however, primarily interested in helping people ventilate emotion and *feel* better, but in showing them how they can truly *get* better and lead to less dysfunctional, less self-defeating, and more self-actualized lives.

Two of the foremost cognitive-behavioral interventionists are Maultsby and Ellis. Maultsby is recognized for rational behavior therapy (RBT) and Ellis for rational emotive therapy (RET). In 1993, Ellis changed the name from Rational-Emotive Therapy (RET) to Rational-Emotive Behavior Therapy (REBT). Maultsby (1975) and Ellis (1973) articulated the role of *interventionist* by demonstrating to troubled clients that through (1) their own thinking, and (2) the use of a structured strategy they can reorder their perceptions and behavior to remove the source of their difficulties. Essentially, Ellis (1979, 1985, 1990) has developed an ABC theory of personality that holds that (A) *activating events* do not directly cause (C) emotional and behavioral *consequences*. Rather, the emotional and behavioral consequences (C) are largely caused by (B) one's *beliefs* about the activating event. The disputation method involves identifying, debating, and challenging irrational beliefs and replacing them with rational beliefs (Ellis, 1975). Thoughts, feelings, and behavior are all interrelated.

The classic model for examining the relationships between thoughts, feelings, and behavior was developed by Ellis (1989): the A-B-C model. Point A is the activating event; point C is the feelings about the event. The critical component between A and C is point B, one's self-talk. Internalized self-talk influences feelings and behavior. It can be rational or irrational, functional or dysfunctional.

Self-statements can become habitual responses to stress or conflict. By cognitively restructuring, the client can learn specific coping skills to restructure thoughts, reduce stress, and increase relatively positive or negative feelings.

Rational Emotive Behavioral Techniques

Technique: *Ellis's A-B-C-D-E Paradigm*

Counseling Intention   To correct distorted thinking or self-defeating belief systems.

Description   Albert Ellis maintained that people upset themselves via their own belief systems. Clients are taught how they falsely attribute their own upsets to outside or activating events. When feeling upset, clients are directed to examine their B (beliefs) instead of blaming the A (activating events).

They are shown that *activating events* (A) do not result automatically in emotional and behavioral *consequences* (C), but that it is mainly the *beliefs* (B) about A that are responsible for the impact at point C. By *disputing* (D) the irrational beliefs at point B, the *effect* (E) is the elimination of negative consequences (C).

The client may be provided with a homework exercise to begin identifying self-defeating feelings such as anger:

A = *Activating event.* Describe a situation about which you became angry.
B = *Beliefs.* What do you tell yourself about the situation?
C = *Consequences, behavioral or emotional.* Describe the upset feeling. Describe what the client did because the client was angry.
D = *Dispute.* Question the client's angry thoughts, expectations, disappointments. Is there a different way of looking at the situation?
E = *Effect.* What would the client like to see happen? What can the client change and what should you accept?

Technique: *Charting Irrational Beliefs*

Counseling Intention   To correct distorted thinking or self-defeating belief systems (Ellis, 1988).

Description   Table 8.1 is helpful in charting irrational beliefs.

TABLE 8.1
Charting Irrational Beliefs

(A) Activating Events—thoughts or feelings that happened just before I felt emotionally disturbed or acted as if I were defeated.

(B) Beliefs—self-defeating talk about the experience or situation.

(C) Consequence of Conditions—disturbed feelings or self-defeating behavior that I produce and would like to change. _____

(B) Beliefs—Irrational Beliefs (IB) leading to my CONSEQUENCES (emotional disturbance or self-defeating behavior). Circle all that apply to these ACTIVATING EVENTS (A).	(D) DISPUTES for each circled IRRATIONAL BELIEF. Examples: *"Why 'must' I do very well?"* *"Where is it written that I am a BAD PERSON?" "Where is the evidence that I 'must' be approved and accepted?"*	(E) EFFECTIVE RATIONAL BELIEFS (RBs) to replace my IRRATIONAL BELIEFS (IBs). *Examples: "I'd 'prefer' to do very well but I don't 'have to'." "I am a person who acted badly, not a bad person." "There is no evidence that I 'have' to be approved, though I would like to be."*
1. I *must* do well or very well!		
2. I am a bad or worthless person when I act weakly or stupidly.		
3. I must be approved or accepted by people I find important.		
4. I am a bad unlovable person if I get rejected.		
5. People must treat me fairly and give me what I need.		
6. People who act immorally are undeserving, rotten people.		
7. People must live up to my expectations or it is terrible.		
8. My life must have few major hassles or troubles.		
9. I can't stand really bad things or very difficult people.		

TABLE 8.1
Continued

10. It's awful or horrible when major things don't go my way.		
11. I can't stand it when life is really unfair.		
12. I need to be loved by someone who matters to me a lot!		
13. I need a good deal of immediate gratification and have to feel miserable when I don't get it!		
14. I should be promoted, I have worked hard.		
15. Everyone I meet should like me 100 percent.		
16. Life should be fair, because I am in control.		
17. Other people should live up to my expectations.		

Source: Ellis (1988) *How to Stubbornly Refuse to Make Yourself Miserable About Anything, Yes Anything.* New York: Kensington Publishing, p. 45. (Reprinted with permission)

Technique: *Identifying Unpleasant Emotions*

Counseling Intention   To identify antecedents to subsequent feelings.

Description   Identify the last time you were feeling a strong, unpleasant emotion. Write the emotion under "C." Under "A," write in the event before the emotion occurred. Under "B," identify what you were thinking between the event and the emotion.

- A = (activating event): "My clients do not implement the action plans developed in therapy."
- B = (my thinking): "Maybe I come on too strongly." "Maybe I'm really a poor therapist." "She really doesn't know what is best for her."
- C = (my feelings and behavior): Self-doubt about skills; anger about client's lack of initiative.

Next, analyze the accuracy of the facts and events written in "A." This can be accomplished through rational self-analysis (i.e., "Where is the evidence that what

I believe is true?"). In addition, one can differentiate between rational and irrational beliefs by answering the following questions:

1. Do the client's beliefs reflect an objective reality? Would a second party perceive the situation in the same way? Are the beliefs exaggerated and personalized?
2. Are the beliefs helpful to the client? (Self-destructive thoughts are usually irrational.)
3. Are the beliefs helpful in reducing conflicts with others or do they foster an "us versus them" mentality?
4. Do the beliefs help or get in the way of short-term or long-term goals?
5. Do the beliefs reduce or enhance emotional conflict?

Write the objective version of the facts and events at "D" below. Only an event that can be recorded by a camera, video camera, or tape recorder is a fact. If the event cannot be recorded, it is probably an opinion, a feeling, or an evaluation. This strategy should help the client see how misperceptions of situations can alter one's self-talk or inner dialogue, and in turn affect one's emotional response. Irrational thoughts lead to negative emotional feelings. Negative emotional feelings ultimately lead to depression (Wilde, 1992, 1996).

Finally, the therapist should have the client decide how he or she would like to feel in the situation described in "D," and enter the feeling under "F." Is it realistic to have a positive emotional response to a stressful situation or is it more appropriate to accept a neutral feeling? Now have the client attend to the "E" section and develop a more rational alternative to the irrational thoughts at "B." The rational alternatives should be acceptable to the client and meet at least three of the five criteria for rational thinking.

This exercise merely outlines some strategies for developing a rational plan of action and changing unwanted feelings and behaviors. This could be reframed in the following manner:

D (objective event): "My client did not carry out his action plan."
E (my rational thinking): "He is responsible for his own behavior."
F (desired feeling or behavior): "Relaxed with continued therapeutic interactions."

Twelve Distressing Myths Revisited

Inherently, people worry and become upset because of the way they interpret their stressors. Yet, people can choose to react rationally (reasonably) or irrationally (unreasonably) to a stressor. Roberts and Guttormson (1990) listed twelve irrational beliefs (myths) to which people commonly cling.

Myth 1: "I must be loved by everyone, and everyone must love everything I do."

Myth 2: "I must be intelligent, competent, and capable in everything I do."

Myth 3: "Some things in the world are bad, wrong, or evil, and I must be punished severely if I see, do, think, or feel them."

Myth 4: "The world is over when things don't turn out the way I want them to."

Myth 5: "I have no control over my own happiness. My happiness depends on what happens to me."

Myth 6: "Worrying about something bad keeps it from happening."

Myth 7: "It's always easier to run away from problems than it is to deal with them."

Myth 8: "You need someone else to depend on. You can't function independently."

Myth 9: "If something bad happened in your past, it must affect you forever."

Myth 10: "If someone else doesn't live his or her life in the way you think he or she should, you must do everything you can to change that person."

Myth 11: "There is only one correct answer to any problem. If that answer isn't found, the consequences will be terrible."

Myth 12: "You can't help feeling the way you do."

These distressing beliefs are complicated when unreasonable demands emerge as unrealistic expectations. Schriner (1990) aptly stated that "Disappointment is the caboose on the train of expectation." Many clients spend a tremendous amount of time and energy wrestling with distorted perceptions of themselves made up of self-criticisms, comparisons with others, apprehension, unrealistic expectations of the future, relentless demands for improvement, defensive excuses for failures, and an array of accompanying self-defeating thoughts and feelings.

Technique: *Eliminating the "Big Ten" Cognitive Distortions*

Counseling Intention To confront irrational thought and related anxiety; to counteract depression, stress, and panic attacks.

Description Crawford and Ellis (1989) have classified irrational beliefs into five categories:

1. Self-defeating beliefs that interfere with basic goals and drives.
2. Highly rigid, dogmatic beliefs that lead to unrealistic preferences and wishes.
3. Antisocial beliefs that cause people to destroy their social groups.
4. Unrealistic beliefs that falsely describe reality.
5. Contradictory beliefs that originate from false premises.

Technique: *A Collective Identification of Irrational Thinking and Suggested Solution for Panic Disorder and Depression*

Counseling Intention   To challenge irrational, self-defeating talk.

Description   Most people who suffer from panic disorders also are depressed. Handly and Neff (1985) outlined and provided solutions to the "big 10" cognitive distortions that affect most anxious people.

Problem 1: Perfectionism.   Often, a high-achieving client may set unreasonably high standards for himself or herself but credit accomplishments to mere luck.

Solution: Don't strive to achieve unrealistically high levels in everything attempted.

Problem 2: Rejectionitis.   The client may have the tendency to exaggerate a single rejection by someone to the point that it affects every dimension of his or her life.

Solution: Prove that this assumption is not true by listing your good qualities, and make another list of people who are like these qualities.

Problem 3: Negative focus.   This is the tendency or habit of letting a negative experience obliterate all the positive dimensions.

Solution: Go to an alpha state of consciousness where the brain wave activity is at a lower frequency than the normal waking state, and picture all the good things about oneself, then select some positive affirmations and repeat them throughout the day.

Problem 4: Refusing the positives.   Refusing the positives expands the "negative focus." A client may tell himself or herself that even "good" things in life are negatives—that is, choosing to be uncomfortable with thinking one is successful, refusing the positive, and inviting depression.

Solution: When you get a compliment or recognition for something well done, say "thanks" and not another word.

Problem 5: The white-is-black phenomenon.   A client may use neutral or even positive facts to make negative conclusions about his or her relationships to others. For example, the client interprets another's action as being particularly hostile to him, when in actuality the person was experiencing some discomfort (e.g., the client assumes that someone didn't return a call because she doesn't like him, when in reality she was out of town and didn't receive the message).

Solution: Think rationally and check reality. Have clients remind themselves that they are not responsible for another person's behavior.

Problem 6: Stretch-or-shrink thinking. The client may either stretch the truth into an "anxiety-producing fiction" (i.e., overreacting when one has done something undesirable) or shrink from attention and accolades until invisible when having done something extraordinarily well.

Solution: Apologize for human mistakes. Acknowledge yourself aloud, sending good messages to your unconscious can result in pleasant dreams and positive imagery.

Problem 7: Creating fictional fantasies. Letting emotions substitute for the truth about what is happening is creating a fantasy.

Solution: Counter fictional fantasies with the acknowledgment that distorted thoughts create negative feelings.

Problem 8: Use emotional transfusion to change feelings at the unconscious level. "Shoulds" and "oughts" cause clients to act in ways they would prefer not to, as they misconstrue responsibilities, expectations, or obligations.

Solution: Recognize that you alone are responsible for your actions.

Problem 9: Mistaken identity. Clients tell themselves that they are bad because of a mistake.

Solution: Try saying "I made a mistake," and let it go.

Problem 10: Saying "It's my fault." The client assumes all blame and responsibility for a negative event, even when no one is responsible. In reality no one can control another person.

Solution: Express your concern, but do not accept responsibility.

Problem 11: Controlling. The desire to be in control of our lives is entirely human; it is hardly irrational, but it can lead to irrational behavior when we are unconsciously manipulated by our self-destructive and self-sabotaging beliefs. To be "in control" means to understand the facts of reality that bear on our life so that we are able to predict, with reasonable accuracy, the consequences of our actions.

Solution: Accept that some things are not within your control.

Technique: *Direct Questioning*

Counseling Technique   To understand different cognitions that may be influencing the emotions of the client (Waters, 1982).

Descriptions   General prompts to use with the client include:

"What were you thinking when_____happened?"
"What sorts of things were you saying to yourself?"
"What name did you call your brother when he_____?"
"Tell me the first thing that comes into your mind when you think
_____."
"Picture yourself back in class; what did you think when _____?"

Technique: *Cognitively Modeled Self-States to Reduce Hair Pulling*

Counseling Intention   To reduce or eliminate self-destructive behavior (Bernard, Kratochwill, & Keefauver, 1983).

Description   Outline the following self-statements for the client.

Problem Definition: "What am I supposed to do?"
Problem Approach: "I'm going to build a protective bubble around me so that nothing worries me until I get my homework done."
Focusing of Attention: "I'd better pay attention to my assignment. What is the next thing I have to do?"
Coping Statements: "Oh, I'm starting to worry about school and I just pulled a hair. I know if I just relax and focus on my work that I won't worry."
Self-Reinforcement: "Hey, that's great. I finished that bit of work. I didn't worry. And I didn't pull my hair out. I knew I could do it!"

Technique: *Internalizing New Skills*

Counseling Intention   To help a client practice and apply skills used in a counseling session (Waters, 1982).

Description   Encourage the client to practice the following homework assignment:

1. Monitor feelings.
2. Make a list of personal demands.
3. Use rational emotive imagery.
4. Practice changing feelings and thoughts in a real situation.

5. Take a responsible risk.
6. Reinforce self through positive self-talk.

Technique: *Perceptions versus Reality*

Counseling Intention To assist the client in assuming personal responsibility for choices and actions; to shift the center of responsibility.

Description Have the client think of an incident that really made him or her angry or resentful, one that he or she still has some feelings about.

1. Have the client, in writing, describe the incident as if others were completely responsible for bringing about the event. Blame them. Make it clearly their fault.
2. Have the client rewrite the incident as if he or she were solely responsible for starting, developing, and getting with the problem. Take full account of what you could have done so that the whole problem would not have arisen.
3. Although the client may feel a sense of unreality about both points of view, have him or her reexamine them and see which one he or she feels most comfortable with. Does it alter the opinion originally held, if he or she accepts the blame or feels like a victim?

Technique: *Conceptual Shift*

Counseling Intention To dismantle a client's damaging pattern of thinking about himself or herself (McMullin, 1986, pp. 85–86).

Description Have the client list all the thoughts connected to a targeted negative emotion:

1. Collapse the thoughts into one major, negative, core belief or theme.
2. List the situations (past and present) that are connected to the core theme.
3. Develop a list of alternative, more positive beliefs for each negative thought.
4. Summarize the positive beliefs into one core theme.
5. Help the client reinterpret the past and present situations in terms of the new perspective. Go through each individual thought and situation and demonstrate how the client misinterprets situations.
6. Have the client practice reviewing more situations and reinterpreting them in terms of the new themes.

Technique: *Making Mistakes*

Counseling Intention   To get the client to give up the demand for perfection in others (Knaus, 1974).

Description   The following statements should be processed and discussed:

1. Everyone will always make mistakes.
2. No one is perfect.
3. Mistakes do not change a person's good qualities.
4. A person is not the same as his performance.
5. People who make mistakes do not deserve to be blamed and punished.
6. People are not bad because they make mistakes.
7. The reasons why people make mistakes are: (a) lack of skill, (b) carelessness or poor judgment, (c) insufficient information, (d) being tired or ill, and (f) irrationality.

Technique: *Interpersonal Cognitive Problem Solving*

Counseling Intentions   To have parents teach interpersonal cognitive problem solving in the context of everyday happenings (Spivack, Platt, & Shure, 1976, p. 210).

Description   Both mother and child engage in a problem-solving style of thinking and communication

Type of Problem   Child engaged in interpersonal conflict.

Specific Problem   Child initiates hurting or grabbing behavior.

1. Why [did you hit him]?
2. [Hitting] is one thing you can do. How did it make [Tommy] feel?
3. What happened when you [hit Peter]? What did Peter do or say?
4. Can you think of another way to [repeat reason child gave why he hit] so that won't happen?
5. [After child answers] That's a different idea. What might happen if you try that?

Technique: *Identifying Personal Rights and*
Changing Irrational Thinking

Counseling Intentions To challenge irrational thinking.

Description List four *rational* thoughts that directly counter your irrational thoughts and underlying ideas.

1. _____
2. _____
3. _____
4. _____

Technique: *Systematic Rationalization Process*

Counseling Intention To help the client cope with stressful life events.

Description Stressors are defined for the client as events that produce aversive symptoms such as feelings of tension, anxiousness, urgency, anger, or concern. Systematic rationalization classifies stressful life events into four quadrants: controllable, uncontrollable, important, and unimportant. It focuses on three steps.

> *Step 1: Identification of stressors.* The client is asked to write down any event, no matter how trivial, that is causing the stress in their lives.
>
> *Step 2: Identification of stressors.* The client classifies each event on the list as controllable or uncontrollable based on his or her perception of personal ability to manage or act on the stressor and as important or unimportant based on the client's personal priorities for each outcome. The therapist learns how the client conceptualizes the stress in his or her life.
>
> *Step 3: Review the classification.* A systematic review of the stressors is conducted. The review begins with stressors perceived as unimportant. Events listed as unimportant whether controllable or uncontrollable can be referred to as hassles (i.e., small life events such as traffic jams, long lines, long waits, bad weather, out-of-order ATM machine, missed flight, or missed train).

Events perceived as important contain issues of personal priority (e.g., job, family, financial security, safety, or orderliness). These stressors are reviewed as two separate classifications: controllable and uncontrollable. Stress reactions for these stressors are accomplished by personal planning and goal setting. Specific action aimed toward managing one or more of these stressors may be assigned to the client as homework. Stress management techniques for important and controllable stressors include stress inoculation, behavioral rehearsal, imagery, and progressive relaxation or other techniques that encourage the client to take responsibility for behavior.

Stressors listed as important and uncontrollable are the most difficult concerns for clients to handle effectively. To reduce the stress associated with important and uncontrollable concerns, the therapists may encourage the client to change his or her perception of these stressors by reclassifying the event. This therapeutic process may include the use of rational emotive therapy, coping skills training, and positive self-talk

Technique: *Daily Activities to Help the Client Give Up Irrational Thinking*

Counseling Intention   To keep the client focused on strategies taught in counseling sessions (Grieger, 1986).

Description   The following activities can be assigned to clients between counseling sessions:

1. *Pleasurable pursuits*—committing time each day to pleasurable pursuits.
2. *Rational-emotive imagery*—vividly picturing difficult events and practicing thinking rationally about them.
3. *Shame-attacking exercises*—performing "silly" or "embarrassing" acts in public to demonstrate that there is no need to feel ashamed.
4. *Courting discomfort*—deliberately doing uncomfortable things, or staying in uncomfortable situations a little longer.
5. *Risk taking*—doing things anxiously feared.
6. *Behavioral rehearsal*—practicing unskilled or fearful things.
7. *Rewarding and penalizing*—rewarding or punishing for doing or not doing something.

Technique: *Depersonalizing Self*

Counseling Intention   To help clients look at themselves as others look at them (McMullin, 1986, pp. 117–118).

Description   Have the client make a list of 20 negative events that he or she has recently experienced, then:

1. Record the hypothesized internal self-deficiencies that the client thinks cause the events (beliefs that caused hyperpersonalization).
2. Teach the client to look for the causes of these events outside himself. Instruct the client in the use of the scientific method: look for stimuli, reinforcements, or environmental contingencies that serve as triggers of negative events. Rewrite all proprioceptive causes as external.
3. Have the client keep a daily log of events, and supposed internal causes and external causes. Teach clients to see themselves and others as objects, subject to environmental influences.
4. Once clients have learned not to take responsibility for these influences, teach them the kinds of problem-solving methods that can be used to modify the environment.

Technique: *Overcoming Resistance to Change*

Counseling Intention   To get the client to confront irrational beliefs and self-defeating behavior (Grieger, 1986).

Description   Resistance often impedes the client from risk taking or taking responsibility for change. Examples of resistance are as follows:

- *Fear of discomfort*—believing that the effort to change is too difficult, that it is easier to drift along with problems than to make the effort to change them.
- *Fears of disclosure and shame*—believing present feelings, actions, or thoughts are inappropriate, and that it would be terrible if anyone else knew it.
- *Feelings of powerlessness and hopelessness*—believing that one is unable to change, that problems are too big to overcome.
- *Fear of change*—believing that the safety and security of present self-defeating behaviors are less risky than change.
- *Fear of failure and disapproval*—believing that one must always succeed, fearing that symptoms may lead to risk failure and disapproval.
- *Self-punishment*—believing one is a bad person and deserves to suffer.
- *Discouragement*—believing that disturbances cannot be overcome.

Technique: *Rational-Emotive Imagery (REI)*

Counseling Intention   To help the client think more rationally and to become less emotionally upset.

Description
Negative Imagery

Picture yourself or fantasize, as vividly and intensely as you can, the details of some unpleasant activating experience (A) that has happened to you or will likely occur in the future. As you strongly imagine this event, let yourself feel distinctly uncomfortable—for example, anxious, depressed, ashamed, or hostile—at "C" (your emotional consequence). Get in touch with this disturbed feeling and let yourself fully experience it for a brief period of time. Don't avoid it; confront it, face it, and feel it.

When you have actually felt this disturbed emotion for a while, push yourself to change this feeing in your gut, so that instead you only feel keenly disappointed, regretful, annoyed, or irritated but not anxious, depressed, guilty, or hostile. Do not think that you cannot do this. You can get in touch with your gut-level feelings and push yourself to change them so that you experience different feelings.

Push yourself only to feel disappointed or irritated; look at what you have done in your head to make yourself have these new, appropriate feelings. Upon close examination, you will recognize that you have in some manner changed your Belief System (or B.S.) at "B," and have thereby changed your emotional Consequences, at "C," so that you now feel regretful or annoyed rather than anxious, depressed, guilty, or hostile.

Let yourself clearly see what you have done, what important changes in your Belief System you have made. Become fully aware of the new beliefs (B) that create your new emotional consequences (C) regarding the unpleasant Activating Experience (A) that you keep imagining or fantasizing. See exactly what beliefs you have changed in your head to make yourself feel badly but not emotionally upset.

Keep repeating the process. Make yourself feel disturbed; then make yourself feel displeased but not disturbed. Keep repeating the process. See exactly what you did in your head to change your feelings. Keep practicing until you can easily, after you fantasized highly unfortunate experiences at "A," feel upset at "C"; change your feelings at "C" to one of disappointment but not disturbance.

Practice REI for at least 10 minutes every day for the next few weeks. You will get to the point where whenever you think of this kind of unpleasant event, or when it actually occurs in practice, you will tend to feel easily and automatically displeased rather than emotionally upset. (Ellis, 1975, pp. 211–212)

Positive Imagery

To employ imagery and thinking, picture to yourself as vividly and intensely as you can the details of some unpleasant activating experience (A) that has happened to you or will likely occur in the future. Picture the situation at "A" at its very worst. Let yourself feel distinctly uncomfortable—anxious, ashamed, depressed—at "C," your emotional consequence. Fully experience this disturbed feeling.

As you feel upset at "C," notice what you keep telling yourself at B (your belief system or B.S.) to make yourself feel disturbed. When you clearly see these Beliefs, dispute them at "D" as you would in the usual kind of Disputing that RET or rational behavior training (RBT) teaches you to do.

Now, as you see these irrational beliefs and vigorously dispute them, strongly fantasize how you would feel and behave after you started giving them up and after you started believing, instead, rational beliefs about what keeps happening to you at "A." Intensely picture yourself (a) disbelieving your irrational beliefs and believing your rational ideas about obnoxious events that may occur at "A"; (b) feeling appropriately displeased and disappointed rather than inappropriately depressed and hostile at "C"; and (c) acting in a concerned instead of an upset manner at "E."

Keep practicing this procedure so that you first imagine something unfortunate or disadvantageous; then make yourself feel depressed, hostile, or otherwise disturbed about your image. Then see what irrational beliefs you hold to create your disturbance; then work on changing these beliefs. Then strongly picture yourself disbelieving these ideas and feelings and acting in accordance with your new rational philosophies of being only concerned and displeased rather than depressed and hostile. (Ellis & Harper, 1975, pp. 36–38)

Perspective for the Therapist: On life experiences

We must insist on talking to patients only about what they actually experience. In other words, go right through the defenses, rather than lose our efforts in helping them strengthen their already strong defenses. The only thing we really deal with in our relationships with patients is their actual life experience—not the stock they came from, their heredity, their genes, their biological propensities to growth. All we deal with is their reaction to their life experience;

> *how much of it isn't integrated; how much they can handle and how much they can't handle, but have to postpone or avoid or deny. And the more infantile the personality, the more they handle by avoidance.*

Elvin Semrad, *The Heart of a Therapist,* 1983, p. 103
(Reprinted with permission)

Technique: *Disputing Irrational Beliefs (DIBS)*

Counseling Intention   To teach clients to seek out, discover, and dispute their irrational beliefs.

Description   To increase rationality and to reduce irrational beliefs, spend at least 10 minutes every day asking the following questions and carefully thinking through the appropriate answers. Write each question on paper, or record the question and answers on a tape recorder.

- What irrational belief do I want to dispute and surrender?—I must always be liked by others.
- Can I rationally support this belief?—No.
- What evidence exists of the falseness of this belief?—Many indications exist that this belief is false: No law of the universe says that everyone must like me.
- Does any evidence exist of the truth of this belief?—No evidence exists for any absolute must that others should like me.
- "What worst things could actually happen to me if I don't get what I think I must?"

Technique: *Disputing Irrational Beliefs by Using "A-FROG"*

Counseling Intention   To provide a five-step thought process for thinking and behaving more rationally (Beck & Emery, 1985).

Description   Use the acronym A-FROG to decide if one is thinking rationally.

> *A*—Does it keep me *alive*?
> *F*—Do I *feel* better as a result?
> *R*—Is it based on *reality*?
> *O*—Does it help me get along with *others*?
> *G*—Does it get me to my *goals*?

Technique   *Rational Self-analysis (RSA)*

Counseling Intention   To provide a systematic way to change unpleasant emotions and to follow up on inappropriate behavior (Sabatino & Smith, 1990).

Description   Record (write or tape record) just what happened—not what you think about it, just a description of the event. Address the following:

> *Self-talk or opinion.* Record what you said to yourself about the event.
> *Emotions and actions.* Record the emotions and actions that you experienced.
> *Rational challenges.* Take each statement you made and substitute a rational statement based upon what you know to be fact. Ask why you tell yourself each of these things.
> *New ways of thinking and feeling.* Record new feelings and the thinking that might lead to solving the problem.

> *Perspective for the Therapist: On fear*
>
> *The world is really not so unknowable. If I but keep my eyes from seeing too much, my ears from hearing too much, my mind from thinking too much, it becomes quite reasonable. I can even persuade myself I see all there is. If I but worship this deity, adhere to this virtue, suffer that pain, insist on that plan, the world becomes quite manageable. If I but hush the voice of possibility both within and about me, the fears grows quieter, I am no longer afraid, so much.*
>
> James F. T. Bugental
> (Reprinted with permission)

Technique: *Coping with Losing a Job*

Counseling Intention   To overcome anger, depression, and hostility.

Description   Most clients really believe that the only emotional and behavioral reaction to losing a job is to automatically feel depressed, angry, and hostile. However, there are alternative emotional responses, which can facilitate getting through the difficult experience of losing a job. Too often people hold rigid beliefs that lay dormant until their job is threatened.

1. When corporations reduce their workforce it should be nice, fair, and gentle.
   Alternative Coping Belief: Work on gracefully tolerating and being strong in the face of insensitive treatment from an employer. Be less sensitive to their insensitive treatment.
2. The client is anxious about job uncertainty. He or she needs to know if his or her job is safe or if it will be terminated.
   Alternative Coping Belief: It is okay to want to know, to wish to know, or to prefer to know the future. Encourage the client to tolerate uncertainty although certainty is preferred.
3. The client cannot stand the long faces and the depressed affect that colleagues are wearing to work each day.
   Alternative Coping Belief: Encourage the client that job uncertainty and job layoffs are dislikeable but highly bearable with the right attitude. Encourage the client to be a model of rational acceptance rather than a bitter, irrational recipient of loss.
4. It is awful and terrible when layoffs happen to people with families, mortgages, and bills.
   Alternative Coping Belief: Encourage the client to change the rules in his or her head and become empowered to be flexible and calm even when the road gets uncertain and rough. Accept the reality of life and prepare for the worst.
5. It would be too uncomfortable to change jobs.
   Alternative Coping Belief: Encourage the client to accept uncomfortable changes and to give up rigid "musts," "shoulds," "have tos," and adopt flexible, scientific beliefs that correspond to reality.
6. The client needs to know what the future holds.
   Alternative Coping Belief: Encourage the client to keep his or her wish to know the future but give up demand to know it, because it only makes the client anxious, angry, and depressed.
7. Clients perceives themselves to be the unlucky ones, and that getting laid off proves they are losers who deserve to be embarrassed.
   Alternative Coping Belief: Encourage clients to acknowledge that losing a job hurts much more they put themselves down for having lost their job.
8. If I lose this job I must find another quickly, easily, and for an equal or better salary than this one.
   Alternative Coping Belief: Encourage the client to avoid believing an inner dialogue of absolute "musts" and avoid "demanding" future job preferences. Misery comes from not accepting reality.

Technique: *Overcoming Panic Attacks*

Counseling Intention To incorporate skills to lessen the effects of a panic attack.

Description Symptoms of a panic attack include a pounding heart, legs feeling weak and trembling, a tight throat, light-headedness, or fears of a heart attack. The anxiety-prone person, rather than ignoring those discomforts, dwells on them, magnifying and prolonging them by thinking: *I must* know precisely why I'm feeling like this, *I must* be certain it's not serious, *I must* never lose control or act crazily, *I must* not do something stupid or look foolish, I must have a guarantee I'm not going to die, *I must* not make myself panic.

> *Step one:* Encourage the client to recognize the *"musts"*—although it would be highly preferable to avoid discomfort, it's never a *must*. The client does not always *have to* feel entirely comfortable, and most people usually don't.
> *Step two:* Encourage the client to confront and dispute persuasively, vigorously, and persistently those unrealistic *musts* until he or she gives them up.

Also, pushing the client to do the things he or she is afraid of doing will reaffirm with these actions that great discomfort is never horrible, but rather tends to diminish when it is consistently faced, rather than avoided.

Technique: *Working toward a Happier Mental Outlook*

Counseling Intention To challenge client's irrational or self-defeating beliefs.

Description As the client follows the acronym "I SAW IT IS A CURSE," the client should be encouraged to express the thoughts behind them and in their own words interpret what they mean. *I SAW IT IS A CURSE* consists of two parts: (1) *I SAW* tells the client what to do, and (2) *IT IS A CURSE* tells the client what irrational or self-defeating beliefs should be challenged.

Do
> *I—inspire* yourself to work on your attitude by remembering that many people have become more involved in life, happier, and more productive by using REBT principles, and that many people have used other commonsense, nonperfectionistic, noncondemning philosophies to enjoy life more.
> *S—set* rational and reasonable goals: Be happy with progress.

A—*accept* behavior in the moment. Work calmly to become more relaxed, change behavior, and gain more of what is wanted.

W—*write* or record some thoughts and progress of growth and self-help.

Challenge

I—*insufficient* allocation of priorities, time, energy, and money to learn to live more happily.

T—*too* hard, too intense trying, which is self-defeating.

A—*absolute*, perfectionistic standards only lead to grief.

C—*childish* catastrophizing. Even though you often say "I can't stand this," no one has died of it.

U—*useless* urgency. It will take as long as it takes to get to where you want to go! Set priorities, allocate time for relaxation, and "smell the roses."

R—*ridiculous rating* of self. We are all alive, we have a tendency to falter, and all of us do! We have so many characteristics and deeds and misdeeds that we cannot be globally rated.

S—*silly* performance shame.

E—*expecting* failure. Just because you have not succeeded in the past does not mean you will not succeed in the future.

Technique: *DEFUSE spelled* DPHEWES

Counseling Intention   To achieve a more optimum sense of well-being.

Description   The following acronym is helpful in overcoming client's irrational "shoulds," "musts," and "oughts."

D—*don't place demands* on self, others, or the world. Demands in self-talk are expressed by terms as "*I must*" or "*he should.*"

P—*prioritize,* plan, subdivide into achievable goals, and then do them (one at a time).

H—*humor* yourself and others; take life less seriously.

E—*exude* relaxed calmness using REBT techniques and calmly accept one unpleasant reality every day of your life.

W—*work* on bad moods and challenge irrationalities, and do tasks at hand.

E—*establish* a routine to tackle problems.

S—*shun* the words "should," "must," and "have to" when used in the sense of being a demand.

REBT is a semantic therapy. That is even though it is quite correct to say that all the signs indicate it *should* rain tomorrow, it is quite illegitimate to say you *should* be able to get the highest score on this test. A better way is to be more accurate: "If I study harder than anybody else, and know more than they do, I will probably receive a high score on the exam. If nobody is extraordinary, neither lucky nor a genius, I may even get the highest score."

REALITY THERAPY AND CHOICE THERAPY

Another rational approach is *reality therapy.* Glasser (1982) conceptualized reality therapy in seven steps, which are cooperative endeavors between the counselor and the client:

1. Make friends, create a relationship to gain support.
2. Deemphasize the client's history and find out what is going on now.
3. Help the client learn to make an evaluation of behavior. Help the client find out whether what he is saying is really helping him.
4. Once the client behavior has been evaluated, explore alternative behaviors that may prove more helpful.
5. Get commitment for a plan of action.
6. Maintain an attitude of "no excuses if you don't do it." The client must learn to be responsible in carrying out the plan.
7. Be tough without punishment. To create a more positive motivation, teach clients to do things without punishing them if they don't.

Reality therapy, with its emphasis on appropriate social behavior and on individual responsibility, is a powerful counseling approach in educational, institutional, corporate, and correctional settings.

Glasser (1999) added another dimension to reality therapy called *choice theory.* Choice theory states that all we do is behave, that almost all behavior is chosen, and that we are driven by our genes to satisfy five basic needs: *survival, love and belonging, power, freedom,* and *fun.* In practice, the most important need is *love and belonging*, as closeness and connectedness with the people we care about is a requisite for satisfying all of the needs. Disconnectedness is the source of almost all client problems such as mental illness, drug addiction, violence, crime, school failure, and spousal and child abuse (Glasser, 1999).

The Ten Axioms of Choice Theory
1. The behavior we can control is our own.
2. All we can give another person is information.
3. All long-lasting psychological problems are relationship problems.
4. The problem relationship is always part of our present life.
5. What happened in the past has everything to do with what we are today, but

we can only satisfy our basic needs right now and plan to continue satisfying them in the future.

6. We can only satisfy our needs by satisfying the pictures in our *quality world*.
7. All we do is behave.
8. All behavior is *total behavior* and is made up of four components: acting, thinking, feeling, and physiology.
9. All total behavior is chosen, but we only have direct control over the acting and thinking components. We can only control our feeling and physiology indirectly through how we choose to act and think.
10. All total behavior is designated by verbs and named by the part that is the most recognizable.

Choice theory is part of reality therapy. Because unsatisfactory or nonexistent connections exist between people, the goal of reality therapy is to help people reconnect. This reconnection almost always starts first with the therapist connecting with the individual. The therapist uses this connection as a model for how the disconnected person can begin to connect with the people he or she needs. To create the relationship vital to reality therapy, the therapist will:

- Focus on the present and avoid discussing the past, because all human problems are caused by unsatisfying present relationships.
- Avoid discussing symptoms and complaints as much as possible, because these are the ways that counselees choose to deal with unsatisfying relationships.
- Understand the concept of *total behavior,* which means focus on what counselees can do directly—act and think. Feelings and physiology can be changed, but only if there is a change in the acting and thinking.
- Avoid criticizing, blaming, or complaining and help client do the same. Clients learn to avoid these extremely harmful *external control behaviors* that destroy relationships.
- Remain nonjudgmental and noncoercive, but encourage clients to judge everything they do by this choice theory axiom: "Is what I am doing getting me closer to the people I need?" If the choice of behaviors is not getting clients closer, then the therapist works to help them find new behaviors that lead to more rewarding connections.
- Focus on specifics. Assess whom clients are disconnected from and work to help them choose reconnecting behaviors. If they are completely disconnected, focus on helping them find a new connection.
- Help clients make specific, workable plans to reconnect with others and follow through on what was planned by helping the client evaluate their progress. Based on their experience, clients may suggest plans, but should not receive the message that there is only one plan. A plan is always open to revision or rejection by the client.

• Be patient and supportive but keep focusing on the source of the problem—
disconnectedness. Clients who have been disconnected for a long time will find
it difficult to reconnect.

Choice theory is a rational approach that focuses on the relationship between
therapist and client with the intent that this relationship will transfer to the client's
own behavioral repertoire so that he or she can make more positive and self-
fulfilling connections with others.

TRANSACTIONAL ANALYSIS

Transactional analysis (TA) is another rational approach to therapy (Berne, 1972).
TA is conceptualized as understanding verbal transactions between people, their
functional or dysfunctional ego states, and their life positions. Essentially, each of
us has three ego states, which together constitute our personality: parent (P), adult
(A), and child (C). The parent ego state is filled with values, injunctions, shoulds
and oughts, good and bad. The adult ego state is the rational, reality-oriented ego
state. The child ego state is conceptualized as the little boy or girl in us who feels,
thinks, acts, and responds in the same way we did when we were children. These
three states of a client's personality communicate interpersonally and
intrapersonally with others in ways that are either curative or dysfunctional.

Transactional analysis has revealed a number of other self-messages that are
illogical and unhealthy (Butler, 1981):

1. ***Driver messages.*** Be perfect, hurry up, try hard, please others, be strong, and
   so on, reflecting unrealistic demands that interfere with our natural preferences and inclinations.
2. ***Stopper messages.*** Ideas that "stop us in our tracks" or "shoot us down" and
   keep us from trying.
   • *Catastrophizing:* "If I said something stupid, it would be terrible." "If she
   rejected me, it would be awful." *Self-put-downs:* "I'm so dumb/boring/ugly/
   weak/selfish/demanding/bossy/irresponsible."
   • *Self-restricting statements:* "I'll speak up *providing* no one's feelings will
   be hurt." "I'd give an opinion *if* I had all the facts." "I'd approach him *if* I
   could think of something witty to say."
   • *Which messages:* "Don't be yourself; they won't like you." "Don't be differ-
   ent/like your father/like a sissy/like a pushy boss/like an egghead professor."
3. ***Illogical thinking.***
   • *False or unfounded conclusions:* "If she doesn't love me, no one will." "He
   loves me so much, he will make the changes I want him to make." "I won't
   be able to find a job and support myself, it's hopeless." "I know they are

making it hard for me and that makes me mad." Eric Berne revealed that some people tend to respond again and again with the same emotional response, such as self-criticism, pessimism, or anger. He called this reoccurring emotion the patient's *racket*. The racket—an emotion based on faulty thinking—becomes a basic part of the personality.

- *Misattribution:* Often clients blame feelings on someone or something else. "You make me so mad." "This setting is depressing." "I did it because I was drinking." Often clients blame the victim.
- *Overgeneralization, exaggeration, or either/or thinking:* Any time a client uses never, always, or everything, he or she is probably overgeneralizing. Another problem is when vague words are used, like "success," "happiness," or "good." If terms like these aren't clearly defined, how do you know if you have reached your goal? Finally, some people use either/or reasoning: "If I'm not *[successful]* yet, I must be a failure." Clearly, irrational thoughts cause unwanted emotions.

Life Scripts

Freud, Berne, and others believed our basic personality and "life scripts" were established by age 6 or so. Other characteristics seem more likely to *change from one stage of life to another:* mood or morale, assertiveness, dominance, independence, alienation, and satisfaction with life. These traits, emotions, or behaviors may be more influenced by the person's life events, situation, or viewpoint (Goleman, 1999).

A *life script* is the unconscious plan or expectation one has for one's life. It reflects the kind of relationships one expects to have with other people. According to transactional analysis, a life script is developed by age 5 or 6, before the adult and parent states are fully developed (Berne, 1972). Our "child," probably the "adaptive child," makes these judgments (the life position) and plans (script) based largely on messages sent by our parents' inner child.

It is these primitive messages (respected, valued, spoiled, neglected, resented), that determine feelings about others and ourselves that produce a script for our lives (Table 8.2). Analyzing *relationships with others* is a central part of transactional analysis (Figure 8.1). Transactional analysis suggests that we live our lives according to one of four *life positions* or life scripts (Harris, 1969).

Four Basic Life Scripts
- **"I'm OK; You're OK."** This life position is the only healthy attribute or attitude. The adult must be realistic, aware, tolerant and maintain control of the child and the parent. A person with such an orientation feels positive.

TABLE 8.2
Injunctions versus Not OK Messages versus OK Messages

Injunctions	Not OK Messages	OK Messages
Don't succeed. Don't feel adequate.	Be perfect!	It's OK to be human and succeed.
Don't be fast and efficient.	Hurry up!	It's OK to take your time.
Don't make it.	Try and try again!	It's OK to just do the best you can.
Don't think and feel what you want; think and feel what I want you to.	Please others, not yourself!	It's OK to consider and respect yourself.
Don't feel.	Be strong!	It's OK to be emotional and need others.

Source. Kahler, A. A. (1974). *Organization and instructional problems of beginning teachers of vocational agriculture.* Ames: Iowa State University, Department of Agricultural Education. (Reprinted with permission)

- **"I'm not OK; You're OK."** This life position requires that others sustain one's position to feel OK. When one feels weak and unable to do many things others can do, the dominant feeling is "not OK." If an "I'm not OK" attitude prevails, the client runs a risk of being anxious, depressed, and passive.
- **"I'm OK; You're not OK."** This life position is a self-centered, self-serving position. If parents are unduly harsh, negligent, inconsistent, or irrational, one learns that others are uncaring, unfair, or unsupportive (i.e., "not OK"). Such a person may certainly feel he or she is better than others. They are likely to be distrustful, aloof, and unconcerned with helping others (who are no good). They may take from others without feeling guilty; or insult, avoid, or hurt others.
- **"I'm not OK; You're not OK."** This life position is the most futile and helpless position of the four. There is no way to turn for help; others won't help the client and the client can't help himself. Nothing seems worthwhile and everything is futile. This is an unhappy state of affairs and, in the extreme, such a person's only recourse may be to withdraw into the utter hopelessness of depression or other emotional disturbances.

Clients have a relationship with themselves as well as with others—"Of all the people you will know in a lifetime, you are the only one you will never lose." This relationship with the "me" inside is crucial; the better we know ourselves, the better the client knows others, because his or her perception of our own self provides us with our primary means of understanding all other humans. As a means of self-assessment, ask: "Are the three parts of my personality reasonably well

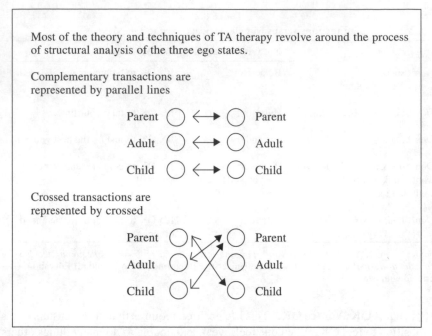

Most of the theory and techniques of TA therapy revolve around the process of structural analysis of the three ego states.

Complementary transactions are represented by parallel lines

Parent ◯ ⟷ ◯ Parent

Adult ◯ ⟷ ◯ Adult

Child ◯ ⟷ ◯ Child

Crossed transactions are represented by crossed

Parent ◯ ◯ Parent

Adult ◯ ◯ Adult

Child ◯ ◯ Child

FIGURE 8.1. Structural Analysis of Ego States

balanced, with the adult in charge?" If not, there may be problems in our intrapersonal and interpersonal relationships.

For this kind of deficiency, the solution is for the adult to recognize the situation and strengthen the weak part so that there is a healthy balance (Table 8.3). If the parent, for instance, is too strong, a client may feel beaten down and guilty.

Game Analysis

Transactional analysis is both a theory of personality and a system for the improvement of personal and social functioning, within the humanistic tradition. Berne (1972) developed a system of analysis that can be applied to the structure of the personality, interpersonal transactions, life plans or scripts, and the "games people play."

Key Concepts in Transactional Analysis

Ego States. Berne made complex interpersonal transactions understandable when he recognized that the human personality is made up of three ego

TABLE 8.3
Underdeveloped and Overdeveloped Ego States

Underdeveloped	Results	Overdeveloped	Results
Parent	Poorly developed conscience	Parent	Overly critical of child and adult
Child	All work and no play	Child	All play, impulsive, angry or sick
Adult	Loss of contact with reality, impulsiveness, or even insanity	Adult	Overly serious, intellectualizing

states; each of which is an entire system of thought, feeling, and behavior from which we interact with each other. The parent, adult, and child ego states and the interaction between them form the foundation of transactional analysis theory. These concepts have spread into many areas of therapy, education, and consulting as practiced today.

Transactions. Transactions refer to the communication exchanges between people. Transactional analysts are trained to recognize which ego states people are transacting from, and to follow the transactional sequences so they can intervene and improve the quality and effectiveness of communication.

Strokes. Berne observed that people need strokes, units of interpersonal recognition, to survive and thrive. Understanding how people give and receive positive and negative strokes and changing unhealthy patterns of stroking is a powerful aspect of work in transactional analysis.

Games People Play. Berne defined certain socially dysfunctional behavioral patterns as "games." These repetitive, devious transactions are intended to obtain strokes but instead they reinforce negative feelings and self-concepts, and mask the direct expression of thoughts and emotions. Berne tagged these games with such instantly recognizable names as "Why Don't You, Yes But," "Now I've Got You, You SOB," and "I'm Only Trying to Help You." Berne's book *Games People Play* achieved wide popular success in the early 1960s.

Life Script. Eric Berne proposed that dysfunctional behavior is the result of self-limiting decisions made in childhood in the interest of survival. Such decisions culminate in what Berne called the *life script,* the pre-conscious life plan that governs the way life is lived out. Changing the life script is the aim of transactional analysis psychotherapy. Replacing violent organizational or societal scripting with cooperative nonviolent behavior is the aim of other applications of transactional analysis.

I'm OK; You're OK. "I'm OK; You're OK" is probably the best-known expression of the purpose of transactional analysis: to establish and reinforce the position that recognizes the value and worth of every person.
Transactional analysts regard people as basically OK and thus capable of
change, growth, and healthy interactions.

Contracts. Transactional analysis practice is based upon mutual contracting
for change. Transactional analysts view people as capable of deciding what
they want for their lives. Accordingly, transactional analysis does its work
on a contractual basis between the client and the therapist, educator, or
consultant.

Analysis of transactions examines both social and psychological forms of
human communication using the ego state model to diagram the types of transactions. Transactions may be open and clear, or combined with ulterior messages.
Their analysis provides a way to understand our "stroking" patterns: how we exchange the level of contact and recognition that all humans need in order to thrive.

Script analysis offers an approach to the question: "How do we get to be the
people we are?" The origins are embedded in the history of our childhoods, families, culture, and life experiences. A life script develops without our being aware
of it, for purposes of survival, approval, and security rather than for self-realiza-
tion. By analyzing the content of our ego states, we can determine the idiosyn-
cratic programming from parents and other influential people and our responses
to this programming that limits our lives.

The analysis of games people play drew the public's attention to TA. People
learn to play games in childhood in response to family and life circumstances.
The motivation in continuing to play these games as adults is the need for stimulus and structure as a substitute for security. Games are predictable patterns of
indirect communication, using ulterior transactions. They are played out of awareness. Games analysis defines these patterns and their consequences.

CONCLUSION

With the advent of rational emotive behavior therapy (REBT), formerly known as
rational emotive therapy (RET), the missing links were scientifically established.
REBT provides the major tools to facilitate the therapy process. REBT theorizes
that emotional and behavioral problems are not caused directly by events but rather
by how one perceives those events. RET theorizes that emotional and behavioral
problems are caused primarily by irrational beliefs that arise when clients intensify strong desires into absolute demands, that is, "musts" and "shoulds." Irrational beliefs impede some clients from working toward their goals, beliefs, and
values; rational beliefs help individuals work toward their goals (Ellis, 1979, 1989).

REBT employs a variety of cognitive, emotive, and behavioral techniques aimed at diminishing emotional and behavioral problems (Ellis, 1985; Ellis & Dryden, 1990). REBT's main intervention is the disputation method, which has been outlined as "any process where a client's irrational beliefs and cognitive distortions are challenged and restructured for a more positive outcome" (Ellis, Sichel, Yeager, DiMattia, & DiGiuseppe, 1989, p. 49). The philosophy of TA and choice theory accentuates that respect and empathic acceptance are essential to psychotherapy. Its practice is based on a contract between client and therapist, in which they take equal responsibility toward common goals. The methods and concepts used are made open to the client in the understanding that power is shared.

Chapter 9

Classic Behavioral Techniques

Perspective for the therapist: On punishment

The commonest technique of control in modern life is punishment. The pattern is familiar: if a man does not behave as you wish, knock him down; if a child misbehaves, spank him; if the people of a country misbehave, bomb them. Legal and police systems are based upon such punishments as fines, flogging, incarceration, and hard labor. Religious control is exerted through penances, threats of excommunication and consignment to hell-fire. . . . The fact that punishment does not permanently reduce a tendency to respond is in agreement with Freud's discovery of the surviving activity of what he called repressed wishes.

B. F. Skinner
Beyond Freedom and Dignity, 1971, p. 45

The basic principles of learning and behavioral change are classics in the school of behavior therapy. Fundamentally, all behavior is learned, whether adaptive or maladaptive. Abnormal behavior is the result of faulty learning experiences, a product of social learning and conditioning. Behavior modification is the goal of therapy. This includes eliminating maladaptive behaviors and learning new effective behaviors. Behavioral techniques have been used with much success to eliminate undesirable behavior such as smoking, overeating, and nail biting, and to improve weight loss, study skills, and coping with stress. Krumboltz and Thoresen (1976) outlined principles for strengthening and developing appropriate behavior as well as eliminating inappropriate behavior. All complex behavior is learned, shaped, and subject to observable laws:

- One can change behavior through *rewards and punishment.*
- Behavior is determined by the *environment,* the consequences or anticipated consequences of that behavior.

221

- Some of what we learn is not the direct result of reinforcers but is rather the result of observing others and the consequences of their actions and *modeling* our behavior.
- Virtually *all work behavior is operant*—it generates consequences in its environment and these consequences in part shape and control behavior.

Behavior modification is defined as the use of rewards or punishments to reduce or eliminate problematic behavior, or to teach an individual new responses to environmental stimuli. Three tools used in behavior modification are positive and negative reinforcement and cueing. The goal of a program of behavior modification is to change and adjust behavior that is inappropriate or undesirable in some way. When embarking on a program of behavior modification it is important is that the undesirable behaviors be isolated and observed. With this awareness, comes a greater goal of understanding the cause and effect of the behaviors, and thus change can be made. In many cases, some form of behavior modification along with cognitive therapy and medication therapy are the preferred methods of treatment for disorders such as attention deficit disorder (ADD), attention deficit hyperactivity disorder (ADHD), conduct disorders, and oppositional defiance disorder. Behavior modification and cognitive therapy are the principal forms of treatment for eating disorders and alcohol or other drug abuse.

Essentially, behavior modification therapy is based on the idea of antecedents (events that occur before a behavior is apparent) and consequences (the events that occur after the behavior occurs). The appropriate behavior is learned by observing and changing both the antecedents and the consequences of the behavior so that the appropriate behavior increases and the inappropriate behavior decreases. The use of rewards to help affect change is called positive reinforcement and the use of punishment—for example, withdrawal of privileges—is called negative reinforcement. A behavioral modification program to change behavior consists of a series of stages. First, an inappropriate behavior is identified and stopped, and then a new behavior must be developed, strengthened, and maintained.

To stop an inappropriate behavior, first the behavior must be observed. To understand the pattern of the behavior it is helpful to chart the behavior: What events precede the behavior? What time of day it is observed? It's important at first to focus on just one or two offending behavior patterns. Once a behavior pattern is recognized and its pattern charted and understood, a system of rewards can then be constructed.

Table 9.1 shows one way to categorize behaviors. Any particular behavior may have aspects fitting in several categories. Fundamentally there are six stages of change:

1. *Precontemplation Stage:* Frequently other people see the problem, but the individual does not; therefore, he or she sees no need for change. Inherently people will try to change only after pressure has been applied by others.

TABLE 9.1
Types of Behavior

Behavior	Description	Examples
Appropriate	Achieves necessary and desired goals without infringing on the rights and needs of others. Includes appropriate social and emotional responses.	Maintains healthy habits; obtains satisfaction for a problem without demeaning others; has appropriate social, emotional, and cognitive skills; is self-sufficient and resilient.
Deficiency	Lacks skill or knowledge needed for performing the behavior; has many social, emotional, or cognitive deficits.	Passive responding in social situations; lack of social, emotional, and cognitive skills; deficient in such skills as assertiveness, problem solving, decision-making, and impulse control.
Excessiveness	Too much of a maladaptive or self-defeating behavior.	Drinking until passed out; overeating; smoking; addicted to sex, the Internet, or gambling; abuses illicit or prescription drugs.
Other Inappropriate	The behavior occurs at a time or place that is inappropriate. If it occurred under other circumstances the behavior would be acceptable.	Bed-wetting; fire setting, exhibitionism; stalking people; shoplifting.
Maladaptive Emotional	Capable of performing but has a stronger than typical autonomic system reaction, most often as fears and anxieties.	Social phobia, shyness, anxiety, panic attacks, obsessive-compulsive disorder, agoraphobia, depression, bipolar disorder.

2. *Contemplation Stage:* The problem has been acknowledged, and the person is beginning to think more seriously about overcoming their maladaptive or self-defeating behavior. He or she may begin weighing the pros and cons of the self-defeating behavior. This stage may last for years.

3. *Preparation Stage:* General goals have been defined and objectives for change have been written down. Goals have been shared with significant people in the client's life.

4. *Action Stage:* This stage requires the greatest commitment on the part of client. Specific guidelines are followed and an optimistic mindset for positive change evolves. Relapse is common at this stage. There is a need to be in this stage for 6 months in order to integrate into the client's lifestyle and behavioral repertoire.

5. *Maintenance Stage:* The client is able to maintain behavior for up to 5 years and strives to prevent relapse.

6. *Termination Stage:* Once a client has maintained a change in behavior for 5 years or more, he or she enters the termination phases and can exit the cycle of change without fear of relapse or failure.

Essentially, to change takes courage and determination, to maintain change takes commitment and routine, and to master change takes the integration of healthy behaviors within one's lifestyle and behavioral repertoire.

BEHAVIOR MODIFICATION PROGRAM STEPS

Assess the Target Behavior

DESCRIBE THE BEHAVIOR

Look for patterns in the behavior by finding the answer to these questions:

- Under what circumstances does the behavior occur and when does it *not* occur?
- What is the pattern that the behavior displays?
- Where does the behavior occur? Only at home? At school? In the presence of particular persons or objects?
- When does it occur? What time of day? What day of week? On weekends or weekdays?
- When the behavior occurs, how long does it endure?
- How intense is the behavior (e.g., is the child talking or screaming)?
- How frequently does it happen? Per hour, per day, per week, per year? (Select the single most meaningful period of time.)
- What was present or occurring 5 to 10 minutes *before* the behavior?
- What was present or occurring within 2 to 3 minutes *after* the behavior?
- Who was present during an instance of the behavior? Describe how these people are related to the subject.
- Describe in very specific behavioral terms what an instance of the behavior looks like. Describe it so an actor could display the exact behavior. Relate what was said as well as what was done and with what. Even seemingly insignificant actions could provide a clue for moderating the behavior.
  1. Not: "He disrupted the class."
  2. Not: "He yelled a lot."
  3. Better: "He spoke in a volume that drowned out my voice and said, 'I want my pencil back.' Then he jumped on his chair and wiggled his hips while pointing at Tim, in the right hand seat. He was laughing and smiling throughout this period."

- Sometimes comments by significant others can be helpful. Favor behavioral examples over summative evaluations.
  1. Not: "He annoys others."
  2. Better: "He interrupts everyone who speaks within a few minutes."

MEASURE THE BEHAVIOR TO GET PRECISE DATA

Methods

- *Frequency:* number of times a response is performed per a unit of time (e.g., day). Example: Subject smokes 24 cigarettes every day.
- A*mount of time:* the length of time a response lasts. This may be measured in terms of
  1. The *duration* of the behavior (from start to finish). Example: Subject takes 2 minutes or 20 minutes to smoke a single cigarette.
  2. The number of *intervals* in which the behavior is observed occurring. Example: Subject only smokes during the 9 AM break, never at any other time (1 interval vs. a cigarette every hour = 18 hours). If the behavior occurs frequently and has a clear beginning and end, then use short intervals (10 to 15 seconds). A behavior lasting less than 5 seconds is too short, as it is different to tell which interval the behavior occurred in. Don't use interval recording if the behavior is "continuous," that is, it persists for long periods of time with no clear beginning or end point (e.g., thumb sucking).
- *Intensity:* the magnitude or size of the response. Example: Does the subject smoke the cigarette down to the filter or take a few puffs and put it out?
- *Latency:* the time that elapses until a response is performed. Example: How long can the subject go before pulling out a cigarette?

IDENTIFY A BASELINE FOR THE BEHAVIOR

Behavior modification is about *real change*. You cannot determine if real change has occurred unless you know what behavior is typical. Typical behavior is the *baseline* against which the success of your intervention is measured. If you fail to collect baseline data, then you have *no way* to tell if your intervention worked. Behaviorists do not rely on memory, which is fallible. Without baseline data you do not have a behavior modification program.

Identifying a baseline means you collect data over a period of time without trying to change the behavior. How long do you collect data? It depends on the characteristics of the behavior. In general, you collect enough that the behavior of interest shows a steady pattern. With some animal behaviors, that might be one hour. With some human behaviors, it may take several weeks.

Commit to the Program

All significant parties should be involved and demonstrate commitment. Encourage participation in decisions by the subject and persons who might have an impact on the success or failure of the program, including parents, teachers, administrators, spouses, children, bosses, and co-workers. Be specific and precise about the behavioral goals

Example of a Precise Goal
• Not: "To eat healthily."
• Better: "To reduce the number of snacks (defined as ice cream, candy, or Twinkies) from one with each meal and one in the evening to one every third day and to increase the number of vegetable portions (as defined by government standards) from one with my evening meal, to six portions per day."

Begin the Program

IDENTIFY POTENTIAL INTERVENTIONS AND SELECT ONE OR SEVERAL THAT MATCH THE TARGET BEHAVIOR

Categorize your target behavior as one of the following, and then develop appropriate interventions.

• Teach a never before performed behavior (*reinforcement: positive and negative*).
• Increase or strengthen an existing behavior (*reinforcement: contingency contract, token economy, modeling*).
• Extend an existing behavior:
  1. To a new environment (*stimulus generalization, stimulus control, modeling*)
  2. To new behaviors (*response generalization, shaping, chaining, fading, prompting, modeling*)
  3. To over time (*maintenance, intermittent reinforcement, modeling*)
• Narrow an existing behavior to limited environments (e.g., only snacking in the kitchen) (also *discrimination training, modeling*).
• Reduce or eliminate the display of an existing behavior (*extinction, time-out, response cost, desensitization, reinforcement of incompatible responses, modeling, punishment*).

Most projects will use a type of reinforcement.

1. Identify appropriate reinforcers for the *individual*.
2. Specify the conditions under which reinforcement can be earned.

3. You already trained any needed data collectors during the baseline. Continue to collect data throughout using the same methods.
4. Apply intervention. Persist with intervention until
   A. Change occurs.
   B. It is clear that change is not going to occur and the method needs evaluation and refinement.
5. Proceed to evaluation.

Graph the Results

Most data collection can be graphed (occasionally a table is more appropriate). Graphs quickly reveal progress or lack thereof. They allow for evaluation of hypotheses as to what happened (or didn't). Small variations in behavior are normal. Judge progress based on viewing multiple data collection periods. (That might mean, for example, looking at a week's worth of data, graphed by days.)

Evaluate the Results and Reach Conclusions

Conclusions will be similar to one of the following:

• The intervention was successful in producing change, as shown by X.
• The intervention was not successful in producing change, as shown by X.
• The data offer a mixed picture. These elements were successful, as shown by X. These elements were not successful, as shown by Y.

A behavior modification program is based on the following issues:

• What behaviors are desired?
• Are these behaviors observable and measurable?
• What reinforces these behaviors?
• When are the reinforcements applied?
• What are the consequences of these reinforcements?
• How can the reinforcement pattern be improved?

Based on the answers to these questions, a behavioral modification program includes the following steps:

• Targeting specific behaviors.
• Analyzing the causes and antecedents of existing behavior or barriers to new behavior.

- Setting explicit, concrete, measurable goals.
- Training.
- Clear reinforcement: praise, recognition, money, etc.
- Concrete continuous feedback.

The key to a successful program of behavior modification is consistency. Expanded behavior intervention programs will increasingly incorporate a variety of efficacious strategies and techniques, some operant, some cognitive-mediational, some observational. Cognitive-behavioral approaches can be integrated to provide the optimal combination of strategies to enhance the adjustment of the client.

PRINCIPLES OF BEHAVIOR MODIFICATION

To Develop a New Behavior

1. *Successive Approximation*: To teach a client to act in a manner in which he has seldom or never before behaved, reward successive steps to the final behavior.
2. *Continuous Reinforcement*: To develop a new behavior that the client has not previously exhibited, arrange for an immediate reward after each correct performance.
3. *Negative Reinforcement:* To increase a client's performance in a particular way, you may arrange for her to avoid or escape a mild aversive situation by improving her behavior or by allowing her to avoid the aversive situation by behaving appropriately.
4. *Modeling:* To teach a client new ways of behaving, allow him to observe a positive role model performing the desired behavior.
5. *Cueing:* To teach a client to remember to act at a specific time, arrange for her to receive a cue for the correct performance just before the action is expected rather than after she has performed it incorrectly.
6. *Discrimination*: To teach a client to act in a particular way under one set of circumstances but not in another, help him to identify the cues that differentiate the circumstances and reward him only when his action is appropriate to the cue.

To Strengthen a New Behavior

7. *Decreasing Reinforcement:* To encourage a client to continue performing an established behavior with few or no rewards, gradually require a longer time period or more correct responses before a correct behavior is rewarded.
8. *Variable Reinforcement*: To improve or increase a client's performance of a certain activity, provide the client with an intermittent reward.

To Maintain an Established Behavior

9. *Substitution:* To change reinforcers when a previously effective reward is no longer controlling behavior, present it just before (or as soon as possible to) the time you present the new, hopefully more effective reward.

To Stop Inappropriate Behavior

10. *Satiation*: To stop a client from acting in a particular way, you may allow her to continue (or insist that she continue) performing the undesired act until she tires of it.
11. *Extinction:* To stop a client from acting in a particular way, you may arrange conditions so that he receives no rewards following the undesired act.
12. *Incompatible Alternative:* To stop a client from acting in a particular way, you may reward an alternative action that is inconsistent with or cannot be performed at the same time as the undesired act.
13. *Punishment:* To stop a client from acting in a certain way, deliver an aversive stimuli immediately after the action occurs. Because punishment results in increased hostility and aggression, it should only be used infrequently and in conjunction with reinforcement.

To Modify Emotional Behavior

14. *Avoidance*: To teach a client to avoid a certain type of situation, simultaneously present to the client the situation to be avoided (or some representation of it) and some aversive condition (or its representation)
15. *Fear Reduction*: To help a client overcome her fear of a particular situation, gradually increase her exposure to the feared situation while she is otherwise comfortable, relaxed, and secure or rewarded.

Providing for Consequences

Consequences are the events that follow immediately after the target behavior and are contingent on the behavior (occur only if the behavior occurs). There are two major kinds of consequences:

1. Reinforcers, which *increase* behavior they follow.
2. Punishers, which *decrease* behavior they follow.

The label, reinforcer or punisher, is given *after* examining the behavior for changes.

- It is *not* given on the basis of how *most* react to the event.
- It is given on the basis of how the behavior of the particular subject reacts to the event. (Krumboltz & Krumboltz, 1972, p. 110–111)

Perspective for the Therapist: On overgeneralized adversiveness

Punishment may result in either overgeneralized adversiveness—as when school becomes aversive for a child who is punished in class—or in unwanted inhibition of desirable as well as undesirable behaviors. Although the technique of removing a misbehaving child from opportunities to gain reinforcement in the classroom would seem more attractive than direct use of aversive stimuli, such time-out techniques can also trigger an aggressive reaction. Excessive use of this type of procedure in the classroom may remove the misbehaving child from exposure to educational experiences and, if used with a child who hates school, it may shape increased "acting-out" behavior.

B. F. Skinner
Beyond Freedom and Dignity, 1971, p. 109

Contingency Contract

A contingency contract is an agreement between a client and counselor that states behavioral or academic goals for the student and reinforcers or rewards that the student will receive contingent upon achievement of these goals. While the target behavior is the bulk of the contract, several other components are vital.

Contract conditions: The client and therapist must decide under what conditions the contract will be in effect.

Contract completion criteria: The criteria describe the level of performance for completion. Does the behavior need only to be achieved once or will it need to be maintained for a period of time (i.e., "client will reduce smoking by 60% for 8 days in a 10 consecutive day period")?

Reinforcers: The contract should include a reinforcer or reward that the client will earn upon contract completion. This should be something the client chooses, within reason. Positive consequences (i.e., rewards) should be delivered immediately upon contract completion.

Review and renegotiation: The contract includes dates on which progress will be reviewed with the client. The therapist may choose to review the contract weekly with the client to help keep him or her on track and to evaluate progress. If there is no progress after a couple of reviews, it may be necessary to renegotiate the contract. Goals may be unreasonable and reinforcers may be inappropriate. It is also appropriate to state a goal date for contract completion.

Language and signatures: The contract should be written in simple, clear language that the client can understand. For example, "reward" should be used instead of "reinforcer." This will make the contract more relevant to the client.

Zirpoli and Melloy (1993, p. 160) make the following recommendations to prevent satiation (i.e., the reinforcer losing appeal for the client):

• Varying the reinforcer or using a different reinforcer for each target behavior.
• Monitoring the amount of reinforcement delivered and using only enough to maintain the target behavior.
• Avoiding edible reinforcers (if you must use edibles, vary and apply them minimally).
• Moving from a constant to an intermittent schedule of reinforcement as soon as possible.
• Moving from primary to secondary reinforcers as soon as possible.

> *Perspective for the Therapist: On behavior*
>
> *Man can be conditioned to behave in almost every desired way;*
> *but only "almost."*
>
> Erich Fromm
> *To Have or To Be,* 1987, p. 36

Technique: *Affirming New Positive Behavior*

Counseling Intention　To strengthen or teach a new behavior.

Description　*Positive Reinforcement Principle.* To increase or enhance a certain activity, provide a reward immediately after each correct performance. The reward is something the person values; it may have material value (e.g., clothes or money), social praise by a support group (e.g., compliments or encouragement), or an opportunity to participate in a pleasant activity (e.g., dining out). The positive reinforcement cycle is "response-then-reward" with the distinct prerequisite that reward does not occur unless the behavior occurs first.

Description　*Token or Point Reward Paradigms.* To maintain the behavior until it is well established in the client's repertoire of positive responses, a point or token system can be established. The token or point system is set up as a contract where the recipient receives points for positive behaviors, accumulates them, and cashes them in for a desirable behavior. This is applicable for increasing such behaviors as assertiveness, weight loss, and nonviolent behavior. For example, after losing so many pounds (such as two pounds a week) and accumulating so many points, one might "cash in" the points for new clothes. The point system gives the client small rewards for the small successes toward the larger goal.

Technique: *Developing New Positive Behavior*

Counseling Intention   To develop new behavior.

Description

Successive approximations principle or *shaping* means each small successive step toward the final behavior is rewarded. This is most applicable when teaching a behavior that someone had never attempted before such as learning the motor skills of riding a bike or learning to ski (e.g., the new skier begins on the beginner's slopes and upon mastery, proceeds to the intermediate and then to the advanced slopes).

Principle of Modeling: Modeling is essentially learning by example or learning by observation. It is teaching a new way of behavior by showing how an effective person performs the desired behavior. This strategy has been successful in assertiveness training, teaching teachers to teach, fear-related behaviors, delinquents, addicts, and helping professionals.

Principle of Cueing: To establish new behavior for a specific time, a cue can be established to signal for the appropriate behavior just before the action is expected.

Discrimination Principle: To encourage a particular behavior under a particular set of circumstances but not another, the client should be assisted in identifying the cues that differentiate the circumstances and establish the reward only when the action is appropriate to the cue.

Technique: *Maintaining New Positive Behavior*

Counseling Intention   To maintain new behavior.

Description

Intermittent Reinforcement: To encourage an individual to continue performing an established behavior with few or no rewards, by gradually and intermittently decreasing the frequency with which the correct behavior is rewarded.

Contingency Contracting: To facilitate a client's goal for behavior change, contingency contracting may be helpful. It can be broken down into six steps:

1. The therapist and client identify the problem to be solved.
2. Data are collected to verify the baseline frequency rate for the occurrence of the undesired behavior.
3. The therapist and the client set mutually acceptable goals.
4. Specific counseling techniques and methods are selected for attaining the goals.
5. The counseling techniques are evaluated for observable and measurable change.
6. Step 4 is repeated if the selected counseling techniques are not effective. If the techniques are effective, a maintenance plan is developed to maintain the new behavior.

Technique: *Stopping Inappropriate Behavior*

Counseling Intention   To stop inappropriate behavior.

Description
Principle of Extinction: Extinction is removing a pleasant consequence, resulting in decreased responding. To stop someone from acting in an undesirable way, try to arrange conditions so that the person receives no rewards following the undesired act.

Principle of Alternative Behavior: This principle for eliminating undesirable behavior involves rewarding an alternative action that is inconsistent with or cannot be performed at the same time as the undesired act. An example could be substituting positive self-talk in the place of negative self-talk.

Principle of Satiation: To decrease a behavior, allow the individual to continue (or insist he or she continue) to perform the undesired act until he or she tires of it.

Technique: *Anger Expression*

Counseling Intention   To get in touch with one's anger; to take responsibility for anger expression.

Description   A prerequisite to expressing anger is the acknowledgment that it does exist. Once the anger is owned, it can be either eliminated through rational disputation or channeled into appropriate more assertive expression. Teaching the client to state "I am angry" over and over, louder and louder, can be used to bring the client in touch with his or her anger.
    This process is particularly successful in a group setting. Pounding rubber

dolls, cushions, pillows, or other indoor-safe toys can be used to express anger in a less threatening way. Behavioral rehearsal then can be taught to the client for future encounters. By rehearsing the desired behavior through role-play with the therapist, the client often feels more competent and successful in future relationships.

It may be helpful to the client to develop a relaxation response when beginning to feel angry or annoyed. Learning stress-inoculation techniques or learning how to express anger assertively may be beneficial. Developing a rational belief system and overcoming irrational beliefs (such as the world should be fair) would be another intervention.

Technique: *Anxiety Management Training*

Counseling Intention   To develop self-control, self-confidence, and self-management of anxiety.

Description   Relaxation training and goal-rehearsal are prerequisite skills in which the client should become proficient prior to anxiety management training. The client is directed to generate anxiety and the concomitant sensations, cognitions, and emotions. Following this anxiety provoking experience, the client is directed to perform the opposite behavior, that is, to elicit relaxation and to dwell on calm sensations, to picture peaceful images, to dispute irrational ideas, and to concentrate on tranquil and relaxing thoughts.

Technique: *Behavior Rehearsal*

Counseling Intention   To assist the client to assimilate new behavior.

Description   Clients often need to practice new behaviors in the confines of a secure therapeutic setting. Through role-play the therapist assumes the role of the individual. The client then can confront (e.g., therapist is the employer; client is the employee), and the client practices the new behavior as an actual encounter. The dialogue should be videotaped so that the therapist and client can critique the playback. Roles are reversed and the same procedure is followed. Behavior rehearsal and video playbacks are continued until the therapist and client are satisfied with the client's performance. To help the client meet his or her goal, the therapist should plan an intervention as follows:

- Specify the target behavior, what the client wants to change.
- Identify the setting or situation for which the skill is needed.
- Construct a hierarchy (from least threatening to most threatening) of settings or situations to practice the targeted skill.

Beginning with the least threatening setting or situation, have the client engage in a rehearsal (role-play) of the targeted skill. Give the client feedback about the strengths or weaknesses of the assimilation of the targeted skill. Feedback can be enhanced with a video playback. Assign homework consisting of in vivo rehearsal of the targeted skill.

Determine when the client has satisfactorily demonstrated the assimilation to the targeted skills and proceed up the hierarchy to client mastery.

Technique: *Thought-Stopping or Thought-Blocking*

Counseling Intention   To eliminate self-defeating or illogical thinking (based on unrealistic fears and assumptions); to control or eliminate negative ideas.

Description   Thought-stopping has proven effective in helping clients who obsessively ruminate on the same thoughts all day long. Clients can learn to cope more effectively in an anxiety-producing situation by practicing what they will say the next time it occurs. They should be encouraged to rehearse appropriate replies, mentally practicing the response. A simple method of combating certain obsessive and intrusive thoughts is simply to scream "STOP" (subvocally) over and over again. The client is instructed to imagine himself or herself in a situation or setting that produces an irrational thought sequence (e.g., "I am in my boss' office with a new idea to present, but he won't give me the time; he really thinks I'm stupid"). The procedure is as follows:

1. Ask the client to verbalize the thoughts that are occurring as he or she imagines the scene.
2. When the client starts to verbalize nonproductive thinking, the therapist interrupts the client with a loud "stop" and handclap or the flicking of the wrists with a rubber band.
3. The client processes what happened in this self-defeating chain when it was abruptly interrupted by the therapist.
4. The procedure is repeated with the client interrupting the nonproductive thinking overtly (aloud) and covertly (imagined).
5. The client is instructed to continue covert and overt interruption to self-defeating thoughts as they occur in his or her daily experiences.

Rathus and Nevid (1977, pp. 33–34) modified the thought-stopping technique listed above by using a tape recorder. The procedure is as follows:

1. Have the client outline clearly the content of the negative ruminative thoughts.
2. Construct two or three statements that oppose the helplessness and self-defeating nature of the ruminations.
3. Have the client record in his or her own voice the strongly stated command "STOP!" Then, while in a comfortable position, have the client purposefully ruminate on the distressing thoughts. Press play on the recorder. The recording disrupts the ruminations and provides assertive, counter-ruminative statements.
4. Repeat the procedure 10 times in a row, three or four times a day for two weeks. After that time frame, use the procedure 10 times in a row once daily for another couple of weeks.

> *Perspective for the Therapist: On wellness*
>
> *Healthy people, research shows, see themselves as liked, wanted, acceptable, able and worthy. Not only do they feel that they are people of dignity and worth, but they behave as though they were. Indeed, it is in this factor of how a person sees himself that we are likely to find the most outstanding differences between high and low self-image people. It is not the people who feel that they are liked and wanted and acceptable and able who fill our prisons and mental hospitals. Rather it is those who feel deeply inadequate, unliked, unwanted, unaccepted, and unable.*
>
> Donald E. Hamachek, *Encounters with the Self,* 1992, p. 63
> London: Thomas Learning

Technique: *Self-management*

Counseling Intention   To empower clients to master and manage their own behavior.

Description   The major difference between self-management and other procedures is that the clients assume major responsibilities for carrying out the program including arranging own their contingencies or reinforcements. To benefit from self-management strategies, clients must use the strategy regularly and consistently. The client should be instructed to do the following:

1. Select and define a behavior to increase or decrease.
2. Self-record the frequency of the behavior for a week to establish a baseline

measure (i.e., the present level before the implementation of self-management procedures).

3. Record (a) the setting in which it occurs, (b) the antecedent events leading to the behavior, and (c) the consequences resulting from the behavior.
4. Using self-monitoring, the client should proceed either to increase or to decrease the baseline of behavior, depending on the client's goal. The self-monitoring should occur for 2 weeks. A contract with the client will reinforce this process.
5. Change the setting and the antecedent events leading up to the target behavior.
6. Change the consequences that reinforce the target behavior.
7. Evaluate the use of self-management on the targeted behavior at the end of the contractual period. Arrange a plan to maintain the new, more desirable behavior.

Technique: *Goal Rehearsal or Coping Imagery*

Counseling Intention   To rehearse a new skill or situation.

Description   Goal-rehearsal implies the deliberate and thorough visualization of each step in the process of assimilating a new behavior. The deliberate picturing or coping imagery of a new situation enhances transfer to the actual event. Clients should be encouraged to be realistic in reaching their goal (i.e., to not expect perfection). For example, an individual may experience a severe panic attack when called on to speak in public. He or she may picture the audience scene vividly, replete with all the anxious feelings toward the situation that may emerge with a feeling of accomplishment if three out of five symptoms are reduced.

Technique: *The Step-up Technique*

Counseling Intention   To decrease anxiety and panic attacks over upcoming events.

Description   Some clients can be paralyzed by anxiety or panic about upcoming events such as a public speech, job interview, or blind date. The step-up technique consists of picturing the worst thing that can possibly happen and then imagining oneself coping with the situation—surviving even the most negative outcome. Once the client successfully pictures himself or herself coping with the most unlikely catastrophes deliberately called into the imagination, anticipatory anxiety tends to recede. When the real situation occurs, the individual may feel less anxious. Difficult cases may require self-instruction training (Lazarus, 1977, p. 240).

Technique: *Self-instruction Training*

Counseling Intention   To directly influence clients to change what they say to themselves.

Description   Self-instruction can break a chain of negative feelings and sensations such as fear, anger, pain, and guilt. Meichenbaum (1977) and Ellis (1962) have shown empirically that negative self-talk contributes to many peoples' failures and anxiety. On the other end of the continuum, the deliberate use of positive, self-creative statements can facilitate successful coping.

Lazarus (1977) cited the following sequence of self-instruction to use with a client who is experiencing anticipatory anxiety over an upcoming event: "I will develop a plan for what I have to do instead of worrying. I will handle the situation one step at a time. If I become anxious, I will pause and take in a few deep breaths. I do not have to eliminate all fear; I can keep it manageable. I will focus on what I need to do. When I control my ideas, I control my fear. It will get easier each time I do it" (p. 238).

Technique: *Systematic Desensitization*

Counseling Intention   To teach anxiety reduction strategies and self-control skills to clients.

Description   According to Wolpe (1982) systematic desensitization is "one of a variety of methods for breaking down neurotic anxiety response habits in piece-meal fashion. A physiological state inhibitory of anxiety is induced in the patient by means of muscle relaxation, and he or she is often then exposed to a weak anxiety-evoking stimulus for a few seconds. If the exposure is repeated several times, the stimulus progressively loses its ability to evoke anxiety. Successively 'stronger' stimuli are then introduced and similarly treated" (p. 133).

Clients experiencing public speaking anxiety, test anxiety, nightmares, fear of flying, fear of death, fear of criticism or rejection, acrophobia (fear of heights), agoraphobia (fear of open places), or other anxiety-provoking situations can often benefit from this approach. In this procedure, events that cause anxiety are recalled in imagination, and then a relaxation technique is used to dissipate the anxiety. With sufficient repetition through practice, the imagined event loses its anxiety-provoking power. At the end of training, when actually faced with the real event, the client will find that it too, just like the imagined event, has lost its power to create anxiety. Systematic desensitization consists of the gradual replacement of a learned fear or anxiety response with a more appropriate response such as the feeling of relaxation or a feeling of being in control. Three steps are involved in the self-administered systematic desensitization procedure:

1. Relaxation training in deep-muscle relaxation or coping responses.
2. Constructing a hierarchy of anxiety-provoking scenes.
3. Pairing deep relaxation with the visualization of scenes from the anxiety hierarchy.

Desensitization should not be used when the client's anxiety is vague or free-floating (Foa, Stekette, & Ascher, 1980). Clients with many fears or with general, pervasive anxiety may benefit more from cognitive change strategies.

Components of systematic desensitization consist of the following:

1. Identification of Anxiety-Provoking Situations.

The counselor and client must ascertain the specific anxiety-provoking situations associated with the fear; specific emotion-provoking situations must be identified. The client can be instructed to observe and to keep a log of the anxiety-provoking situations as they occur during the week, noting what was going on, where and with whom, and rating the level of anxiety on a scale of 1 (low) to 10 (high).

2. Construction of Hierarchy of Stimulus Situations.

A hierarchy typically contains 10 to 20 items of aversive situations. The client and the counselor can begin generating items during the session. The client can be instructed to generate items during the following week on 3 × 5 inch index cards. The cards then can be rank ordered from the least stressful situation at the bottom and successfully more stressful items in an ascending order (i.e., from least to most anxiety provoking). See Table 9.2 for an example.

3. Selection and Teaching of Counterconditioning or Coping Responses.

For desensitization to be successful, the client must learn to respond in a way that either inhibits anxiety or copes with anxiety. The counselor selects the most appropriate counterconditioning or coping response and trains the client in the procedure. The anxiety-inhibiting or counterconditioning response most used in desensitization is deep-muscle relaxation. Other examples of counterconditioning or coping responses include emotive imagery (focusing on pleasant scenes during desensitization), meditation (focus on breathing and counting), assertion responses, music, and coping thoughts (whisper or subvocalize coping statements, e.g., "I can do this"). Teaching muscle-relaxation response will take several sessions to complete. Identification of hierarchy items should not occur simultaneously with relaxation; however, teaching counterconditioning or coping response can occur simultaneously with hierarchy construction. Teaching should be continued until the client can discriminate different levels of anxiety and can achieve a state of relaxation. It is helpful to have the client rate the felt level of stress or anxiety on a scale of 1 to 10 before and after each teaching session. Daily homework practice also should be a requirement.

4. Evaluation of Client's Capacity to Generate Images.

The client's capacity to generate images is critical to the success of this procedure. Marquis, Morgan, and Piaget (1973) proposed four criteria for creating effective imagery: the client must be able to imagine the scene completely with detail to touch, sound, smell, and sight sensations; the scene should be imagined in such a way that the client is a participant not an observer; the client should be able to switch a scene on and off upon instruction; and the client should be able to hold a particular scene as instructed without drifting off or changing the scene (p. 10).

Each scene in the hierarchy is paired with the counterconditioning or coping response so that the client's anxiety is inhibited or diminished. Each scene-presentation session should be preceded by a training session involving the designated counterconditioning or coping response. Successive scene presentation always begins with the last item successfully completed at the preceding session. Typically, when the client visualizes an item and reports anxiety associated with the visualization, the client is instructed to remove or stop the image, then to relax away the tension. A helpful procedure is to have a signaling system between the counselor and the client. One method advocated by Wolpe (1982, p. 57) is to instruct the client to raise the left index finger one inch as soon as a clear image of the item is formed. Wolpe presented the item for a specified time (usually between 7 to 10 seconds) and then asks the client to stop the image and to rate the level of anxiety felt during the visualization on a scale of 1 to 10. An alternative approach is to have client imagine the scene and to indicate when anxiety is felt by raising an index finger.

5. Steps in Gradually Prolonging Exposure to an Anxiety-Provoking Situation.

Rathus and Nevid (1977) suggested reducing some fears by gradually prolonging exposure to the anxiety-provoking situation. Fears amenable to these conditions include fear of being in a small room, fear of hospital rooms, and fears of handling sharp tools.

First, ascertain that the target situation or thing meets two requirements: (a) the client can tolerate brief exposure to the target, and (b) the client has complete control over the duration of exposure to the target. Create a situation in which the client can readily expose himself or herself to the target and then readily remove self. The client then places himself or herself in the target situation until he or she begins to feel discomfort. The client should maintain self in the situation for only a few moments longer. The client leaves the situation and relaxes, breathing deeply and focusing on a peaceful setting.

After re-achieving relaxation, the client should return to the fear-inducing situation until discomfort is experienced. Remain a few minutes longer and then leave. Through gradually prolonging exposure to a fear-inducing situation, and then allowing the physical sensations of fear either to dissipate or to be replaced by the physical sensation of relaxation, ability to remain in the anxiety-provoking situation will become stronger.

6. Homework and Follow-up.

Homework should include daily practice of the selected relaxation procedure and visualization of the hierarchy items completed to date. The client also should be encouraged to participate in real-life situations that correspond to situations covered in hierarchy-item visualization during counseling sessions.

TABLE 9.2
Sample Hierarchy: Test Anxiety

1 = Least Anxiety-provoking situation.
18 = Most anxiety-provoking situation.

1. Taking a course examination three months from now.
2. Two months before taking course examination.
3. One month before taking course examination.
4. Three weeks before taking course examination.
5. Two weeks before taking course examination.
6. One week before taking course examination.
7. Four days before taking course examination.
8. Three days before taking course examination.
9. Two days before taking course examination.
10. One day before taking course examination.
11. Morning of taking course examination.
12. Three hours before taking course examination.
13. Two hours before taking course examination.
14. One hour before taking course examination.
15. Thirty minutes before taking course examination.
16. Entering building where course examination is to be given.
17. Entering room where course examination is to be given.
18. Examiner walks in the room with course examination.

Note: Least anxiety-provoking situation = 1; most anxiety provoking = 18

Technique: *Confronting Shyness*

Counseling Intention   To assist the client in becoming more assertive (Zimbardo, 1977).

Description   Three simple guidelines can be considered when assertive behavior has implications.

1. The best way to get what you want is to ask for it.
2. The best way to get someone to stop doing something you do not want the person to do is to tell him or her how those actions make you feel.

Assertiveness implies a special type of self-disclosure. Do not avoid expressing negative feelings. Negative feelings are just as important as positive ones. Focus on first-person "I" language to signify that the statement you are making is an indication of your own feelings (Wassmer, 1978).

Technique: *Cost and Benefits of Shyness*

Counseling Intention   To assess missed opportunities for growth (Zimbardo, 1977, pp. 143–144).

Description   Does shyness cost anything? Has the client missed any opportunities or passed by any unique experiences because he or she is shy? Have the client draw up itemized costs (Table 9.3).

TABLE 9.3
Shyness Costs

Time of Your Life	Valued Event or Opportunity That Was Delayed or Diminished	Personal Consequence to You
1.		

Technique: *Shyness Journal*

Counseling Intention   To evaluate dimensions of shyness (Zimbardo, 1977).

Description   Keep a journal of the times you feel shy. Write down the time, what happened, your reaction, and the consequences for you (Table 9.4).

TABLE 9.4
Shyness Journal

Time	Situation or Setting	Physical Symptoms	Mental Notation Reactions	(+) (−)
3rd Bell	U.S. Government class current events	Heart pounding nervous, avoiding eye contact	"I can't remember anything that I read this morning."	"I've lost another opportunity for my grade." Anxiety; panic

Technique: *Undoing Negative Self-talk*

Counseling Intention   To identify circumstances around negative inner dialogue.

Description   Have the client make a list of his or her weaknesses; put them on the left side of the page. Then put the opposite positive statements on the right side. See Table 9.5 for an example.

TABLE 9.5
Undoing Negative Self-Talk

Weaknesses	Truth
"No one who knows me likes me."	"Everyone who really knows me, like Jake, Jan, and Jessica, likes me."
"There are few things about me that are attractive."	"I have a lot of attractive features— my eyes, my hair, and my teeth."

Technique: *Writing Yourself a Letter*

Counseling Intention   To identify and validate personal attributes that are positive.

Description   Write yourself a letter focusing on your positive attributes or record a message about your successes, hopes, and possibilities and play it back to listen to it.

Technique: *First-Time Talking*

Counseling Intention   To focus on critical social skills.

Description   If you find that you have a difficult time talking to "anyone," try some of the following less threatening experiences.

- Call information and ask for the telephone numbers of people you want to call. Thank the operator and note his or her reaction.
- Call the local discount department store and check on the price of something advertised in the paper.
- Call a radio talk show, compliment their format and then ask a question.
- Call a local movie theater and ask for the discounted show times.
- Call the library and ask the reference librarian some question about the population in your town or the United States.
- Call a restaurant and make reservations for four, then call back within the hour and cancel them. Thank the reservation desk and note their reaction.

Technique: *Saying Hello*

Counseling Intention   To begin an experiential hierarchy of anxiety-provoking situations (Zimbardo, 1977).

Description   On campus, in hallways at school, or at work, smile and say hello to people you do not know.

Technique: *Beginning a Dialogue with a Stranger*

Counseling Intention   To continue structured interpersonal experiences (Zimbardo, 1977).

Description   An ideal way to practice initial conversational skills is to initiate a safe conversation with strangers in public places, such as grocery store lines, theater lines, the post office, a doctor's waiting room, lottery lines, the bank, the library, or the lunchroom. Start a conversation about a "common experience": "It looks like mystery meat for lunch again." "I hope this will be my lucky lotto ticket." "Have you seen *Sleepless in Seattle* [or a recently released movie]?

Technique: *Giving and Accepting Compliments*

Counseling Intention   To provide an opportunity to integrate social skills into interpersonal relationships.

Description   Giving and accepting compliments is an easy way to start a conversation and make the other person feel good about themselves. Yet it is probably the most overlooked "ice breaker" between people. Suggestions on items about which to comment include the following:

> What a person is wearing—"That's a cool jacket."
> How a person looks—"I like your haircut."
> A skill—"You sure know how to catch those waves."
> Personality trait—"I love your laugh."
> Possessions—"That car is awesome!"

To get further into the conversation, simply ask a question: "What an awesome car. How long have you had it?"

Technique: *Starting a Conversation*

Counseling Intention   To identify comfort levels in interacting with others.

Description   A conversation can be started in a number of ways. Choose the one that is most appropriate and comfortable for you.

- Introduce yourself. "Hello, my name is _____." (Practice this in a mirror at home.) This is best practiced when you are at gatherings where everyone is a stranger to you. Give a compliment and then follow it up with a question. "That's a terrific suit. Where did you get it?"
- Request help. Make it obvious you need it and be sure the other person can provide it. "Last time I went to this library, I used the card catalogue. How can I find the works of Carl Rogers with this search engine?"
- Try honesty and self-disclosure. When you make an obviously personal statement, it will create a positive, sympathetic response. Be honest and say, "I'm not sure what I'm doing here. I'm really quite shy."
- Cultivate your normal social graces. "Looks like you need a refill; let me get it for you; I'm headed that way." "Here, let me help you with those groceries."

Technique: *Keeping the Conversation Going*

Counseling Intention   To provide the client with strategies to sustain a conversation (Zimbardo, 1977, p. 180).

Description   Once you have initiated a conversation, there are several techniques you can use to keep the conversation going:

1. Ask a question that is either factual ("Can you believe how poorly the Redskins look this year?") or personal ("How do you feel about gun control?"). Offer one of your own personal stories or opinions.
2. Read a lot about some political or cultural issues and become knowledgeable about them, for example, the national deficit or violence in society. Come up with a few interesting things that have happened to you recently and turn them into brief interesting stories, for example, registering for classes, incidents on the job, a new video game, learning to surf or rollerblade, or encounters with teachers, parents, brothers, and sisters. When you meet people, be ready with several stories to tell or interesting comments to make. Practice ahead of time in the mirror or on a tape recorder. Get the other person to talk about himself or herself—his or her interests, hobbies, work, or education.
3. Express interest in the other person's expertise. "How were you able to land a job like that?" "How did you make it through Gaskin's class?"
4. Above all, share your reactions to what is taking place at that moment while you are interacting. Relate your thoughts or feelings about what the other person has said or done.

Technique: *Becoming More Outgoing*

Counseling Intention   To increase the client's interpersonal repertoire of experiences.

Description   Start with the easiest reaching-out exercise and progress to those more difficult. Record your reactions to each of these opportunities.

- Introduce yourself to a new person in one of your classes.
- Invite someone who is going your way to walk with you.
- Ask someone you do not know if you can borrow some money. Arrange to pay them back.

- Find someone of the opposite sex in your class. Call him or her on the phone and ask about the latest class assignment.
- Stand in line at a grocery store. Start a conversation about the line with the person near you.
- Ask three people for directions.
- Go to the beach, swimming pool, or sports stadium and converse with two or three strangers you meet.
- Notice someone who needs help in school or class. Offer to help.
- Invite someone to eat with you.
- Say "Hi" to five new people during the week. Try to provoke a smile and return "Hi" from them.

Technique: *Making a Date with the Opposite Sex*

Counseling Intention   To decrease irrational thoughts of rejection.

Description   Dating is a social contact that is anxiety provoking for many. Shy daters feel more vulnerable to irrational thoughts of rejection.

- Make your date by telephone initially. Be prepared ahead of time and have two specific activities in mind.
- When you contact the person by phone, identify yourself by name and explain when you met (if applicable). "This is Jim Thompson. I met you at the year-book signing party."
- Be sure you are recognized.
- Pay the person a compliment related to your last meeting, one that recognizes his or her talent, values, or position on an issue. "You really did a great job designing the cover of the yearbook."
- Be assertive in requesting a date: "I was wondering if you'd like to come to a movie with me this Saturday?" Be specific in your request, state the activity in mind, and state the time it will take place.
- If "yes," decide together on the movie and the time to meet. End the conversation smoothly, politely, and quickly. If "no," suggest an alternative such as a more informal get together. "How about meeting for drinks after work on Monday—my treat?"
- If the answer is still "no," politely end the conversation. Refusal is not necessarily rejection. There may not be enough interest or there may be previous commitments—school, work, or family commitments.

Technique: *Anxiety Hierarchy for Fear of Flying*

Counseling Intention   To reduce anxiety and gain some control over an anxiety-provoking situation.

Description   Create about 16 or 17 anxiety-provoking situations to create the hierarchy, ending up with about 10 to 15 items in your final version. To aid in sorting the items, write each one on a separate index card. Grade the anxiety of each item by assigning it a number on a scale from 0 to 100, where 100 is the highest level of anxiety imaginable and 0 is no anxiety (complete relaxation). Write this number on the back of the index card for the item being graded. When each item has an anxiety grade, sort the cards into 5 piles. Each pile will represent a different category of anxiety (Table 9.6).

    The goal is to end up with at least two items in each pile. Combine all the cards into one pile that is ordered from lowest to highest anxiety to create a personal *"fear of flying anxiety hierarchy."* Set the cards aside for one day. On the next day, shuffle the index cards to re-order them without looking at the grades on the back of the cards. Then check the grades to see if the second ordering is the same as the first. If not, make some adjustments.

SAMPLE FEAR OF FLYING ANXIETY HIERARCHY

The following is a sample *"fear of flying"* hierarchy to help clients develop their own hierarchy.

- Making reservations
- Driving to the airport
- Realizing you have to make a flight
- Checking in
- Boarding the plane

TABLE 9.6
Anxiety Hierarchy

Pile	Anxiety Grade
Low Anxiety	1–19
Medium Low Anxiety	20–39
Medium Anxiety	40–59
Medium High Anxiety	60–79
High Anxiety	80–100

- Taking off
- Waiting for boarding
- Taxiing
- In-flight service
- Moving around the cabin
- Climbing out
- Descending
- Waiting for departure
- Landing
- Turbulence

OVERVIEW OF THE PAIRING PROCEDURE

1. The overall goal of systematic desensitization is to reduce the ability of certain situations that cause anxiety. Confront each item of the anxiety hierarchy while the client is in a deep state of relaxation.
2. The systematic desensitization sessions *should not exceed 30 minutes.* Do not desensitize for *more than three of your anxiety hierarchy items per session.*
3. Each session (except the first one) should begin with *the last item from the previous session.* That is, if the last item was successfully desensitized, review it in the next session, and if it was not successfully desensitized, begin with it in the next session.
4 Progress will depend on how many times a week the client practices. A schedule of two sessions per day, every day, would be more ambitious than most people would attempt. Once a day five times a week would be admirable; two times a week would be average. Consider Table 9.7 as a plan for an anxiety hierarchy consisting of 15 items.

With a schedule of two sessions per week, the desensitization plan will be completed in about 3½ weeks. Using a schedule of five sessions per week, the desensitization plan will be completed in about 1½ weeks.

TABLE 9.7
Pairing Sessions

Session	Item Numbers
1	1–3
2	3–5
3	5–7
4	7–9
5	9–11
6	11–13
7	13–15

Technique: *The Self-administered Systematic Desensitization Procedure*

Counseling Intention   To empower the client outside of therapy.

Description   The self-administered systematic desensitization procedure consists of seven steps that are repeated for each item of your *"fear of flying"* anxiety hierarchy. The task will be to work through each item of the anxiety hierarchy following these seven steps.

> *Step 1.* Induce relaxation using a preferred relaxation technique.
>
> *Step 2.* Read the appropriate item from your hierarchy. (In the first session, this will be the first item in the hierarchy. In all other sessions, this will be the last item from the previous session.)
>
> *Step 3.* Imagine the situation for a tolerable time.
>
> *Step 4.* Stop imagining the situation and determine the level of anxiety that is experienced (on a 0–100 scale). Reestablish relaxation again and relax for about 30 seconds.
>
> *Step 5.* Re-read the description of the situation. Imagine the scene for a tolerable time.
>
> *Step 6.* Stop and again determine the level of anxiety. If experiencing any anxiety, return to Step 2. If feeling no anxiety, go on to Step 7.
>
> *Step 7.* Move on to the next item of the hierarchy. Repeat the above procedure for this next item, beginning with Step 1. End each session with several minutes of relaxation.

Research has shown that long-term success in overcoming a fear of flying depends on taking an actual flight (in vivo) after treatment is complete. Some people call it a graduation flight. Before each flight, work through the anxiety hierarchy to reinforce the ability to remain relaxed. Above all, remember to practice relaxation techniques on a daily basis, to both cope with daily stress and also improvise short desensitization sessions as needed.

Technique: *The Family Chip System*

Counseling Intention   To provide immediate reward for appropriate behavior and immediate consequences for inappropriate behavior (Myers, 2000).

Description

1. Purchase a box of poker chips.

2. Hold a family meeting to discuss the need for the program. Tell the children that it will help them to learn to be in charge of themselves. Tell older children that this system is similar to what adults experience: (1) Adults earn money for working; (2) Adults have to pay fines for breaking rules like speeding or making a late payment; (3) Adults spend their money on things they need as well as a few things they want.

3. Develop a list of behaviors they will earn chips for. Start with the morning and then go throughout the day looking for behaviors to reward. Some possibilities are:
   - Getting up on time
   - Brushing teeth
   - Getting ready for school on time
   - Playing nicely with brother or sister
   - Completing chores such as feeding a pet or taking out the trash
   - Saying please and thank you
   - Doing things the first time they are asked
   - Doing homework without a fuss
   - Getting ready for bed on time
   - Going to bed on time
   - Cleaning bedroom

4. Agree on a list of behaviors that result in a loss of chips. These can include behaviors that are oppositional, defiant, or disruptive. Some examples are:
   - Tantrums
   - Yelling
   - Screaming
   - Fighting
   - Arguing
   - Throwing things
   - Jumping on the furniture
   - Getting up after bed time
   - Swearing
   - Putting others down

5. Agree on a list of privileges they will earn and pay for with chips. Some privileges will be bought for the day, others will be bought for a period of time (usually a half hour). These can include:
   - Watching TV
   - Playing outside
   - Computer time
   - Staying up late
   - Playing a game with a parent
   - Having a friend over to spend the night
   - Trip to a favorite fast food restaurant

6. Assign point values to each item on the list (Table 9.8).
7. Post the list of behaviors and chips earned in a convenient place.
8. Let your child decorate a paper cup in which to keep their chips. Place the "bank's" chips in a jar or bowl and put it in a place that is out of reach of children.
9. Practice giving and receiving chips before starting the program. The practice should be based on the rules for parent and children provided below.

Rules for Parents When Giving Chips
1. Be near your child and able to touch him (not 20 feet or two rooms away).
2. Look at your child and smile.
3. Use a pleasant voice tone.
4. Make sure your child is facing you and looking at you.
5. Praise your child: "Hey that's great. You're really doing a nice job. That's really helping me." Reward your child with chips: "Here are two chips for doing a great job."
6. Describe the appropriate behavior for your child so he know exactly what behavior he is being praised and rewarded for.
7. Hug your child occasionally or use some other form of positive touch.
8. Have your child acknowledge you, such as "Thanks Mom" or "OK."

TABLE 9.8
Sample Chip Program

Earn Chips	
Making bed	2
Picking up bedroom	2
Brushing teeth	2
Setting the table	4
Being ready for bed on time	2
Going to bed on time	2
Doing things first time asked	1
Saying please and thank you	1
Lose Chips	
Throwing things	4 + Time out
Tantrums	4 + Time out
Arguing	2
Interrupting	2
Running in the house	2
Privileges to Spend Chips on	
Watching TV	5 chips per half hour
Playing outside	5 chips
Having a friend over	5 chips for the day
Going to friends' house	10 chips
Playing game with parent	5 chips

Rules for Parents When Taking away Chips

1. Be near you child and able to touch him.
2. Look at your child and smile.
3. Use a pleasant voice tone.
4. Make sure your child is facing you and looking at you.
5. Explain what was inappropriate, such as "Remember you are not allowed to run in the house because it is not safe" or "You need to learn not to yell and scream so we can enjoy being together at home."
6. Be sympathetic. "I know it's hard to lose chips but that's the rule."
7. Give your child the chip fine.
8. Make sure your child gives you the appropriate chips.
9. Prompting the appropriate responses will sometimes be necessary. For example, "Come on, give me a smile—that's right."
10. If a chip loss is taken very well by your child, it is a good idea to give him back a chip or two.
11. If your child is too mad or upset to give you the chips, don't force the issue. Place your child in time out (to cool off) and then get the chips.

Rules for Children When Getting Chips

1. You should be facing your parents, looking at them and smiling.
2. You should acknowledge the chips by saying "OK," "Thanks," or something else pleasant.
3. The chips should be put in a specified container. (Any chips left lying around are lost.)

Rules For Children When Losing Chips

1. You should face your parents, look at them and smile (not frown).
2. You should acknowledge the chip loss with "OK" or "All right," and "I'll get the chips," etc. (You must keep looking at them and be pleasant.)
3. You should give the chips to your parents pleasantly.

CONCLUSION

Fundamentally, behavior modification therapy is based on the idea of antecedents (events that occur before a behavior is apparent) and consequences (the events that occur after the behavior occurs). The appropriate behavior is learned by observing and changing both the antecedents and the consequences of the behavior so that the appropriate behavior increases and the inappropriate behavior decreases. The use of rewards to help affect change is called positive reinforcement and the use of punishment (for example, withdrawal of privileges) is called negative reinforcement. A behavioral modification program to change behavior consists of a series of stages. First, an inappropriate behavior is identified and stopped, and then a new behavior must be developed, strengthened, and maintained.

Chapter 10

Person-Centered Techniques and Psychoeducational Counseling Approaches

Perspective for the Therapist: On relationships

The degree to which I can create relationships which facilitate the growth of others as separate persons is a measure of the growth I have achieved in myself.

Carl Rogers, *A Way of Being,* 1980, p. 16
(Reprinted with permission)

Three conditions constitute a growth-promoting climate, whether speaking of the relationship between therapist and client, parent and child, leader and group, teacher and student, administrator and staff, or employer and employee. The first condition is genuineness—realness or congruence. The more the therapist is authentic in the therapeutic relationship (i.e., putting up no professional front or personal façade), the greater the likelihood that the client will change and grow in a constructive manner. The second condition is a climate for change with unconditional positive regard. It means that when the therapist is experiencing a positive, nonjudgmental, accepting attitude toward whatever the client is at that moment, therapeutic movement or change is more likely. Finally, the third condition is empathic understanding. This means that the therapist senses accurately the feelings and personal meanings that are being experienced by the client and communicates this acceptant understanding to the client (Rogers, 1986). A set of central values that are implicit or explicit in Rogers' theoretical writings are central to the person-centered approach:

1. Human nature is basically constructive.
2. Human nature is basically social.

3. Self-regard is a basic human need and self-regard, autonomy, and individual sensitivity are to be protected in helping relationships.
4. People are basically motivated to perceive realistically and to pursue the truth of situations.
5. Perceptions are a major determinant of personal experience and behavior, and thus to understand people one must attempt to understand them empathically.
6. The individual person is the basic unit and the individual should be addressed (not groups, families, organizations, etc.) in situations intended to foster growth.
7. The concept of the whole person is valid.
8. People are realizing and protecting themselves as best they can at any given time and under the internal and external circumstances that exist at that time.
9. The pursuit of control or authority over other people must be abdicated, and instead a commitment must be made to strive to share power and control.
10. In helping relationships, the helper is committed to honesty in relation to him/herself. This honesty is a major means for helpers to maintain and enhance their mental and emotional health and the health of their relationships.

Carl Rogers's basic notion was that we are all struggling to become our "real," true, unique selves. What stands in our way? It was the tendency to deny our own needs and feelings, to pretend to be someone we aren't, to avoid facing our true self. Person-centered counseling assumes that each individual is endowed with the urge to expand, to develop, to mature, and to reach self-actualization (Hansen, Stevic, & Warner, 1986). The only major therapeutic approach that relies on the counselee's innate movement toward growth. Individuals are viewed as self-healing, only needing a warm, supportive environment to reach higher levels of self-fulfillment.

The counselor-client relationship continues to be considered a vital ingredient in psychotherapy (Gelso & Carter, 1985; Henry, Schacht, & Strupp, 1986). Counseling relationships differ from other relationships. In daily relationships between family and friends, for example, communication is reciprocal, focusing on give-and-take statements that may offer advice, judgments, or personal perspectives. The major barrier to interpersonal communication lies in our inherent tendency to judge others—that is, to approve or disapprove of the statements of the other person. In the counseling relationship, however, communication is focused on the person experiencing difficulty and is nonreciprocal. Rogers (1986) described the three facilitative conditions as (1) "genuineness, realness, or congruence," (2) "acceptance, or caring, or prizing-unconditional positive regard," and (3) "empathic understanding." Rogers maintained that there is a body of steadily mounting research evidence that, by and large, supports the view that when these facilitative conditions are present, changes in personality and behavior do indeed occur. Such research has been carried on in the United States and other countries from 1949 to the present.

Studies have been made of changes in attitude and behavior in psychotherapy, in degree of learning in school, and in the behavior of schizophrenics. In general they confirm Rogers's ideas (Rogers, 1986, p. 198). A number of studies have reported improved psychological adjustment, greater tolerance for frustration, decreased defensiveness, accelerated learning, and also less tangible improvements such as increased self-esteem, and congruence between one's ideal and real self. The works of Carkhuff and Berenson (1967) and Truax and Carkhuff (1967) have validated the important contributions that the variables of empathy, respect, and genuineness make to the counseling process.

PERSON-CENTERED COUNSELING

Researchers have acknowledged that conditions proposed by Rogers for counseling are sufficient to bring change to the client. Through person-centered counseling, clients have enhanced their self-esteem and also "tend to shift the basis for their standards from other people to themselves" (Corsini & Wedding, 1989, p. 157). One major difference between person-centered counseling and other approaches is the increased responsibility placed upon the client compared with that assumed by the counselor (Brammer & Shostrom, 1982). Core Rogerian concepts have become fundamental conditions in the counseling and therapeutic relationship today.

Unconditional Positive Regard

Possessing unconditional positive regard is accepting the client without judging the behavior, event, or feeling as good or bad. Verbal sharing responses to communicate positive regard might include, "I really look forward to our talks together."

Empathy

Empathy is the ability to sense and identify the feelings of others and to communicate it to the client from his or her point of view—that is, entering the client's frame of reference. The conceptual importance of empathy is not unique to Rogerian-related approaches. It has been adapted by others under a different nomenclature. Special references to empathy are apparent in approaches such as Adlerian psychotherapy (Dinkmeyer, Pew, & Dinkmeyer, 1979) and developmental counseling and therapy (Blocher, 1974; Ivey, 1986).

In addition, even though behavioral therapy (Krumboltz & Thoresen, 1976) and cognitive therapy (Bedrosian & Beck, 1980) put less emphasis on counselor-client relationships, they do focus on the use of empathy to understand the client's problem accurately. Even Ellis's rational emotive behavioral therapy regards empathy as an important counseling component.

Patterson (1986) has emphasized empathic understanding as one of the core elements in relationships common to most therapeutic systems. Brammer and Shostrom (1968) delineated that responding with empathy is "an attempt to think with rather than for or about the client" (p. 180). For example, if a client says, "I've tried to get along with my boss, but it never works out. She's too hard on me," an empathic response could be "You feel discouraged about your unsuccessful attempts to get along with your boss." In contrast, if the counselor responded with "You should try harder," the counselor is responding from his or her own frame of reference. The communication formula for basic empathy (Egan, 1990), for responding verbally to the client's feelings about concern, uses a statement that identifies the client's feelings and the content of the situation:

"I feel _____ [fill in the right category of emotion and the right intensity] because_____ [fill in the experiences, behaviors, or both that elicit the feeling or emotions]."
Sample response: "You feel frustrated because your boss doesn't trust you to run the operations when he is out of town."

Perspective for the Therapist: On low levels of empathy

Low levels of empathy is related to a slight worsening in adjustment and pathology. If no one understands me, if no one can grasp what these experiences are like, then I am indeed in a bad way . . . more abnormal than I thought.

Carl Rogers
A Way of Being, 1980, p. 37

Genuineness

Genuineness is the ability to be authentic or "real" with others. The counselor does not distort communication, hide motives, operate from hidden agendas, or become pretentious or defensive. Genuineness means being oneself, not playing a role. The counselor's actions and words match his or her feelings both verbally and nonverbally.

Active or Reflective Listening

Listening is an art. Full attention is given both to what the client is saying and to other nonverbal cues such as posture and facial expression. Attending is a precondition to helping. An active listener feeds back what has been said in his or her own words for three reasons: (1) to make sure that he or she understands correctly, (2) to reassure the client that he or she was heard, and (3) to facilitate more disclosure on the part of the client. Identifying feelings communicates to clients that the counselor is listening and encourages them express themselves more freely. This facilitates the focus on key issues for working out a satisfactory solution. McKay, Davis, and Fanning (1983) maintained that active listening requires the counselor's participation as a collaborator in the communication process through paraphrasing, clarifying, and feedback.

Paraphrasing Responses

The therapist states in his or her own words what the client has actually said, using such lead-ins as

- "What I hear you saying is . . ."
- "In other words . . ."
- "So basically now your feeling is . . ."
- "Let me understand what is going on with you, which is . . ."
- "Do you mean . . . ?"

The counselor should paraphrase when the client says something of any importance. The benefits of paraphrasing in the counseling relationship are that clients deeply appreciate feeling heard:

- Paraphrasing stops escalating anger and cools down crises.
- Paraphrasing stops miscommunication (false assumptions, errors, and misinterpretations are corrected in the counseling session).
- Paraphrasing helps the counselor remember what was said.
- Paraphrasing inhibits blocks to listening on the part of the counselor, such as judging, comparing, advising, or the preoccupation of other thoughts (McKay, Davis, & Fanning, 1983, p. 24).

Clarifying Responses

Clarifying compliments paraphrasing responses by asking questions to clearly understand the client beyond vague generalities. The counselor uses these clarifying responses to understand events in the context of how the client thinks and how the client feels about the problem.

Feedback

During the counseling interview, feedback provides the counselor with an opportunity to share what was thought, felt, or sensed, and to check perceptions. To check perceptions, the counselor frames what was heard and perceived into a tentative description. For example,

- "I want to understand how you feel. Is this (giving a description) the way you feel?"
- "As I listened to what you said, it seems like [counselor description] _____ is what is really happening in this situation."

Feedback is nonjudgmental and should be honest, supportive, and in the here-and-now.

> *Perspective for the Therapist: On client responsibility*
>
> *First of all, the client in therapy moves toward being autonomous. By this I mean that gradually he chooses the goals toward which he wants to move. He becomes responsible for himself. He decides what activities and ways of behaving have meaning for him, and what do not.*
>
> Carl Rogers, *On Becoming a Person,* 1961, p. 36

Congruence

Congruence requires the counselor to be transparent to the client; that is, if the counselor is feeling angered by the client's communication, it would be incongruent to deny these feelings or to try to hide them from the client. Sometimes trying to be congruent may conflict with trying to be nonjudgmental, illustrating how difficult it is to provide relationship conditions that are facilitative. To be an effective communicator, the counselor must attend to both verbal and nonverbal communication. Collectively,

> 70% of what we communicate is through body language,
> 23% of what we communicate is through tone of voice, and
> 7% of what we communicate is through words (Glasser, 1985).

Listening for Feeling

Effective communication involves the thorough understanding of the other person's world (listening) and conveying that understanding to that person (responding). Through accurate listening and responding, barriers that hinder mutual understanding can be broken down (Dinkmeyer & Losoncy, 1980). Identifying and verbalizing the feelings in messages are framed with responses such as "sounds like," "you are kind of feeling," "your feeling now is that," or "if I'm hearing you correctly."

Listening with Empathy

Empathy means that the counselor recognizes that "this is hard to hear, but this is another human being trying to live." The counselor should ask himself or herself: "How did this belief or this decision, though it eventually may fail, lower this person's anxiety or get some needs met?" McKay, Davis, and Fanning (1983) suggested that if listening with empathy is difficult, the counselor should ask these questions:

- What need is the self-defeating behavior coming from?
- What danger or anxiety is the person experiencing?
- What is he or she asking for?

Listening with Openness

The counselor needs to hear the whole communication before judging; more information may be disclosed later and all the information may not be present.

Listening with Awareness

Awareness is accomplished by comparing the client's verbal and nonverbal communication with tone of voice, emphasis, facial expression, and posture for any mismatch between expression and content. Brigman and Earley (1990) maintained that, in order to have a satisfying relationship with others, a client must learn to communicate effectively. Much of our ineffective communication practices involve nagging, reminding, criticizing, threatening, lecturing, advising, and ridiculing.

Respect

Respect is an interpersonal skill that demonstrates an appreciation of the uniqueness of others, tolerance of differences, and willingness to interact with others equally.

Concreteness

Concreteness is demonstrated with specific, clear, and unambiguous communication—one uses *"I-messages"* rather than *"You-messages"* (Table 10.1). One uses I-messages to take responsibility for feelings, emotions, and actions. Effective communication messages involve three components: (1) owning feelings, (2) sending feelings, and (3) describing behavior. Sending a feeling message adheres to the following communication formula: Ownership + Feeling Word + Description of Behavior = Feeling Message. For example: "I [ownership] am anxious [feeling word] about sending in my tax return on time [description of behavior]."

Immediacy

Immediacy is the ability to discuss openly what is happening in the here-and-now as well as the ability to use constructive confrontation.

Self-disclosure

Self-disclosure is the willingness to share personal experience with others without being critical or judgmental. Self-disclosure facilitates intimacy and self-exploration. Self-exploration also can occur on three levels:

TABLE 10.1
I-Messages versus You-Messages

"I Message"	"You Message"
Respects the individual's integrity.	Does not respect the individual's integrity.
Identifies one's feelings.	Instills blame and anger.
Reflects the individual's needs in the here-and-now.	Criticizes and focuses on the then-and-there.

Level 1: Clients talk of others and things related to themselves, such as general events and ideas, global conceptual ideas, universal and public issues, and historical perspectives in the "there and then."

Level 2: The client will talk of self and ideas as related to others, such as personal events and opinions, personal goals, perspectives for the future with significant others or peers in the "there and then."

Level 3: The client begins to talk about self and related feelings as they impact on self-experience, with attention to personal meanings, feelings, and perceptions in the "here and now."

Confrontation

Confrontation is the ability to tell others about their behavior and its impact on oneself without being aggressive, critical, judgmental, or defensive. Confrontation is an open, sincere identification of one's self-defeating patterns, behavior, thoughts, feelings, or actions that may interfere with interpersonal relationships. Confronting an individual's discrepancies, at the minimum, leads to greater awareness of the reality that the particular behavior is helping or hindering interpersonal relationships.

Warmth

Warmth is the ability to be open, friendly, and accepting of others with nonverbal communication that conveys congruent signals of openness and readiness to listen. The person-centered approach of Carl Rogers has the potential to be applied to a variety of educational, psychological, political, industrial, managerial, recreational, medical, and other settings (Purkey & Schmidt, 1990, p. 129). This counseling model is especially important for self-acceptance by those who have a physical disability. In particular the self-acceptance of children who have disabilities is needed to assist this population in their efforts to move toward greater use of the potential they possess (Williams & Lair, 1991, p. 202).

Technique: *The use of "I-Messages"*

Counseling Intention   To respond assertively and for resolving interpersonal conflicts.

Description   Alberti and Emmons (1986) identified a three-step empathic assertive response model:

1. Let the person know you understand his or her position: "I know it's not your fault."
2. Let the person know your position (what the conflict is): "But I ordered my steak well done not medium rare."
3. Tell the person what you want or what you plan to do: "I would like you to take it back and have it cooked some more."

The communication formula for an assertive response is *"I know [the other person's position] but [my position] and [what I want]."*

Technique: *The Companion*

Counseling Intention   To feel the personal presence of a loving, caring companion; to fulfill a profound emotional need (Schriner, 1990, p. 77).

Description   Imagine that a deeply caring and insightful person is standing beside you, touching you in a reassuring manner and offering words of encouragement. You listen, perhaps writing down the suggestions. Then you go on with your activities, knowing you can come back for advice and support any time you choose.

Technique: *Repeating the Obvious*

Counseling Intention   To clarify our thinking or redirect our feelings about a problem situation (Schriner, 1990).

Description   Two kinds of obvious statements are especially valuable to repeat:

1. *"I understand" statements.* We can explain why we have a problem or an unhappy feeling: "Of course I'm feeling anxious—I always feel nervous speaking in front of people. This always happens to me." Or "My client's boss is prone to mood swings; this just must be one of my boss's days."
2. *"I can" statements.* Repeating what we do to alleviate our problems is empowering and reassuring: "I can remind myself to breathe deeply and to recall how I have been successful in past situations." Or "If my boss is still irritable after three days, I can request a personal conference."

Several writers have developed lists of more than 100 "assertive rights." The most basic ones include:

- The right to act in ways that promote your dignity and self-respect as long as others' rights are not violated in the process.
- The right to be treated with respect.
- The right to say "no" and not feel guilty.
- The right to experience and express your feelings.
- The right to take time and to slow down and think.
- The right to change your mind.
- The right to ask for what you want.
- The right to ask for information.
- The right to make mistakes.
- The right to feel good about yourself.

Technique: *Assertiveness Skills*

Counseling Intention   To be in control; to ignore irrational fears or anxieties; to express feelings; to ask for support or assistance.

Description   The following are different ways to be in control:

1. Don't be afraid to say "no." Saying "no" is acceptable.
2. Make eye contact and maintain an open posture.
3. Repeat your request to reinforce your position. State your demand over and over again to transcend the barrier of resistance or the barrier of avoidance.
4. State your goal clearly. Be sensitive to the needs of others, but be firm in expressing what you need and what you want.
5. Recognize the needs of others and reassure them that you are aware of their position on their point of view.
6. Regulate your pitch and tone of voice to communicate a firm, controlled position.
7. Stand straight and thank the person for listening to your request.

Creating more assertive dialogue is represented in Table 10.2.

Technique: *Different Ways to Refuse a Request*

Counseling Intention   To provide alternatives to saying "no" to a request.

TABLE 10.2
A Continuum of Assertiveness

From Less Assertive	To More Assertive
"I'm going to . . ." "I will . . ."	"I've decided to . . ."
"One day I'm going to . . ."	"My goal is to_____by_____."
"I don't think . . ."	"I think that . . . My thoughts are . . .
"I can't do it . . ."	"I want to do it . . ."

Description   The following are different ways to refuse a request:

1. Simply say "no."
2. Use an "I want" statement; for example, "No, I don't want to loan you my car, I may need it."
3. Use an "I feel" statement; for example, "No, I just wouldn't feel comfortable parting with it right now."
4. Use an "empathetic assertion" statement; for example, "I can see you're in a bind, but I can't loan you my car tonight."
5. Use a "mixed feelings" statement; for example, "Part of me says let you have my car this evening, and the other part is saying 'No, I may need it and you will be stranded.'"

Technique: *Inner Processing of Personal Feelings*

Counseling Intention   To assess emotional well-being.

Description   Go inside yourself and identify *how* you feel. (Are you feeling depressed, disappointed, nervous)?

1. Go inside yourself and identify *what* you feel. (Are you experiencing anger, frustration, or lack of control)?
2. Identify what happened to make you feel this way. (Was it a particular event, a phobia, behavior of another, or an uncontrollable situation)?
3. Make a mental list of ways you could express your feelings, or identify ways you could act.
4. Choose the best way for the current circumstances. Carry out your choice.

Technique: *Inner Processing of How Another Person Is Feeling*

Counseling Intention   To empathetically assess how another person may feel.

Description   Observe the other person's behavior and actions.

1. Pause and listen to gain an understanding of what the other person is saying.
2. Identify with your inner dialogue, the feelings you think the other person is having. (Inner dialogue to self: He must feel embarrassed.)
3. Mentally list specific feelings you think the other person is experiencing.
4. Decide if you need to do a *perception check* to verify the other person's experience.
5. Use *reflection skills* to verify the feelings the other person has, to show that you understand.

Technique: *Handling the Perennial Dilemma of Peer Pressure*

Counseling Intention   To learn peer pressure refusal skills.

Description   Use the following steps:

1. Listen to what someone wants you to do and give it a name (e.g., underage drinking, stealing, cutting class, getting a false ID, calling in sick from work, cheating on taxes).
2. Think about what would happen if you were caught. What would be the consequences (e.g., suspension from school, committing a felony, getting a DUI)?
3. Think about what you want or need to do (e.g., walk away, suggest an alternative, blow it off).
4. Examine possible consequences and rank them from 1 to 10 (1 = least; 10 = most).
5. Decide what to do to maintain your best interest.
6. Explain to others your needs and wants (e.g., I need to stay straight; I want to avoid trouble).

Technique: *Peer Pressure Refusal Skills*

Counseling Intention   To become assertive in resisting peer pressure.

Description   A list of "one-liners" to peer pressure could include the following:

- Invent a routine excuse, such as "I have to be at work at that time."
- Use delay tactics: "I'm not ready."
- Walk away and avoid the situation.
- Shift the blame and try to make the pressure group feel guilty.
- Act ignorant about how to do something.
- Identify the other things that are more important to do at the moment.
- Get away from the situation as soon as possible.
- Take control of the situation. "I don't want to do it."
- Ask them to justify why you should do what they want you to do. "What is in it for me?"

Technique: *Dealing with Fear and Anxiety*

Counseling Intention   To assess the source of fear and anxiety.

Description   Think about what is causing the fear or anxiety.

1. Is the situation in your control? Is there an alternative solution?
2. Is this situation life threatening? Do a perception check with someone else. Are they experiencing the same discomfort?
3. Talk with someone, leave the situation, or approach the situation gradually.
4. Take steps to reduce your fear or anxiety. Ask yourself the following questions:
   - Is it really a big deal?
   - Is this worse than what I handled before?
   - Will this seem important two weeks from now?
   - What is the worst thing likely to happen, and will I be able to cope with that?

Technique: *Communicating to Enhance Relationships*

Counseling Intention   To identify communication skills that would enhance interpersonal relationships.

Description   To enhance relationships, try the following strategies:

> ***Speak directly.*** Tell your partner what you want (e.g., "I want to go to the game with you on Saturday").

Distinguish between needs and wants. Needs are the minimum requirement for the relationship to exist. Wants are things that enhance the relationship.

Listen actively and attentively. Maintain a relationship where feelings are shared, along with hopes and dreams without the fear of condemnation.

Fight fairly. State your feelings using I-messages, and learn how to respond assertively, such as "I think" or "I feel."

Focus on behavior, not personality. Concretely describe the problem behavior.

Avoid gunny sacking. Don't save up all your hurt feelings and hostilities and let them accumulate to one explosive episode. Deal with significant issues when they occur. Stay in the here-and-now. Bringing up the past is disrespectful and merely brings on more hostility. Work so that both parties win. Lasting relationships require daily maintenance and fine tuning.

Technique: *Positive Affirmations*

Counseling Intention   To increase intrapersonal well-being and self-esteem.

Description   Many people are limited by their negative thinking: "I can't" or "I don't deserve." Negative beliefs are blocks to positive action. Sometimes you must consciously work to maintain good feelings about yourself. Remind yourself that day-to-day life has its ups-and-downs.

Guidelines for Positive Affirmation
1. Begin with the words "I am."
2. Include your name in the affirmation.
3. Include positive feeling words such as enthusiastic, awesome, tremendous.
4. Phrase it in the present tense.
5. Keep the statements short.
6. Incorporate your strengths within your affirmations.
7. Choose action words.
8. Choose positive words.
9. Include a feeling word to motivate action (I am happy when I receive compliments).
10. Once you have constructed an affirmation, close your eyes, repeat the affirmation several times (at least three), and notice what inner picture it creates. If the picture it creates matches your desired outcome, your affirmation is a good one.

Technique: *Poor and Good Listening Characteristics*

Counseling Intention   To identify positive and negative listening characteristics.

Description

Poor Listening Characteristics
- Interrupting
- Looking at the clock
- Taking the focus off the topic by talking about yourself
- Acting bored
- Poor posture
- Joking or trying to top the person with another story

Good Listening Characteristics
- Maintaining eye contact
- Paraphrasing what the other person said
- Asking relevant questions
- Nodding
- Using body language that shows interest

Technique: *Using I-Messages, You-Messages, and We-Messages*

Counseling Intention   To differentiate messages that hinder or help with communication.

Description   I-Messages express thoughts, feelings, wants, needs, expectations; for example:

- I think Jennifer is the best candidate for the job.
- I feel disappointed that you are behind.
- I am put at a disadvantage when I don't receive the information on time.
- I want you to give me an explanation for your absence for practice.
- I need your help.
- I expect you to inform me when you change shifts with someone.
- I would prefer that you talk with me rather than write a note.

You-messages can express empathy or understanding of the other person's dilemma, and sympathetically describes the other person's behavior; for example:

- You are feeling a great deal of pressure.
- Your position has some positive points.
- You handled the conflict very well.

We-messages express alternatives, compromises, and mutual problem solving; for example:

- We have three options: work through lunch, work late, or come in early.
- How can we solve the conflict with the team to our mutual satisfaction?
- We've decided to have the luncheon instead of the breakfast.

Technique: *Confirming Interpersonal Hunches about Others*

Counseling Intention   To understand relationships and feelings about others.

Description   What you think someone thinks about you, and what you think about that person, are powerful determinants about how you will relate to and interact with each other. Some of the following relationship skills may help:

1. If both of you disagree about how you perceive of each other, reserve judgment and make more observations of each other's behavior.
2. If you feel misunderstood, try to change the other person's experience with you. Let them see another side of you.
3. Try to change your behavior.
4. Try to change the other person's behavior, or help him or her make the desired changes.
5. Try to change your views of the other person.
6. Become more aware of your needs and wants.
7. Start a crusade to be better understood by others.

Technique: *Clarification and Reflection*

Counseling Intention   To understand someone else's feelings through clarification and reflection.

Description   To clarify and reflect back to another person, remember the following acronyms:

FAT
>   **F**eelings
>   **A**ctions
>   **T**houghts

CPR
>   **C**larify
>   **P**araphrase
>   **R**eflect

Technique: *Active Listening*

Counseling Intention   To listen to the feeling under the words.

Description   Listen for the feelings under the words:

1. Identify discrepancies in behavior.
2. Summarize target issues.
3. Use silence to encourage responses from others.
4. Paraphrase the essence of what was said.
5. Obtain feedback about perceptions versus realities.
6. Reflect similarities in behaviors and thoughts.
7. Check for accuracy of the presenting problem.
8. Ask questions to gain better clarification.

Technique: *The Assertive Response*

Counseling Intention   To communicate needs more assertively and less aggressively.

Description
>   Step 1: "When . . . " (Concretely describe the other person's behavior.)
>   Step 2: "The effects are . . . " (Describe objectively how the other person's actions have affected you.)
>   Step 3: "I feel . . . " (Accurately describe your feelings).
>   Step 4: "I prefer . . . " (Suggest what you would like to see happen.)

Example

Step 1: When you are late picking me up for work in the morning.

Step 2: I am always late and my boss will probably put it on my evaluation.

Step 3: I feel hurt and angry at you.

Step 4: I am hoping that we could make plans so that I don't have to be late anymore.

Technique: *Supporting*

Counseling Intention   To help others feel better about themselves and eliminate unnecessary stress.

Description   Supporting is a communication skill to help people feel better about themselves by soothing and reducing tension.

1. Actively listen to the message the person is sending (i.e., listen for the feelings under the words).
2. Try to empathize with the person's feeling (i.e., try to walk in their shoes).
3. Paraphrase a reply that is in harmony with the other person's feelings.
4. Support the other person by indicating your willingness to be of help if possible.

Example

> *"I've been on my fifth interview and I have yet to find a job."*
>
> *"I can understand your disappointment; you've really worked hard. Let's practice an interview session and I'll record it. Then, we can play it back and see how you look in an interview situation."*

Technique: *Describing Feelings and Empathizing*

Counseling Intention   To communicate your needs and wants effectively to others.

Description   Describing feelings is putting your emotional state into words so that others can understand your perspective.

1. Get in touch with the feelings you are currently experiencing. Identify them specifically—angry, embarrassed, helpless, tired, lonely.
2. Acknowledge those feelings.
3. Make sure the statement you make to someone else contains the emotion you feel.
4. Share the feeling and your behavioral reaction.

Example

"I felt rejected and alone when you broke your date with me."

Empathizing is being able to identify another's feeling and responding to it as if it were your own.

1. Listen actively to what the person is saying (i.e., understand the feeling under the words).
2. Try to recall or imagine what you would feel like under those same conditions or circumstances.
3. Respond with the appropriate feeling words to share your own sensitivity to another person's circumstance.

Example

"I feel so stupid in Herr Bradshaw's class, everyone is passing his German vocabulary test but me."

"Yeah, I can understand, it's a very helpless feeling. Maybe we can quiz each other for the next test?"

Technique: *Self-Disclosure*

Counseling Intention   To self-disclose appropriate information to build a more intimate relationship.

Description   Self-disclosure is sharing personal feelings, ideas, experiences that are unknown to another person. Personal sharing builds relationships with others if it is reciprocated. Acceptance by friends and others increases your self-acceptance, and makes you more perceptive, more extroverted, more trusting, and more positive toward others.

Tell a friend some facts about your family, work, school, or hobbies. Determine the level of risk. On a scale from 1 to 10, how risky is this information you disclose to someone else?

If appropriate, move to a deeper level of self-disclosure. Encourage mutual disclosure from the other person (e.g., "Do you get the same feeling that I do about Mr. Cohen's class?").

1. Refrain from revealing intimate self-disclosures to short-time acquaintances.
2. Start and continue self-disclosure only if the other person reciprocates it.
3. Understand that individuals share personal information differently and people's attitude about disclosure varies.

Example

While being pressured to try some crack cocaine, Bill responds, "You know my stepfather, but not my real dad. My real dad is doing time for dealing and doing drugs. I prefer not to end up like him."

Self-disclosure should include four clear statements:

1. I see the situation this way . . .
2. I conclude . . .
3. I feel . . .
4. I prefer . . .

Technique: *"Carefronting" (Confronting Self-defeating Behavior)*

Counseling Intention   To confront self-defeating or life-threatening behavior in a caring way.

Description   People need to hear that you care about their well-being. It must be a genuine concern if confronting is to be effective; hence, a better term is "carefronting." Examples might include:

"The concerns I have about you are because I care about you and our relationship. I care about you too much to let this go and not say anything about what I see happening."

Then state the behavior—how you feel—and then reiterate your caring and concern.

Other Guidelines

1. Maintain a sense of calm. Be simple and direct. Don't circumvent the issue or behavior. Speak to the point. Don't become emotional. It is all right to show your feelings, but anger should not be directed at the person.
2. Keep on the subject and be specific. Talk about the problem and specific ways it has affected the person's behavior.
3. Be prepared for promises, excuses, and counter-accusations (especially when confronting drinking behavior). Denial and resistance to receiving help may occur.
4. Admit the problem and face it.
5. Find a good source of reliable information and learn it.

Technique: *Listening with Empathy*

Counseling Intention   To understand the feelings under the words.

Description   Empathy is a skill that can be acquired through practice. It involves hearing who the person is, how he or she feels about himself or the situation. It involves four steps:

1. Listen for feeling, both verbal cues and nonverbal cues.
2. Acknowledge his or her feelings. Identify what you see or hear (e.g., you sound irritated, angry, confused).
3. Clarify feelings. Use phrases like "What I hear you feeling is something like . . ." or "Can you give me an example?"
4. Check it out. Paraphrase: "Let's see if I understand; what you are saying is . . ."

Technique: *Paraphrasing*

Counseling Intention   To convey to another person that you understand the meaning of what he or she has said, paraphrase what you heard in your own words.

Description
1. Listen actively and carefully.
2. Pause to determine what the message means to *you*.
3. Restate the meaning you got from the message using your own words.

4. Obtain a confirmation from the other person that the meaning you conveyed was correct.

Example

Bill says, "My chemistry teacher just assigned three more chapters for the test tomorrow and I am scheduled to work tonight."

Jill replies, "If I understand you right, you feel stressed and overwhelmed about what you need to do."

Technique: *Making Intention Statements*

Counseling Intention   To express commitments, expectations, and limitation.

Description   Intention statements let others know more about your immediate or long-range commitments or expectations. An intention statement is a way of being *direct* about what you would or would not like for yourself, or what you would or would not like to do. Intention statements begin with words like:

"I want . . ."
"I would like . . ."
"I intend . . ."

Examples
- "I want to be with you today, but I don't want to spend all our time shopping."
- "I'd like to do my studying in the afternoon, then catch the game this evening."
- "I'd like to be with you, but I want to be with my family tonight too, because it's my brother's birthday. And I want to spend this afternoon in the library working on my paper."

Technique: *Confrontation Guidelines*

Counseling Intention   To gently bring to the attention of someone else that a behavior needs to be changed.

Description
1. Be flexible and reasonable in your expectations about the outcome of the confrontation. It is more reasonable to ask for an apology about one's actions

rather than changing their personality. "The most important thing is that he knows what an inconvenience he caused me."

2. Confronting at the right time and in the right place is critical to a successful confrontation. Privacy and easy access to each other will usually improve the impact, unless you are concerned about a physical confrontation.
3. Talk directly to the person you are confronting. "I really need to tell you something important that concerns me. Can we talk?"
4. Talk clearly and calmly. If the person is unable to listen, wait until he or she is in a more receptive emotional state.
5. Refer directly to the issue. "Remember when we were supposed to meet at the mall last Saturday?"
6. Explain how the person's behavior affected you. Use I-Messages. "I get frustrated and impatient when you keep me waiting."
7. Listen actively to the other person's viewpoint. Try to put yourself in his or her shoes.
8. Ask for cooperation and openness. This will test the person's flexibility and receptivity to improve or change. "Will you hear me out?" or "Would you be willing to change the way you treat me?"
9. Summarize what you both need to do to resolve the problem. "I need to know that you will avoid being late again."

Technique: *"I-Language" Assertion*

Counseling Intention   To enhance one's ability to communicate difficult feelings.

Description   "I-language" assertion is helpful in expressing difficult negative feelings. It involves a four-part statement:

1. Objectively describe the other person's behavior or the situation that interferes with you.
2. Describe how the other person's behavior or the situation concretely affects your life, such as costing you additional time, money, or effort.
3. Describe your own feelings.
4. Describe what you want the other person to do, such as providing an explanation, changing behavior, apologizing, offering suggestions for solving the problem, or giving a reaction to what was said.

Example

> *"When you cancel a meeting with just a few hours' notice, I don't have enough time to make other arrangements and I'm left with empty down-time. I feel irritated and unproductive. We need to make other arrangements about changing meetings at the last minute."*

Technique: *"I-Want" Statements*

Counseling Intention   To clarify what all parties want in a situation.

Description   I-want statements help you to clarify to both yourself and others what you really want. It gives the other person information that is necessary to know how to fulfill your wants. It relieves you from the conflict of wanting, being afraid to ask, and worrying about whether the other person will do what you want.

Use I-want statements when you say, "I want to do this," or "I want you to do this," while referring to a specific behavior.

Example

> "I want to know what I did to make you so angry, but I don't want you to call me names."

I-want statements can be framed as follows:

1. Instead of going to the movies, I want to just stay home and rent a video.
2. Rate your want on a scale of 1 to 10, "I want to go to the movies in the mall. It's a strong preference—about an 8."
3. State what your I-want statement means and what it doesn't mean. "I want to go to the movies sometime in the next two weeks. That's just for information; no pressure if you can't make it this weekend."

Technique: *Empathic Assertion*

Counseling Intention   To assertively communicate empathic understanding.

Description   Empathic assertion can be used to convey some sensitivity toward a person. It consists of a two-part statement. The first part states your recognition of the other person, making a recognition statement involving one of the following areas:

- His/her situation (e.g., pressures, difficulties, lack of awareness)
- His/her feelings (e.g., sad, mad, angry, scared)
- His/her wants (e.g., to get a higher grade, a better job)
- His/her beliefs (e.g., that he/she has been unfairly treated, singled out)

A recognition statement simply indicates that you see, hear, acknowledge, and realize the situation, feelings, wants, desires, or beliefs of the other person.

The second part of the empathic assertion is describing your situation, feelings, wants, or beliefs. Describe what you understand.

Example

> *"I can understand you are upset with me and probably not in the mood to discuss this right now. I would very much like to talk it over when you're ready."*

Technique: *Mirroring*

Counseling Intention   To understand the thoughts and feelings of a complaint.

Description   One method for effective emotional listening is called *"mirroring."* One person makes a complaint; the other person repeats it back in his or her own words, trying to capture not just the thought, but also the feelings that go with it. The partner mirroring checks with the other to be sure the restatement is on target, and if not, tries again until it is right.

Technique: *Communicating Feelings in a Non-blaming Manner*

Counseling Intention   To increase negotiation skills.

Description   Negotiation language proceeds as follows:

"When you said or did _____, "I felt _____."
"Can you tell me what you meant?"
"What I would like is _____."
"How can we work this out?"

Technique: *Interpretive Confrontation*

Counseling Intention   To gain better insight into oneself.

Description   Interpretive confrontation can provide insight into oneself—a critical component of mental health. Interpretation can enhance personal growth if the information is communicated with skill, integrity, and empathy.

Characteristics of an Interpretive Confrontation
Empathy. Understand the issues that are central to the other person's behavior and life style.

Timing. The confrontation should be timed to prevent the receiver from becoming defensive.

Relatedness. The confrontation should be related to the situation in which both parties are engaged.

Concise. The confrontation should be concisely stated and to the point.

Genuine. The person who is confronting must be able to communicate with genuine interest and concern for the well-being of the other party.

Tentative. The interpretation is a suggestion about the other person's behavior, not an absolute fact.

Technique: *Self-Talk to Maintain Composure*

Counseling Intention   To manage stress with positive self-talk.

Description   Self-talk statements should be generated and internalized *before, during,* and *after* the situation:

Before: Take a minute to become more centered. "What is it that I want to do?"

During: Take a moment to exhale. Take things one step at a time. "People get irritated. It's nothing more than that." Clearly say what you want. Don't raise your voice.

After: On a scale of 1 to 10, rate the experience. " I handled that with a 7. I'm getting better at this every time I try."

Technique: *Working through Disappointment When a Mistake Has Been Made*

Counseling Intention   To make the best of a bad decision.

Description   First, a mistake is evidence that someone tried to accomplish something. View a mistake as an opportunity rather than a crisis. A mistake can be an opportunity in disguise. Many people have discovered new opportunities by accident. Accept your mistake and learn to forgive yourself. Obsessing over what you could have done or should have said is wasted energy. Take a personal inventory of your personal costs versus benefits. Are you spending more energy than it is worth?

Technique: *The Compassionate Response*

Counseling Intention   To forgive, accept, and lower expectations.

Description   It is important to recognize that if we have no expectations we will not be disappointed. Responding to someone with compassion requires understanding, acceptance, and forgiveness. Ask yourself:

• What *need* was the person trying to meet through his or her actions?
• What *personal beliefs* influenced his or her actions?
• What *pain, hurt, or other feelings* influenced his or her actions?
• Am I judging someone because of my own expectations?
• You can let go and forgive this person for their actions, or you can hold on to the anger and destroy the relationship.

Technique: *Paraphrasing Responses*

Counseling Intention   To gain insight about how others are feeling.

Descriptions   Paraphrasing means to state in your own words what the person has actually said using a lead-in such as "What I hear you saying is," "In other words," "So basically how you feel is," or "Let me understand what is going on with you."

The benefits of paraphrasing in relationships are that:

1. People deeply appreciate feeling heard.
2. Paraphrasing deescalates anger and cools down a crisis.
3. Paraphrasing stops miscommunication, false assumptions, and errors in meaning.
4. Paraphrasing helps you remember what was said.
5. Paraphrasing inhibits blocks to listening.

Technique: *Turning You-Statements into I-Statements*

Counseling Intention   To expressed repressed feeling and emotions.

Description   Suppressing or denying feelings leads to several problems: (1) increased irritability and conflicts with others, (2) difficulty resolving interpersonal problems, and (3) distorted perceptions. I-statements do not judge, blame, or threaten; they essentially clarify how you feel (Table 10.3).

TABLE 10.3
You-Statements versus I-Statements

Examples of You-statements	Examples of I-Statements
Blaming	
"You tick me off."	*"I feel angry."*
Judging and Labeling	
"You are an arrogant jerk."	*"I feel hurt when you criticize."*
Accusing	
"You don't care about anyone."	*"I feel neglected."*
Ordering	
"You shut up."	*"I feel hurt when you yell."*
Arguing	
"You don't know anything."	*"I feel this option is possible."*
Threatening	
"You had better."	*"I'd like it if you would . . ."*
Moralizing	
"You should do . . ."	*"I think this would be . . ."*
Analyzing	
"You can't stand to leave."	*"I feel disappointed that you are reluctant to leave."*

THE PSYCHOEDUCATIONAL LIFE SKILL
INTERVENTION TECHNIQUE

The Psychoeductional Life Skill Intervention Model enhances social, emotional, and cognitive skills. The indicators of emotional deficits manifest themselves in increased incidents of violence, suicide, and homicides. Social deficits manifest themselves as poor peer relations and an inability to resolve conflicts and to manage anger. Cognitive deficits place clients at a disadvantage academically and reduce their career options, making them more vulnerable to criminal influences because they do not have the marketable skills to compete in a global economy.

The Pychoeducational Life Skills Intervention Model follows a five-step learning model: (1) instruction (teach), (2) modeling (show), (3) role-play (practice), (4) feedback (reinforce), and (5) "ownwork" (apply the skill outside the group setting). Modeling, feedback, role-playing, instruction, situation logs, and ownwork assignments are used to reinforce desired behavior. The term *ownwork* is used rather than homework to reinforce one's own responsibility for changing behavior, as the term *homework* is often associated with isolated drudgery. The Psychoeducational Life Skill Intervention Model is a more comprehensive and systematic approach to the remediation and enhancement of interpersonal and intrapersonal effectiveness. This comprehensive skill delivery system emphasizes a psychoeducational life skill promotion and enhancement model in which (1) help is provided by a counselor or therapist, (2) a client's difficulties are seen as gaps in knowledge or experiences rather than being viewed as maladaptive behavior through a deficit lens, and (3) the client is active in the design of his or her life skill development and management plan. An experiential group approach rather than a didactic one-on-one approach is the most successful way to diminish self-defeating behavior. The instructional psychoeducational intervention techniques are derived from social learning theory. Social skills are acquired primarily through learning (e.g., by observing, modeling, rehearsing, and providing feedback) and are maximized through social reinforcement (e.g., positive responses from one's social environment). Behavioral rehearsal and coaching reinforce learning.

The Psychoeducational Life Skill Intervention Process

The psychoeducational group leader assumes the role of director, teacher, model, evaluator, encourager, motivator, facilitator, and protector. Role-playing within the Psychoeducational Life Skill Intervention Model provides several opportunities: (1) to try out, rehearse, and practice new learning in a safe setting, (2) to discover how comfortable new behaviors can become, (3) to assess which alternative actions work best, and (4) to practice and repractice new learning by reality testing. Role-playing is a fundamental force of *self-development* and *interpersonal learning*.

Five-Step Process to the Psychoeducational Life Skill Intervention Model

The steps are outlined according to what the group leader should say and do to help the client youth integrate social, emotional, and cognitive skills into his or her behavioral repertoire.

STEP 1: PRESENT AN OVERVIEW OF THE SOCIAL, EMOTIONAL, OR COGNITIVE SKILL

In the instructional portion of the process, a vignette (5 to 10 minutes) is presented to teach the social, emotional, or cognitive skill. Introduction to the benefits of the skill in enhancing relationships, as well as the pitfalls for not learning the skill are also presented. The following are suggested instructional overviews for the social skill of assertiveness:

Example: Social Literacy Skill: Understanding Your Assertive Rights
We all have rights:

- To decide how to lead our lives.
- To express thoughts, actions, and feelings.
- To have our own values, beliefs, opinions, and emotions.
- To tell others how we wish to be treated.
- To say, "I don't know," or "I don't understand."
- To ask for information or help.
- To have thoughts, feelings, and rights respected.
- To be listened to, heard, and taken seriously.
- To ask for what is wanted.
- To make mistakes.
- To ask for more information.
- To say "no" without feeling guilty.
- To make a decision whether to participate.
- To be assertive without regrets.

Social Literacy Skill: Components of Assertiveness
Very often, people who are aggressive do not have within themselves the interpersonal repertoire to express themselves assertively. There are essentially six attributes that are specific to assertiveness:

1. *Self-awareness:* a developed knowledge of one's goals, aspirations, interpersonal and intrapersonal behavior, and the reasons for them. Realize where changes are needed and believe in your rights.
2. *Self-acceptance:* self-awareness that acknowledges one's own particular strengths and weaknesses.
3. *Honesty:* congruency between verbal and nonverbal thoughts, feelings, actions, and intentions.
4. *Empathy:* sensitivity and acceptance of other's feelings, behavior, and actions—the ability to walk in the other person's shoes.
5. *Responsibility:* assuming ownership for thoughts, feelings, actions, needs, goals, and expectations.
6. *Equality:* accepting another person as equal with a willingness to negotiate with their needs, wants, or desires.

After the overview, a question can help the members define the skill in their own words. Use language such as:

• Who can define *assertiveness*? What does being *assertive* mean to you?"
• How is assertiveness different from aggressiveness?"

Make a statement about what will follow the modeling of the skill.

• "After we see the examples of the skill, we will talk about how you can use the skill."

Distribute skill cards and ask a member to read the behavioral steps aloud. Ask members to follow each step as the skill is modeled.

STEP 2: MODEL THE BEHAVIOR FOLLOWING THE STEPS LISTED ON A FLIPCHART OR CHALKBOARD.

Moving into the experiential component, the leader models for the group members what he or she considers to be appropriate mastery of the skill. This enables group members to visualize the process. The model can be a live demonstration or a simulation media presentation. Identify and discuss the steps.

Example: Social Literacy Skill: Assertiveness
Lack of assertiveness is one reason why conflicts occur in relationships. To foster understanding and cooperation rather than resentment and resistance:

• Be direct. Deliver your message directly to the person with whom you are in conflict with, not to a second party (avoid the he said/she said trap).

- Take ownership for your message. Explain that your message comes from your point of view. Use personalized I-statements such as "I don't agree with you" rather than "You're wrong."
- State what you want, think, and feel as specifically as possible. Preface statements with
  "I have a need."
  "I want to . . ."
  "Would you consider . . ?"
  "I have a different opinion, I think that . . ."
  "I don't want you to . . ."
  "I have mixed reactions for these reasons . . ."

Here is an example.

> *Step 1:* Concretely describe the other person's behavior: When you are late picking me up for school in the morning.
>
> *Step 2:* Describe objectively how the other person's actions have affected you (the effects): I am always late for first bell and I always get detention.
>
> *Step 3:* Accurately describe your feelings. I feel hurt and angry with you.
>
> *Step 4:* Suggest what you would like to see happen: I am hoping that we could make plans so that I don't have to be late anymore.

- Ask for feedback to correct any misperceptions. Encourage others to be clear, direct, and specific in their feedback to you: "Am I being clear?" "How do you perceive the situation?" "What do you want to do about this?"

STEP 3: INVITE DISCUSSION OF THE SKILL THAT IS MODELED

Ask clients, "Did any of the situations you observed remind you of times that you had to use the skill?" Encourage a dialogue about skill usage and barriers to implementation among group members.

STEP 4: ORGANIZE A ROLE-PLAY BETWEEN TWO GROUP MEMBERS

Designate one member as the *behavior-rehearsing member* (i.e., the individual who will be working on integrating a specific social, emotional, or cognitive skill). Go over guidelines for role-playing:

1. Role-playing gives a perspective on troublesome behavior.
   - It is a tool to bring a specific skill and its consequences into focus.
   - By rehearsing a new skill, a client will be able to feel some of the same reactions that will be present when the behavior occurs outside the group in a real setting.

2. Role-playing is intended to give clients experience in practicing skills and in discussing and identifying effective and ineffective behavior.
3. Practice will enhance confidence and comfortable level in real life settings.
4. The more real the role-playing, the more the emotional involvement, which will increase what is learned.
5. Real-life situations make it possible for clients to try ways of handling situations without suffering any serious consequences if the methods fail.

Ask the behavior-rehearsing member to choose a *partner* — someone in the group that reminds him or her of the person with whom they would most likely use the skill. For example, ask "Which member of the group reminds you of that person in some way?" or "Which member of the group would you feel most comfortable doing the role-playing with?" If no one is identified, ask someone to volunteer to rehearse the skill with the behavior-rehearsing member.

Set the stage for the role-play, including setting, props, and furniture, if necessary. Ask questions such as, "Where will you be talking?" "What will be the time of day?" and "What will you be doing?"

Review with the behavior-rehearsing member what should be said and done during the role play, such as "What will be the first step of the skill?" and "What will you do if your partner does _____?"

Provide final instructions to the behavior-rehearsing member and the partner:

• To the behavior-rehearsing member: "Try to follow the steps as best you can."
• To the partner: "Try to play the part the best that you can by concentrating on what you think you would do when the practicing member follows the steps."

Direct the remaining members of the group to be observers of the process. Their role is to provide feedback to the behavior-rehearsing member and the partner after the exercise. When the role-play begins, one group member can stand at chalkboard or flipchart to point out each step for the role-playing team. Coach and prompt role-players when needed.

STEP 5: ELICIT FEEDBACK FROM GROUP MEMBERS AND PROCESSES AFTER THE EXERCISE IS COMPLETED

Generous praise should be mixed with constructive suggestions. Avoid blame and criticism. The focus should be on how to improve. Suggestions should be achievable with practice. The social literacy skill of giving constructive feedback is an integrated part of every psychoeducational life skill intervention model. The suggested dialogue for giving constructive feedback another social literacy skill is as follows:

1. Ask permission. Ask the person if he or she would like some feedback. (If no, wait for a more appropriate time; if yes, proceed.)
2. Say something positive to the person before you deliver the sensitive information.
3. Describe the behavior.
4. Focus on behavior the person can change, not on the person's personality.
5. Be specific about the behavior and verifiable. (Have other people complained?)
6. Include some suggestion for improvement.
7. Go slowly. True behavior change occurs over time.

Important Considerations for the Feedback Process
The behavior-rehearsing member is instructed to wait until everyone's comments have been heard. The partner processes his or her role, feelings, and reactions to the behavior-rehearsing member. Observers are asked to report on how well the behavioral steps were followed, as well as on their specific likes and dislikes, and comments about the role of the behavior-rehearsing member and the partner.

Process the group comments with the behavior-rehearsing member. The behavior-rehearsing member is asked to respond to how well he or she did in following the behavioral steps of the skill. For example, "On a scale from 1 to 10, how satisfied were you about following the steps?"

STEP 6: ENCOURAGE FOLLOW-THROUGH AND TRANSFER OF LEARNING
TO OTHER SOCIAL, EMOTIONAL, OR COGNITIVE SETTINGS

This is a critical component: Participants need to transfer newly developed life skills to personally relevant life situations. The behavior-rehearsing member is assigned "ownwork" to practice and apply the skill in real life. (Ownwork is like homework, a task that is assigned for the behavior-rehearsing member to try out between sessions.)

Ownwork
Group members are assigned to look for situations relevant to the skill they might role-play during the next group meeting. Ask the behavior-rehearsing member how, when, and with whom he or she might attempt the behavioral steps prior to the next group meeting. Assign the Ownwork report (Figure 10.1), a written commitment from the practicing member to try out the new skill and report back to the group at the next group meeting. Discuss how and where the skill will be used. Set a specific goal to use the skill outside the group.

Ownwork is assigned to enhance the work of the session; and to keep behavior-rehearsing members aware of the life skills they wish to enhance. The ultimate goal is to practice new behaviors in a variety of natural settings. Ownwork puts the onus of responsibility for change on behavior-rehearsing member—they must do ownwork to resolve the problem. The following examples are appropriate ownwork assignments.

- *Experiential/behavioral assignments.* Assignments to perform specific actions between sessions. A behavioral assignment for lack of assertiveness may be to instruct the behavior-rehearsing member to say "no" to unreasonable requests from others.
- *Interpersonal assignments.* Assignments to enhance perceived communication difficulties by writing down unpleasant dialogues with others. These dialogues can be reviewed during the next session to show how someone inadvertently triggers rejection, criticism, and hostilities in others.
- *Thinking assignments.* Assignments such as making a list of things that are helpful to think about, and practice in thinking these new thoughts throughout the day. A person with low self-esteem can be instructed to spend time thinking about his or her proudest accomplishments.
- *Writing assignments.* Assignments such as writing in a journal or diary help participants develop an outlet for their feelings while away from the sessions. A diary can list for each day the frequency of new behaviors that are practiced.
- *Solution-focused assignments.* Assignments that actively seek solutions to problems identified in the sessions. Clients could seek a resolution to an interpersonal problem by negotiating or resolving a conflict with another person.

Example: Psychoeducational Session
Teaching the Social Skill: Maintaining Impulse Control
1. Instruction
   - *Question:* How would you define impulse control? *Impulse control* is learning to stop and look at the consequences of your actions before you commit yourself to something. It is the ability to stop and think who else is going to be affected by your actions and what the consequences will be. Is it worth it?
   - *Simulation:* Shelly is constantly overcommitting herself by being impulsive. She has a problem saying no and working within the boundaries that are comfortable for her. When she is asked to do something, she will say yes even if she does not have the time or resources to complete the task. Shelly was looking at the course schedule book for the fall, saw a class that looked interesting, so she signed up for it. She was already taking 15 graduate hours and working 20 hours per week. She is feeling extremely stressed because of her overload of classes and she is not sure if she will get her assignments completed on time. How can we help?
   - *Signs of Loss of Control*
     1. Acting impulsively consumes lots of energy and resources.
     2. You feel driven, impelled, and think of nothing else.

   3. You feel like the decision is the only possible answer, and you let it take over all rational thinking.
- *Control Strategies*
  1. Ask yourself who else is going to be affected by this behavior?
  2. How are they going to be affected by what you do?
  3. Delay the action. Give yourself some time to think through the decision so that you can see the consequences and alternatives. Remember, choice is important.
  4. Find a way to buy time so that you can think about your actions.
  5. Think back to the past and consider the situations you had to get yourself out of because of being too impulsive.

2. Modeling
- *Self-Help Strategies*
  1. Reward yourself each time you stop and think through a situation instead of acting impulsively.
  2. Keep a journal and record your feelings about decisions you make and whether you made those decisions impulsively.
  3. Write yourself a bill of rights and read it when you get ready to make decisions.
- *Reminders for Yourself*
  Having a choice is critical. It allows you freedom to act or not to act. It puts you in charge of yourself. If you always do what you've always done, you will always get what you've always gotten.
- *Consequences of Acting Impulsively*
  1. The consequences of acting impulsively are: confusion, self-loathing, and feeling out of control.
  2. The results of acting impulsively are that you spend a tremendous amount of time trying to resolve conflicts, mend relationships, or balance time and money.

3. Role-Play Simulation
   Shelly: Hey Beth, I just saw this great course in the fall catalog. I think I will take it.

   Beth: Shelly, how many hours of classes are you already taking?

   Shelly: Fifteen, but this course sounds interesting and I really want to take it.

   Beth: Shelly, I realize you really want to take it and it sounds interesting, but is it something that you can handle right now with work and school?

   Shelly: It will mean more homework and being up late at night, but I really think I can do it.

   Beth: Shelly, remember last semester how stressed you were during finals? Do you want that again?

Shelly: No, but Beth you don't understand. I really want to take this class.

Beth: Look at your "plus versus minus" ratio. How is it going to benefit you and how is it going to impact your family?

Shelly: It's going to help me with general knowledge but not toward my degree. I hadn't thought about my family.

Beth: Shelly, do you think you could wait until tomorrow and make your decision? That way you could talk it over with Brian and the kids and think more about it.

Shelly: I guess I could, but what if it's full by then?

Beth: Shelly, what if it is? Will you still be able to graduate and could you take it later?

Shelly: You've got a point. I'll think about it and talk it over with Brian.

4. Feedback

Elicit feedback from group members as outlined in the process above, focusing on the behavior not the personality of the role-playing member.

5. Ownwork Assignment

Assign Shelly to complete a *decision-balance matrix* (Table 10.4). Have Shelly look at the aspects of her life and determine how her decision to take on more coursework would affect her.

Have Shelly analyze the time commitment for the course requirements: how many research papers per class, readings per class, and special projects. Merge those commitments with family and job responsibilities. Bottom line: Are there enough hours in the week to do everything she will be obligated to do? Ownwork assignments serve to strengthen behavior rehearsal of skills between sessions.

TABLE 10.4
Decision-Balance Matrix

	Personal Time Commitment for Self and Others	
	Positive Consequences (+)	**Negative Consequences** (−)
Social and family relationships		
Academic responsibilities		
Job and career responsibilities		
Leisure-time pursuits		
Church/synagogue/community obligations		

Name _____   Date Assigned _____
                                   Date Completed _____

Instructions: Your social skills ownwork is an assignment that follows the lesson that has been taught. You need to practice the social skill five times with other people or peers. (1) Write a description of what happened, when it happened, and where it happened in each practice example. (2) Record what you said and did. (3) Record what the other person said and did.

Behavioral Definition _____

_____

What Happened?

What You Said and Did   *What the Other Person Said and Did*

1.
2.
3.
4.

FIGURE 10.1. Life Skill: Ownwork Form

Ownwork in psychoeducational group is different from homework in academic domains. Ownwork in psychoeducational group is perhaps more critical to provide generalization, transfer, and reinforcement to other social settings to bring back to the group to share successes.

CONCLUSION

Person-centered, client-centered, or Rogerian therapy is America's first distinctively indigenous school of counseling. It was conceived, nurtured, and articulated by the ambitious work of a single man, Carl Rogers. Therapists and counselors have incorporated the constructs of empathy, congruence, and unconditional positive regard in all counseling genres. They are the fundamental foundation for a therapeutic relationship and truly "a way of being."

Chapter 11

Conflict Mediation and Conflict Resolution Techniques

Individuals who witnessed or experienced excessive conflict in their families, such as in abusive or alcoholic homes, are particularly prone to view conflict as only destructive. They either may become aggressive when resolving conflicts or retreat completely from a conflict situation. Conflict is destructive when it:

- Results in no decision or new coping behaviors and the problem remains.
- Diverts energy from more important activities and issues.
- Destroys the morale of individuals and groups.
- Reinforces poor self-concept.
- Divides people even more and polarizes groups.
- Produces irresponsible behavior.

Conflict is constructive when it:
- Increases the involvement of everyone affected by the conflict.
- Opens up discussion of issues resulting in clarification.
- Identifies alternative solutions.
- Results in the solution of a problem.
- Serves as release of pent-up emotions, anxiety, and stress.
- Builds cohesiveness among group members.
- Helps individuals and groups to grow personally and apply their knowledge to future conflicts.

Main and Roark (1975) and Roark (1978, p. 402) outlined a five-step process of conflict resolution for dealing with emotion-laden interpersonal conflict:

1. At the beginning, each conflictee describes the situation from his or her perspective. Participants should restrict their account of the situation with cognitive descriptions, strictly avoiding emotional connotations. The outcome of this step is to achieve consensus and mutual understanding regarding the description of the conflict situation as the starting point for conflict resolution.
2. Next, each conflictee describes his or her feelings regarding the conflict. It is important to avoid escalating the conflict with statements of blame. The outcome of this statement is to have conflictees understand one another's feelings and needs.
3. Prefaced by information and understanding from the first two steps, conflictees formulate and describe a situation acceptable to everyone. The outcome of this step should be a) agreement on perceptions of the conflict, b) understanding of one another's feelings regarding the conflict, and c) agreement on what the situation would be if the conflict was significantly reduced.
4. At this juncture, changes necessary to achieve the desired situation are agreed upon. Each conflictee should list the changes he or she is willing to make as well as verbalize and understand what the other is willing to do.
5. Finally, a detailed agenda should be formulated, including follow-up plans and specific dates for the accomplishment of all tasks.

Technique: *DESC Script (Describe, Express, Specify, Consequences)*

Counseling Intention   To develop a formula for conflict resolution, negotiation, and assertiveness.

Description   Bower and Bower (1976) provided the following technique or guidelines for handling interpersonal conflicts. It consists of four key elements: (D) Describe, (E) Express, (S) Specify, and (C) Choose consequences.

Describe: Begin your dialogue by describing as specifically and objectively as possible the behavior or situation that is bothersome to you. Use concrete terms. Describe a specified time, place, and frequency of action. Describe the action, not the motive.

Express: Say what you feel and think about this behavior. Explain the effect of this behavior on you. Empathize with the other person's feelings. Express them calmly. State feelings in a positive manner, for example, as relating to a goal to be achieved.

Specify: Ask for a different, specific behavior, or specify what behavior you would prefer or need in this particular situation. Request only one or two changes at one time. Specify the concrete actions you want to see stopped and those you want to see performed. Take into account whether or not the other person can meet your request without suffering large losses. Specify (if appropriate to the situation) what behavior you are willing to change to make the agreement.

Choose consequences: State concretely and simply what positive and negative consequences you are prepared to carry through if your preferences are not met. Make the consequences explicit. Give a positive reward for change in the desired direction. Select something that is desirable and reinforcing.

Consider the impact of these consequences on yourself and on others involved in the situation. Sometimes you have to specify the negative consequences of not following changes. In one example situation, Jessica's father tries to give her advice (to the point of nagging) about what she should do in school, who she should and should not date, and who she should have as friends. Jessica loves and respects her father's concern for her, but she would like to make her own decisions without her father's constant nagging and interference. Jessica decides to outline a DESC script to use in dealing with her dad.

Describe: (The description should be concise, accurate, directed toward a single point, carefully worded, objective, and nonaccusing.) "Dad, you have been giving me detailed advice about what you think I should study in school, how you think I should choose my friends, and what guys I should date."

Express: (Express how it makes you feel; be positive and focus on common goals; do not provoke feelings of guilt.) "I know you want the best for me, and your intentions are well meaning. I feel like you are treating me like a child. I'm older now, and I can think for myself."

Specify: (Specify an alternative behavior instead of the current one.) "Please stop giving me advice unless I specifically ask for it. Trust me to be responsible for myself and allow me to learn on my own."

Consequences: (Let the other person know how you intend to follow through on your request for behavior change. The consequences consist of two parts: rewards if he or she accedes to your request and punishments if the individual fails to go along with it.) "We will get along much better if you will let me have more freedom to make my own decisions. I think you will be proud of how responsible I can be" (positive consequence). "If you continue to give me advice when I don't ask for it, I will gently remind you of our agreement, the first time. If you continue after this, I will just turn and leave the room" (negative consequences).

In most cases, if a DESC script is prepared and followed through with a clear calm statement, the other person will listen and probably respond favorably. If the script does not provide the desired result, the client can follow through on the consequences without feeling frustrated or helpless.

Technique: *Locating "Pinch Points" That Provoke Aggressive Responses*

Counseling Intention   To help the client stop the internal process that triggers aggressive behavior.

Description   One way to keep track of aggressive behavior is to keep a log. In the daily log, the client should note the following:

1. Aggressive comments or actions.
2. A precise description of what the other person did or said just before the aggression.
3. In addition to anger, any other feelings experienced.
4. Thoughts and internal dialogue.
5. Body language just prior to the aggressive reaction.

Technique: *Guided Conflict Imagery*

Counseling Intention   To facilitate awareness of strategies for dealing with conflict situations; to examine methods of responding to conflict.

Description   Ask the client to get comfortable, close his or her eyes, get in touch with him or herself at the present moment, and relax. The guided imagery is as follows:

> *"You are walking down a long hallway and begin to notice a familiar face coming in your direction. Suddenly, you recognize that it is the person with whom you are in most conflict at the present time. You realize that you must decide quickly how to respond to the person. As he or she comes closer, a number of alternatives flash through your head. Decide right now what you will do and then imagine what will happen."*
> *(Pause to allow the images and the response to develop.)*
>
> --
>
> *It's over now. The person has gone. How do you feel? What did you say? How satisfied were you with how the interchange went? What did you say to yourself?*

> *(Pause to allow the client to process and identify the internal dialogue.)*
>
> --
>
> *Return to the present. Gradually become aware of any tension in your body. . . your breathing . . . the sounds in the room . . . and finally open your eyes when you feel ready.*

Ask the client (or group members) to spend five minutes writing: (1) the alternative ways of acting they had considered, (2) the one the client chose to act upon, and (3) the level of satisfaction he or she felt as to the outcome of the choice on scale of 1 to 10.

> *Perspective for the Therapist: On inferiority*
>
> *To be a human being means to possess a feeling of inferiority which constantly presses toward its own conquest. The paths to victory are as different in a thousand ways as the chosen goals of perfection. The greater the feeling of inferiority that has been experienced, the more powerful is the urge to conquest, and the more violent the emotional agitation.*
>
> Alfred Adler
> *The Neurotic Constitution*, 1972, p. 16

Technique: *Resolving Conflicts Cooperatively*

Counseling Intention   To assist clients in conflict to express feelings and interpersonal conflict.

Description   The two individuals who are angry with each other sit opposite each other with knees touching. Instruct them to look at each other in the eyes as they talk, talking directly to each other and not about the other. Each will state his or her viewpoint and feelings. One person begins by stating the problem as he or she sees it and also says how he or she feels: "I feel [description of feeling] when you [description of behavior]." The other person is not to share his or her viewpoint at this time. He or she is only to repeat what he or she heard the other person say. The listener who repeated the problem and feelings is to confirm with the other person that everything was stated basically as the other said it.

The second person is provided with the same chance to state the problem. Encourage the two to do any of the following: agree to disagree, compromise and come to a solution, seek forgiveness if wrong or forgive if wronged, or accept the other's viewpoint.

Technique: *Assuming Responsibility for Choices and Actions*

Counseling Intention   To shift the center of responsibility or ownership to a problem.

Description   Direct the client to think of an incident that really made him or her angry or resentful, one about which he or she still has strong feelings. In writing, describe the incident as if others were completely responsible for bringing about the event. Blame them. Make it clearly their fault. Now rewrite the incident as if you were solely responsible for starting, developing, and getting stuck with the problem. Take full account of what you could have done so that the whole problem would not have arisen. Process with the client the issues of blame, responsibility, and victimization.

Technique: *Resent, Expect, Appreciate*

Counseling Intention   To word with bipolarities, or splits in the personality, by bringing each side into awareness; to become aware of expectations and mixed feelings held about others.

Description   Have the client list three of his or her closest friends. For each individual, have the client think of one thing that he or she resents, one thing that is expected that the offending person change, and one thing that is appreciated about the person (Table 11.1). Process how to resent and appreciate a person at the same time, how to be aware of the mixed feelings he or she may have toward others, and how to integrate opposing thoughts or feelings.

Technique: *How to Handle a Verbal Attack*

Counseling Intention   To maintain composure during a conflict.

TABLE 11.1
Resent, Expect, Appreciate

"I Resent"	"I Expect"	"I Appreciate"
"that you break a lot of promises."	"you to keep your word."	"how easygoing you are and your sense of humor."

Description   Internally process the following:

1. Find out where the other person is coming from.
   • "What are your feelings about . . . ?"
   • "What would you like me to know?"
   • "How can I help?"
2. Study the other person's power.
   • "You seem upset because I hear/see . . . "
   • "What I hear you saying is . . . "
3. Hold onto this power, step out of the way, and encourage it to move past you without letting it get to you.
   • "You want me to hear that you are feeling *X* about *Y* because *Z*?"
4. If this fails, walk away without saying another word.
   • Stay quiet for a moment. If you can't walk away, at least say nothing, and keep your cool until you can talk it out with the support of another person.
   • Simply say "We'll talk later."

Technique: *Coping with Anger*

Counseling Intention   To maintain self-control.

Description   First, accept your emotional arousal and try to assess your personal condition (accept that you are upset). Second, pause, to collect yourself and try to gain your composure through a relaxation response (counting from 1 to 10). Third, think about your choices of emotional expression. Fourth, do something to express the emotional tension

Technique: *Inner Processing How Another Person Might Feel*

Counseling Intention   To use empathy to resolve conflict.

1. Observe the other person's behavior and actions.
2. Pause and listen to gain an understanding of what the other person is saying.
3. Identify with your inner dialogue, the feelings you think the other person is having. (Inner dialogue to self: He must feel embarrassed.)
4. Mentally, list specific feelings you think the other person is experiencing.
5. Decide if you need to do a *perception check* to verify their experience.
6. Use *reflection skills* to verify the feelings the other person is having to show that you understand.

Technique: *Toning Down Heated Remarks*

Counseling Intention   To diffuse a potential conflict.

Description   When someone is angry and emotional they often use strong, negative feelings to talk about the individual. To create a greater state of calm, it is helpful to restate the information in more neutral words.

Example

> *"I hate Jim. He makes me sick. He can never make a decision and he always berates colleagues in staff meetings."*
>
> Restate: *"I am upset with Jim because he is indecisive and sometimes critical of others."*

Technique: *Steps to Anger Management*

Counseling Intention   To maintain control of behavior.

Description   "I can keep my power. I can choose what I think and how I act. I am responsible for my day. Peace begins with me."

1. *Recognize* that you are angry.
2. *Accept* your feelings.
3. Stop do a quieting response (QR) *relaxation.*
4. *Think* about way to express the anger.
5. Prepare.
6. Problem solve.
7. Plan.
8. *Evaluate* the consequences.
9. Identify and invite alternatives.
10. Instead of insults, imagine successes.
11. *Choose* the best way; name your feeling; negotiate.
12. *Express* the anger in a helpful way.

Technique: *Enhancing Relationship Skills*

Counseling Intention   To identify roadblocks to healthy relationships.

Description

1. Problems can be defined and thought about carefully.
2. Problems are different from people, and peoples' problems are different.
3. Roadblocks to communication can be eliminated.
4. Specific skills can help remove conflict: using "I-Messages," helpful criticism, problem solving, brainstorming, anger management, and assertiveness.

Friendliness helps reduce conflicts and improve relationships.

Technique: *Communicating to Enhance Relationships and Avoid Conflict*

Counseling Intention   To enhance relationships try the following strategies:

- *Speak directly.* Telling your partner what you want (e.g., "I want to go to the game with you on Saturday").
- *Distinguish between needs and wants.* Needs are the minimum requirement for the relationship to exist. Wants are things that enhance the relationship.
- *Listen actively and attentively.* Maintain a relationship where feelings are shared, along with hopes and dreams, without the fear of condemnation.
- *Fight fairly.* State your feelings using I-messages, and learn how to respond assertively, such as "I think" and "I feel."
- *Focus on behavior not personality.* Concretely describe the problem behavior.
- *Avoid gunny sacking.* Don't save up all your hurt feelings and hostilities and let them accumulate to one explosive episode. Deal with significant issues when they occur. Stay in the here-and-now. Bringing up the past is disrespectful and merely brings on more hostility. Work so that both parties win. Lasting relationships require daily maintenance and fine-tuning.

Technique: *Dealing with Rumors and False Accusation*

Counseling Intention   To eliminate incongruency between actions and intentions.

Description

- Acknowledge the rumor. Is it accurate or is it false?
- Is it intended to hurt you or help you? Was the motivation constructive or destructive?
- Maintain your composure. Evaluate if someone else started the rumor. Is it a true or false accusation?
- Think about the ways to answer the accusation(s) without being defensive or angry. You can:
  1. Deny it and walk away.
  2. Express your side of the rumor, and explain your own behavior.
  3. Correct perceptions held by others.
  4. Assert yourself.
  5. Apologize for what has occurred.
  6. Express your regrets and offer to make up for what happened.
  7. Review your options, and choose the best one for the situation.

Technique: *Preparing for a Difficult Conversation*

Counseling Intention   To anticipate actions that result from conflict.

Description

1. Prepare what you are going to say. Write it down. Read it and revise it for tone and content.
2. Think about how you will feel during the conversation (e.g., tense, nervous, afraid).
3. Plan your self-talk (your inner dialogue). What will you say to yourself to keep yourself calm and composed?
4. Think about how the other person will feel (e.g., angry, cold, aloof, inattentive).
5. Practice what you want to say.
6. Think about what the other person might say back to you.
7. Think about other issues that may come up during the course of the conversation.
8. Choose your best approach and do it.

Technique: *"Carefronting" (Confronting Self-defeating Behavior)*

Counseling Intention   To bring self-defeating behavior into awareness.

Description   People need to hear you care about their well-being. It must be a genuine concern if confronting is to be effective; hence, a better term is "carefronting." Examples might include:

- "The concerns I have about you are because I care about you and our relationship."
- "I care about you too much to let this go and not say anything about what I see happening."

Then state the behavior—how you feel—and then reiterate your caring and concern. Other guidelines include the following:

- Maintain a sense of calm. Be simple and direct. Don't circumvent the issue or behavior. Speak to the point. Don't become emotional. It is all right to show your feelings, but anger should not be directed at the person.
- Keep on the subject and be specific. Talk about the problem and specific ways it has affected the person's behavior.
- Be prepared for promises, excuses, and counter-accusations (especially when confronting drinking behavior). Denial and resistance to receiving help may occur.
- Admit the problem and face it.
- Find a good source of reliable information and learn it.

Technique: *How to Let Someone Know They're Bothering You*

Counseling Intention   To explain your needs to someone else.

1. Keep a serious facial expression and straight posture. Maintain eye contact. Use a serious tone of voice.
2. Ask if you could talk to the person for a moment.
3. First say something positive. "I like . . ."
4. Tell the person what's bothering you—make it an "I-Message": "When you do [specify behavior], I feel . [emotion] because I [consequence]."
5. The other person responds (may be defensive or deny the problem).
6. Do some active listening—let the other person know you heard what they said.
   - Paraphrase—Repeat what they said in a little different way.
   - Reflect feelings—Say how you think they feel (e.g., "You really seem to be angry.")

- Ask for more information (how, what, when, where).
- Check out your understanding of what they said ("Do you mean . . .?").

7. Ask if the person understood what you said, and if not, explain again.
8. Problem solve—give the person suggestions for changing. Be specific. Ask for a small behavior change. Work toward a compromise.
9. Give the person a reason for changing. Tell the person what the positive consequences will be if they agree to your request and what the negative consequences will be if they don't (optional). Do not make threats or offer a reward that you can't or do not want to give.
10. Thank the person for listening.

Technique: *Making Intention Statements*

Counseling Intention   To provide statements that let others know more about your immediate or long-range commitments or expectations.

Description   An intention statement is a way of being direct about what you would or would not like for yourself, or what you would or would not like to do. Intention statements begin with words like:

- I want
- I would like
- I intend
- I need

An intention statement is a way of being *direct* about what you would or would not like for yourself, or about what you would or would not like to do.

Example
- "I want to be with you today, but I don't want to spend all our time shopping."
- "I'd like to do my studying in the afternoon, then catch the game this evening."
- "I'd like to be with you, but I want to be with my family tonight too, because it's my brother's birthday. And I want to spend this afternoon in the library working on my paper."

Technique: *Making Action Statements*

Counseling Intention   Making action statements simply involves describing your actions, your behaviors to others—what you have done, are doing, or will do.

Description   An action statements put words to some of your behavior in a simple, descriptive way. Action statements refer to your past, current, or future actions and are expressed using "being" verbs: was, am, will. It is a skill because it requires:

1. Awareness of your own behavior.
2. Awareness of the possible impact of this behavior on others.
3. Remembering to do it.

Action statements about the future are particularly important because they *involve a commitment* to do or not do something.

Statements of commitment to action start with "I will" rather than "I might."

- "I will try to call you this morning."
- "I will do it by Friday."
- "I will be there at 6:00 PM, sharp."

Technique: *Confrontation Guidelines*

Counseling Intention   To be more assertive about expectations and behavior.

Description

1. Be flexible and reasonable in your expectations about the outcome of the confrontation. It is more reasonable to ask for an apology for peoples' actions than to change their personality. "The most important thing is that he knows what an inconvenience he caused me."
2. Confronting at the right time and in the right place is critical to a successful confrontation. Privacy and easy access to each other will usually improve the impact, unless you are concerned about a physical confrontation.
3. Talk directly to the person you are confronting. "I really need to tell you something important that concerns me. Can we talk?"
4. Talk clearly and calmly. If the person is unable to listen, wait until he is in a more receptive emotional state.
5. Refer directly to the issue. "Remember when we were supposed to meet at the mall last Saturday?"
6. Explain how the person's behavior affected you. Use I-messages. "I get frustrated and impatient when you keep me waiting."
7. Listen actively to the other person's viewpoint. Try to put yourself in that person's shoes.

8. Ask for cooperation and openness. This will test the person's flexibility and receptivity to improve or change. "Will you hear me out? Would you be willing to change the way you treat me?"
9. Summarize what you both need to do to resolve the problem. "I need to know that you will avoid being late again."

Technique: *Fair Fighting*

Counseling Intention   To resolve conflicts more constructively.

Description   The sequence of the process of *fair fighting* fosters better relationship skills.

1. *Ask permission to fight.* Jessica says, "Ryan, I'd like to share something that is really upsetting me."
2. *Present one specific complaint.* "I'm really angry at you for not taking me to the mall with you."
3. *Ask the other person for feedback.* "Okay, I understand that you're really mad at me because I didn't take you to the mall."
4. *Thank the person for listening and understanding how you feel.* "Thank you for listening to me."
5. *Make a specific request for a change in behavior.* "Next time, I'd like you to ask me if I want to go to the mall instead of taking it for granted that I don't want to go."
6. *Ask the person for feedback.* Be sure you were understood. "Okay, Jessica next time I'll ask."
7. *Reaffirm your feelings of appreciation.*

Technique: *Negotiating a Conflict of Interest*

Counseling Intention   To assess the amount of conflict.

Description   When striving for the same goals, sometimes there are conflicts of interest. Cooperators resolve conflicts as partners, not as adversaries. Below are listed the six steps in negotiating conflict of interests:

1. Describe what each person wants.
2. Describe how each person feels.

3. Exchange reasons for positions.
4. Understand each other's perspective.
5. Invent options for mutual benefit.
6. Reach a wise agreement.

Technique: *Conventional Arbitration*

Counseling Intention   To increase the mediation process.

Description   Mediation is an extension of negotiation; the mediator assists disputants in negotiating a constructive resolution. In contrast, with arbitration, an outside person makes a judgment; the arbitrator does not assist the disputants in improving their conflict. Disputants leave the decision to the arbitrator who hears both sides and then makes a decision. It goes as follows:

1. Both persons agree to abide by the arbitrator's decision. Agreement is based on the assumption that after disputants have presented their side of the conflict, the arbitrator will be able to make a fair decision. The arbitrator should be familiar with the subject matter of the case and have access to all available documents and evidence.
2. Both persons agree to abide by the arbitrator's decision. Agreement is based on the assumption that after disputants have presented their side of the conflict, the arbitrator can begin with an understanding of what the focus of the decision should be.
3. Each person defines the problem. Both have the opportunity to tell his or her side of the conflict.
4. Each person presents his or her case, with documented evidence to support it. No interruptions are allowed.
5. Each person has an opportunity to refute the other's contentions. After one person has presented his or her case, the other may attempt to refute the person's contentions. Both have a turn to show the arbitrator a different perspective on the issues.
6. The arbitrator makes a decision. After both persons have presented their case, refuted the other person's case, and given a closing statement, the arbitrator decides what to do. Usually, the decision is a win-lose situation—one side wins, the other loses. Winning or losing is secondary to having had the fair opportunity to be heard.

Technique: *Negotiation*

Counseling Intention   To outline the process of negotiation.

Description   The following apply to negotiation:

Ground Rules
1. Each person takes a turn saying the rules.
   - No interrupting
   - No name calling
   - Be honest
   - Work hard to solve the problem

Defining the Problem
2. Decide who will talk first.
3. Person 1 tells what happened.
   Person 2 *restates* and asks how 1 *feels*.
4. Person 2 tells what happened.
   Person 1 *restates* and asks how 2 *feels*.

Finding Solutions
5. Person 1 gives a solution.
6. Person 2 agrees or gives another solution.
7. Each person continues to give solutions until agreement is reached. (There must be a solution for each part of the problem.)
8. Each person says what the solutions are.
9. Each says what can be done to keep the problem from happening again.

Technique: *Maintaining Peace during Conflict Resolution Situations*

Counseling Intention   To create a win-win situation.

Description   Use the acronym ***RESOLUTION***

   R   Respect the other person's right to disagree.
   E   Express your honest concerns.
   S   Share common interest.
   O   Open up to different points of view.
   L   Listen attentively.
   U   Understand the major issues.

T   Think about all the consequences.
I   Investigate alternatives and solutions.
O   Offer a compromise.
N   Negotiate for mutual benefits.

Technique: *Knowing When, Where, and How to Resolve Conflicts—A Self-Assessment*

Counseling Intention   To prepare for a conflict situation.

Description   Steps to consider when you are planning how to handle a situation that upsets you, a self-assessment.

1. Have a chosen time and place where both of you can feel free to discuss the problem.
2. Ask yourself, "Have I tried to find out how the other person sees and feels about the conflict?" Ask questions to get his or her point of view. Put yourself in the other person's shoes. Understanding will begin to replace anger.
3. Ask yourself, "Have I asked the other person to listen to my point of view?" Be specific and accurate about what was said and done, explaining why you are upset. Use I-statements: "I feel X when you Y because Z."
4. Ask yourself, "Have I made it clear to the other person exactly what I want to be different?" Did you make it clear that you are willing to change too?
5. Ask yourself, "Have I asked the other person to tell me exactly what he would like me to do differently?" (without implying that you will do whatever he or she wants).
6. Have the two of you agreed on a mutually acceptable solution to your difficulty? Are you sure he or she knows exactly what you have in mind? Do you know exactly what he or she thinks the plan is? Should you put the agreement in writing?
7. Do you have a plan to check with each other, after a given time, to make sure your compromise is working out?
8. Have you shown your appreciation for the positive changes the other person has carried out?

Technique: *3R Strategy*

Counseling Intention   To eliminate long-standing resentment.

Description   This structured technique is useful in cases of long-standing disagreement and dislike. There are three steps: resentment, request, and recognition.

1. *Resentment.* Each person states what he or she dislikes about the other and outlines everything done to cause the resentment.
2. *Request.* Each person tells the other what to do to solve the problem.
3. *Recognition.* Both parties negotiate which requests they would be willing to meet. The session ends with each party stating what qualities they like or find admirable in each other.

This strategy requires a firm mediator to manage exposed emotions. It is very useful for clearing the air when individuals have built up a lot of resentment toward one another.

Technique: *Coping Thoughts for Anger Reactions*

Counseling Intention   To internalize skills when responding to someone's anger.

Description
1. Preparing for an anger reaction.
   - This is going to upset me, but I know how to deal with it.
   - What is it that I have to do?
   - I can work out a plan to handle this.
   - If I find myself getting upset, I'll know what to do.
   - Try not to take this too seriously.
   - This could be a testy situation, but I believe in myself.
   - Time for a few deep breaths for relaxation.
   - Easy does it; remember to keep my sense of humor.
2. Conflict occurs.
   - Stay calm. Just continue to relax.
   - As long as I keep my cool, I'm in control.
   - I don't need to prove myself.
   - There is no point in getting mad.
   - I'm not going to let him get to me.
   - Look for the positives: I won't assume the worst or jump to conclusions.
   - There is no need to doubt myself. What he says doesn't matter.
   - I can't change him with anger; I'll just upset myself.
   - I'm on top of this situation, and it's under control.

Technique: *Preparing for a Potential Conflict*

Counseling Intention   To avoid a conflict.

Description   The following self-talk can help prepare for and avoid a conflict.

- What is it that you have to do?
- You can work out a plan to handle this.
- You can manage this situation. You know how to regulate your anger.
- If you find yourself getting upset, you'll know what to do.
- There won't be any need for an argument.
- Time for a few deep breaths of relaxation. Feel comfortable, relaxed, and at ease.
- This could be a testy situation, but you believe in yourself.

Technique: *Confronting a Conflict*

Counseling Intention   To resolve a conflict.

Description   The following statements can help resolve a conflict.

1. Stay calm. Continue to relax. Breathe deeply.
2. As long as you keep your cool, you're in control.
3. Don't take it personally.
4. Keep focused on what you need to do.
5. You don't need to prove yourself.
6. There is no point in getting mad.
7. Don't let the situation get the best of you. This too will pass.

Technique: *Coping with Agitation*

Counseling Intention   To internalize coping skills.

Description   Being agitated is part of life. Handling agitation will increases your well-being. The following self-statements may help.

- Your muscles are starting to feel tight. It's time to relax and slow down.
- Getting upset won't help.

- It is reasonable to get annoyed, but keep it in control.
- Time to take a deep breath.
- Your anger is a signal of what you need to do. It's time to talk yourself out of being agitated.
- Try a cooperative approach. Maybe both of you are right.

Technique: *Skills to Handle Conflict and Anger*

Counseling Intention   To gain control of a situation.

Description   There are seven skills to process when angry and in conflict. It is important to *RETHINK* to gain control of the situation.

R—Recognize
- When you feel angry
- What makes your parents, teachers, friends, and siblings angry.
- When anger is a cover for other emotions such as fear, stress, anxiety, embarrassment, humiliation, or shame.

E—Empathize
- Try to see the other person's point of view; step into their shoes.
- Learn to use I-messages "I feel *X* because *Y.*"

T—Think
- Anger comes from our perception about situations or events.
- Think about how you interpret what the other person said.
- What can you tell yourself about what you feel?
- How can you handle your frustration and disappointment?
- Can you change your outlook?
- Can you reframe the situation to find a constructive solution?

H—Hear
- Listen to what the other person is saying to understand where he or she is coming from.
- Show that you are listening by establishing eye contact and giving feedback.

I—Integrate
- Integrate love and respect when conveying your anger (e.g. "I'm angry with you, but I want us to remain friends."

N—Notice
• Your body's reaction when you become angry.
• How you gain control of your behavior and how you calm yourself.

K—Keep
• Keep your attention in the hear-and-now.
• Keep from bringing up the past. Bringing up the past is disrespectful.
• Focus on the behavior that is causing difficulty, not on the personalities involved.

Source: National Institute of Mental Health (Reprinted with permission)

Technique: *I-Language Assertion*

Counseling Intention   To express negative feelings assertively.

Description   *I-language assertion* is helpful in expressing difficult negative feelings. It involves a four-part statement:

1. Objectively describe the other person's behavior or the situation that interferes with you.
2. Describe how the other person's behavior or the situation concretely affects your life, such as costing you additional time, money, or effort.
3. Describe your own feelings.
4. Describe what you want the other person to do, such as provide an explanation, change behavior, apologize, offer suggestions for solving the problem, or give a reaction to what was said.

Example

> *"When you cancel a meeting with just a few hours notice, I don't have enough time to make other arrangements and I'm left with empty down time. I feel irritated and unproductive. We need to make other arrangements about changing meetings at the last minute."*

Technique: *I-Want Statements*

Counseling Intention   To clarify needs and wants.

Description   *I-want statements* help you to clarify to both yourself and others what you really want. It gives the other person information that is necessary to know how to fulfill your wants. It relieves you from the conflict of wanting, being afraid to ask, and worrying whether the other person will do what you want.

Use I-want statements, "I want to do this" or "I want you to do this, "while referring to a specific behavior.

Example

> *"I want to know what I did to make you so angry, but I don't want you to call me names."*

I-want statements can be framed as follows:
1. State your want: "Instead of going to the movies, I want to just stay home and rent a video."
2. Rate your want on a scale of 1 to 10: "I want to go to the movies in the mall; it's a strong preference—-about an 8."
3. State what your I-want statement means and what it doesn't mean: "I want to go to the movies sometime in the next two weeks. That's just for information; no pressure if you can't make it this weekend."

Technique: *Empathic Assertion*

Counseling Intention   To respond to others with assertiveness and empathy.

Description   Empathic assertion can be used to convey some sensitivity toward a person. It consists of a two-part statement. The first part states your recognition of the other person, making a recognition statement involving one of the following areas:

- His/her situation (e.g., pressures, difficulties, lack of awareness)
- His/her feelings (e.g., sad, mad, angry, scared)
- His/her wants (e.g., to get a higher grade, a better job)
- His/her beliefs (e.g., that he/she has been unfairly treated, singled-out)

A recognition statement simply indicates that you see, hear, and acknowledge the situation, feelings, wants, desires, or beliefs of the other person.

The second part of the empathic assertion describe your situation, feelings, wants, or beliefs. Describe what you understand.

Example

> *"I can understand you are upset with me and probably not in the mood to discuss it right now. I would very much like to talk it over when you're ready."*

Technique: *Confrontive Assertion*

Counseling Intention   To have others follow through on their commitments.

Description   The confrontive assertion is helpful when you have previously asserted yourself and the other person has agreed to change his or her behavior, but has not followed through with the agreement. You point out the *discrepancy* rather than confront the *person*. It is appropriate to use this technique when a person's words contradict his or her actions or behaviors. The confrontive assertion has three parts:

1. Objectively describe what the other person said would be done.
2. Describe what the other person actually did do.
3. Express what you want.

Example

> *"I was supposed to review the article before it was sent to the typesetter. But I see the typesetter is working on it as we speak. Before he finishes it, I want to review the article and make the corrections I think are needed. In the future I want to have the opportunity to review the article before it goes to the typesetter."*

Technique: *Stop the Action/Accept the Feelings*

Counseling Intention   To contain outbursts of hostile behavior.

Description   When confronted with an outburst of hostile behavior, the recommended assertion procedure is to act quickly.

1. Stop the action.
2. Don't become emotionally involved yourself.
3. Accept the feeling.
4. Suggest alternative behaviors if possible.

Technique: *Avoiding Conflict By Paraphrasing*

Counseling Intention   To clarify points of view.

Description   Paraphrasing in conflict mediation clarifies the views of the problem and the feelings about it. It is important to listen attentively and summarize accurately using the following techniques:

• Restate the facts and summarize the events. Follow paraphrasing rules: Put yourself in the other person's shoes, state the other person's ideas and feelings in your own words, use *you* to begin your statements (e.g., *you want, you feel,* and *you think),* and show understanding and acceptance through nonverbal behaviors such as tone of voice, facial expressions, gestures, eye contact, and posture.
• Reflect feelings. Pay attention to the emotional element in each person's position. Use the statement, *"You feel [name the feeling] because [explain why]."*
• Offer alternatives.
• Reach a compromise.
• Agree on a solution.

Technique: *Reframing a Conflict*

Counseling Intention   To reframe perceptions between people.

Description   Reframing means thinking of the conflict and the other person's actions from another angle. There are a number of ways to reframe perceptions:

• View the conflict as a mutual problem to be jointly solved rather than a win-lose situation.
• Change perspectives.
• Distinguish between the intent of an action and the actual result of the action.
• Continue to differentiate between one's interest and reasoning. Seeking information about the other person's reasoning will result in a new "frame" emerging.
• Explore the multiple meanings of any one behavior. Ask: "What else might that behavior mean?"

Technique: *Dealing with Teasing*

Counseling Intention   To diffuse teasing or bullying behaviors.

Description   People tease other for a variety of reasons such as anger, revenge, power, attention, or feeling important. Teasing can be handled as follows.

- Use an I-message.
- Have a ready answer to respond.
- Walk away.
- Go somewhere near friends or adults.
- Don't tease back.
- Don't overreact.
- Don't join a group in teasing.
- Don't be afraid to help someone who is being teased.
- Change your inner dialogue with positive affirmations.

Technique: *What to Do When You Are Angry*

Counseling Intention   To recognize and process angry feelings.

Description
1. Recognize angry feelings.
   - Identify how your body feels.
2. Try to calm down.
   - Take in three deep breaths.
   - Count backward slowly.
   - Think pleasant thoughts.
   - Tell yourself to stay calm, that it is not worth it.
3. Talk aloud to solve the problem.
4. Think about the situation later.
   - What exactly made you angry?
   - Were you in control? Or with the situation out of your control?
   - Were you pleased with what you did?
   - Could you have done things differently?
   - Did you do your best under the circumstances?

Technique: *The XYZ Formula for a Complaint*

Counseling Intention   To describe offensive behavior constructively (Goleman, 1999).

Description   Criticisms are usually voiced as personal attacks rather than complaints. They create defensiveness or passive resistance that comes from feeling unfairly treated. Such criticism displays an ignorance of the feelings it will trigger in those who receive it, and the devastating effect those feelings will have on motivation, energy, and confidence in doing things well.

Example

"When you did X, it made me feel Y, and I'd rather you did Z instead."
"When you didn't call to tell me you were going to be late for dinner, I felt unappreciated and angry. I wish you would call to let me know you'll be late."

Technique: *The Artful Critique*

Counseling Intention   To specify behavior change.

Description   The artful critique follows:

- *Be specific.* Pick a specific incident that needs changing. Focus on the specifics, saying what the person did well, what was done poorly, and how it could be changed.
- *Offer a solution.* Point to a way to solve the problem.
- *Be present.* Deliver the critique in private, face to face.
- *Be sensitive.* Use empathy to structure the impact of what you say, and how you say it.

Technique: *Communicating Feelings in a Non-Blaming Manner*

Counseling Intention   To express feelings and negotiate change.

Description   Negotiation language proceeds as follows:

- "When you said or did *X*, I felt *Y*."
- "Can you tell me what you meant?"
- "What I would like is _____."
- "How can we work this out?"

Technique: *Setting Boundaries with Others*

Counseling Intention   To set limitations to enabling behaviors.

Description   Setting boundaries includes the following:

- I have the right to say "no," "I don't know," or "I need to think about that."
- I have the right to act without providing excuses or justifications.
- I have the right to change my mind.
- I have the right to put myself first when it feels appropriate.
- I have the right to make mistakes and be responsible for them.
- I have the right to ignore the advice of others.
- I am not responsible for anticipating the needs of others.
- I have the right to ask for help or emotional support.
- I have the right to ask for information.

Technique: *Strategies to Manage Anger More Appropriately*

Counseling Intention   To use more appropriate ways to manage anger.

Description   Anger is a strong emotion that needs to be expressed in an appropriate manner. Anger management is a life skill to cope with angry feelings. Some useful strategies follow.

1. Acknowledge to yourself that you are angry.
2. Get in touch with your feelings and physical sensations.
3. Take a few deep breaths and try to calm yourself using some coping self-statements:
   - "I'm under control. I can handle this."
   - "I can stay calm. I can relax."
   - "Don't get bent out of shape."
   - "Just roll with the punches."

4. Think about ways to suppress or express the anger.
   - Are you overreacting?
   - Could you lighten up?
   - Have you looked at the other person's point of view?
   - Are you blaming others when you are really angry with yourself?
   - Could you delay your angry response in order to give yourself time to cool off?
5. Use this formula to express your anger in a helpful way:
   "When *X* happens, I feel *Y*. I would feel better if *Z* would happen."

Example

> *"When you read while I'm talking to you, I feel that you aren't listening to me. I would feel better if you would look at me when I am talking to you."*

Technique: *Interpretive Confrontation*

Counseling Intention   To gain insight to oneself and to enhance personal growth.

Description   Interpretive confrontation can provide insight to oneself—a critical component of mental health. Interpretation can enhance personal growth when the information is communicated with skill, integrity, and empathy. The characteristics of an interpretive confrontation are:

- *Empathy.* Understand the issues that are central to the other person's behavior and lifestyle.
- *Timing.* The confrontation should be timed to prevent the receiver from becoming defensive.
- *Relatedness.* The confrontation should be related to the situation in which both parties are engaged.
- *Concise.* The confrontation should be concisely stated and to the point.
- *Genuine.* The person who is confronting must be able to communicate with genuine interest and concern for the well-being of the other party.
- *Tentative.* The interpretation is a suggestion about the other person's behavior, not an absolute fact.

Technique: *Self-Talk to Maintain Composure*

Counseling Intention   To maintain self-control.

Description   Self-talk statements should be generated that would be useful *before, during,* and *after* the situation.

Before: Take a minute to become more centered. "What is it that I want to do?"

During: Take a moment to exhale. Take things one step at a time. "People get irritated. It's nothing more than that. Clearly say what you want. Don't raise your voice."

After: On a scale of 1 to 10, assess your reactions. "I handled that with a 6. I'm getting better at this every time I try."

Technique: *Maintaining Your Personal Power*

Counseling Intention   To identify your personal anger responses.

Description   It is not easy to maintain your personal power when you are being taunted to fight by friends. Learn to identify your personal anger response components by answering the following questions.

- What are they doing that is getting to me? (Assess the environmental triggers.)
- How am I feeling inside? (Note the physiological feelings of anger.)
- What am I saying to myself? (Cognitive—stay cool, and he'll be the fool.)
- What am I going to do? (Behavioral—keep your distance but maintain eye contact.)
- Will this make a difference next week?

Technique: *Don't Take It Personally*

Counseling Intention   To gain more control of the way you think about situations.

Description   Sometimes it is helpful to modify your cognitive set (the way you think about situations) to gain more control of your feelings. When environmental demands are uncontrollable, anger management needs to be focused on changing your cognitive set so that the situation can be tolerated more easily. Consider the following self-questions:

- What need of hers might be making her say those things to me?
- What values might be influencing what he says?
- How does her background influence how she treats me?

Coping Self-statements to Remain Calm
- You can take anything he says.
- She can't get to you unless you let her.

Technique: *Getting Out of the Middle of Dueling Relationships*

Counseling Intention   To free oneself from enmeshed relationships.

Description   Sometimes, with all good intentions, you become caught in the middle of the needs of two people you care about. You may try to rescue both people, to the detriment of your relationship with each person. To leave a triangulated relationship gracefully, it may be helpful to de-stress, defuse, detach, and distance yourself from an otherwise toxic relationship.

1. *De-stress.* Is your involvement with each individual stressful? Is your anxiety level increasing? It may be time to make a decision to get out of the triangle.
2. *Defuse.* Are you constantly reacting to what the other person is saying and revealing? Is your energy level depleting needlessly? Perhaps it is time calm down and stop reacting emotionally to the needs of both parties. Step back and be a listener and observer.
3. *Disengage.* Are you trying to fix things? Are you trying to control people? Take your focus off the other two sides of the triangle. Consider your own emotional needs, your own importance, and your opportunity for personal growth.
4. *Distance.* Leave the relationships and get the emotional distance to separate and reorganize your position. Be prepared for a pull on your "heart strings" to put you back into the middle of things again.

Technique: *Using Self-Control Techniques*

Counseling Intention   To maintain self-control.

Description   Maintaining self-control is a skill that may take some time and practice to learn. It is not easy maintaining grace under fire. Listed below are some self-control techniques.

- Avoid frustrating situations by noting where you have become angry in the past.
- Reduce your anger by consciously taking time to focus on other emotions that are more passive, avoiding the weapons of aggression.
- Respond calmly to an aggressor with empathy, unprovocative comments, or with no response at all.
- If angry, concentrate on the undesirable consequences of becoming aggressive. Tell yourself that you are not going to give anyone the satisfaction of seeing you get upset.
- Review your present circumstances and try to understand the motives or point of view of the other person.

Teach yourself to be empathetic, forgiving of others, and tolerant of individual differences.

Technique: *Aggression Control Methods*

Counseling Intention   To maintain composure.

Description   Prevention of anger and control of anger are methods that can be learned.

- *Reduce your frustrations.* Try to avoid topics of conversation, personal opinions, or situations that *grate on you.*
- *Reduce the environmental settings.* Avoid aggressive subcultures, gangs, hostile friends, television violence, or violence in other forms of media such as the movies or music.
- *Cultivate new friends.* Associate with people who are not quick tempered, hostile, prejudiced, or agitators.

- *Disclose some of your own anxiety.* Rather than being abrasive or rude, try a comment such as "I'm having a bad day," "I'm stressed out," or "I'm upset" to change the context and soften your remarks.
- *Control anger through stress management.* Use problem-solving methods, I-messages, or positive self-talk.
- *Stop hostile fantasy building.* Preoccupation with frustrating situations increases anger. Move out of the situation or use thought-stopping techniques.

Technique: *Writing a Learning History of Angry Reactions*

Counseling Intention   To assess personal reactions to anger.

Description   Have the client take two weeks to carefully and systematically record anger-causing thoughts to become aware of the common but subtle triggers of emotional reactions and how to avoid future conflict. A learning history of the behavior or angry reactions should include the following:

1. Record the specific situations that "set you off."
2. Record the nature and intensity of your anger.
3. Note your thoughts and feelings of the situation immediately before and during the anger.
4. List what self-control methods you used and how well they worked.
5. Record the consequences and how others responded following your emotional reaction.

Evaluate the payoffs you get from your anger, clarify to yourself the purpose of your aggression, and give up some of your unhealthy payoffs.

Technique: *Three Quick Questions to Suppress or Express Anger*

Counseling Intention   To gain control of anger reactions.

Description   Have the client ask himself or herself the following questions:

1. Is this worthy of my attention?
2. Am I justified in being angry?
3. Can I do something about it without anyone getting hurt?

If yes, express your feelings and try to do something. If no, suppress your feelings by attending to something else, meditating, or using thought stopping or positive imagery.

Technique: *Self-Control Techniques for Anger Management*

Counseling Intention   To increase feelings of control.

Description   There are two distinct ways of managing anger: prevent it or control it. Strategies that may be helpful are as follows:

- Avoid frustrating situations by noting where and when you got angry in the past.
- Reduce your anger by taking time to focus on pleasurable emotions, avoiding weapons of aggression, and attending to other matters.
- Respond calmly to an aggressor or make no response at all.
- If your inner anger begins to escalate, concentrate on the undesirable consequences of becoming aggressive. You self-talk could be "Why give him the satisfaction of knowing I'm upset?" or "It isn't worth it."
- Try to understand the motives of the other person, to be tolerant of differences, and to be sensitive to human weakness.

Technique: *How to Calm an Angry Person*

Counseling Intention   To help others maintain control.

Description   The Institute of Mental Health provides a brief list of strategies to use to calm an angry person.

- Reduce the noise level.
- Keep calm yourself.
- Acknowledge that the irate person has been wronged (if true) or acknowledge their feelings without passing judgment.
- Ask them to explain the situation (so that you can diplomatically correct errors).
- Listen to their complaints without counterattacking.
- Explain your feelings with non-blaming "I-statements"
- Show that you care but set limits on violence. ("I'd like to work it out with you, but I'll call the authorities if you can't control yourself.")

Technique: *How to Handle a Bully*

Counseling Intention   To avoid being victimized.

Description   Victims of violence often use poor "survival strategies" such as (1) denial of the abuse ("It didn't happen"), (2) minimizing the action ("It doesn't matter, I'm OK"), or (3) self-blame ("It's my fault"). Repeated abuse leaves the victim more helpless and more willing to accept the blame. As the abusing cycle escalates (such as in battered women) the victim may kill their abuser (often in kill-or-be-killed situations).

Rule 1: If someone seriously threatens you, protect yourself immediately.

How to Handle a Bully
- Avoid them.
- Be assertive, "If you continue to harass me I will notify [personnel, the teacher, the police]."
- Find a support network and jointly confront the bully, demanding that he or she stop.
- Practice the social skills of assertiveness.
- Join a self-defense class to build self-confidence and strength.

Technique: *Rules to Increase the Effectiveness of Fair Fighting for Change*

Counseling Technique   To express anger without hurting a relationship.

Description   Fair fighting strategies allow people to express their anger clearly and directly without hurting the relationship.

Step 1: Make sure there is a conflict. Ask yourself, "What behavior do I want changed?"

Step 2: Arrange a specific time for a fair fight for change. "I want to take some time after class to share my feelings and see if we can make some changes."

Step 3: Clearly state what problem behavior you want to see changed. "I want to discuss this bill for $300."

Step 4: Make I-statements to express your current feelings and to accept responsibility for your feelings in the here-and-now.

Step 5: State what specific change of behavior you would like to happen.

Make fair changes that are practical and specific. "Don't run the bill up so high. Try to use your e-mail more."

Step 6: Indicate the reasons and consequences for the requested changes. Give your rationale for the changes you want made. Also, express how you feel and what you will do if the changes are not made. "Our budget can't afford such high monthly bills. If you continue to run the phone bill up, we won't be able to afford to go to Texas for spring break."

Step 7: Negotiate a compromise and make sure the agreement is understood. The listening partner responds and proposes his or her own changes or conditions so that a fair and workable agreement can be made.

Step 8: Put the incident in the past. Show appreciation for each other and for the efforts made for change.

Technique: *Aggression and Self-Assertion 1*

Counseling Intention   To see how participants handle self-assertion and conflict resolution.

Description   Members take turns portraying one of the following situations.

_____A customer in a restaurant complains about the food.

_____A customer complains to a hairdresser that her or his hair has been cut badly.

_____An employee comes to the personnel department and asks for a raise.

_____A telemarketer tries to sell a time-share.

_____A train conductor discovers a passenger whose pass has expired.

_____A father shouts at his daughter for coming home late.

_____An unemployed son asks his parents for pocket money.

_____Parents catch their daughter smoking marijuana.

_____A gang of teenage girls gets caught trying to steal something from a store.

_____A girl is tormented by some friends of her brothers.

_____A group of boys bullies a boy who is much younger.

_____Several people have an argument because they all want to watch different television shows.

_____Two drivers have a slight collision. They argue about how it happened. Some witnesses join in.

_____A family has an argument because the front door key is lost.

Process how the conflicts were resolved. Do some people assert their own interests without considering others? Do some people sacrifice their own interests? Do people compromise? How do people express their individual needs—objectively, clearly, humorously, hurtfully, or angrily?

Technique: *Aggression and Self-Assertion II*

Counseling Intention   To observe how members reach their goal.

Description   Members divide into two groups of equal size and stand facing each other with their backs against the wall. At a given signal players in one group try to reach the opposite wall, while members of the other group try to stop them.

Process the experience. How do players individually or jointly attempt to reach the wall, or prevent their opponents from reaching it?

Technique: *Aggression and Self-Assertion III*

Counseling Intention   To make one's interests clear and assert self against the group.

Description   All members except one link arms and form a tight circle. The lone member stands in the middle and tries to get out. Process how the member tried to get out. Does he or she use persuasive argument, bribes, or physical force?

Technique: *The Human Machine*

Counseling Intention   To observe aggression and self-assertion.

Description   The group has to produce a machine. First, members choose an inventor who has the idea for the machine, and an engineer and several workers who build the machine out of the rest of the members according to the inventor's instructions.

The machine is then set into motion; members accompany and punctuate their movement with noises. One player then destroys the machine.

Process the experience. Who chooses to destroy the machine? How does he or she do it? How do group members react to the destruction? Do they defend themselves, try to stay together, or allow it to happen?

Technique: *The Pushing Encounter*

Counseling Intention   To observe aggression and self-assertion.

Description   Two players stand facing each other; they place the palms of their hands together and clench their fingers. At a given signal they try to push each other backward, away from the spot where they are standing. They may break off the struggle any time they choose.

Process
- Why is the struggle broken off—because of exhaustion, satisfaction, sense of inferiority, or resignation?
- How does the member who gave up feel?
- How does the winner behave?

> *Perspective for the Therapist: On blame*
>
> *We create the situations and then we give our power away by blaming the other person for our frustration. No person, no place and no thing has any power over us for "WE" are the only thinkers in our mind.*
>
> Louise Hay
> *You Can Heal Your Life,* 1987, p. 1

CONCLUSION

Our country is becoming more and more culturally diverse. Increasing diversity often encourages intolerance, as well as ethnic and racial profiling. It is estimated that, by the year 2050, no more than 50% of the population will be of Anglo ancestry. In addition, advances in technologies have increased each person's ability and likelihood of interacting with people of cultural backgrounds quite different from his or her own. To understand how many different subcultures exist in the United States one must consider that subcultures exist according to gender, socioeconomic status, age, race, religion, ethnic heritage, and sexual orientation. The difficulty for many subcultures is that if they do not have the same physical characteristics, values, customs, or beliefs as the dominant culture, their culture is devalued and members may even be oppressed or subjugated by the dominant cultural structure.

Chapter 12

Stress and Stress Reduction Techniques

The twenty-first century is the age of noise. The din penetrates the mind filling it with a babble of distraction—new items, mutually irrelevant bits of information, blasts of music, continually repeated doses of drama that bring no catharsis merely create a craving for daily emotional purging.

Aldous Huxley
Silence, Liberty & Peace, 1946, p 24

THE LINK BETWEEN LIFE STRESS AND PSYCHOPATHOLOGY

The National Institute of Mental Health has concluded that the link of "life stress" to psychopathology is well supported in the literature. The current quest, however, is to delineate how life stress impairs one's health and well-being. As a conceptual framework, Klerman and Weissman (1985, p. 56) provided a working definition of stress and its related nomenclature:

* *Stress*—hypothesized psychological, emotional, or physical changes as the result of the stressor.
* *Stressors*—stressful environmental changes, particularly circumstances requiring changes in patterns, routines, or interactions.
* *Stress response*—the behavioral, psychological, emotional, physical, or cognitive responses experienced in an attempt to cope, adapt, or survive.
* *Adverse health consequences*—increased susceptibility to physical illness or emotional disorders.

333

TABLE 12.1
The Equation of Emotional or Behavioral Disorder

Incidence of emotional or behavioral disorder = Stress + Physical, emotional,
social, and cognitive vulnerability

Coping skill + Social support + Self-esteem

Stressors become a causative or moderating influence, interacting with personal dispositions and factors in the social environment (Dohrenwend & Dohrenwend, 1985). Stress management, stress reduction, and stress relief procedures are viable intervention strategies. An individual's risk of psychopathology is intensified by the presence of debilitating stress and physical handicaps and is diminished if an individual has reliable coping skills, a positive sense of self, and perceives the existence of social support in the immediate environment. From the perspective of the individual, wellness can be assessed with the equation shown in Table 12.1. There also is an environmental-centered analogue equation, shown in Table 12.2, that focuses on risk of psychopathology in a population (Albee, 1982).

Psychopathology is less likely to occur in a population if there are socialization practices that teach and promote social competence, supportive resources available in the environment, and opportunities available for people to form constructive, positive social bonds and identities connected with the mainstream of society. Both equations are interdependent and reflect the paramount need for stress-related interventions that are multidimensional (Elias, 1989). Some symptoms of stress are found in Table 12.3.

STRESS OF THERAPEUTIC WORK

Psychotherapy often creates stress for practitioners. Among the most stressful aspects of therapy according to Hellman, Morrison, and Abramowitz (1986) were doubt about one's effectiveness, problems in scheduling, becoming too involved

TABLE 12.2
Likelihood of Emotional Disorder in a Population

Likelihood of disorder in a population = Stressors + Risk factors in the environment

Socialization practices + Social support resources + Opportunities for connectedness

TABLE 12.3
Symptoms of Stress

Nervous tic	Constipation or diarrhea
Muscular aches	Decreased libido
Increase or decrease in appetite	High blood pressure
Increased smoking	Dry mouth
Sleep disorder	Irritability
Increased perspiration	Lethargy or fatigue
Stammering or stuttering	Cold, clammy hands
Nausea or gastrointestinal distress	Depression
Grinding teeth	Fear, panic, or anxiety
Headaches	Restlessness
Skin disorders	Other coping manifestations
Crying spells	

in work, becoming depleted, and having difficulties in managing relationships with clients. The five types of client behaviors that cause the most stress for therapists were suicide threats, resistance, expression of negative feelings, passive-aggressive behavior, and psychopathological acts.

Concurrently, the growing concern for American youth over adolescent suicide, substance abuse, alienation, depression, family dysfunction, teen pregnancy, HIV/AIDS, violence, and escalating dropout rates demonstrates the critical need for responsible adults to establish close, caring relationships with young people. Debilitating stress accompanies all of these conditions, which in turn foster adverse health consequences (William T. Grant Commission on Work, Family, and Citizenship, 1988).

Perspective for the Therapist: On the therapeutic role

In the face of incredible emotional arousal—anger, sadness, panic, despondency, conflict—the therapist is expected to maintain neutrality, detachment, frustration tolerance, empathy, alertness, interest, and impulse control without feeling depleted, deprived, and isolated. As if such demands are not enough, we are also supposed to be charming and invigorated by the time we get home. Since our friends and family know what we do for a living, they have greater expectations that we will be inhumanly patient, forgiving, and compromising during those instances when they have us locked in battle.

Sigmund Freud
*The Complete Letters of Sigmund Freud to Wilhelm Fliess,
1887–1904,* edited by J. M. Masson, 1985, p. 104

IMPROVING RELATIONSHIPS WITH OUR ENVIRONMENT

Seasonal Affective Disorder

Seasonal affective disorder (SAD) is a mood disorder characterized by recurrent fall and winter depressions alternating with nondepressed periods in spring and summer (Rosenthal, Sack, Gillin, Lewy, Goodwin, Davenport, Mueller, Newsome, & Wehr, 1984). Experts believe 10 million Americans may be severely afflicted with these symptoms, whereas 25 million others may suffer to a milder degree. Rosenthal and Wehr (1987) provide the following operational criteria for a diagnosis of seasonal affective disorder:

1. A history of at least one major depressive episode, according to Spitzer, Endicott, and Robins (1978).
2. Regularly occurring fall-winter depressions (at least two occurring during consecutive winters) alternating with nondepressed periods during spring and summer.
3. No other major psychiatric disorder.
4. No psychosocial variables accounting for the regular changes in mood.

These criteria have been modified and included in DSM-IV (American Psychiatric Association, 1994) as "seasonal pattern," a descriptor that may qualify any recurrent mood disorder. Seasonal depressions are accompanied by a distinctive constellation of symptoms such as hypersomnia, overeating, carbohydrate craving, weight gain, fatigue, and social withdrawal. It is triggered by light deficiency and responds to a novel type of treatment, phototherapy. Researchers have shown a strong association between the seasons and the incidence of depression, mania, suicides, and suicide attempts.

Phototherapy: Light as a Therapeutic Agent

Bright artificial light has antidepressant effects on SAD. The effectiveness of light in treating SAD was first shown by researchers at the National Institute of Mental Health in the early 1980s. Clients who are being treated for SAD typically receive two hours of phototherapy per day. The light source most frequently used has been full-spectrum fluorescent light (Vitalite®, Six Powertwist®). Eight regular 40-watt tubes inserted into a rectangular metal fixture, approximately 2 × 4 feet, with a reflecting surface behind them, also may work. The light intensity should be 5 to 10 times brighter than ordinary room lighting. Clients simply sit close to the light box with lights on and eyes open.

Rosenthal, Carpenter, and James (1986) suggested that bright light might exert its antidepressant effects by the suppression of melatonin secretion. Lewy, Sack, and Miller (1987) have suggested that light exerts its antidepressant effects by means of its circadian phase-shifting properties, a theory that continues to be researched. In addition, it appears as though certain individuals have a neuro-chemical vulnerability (perhaps genetically determined), which, in the absence of adequate environmental light exposure, produces the behavioral changes seen in SAD.

Bright light, probably acting via the eye and presumably retinohypothalamic projections, appears capable of reversing this biochemical abnormality if the light is of high enough intensity and is used regularly and for sufficient duration (Rosenthal, 1989, p. 3). Bright artificial light may be capable of shifting the timing of circadian rhythms in humans, which may be helpful in conditions of abnormal circadian rhythms, such as jet lag, shift work fatigue, or chronic reactions as in delayed sleep phase syndrome and SAD. Scientists at the National Institute of Mental Health have demonstrated successful treatment using full spectrum fluorescent lights placed on the floor. Bright light relieves SAD symptoms through alterations in hormone production and body chemistry.

TECHNIQUES FOR MANAGING STRESS

Techniques like progressive muscle relaxation training (PMRT), biofeedback, self-hypnosis, rhythmic breathing, and exercise can elicit the relaxation response. Relaxation training can reduce physiological arousal and attenuate the effects of chronic stress. Various meditative techniques for therapeutic purposes have been studied (Benson, 1974; Goldman, 1976; Goldman & Schwartz, 1976; Heider, 1985; Maharishi, 1972).

Meditation

By relaxing the body and calming the mind, meditation seeks to alleviate the harmful effects of tension and stress—factors that are known to aggravate a number of medical conditions. Although meditation has its roots in Eastern religious practices, its health benefits are independent of its spiritual aspects. Meditation has measurable effects on the pattern of electrical impulses flowing through the brain. Studies with an electroencephalograph (EEG) show that it boosts the intensity of the alpha waves associated with quiet, receptive states to levels not even seen during sleep. Other studies show increased synchronization of brain waves between the two hemispheres of the brain during meditation, lower levels of stress hormones, and improved circulation. Levels of lactic acid, a potential by-product of tension and anxiety, drop after meditation. When practiced for an extended period of time, meditation has also been found to reduce oxygen consumption, slow the heart rate, and bring down blood pressure. Devotees of meditation often claim that it improves their memory and other mental abilities, protects them from disease, and reduces their use of alcohol and drugs.

The practice of meditation can be categorized by the dimension of human experience: (1) intellectual, as in trying to achieve a greater mental consciousness of reality; (2) emotional, as in trying to expand to greater awareness of positive emotion; (3) physical, as in trying to become completely absorbed in physical movement; and (4) action, as in the practice of a particular skill or technique (LeShan, 1974). Weinhold (1987) listed the benefits of reaching an altered state of consciousness:

- To experience a state of ecstasy.
- To gain spiritual insights.
- To escape from pain and suffering.
- To obtain new creative ideas.
- To improve health or alleviate illness.
- To increase sensory acuity. (pp. 14–17)

Meditation takes on many forms. One simple method is to select a quiet place for a few minutes a day for prolonged reflective thought or contemplation and clear one's mind of all conscious thoughts and concentrate on a particular sound, image, object, or word. Some approaches to meditation emphasize restricting of consciousness, whereas others stress consciousness expansion. Experienced meditators are able to produce major changes in their physiological functioning such as reduced heart rate, slowed respiration, and changes in brain waves. Ultimately the outcome is to reach an inner harmony, a peace within one's self through the use of positive self-suggestions.

Technique: *Meditation*

Counseling Intention   To reduce stress among clients; to empower them to gain control over self-defeating behaviors that manifest a chronic stress response; to evoke the relaxation technique with meditation (Devi, 1963, p. 126).

Description   The client uses a candle as a fixation point.

1. Now keep your eyes upon the flame and don't let them wander.
2. Start breathing rhythmically.
3. Next close your eyes, and try to retain the impression of the flame. You can

visualize it clearly, hold the picture, but if the light eludes you, open your eyes for another look at the light.
4. Close them again and see if you are able to envision the flame this time. Repeat this until you are able to capture and hold the impression.

If you are still unsuccessful, try the same procedure again the following day, and continue trying until you have succeeded. Do not hurry or force anything—do not try too intensively. Remember that it is most important to remain inwardly relaxed and motionless.

Technique: *Harvard Meditation for Relaxation*

Counseling Intention   To evoke the relaxation response using the Harvard meditation technique (Benson, 1974).

Description   Have the client do the following:
1. Select a quiet environment where you will not be distracted or disturbed.
2. Select two times during the day when you can afford 10 or 20 minutes of uninterrupted time. For some people a good time is before breakfast or before dinner. A particularly good time is when you are experiencing stress.
3. Find a comfortable chair, or sit in a position in which you feel at ease
4. Loosen any tight clothing; take off your shoes or related clothing that may be uncomfortable.
5. Close your eyes. Begin to relax by thinking of relaxing while successively thinking about your feet, legs, trunk, body, arms, neck, and head.
6. Breathe through your nose and become aware of your breathing.
7. Say a simple one- or two-syllable word to yourself as you breathe out. Almost any word will do. Words some people like are *gohum, carim, shaim,* or *sharin.* A word without meaning works best.
8. Breathe easily and naturally. Ignore worries, ideas, or anxieties as you meditate. Keep repeating your word. After you finished meditating, sit quietly for a minute with your eyes closed then with your eyes open.

Technique: *Increasing Sensory Awareness*

Counseling Intention   To heighten sensory awareness.

Description   Have the client do the following:

1. Go to a location where you feel comfortable, preferably outside.
2. Focus your eyes on an object—a tree, a rock, a picture—as if you have never seen it before.
3. Become aware of its size, shape, color, and texture.
4. Now allow it to fade away and let the background come into focus.
5. Repeat this with other objects or, if you are calm, stay there and let your mind and senses rest.
6. Focus your attention on listening to the sounds around you. Which sounds are constant? Which are intermittent? Be aware of their intensity, pitch, and rhythm.

Try repeating these experiments every day for at least 10 minutes. Choose different settings and objects to contemplate. Active observing and listening allows the client to become more aware of odors, tastes, and textures as well. Heightening your sensory awareness is a form of meditation that will not only help you to relax but will also allow you to appreciate more fully the world around you.

Technique: *Evoking Relaxation Techniques Autogenically*

Counseling Intention   To evoke the relaxation technique autogenically.

Description   With autogenic or self-directed relaxation techniques, the client is urged to relieve tension by saying that he or she feels calm, relaxed, or warm. The client is guided to use his or her creative awareness and repeat self-statements as he or she feels and experiences deep relaxation.

The following outline of self-statements (to repeat at least two times each) are directed to the client's entire body, beginning with legs and arms:

1. Slow breathing. "I take a slow deep breath."
2. Slight tension, then release. "I feel slight tension in my foot, and now I am completely relaxed."
3. Feeling warm and heavy. "My foot feels warm and heavy."
4. Flow of warmth. "Warmth flows from my arm to my chest."
5. Rate of heartbeat. "My heartbeat is calm and regular."
6. Quiet mind. "My mind is quiet and still."
7. Separation from surroundings. "I withdraw my mind from my environment. I feel calm quiet, still. My thoughts are turned completely inward."
8. Peace and harmony. "My body and my mind are in perfect harmony."
9. Closing statement. "I am now calm, quiet, and renewed with energy."

Autogenic or self-directed relaxation can be used in mental training (Zilbergeld & Lazarus, 1987); for tension release leading to better sleep; in management of stress and increased efficiency (Carrington, 1977); in treatment of neurotic, compulsive, and depressive disorders (Romen, 1981); and in achieving a state of optimum health (Pelletier, 1980).

Biofeedback Sensory Awareness Techniques

Technique: *Self-Management through Biofeedback*

Counseling Intention To integrate self-management through biofeedback.

Description Biofeedback refers to a continuous aural or visual report of changes in bodily reactions brought about by changes in thoughts and emotions (Marcer, 1986). After they have been provided information about a bodily state frequently enough, clients can learn to recognize the link between thoughts, feelings, and physical reactions. Self-management is a technique developed to empower people to feel better by changing destructive habits or inefficient patterns of coping into positive behaviors.

It is essentially a step-by-step process for self-control and makes use of many of the same techniques used by behavior therapists. Biofeedback involves providing people with information about physiological process of which they are normally aware. With the benefit of this information, people can learn to bring under voluntary control physiological conditions that may be harmful to their health. Biofeedback training can be thought of as a three-step learning process:

1. Developing increased awareness of body states.
2. Learning voluntary control over these states.
3. Learning to use these new skills in everyday life.

The goal is for individuals to eventually learn to exercise this voluntary control without the use of biofeedback instruments so that they can apply their newly acquired skills to their daily lives in a manner that allows them to control their stress responses. From this perspective, biofeedback is basically a return of responsibility for one's health to the individual rather than to a caregiver.

Biofeedback and relaxation training techniques have found wide application and success in the treatment of anxiety states, diabetes, tension headaches, and migraine headaches. Biofeedback and relaxation techniques also are being applied in treating such varied conditions as hypertension, cardiac arrhythmia, stroke, epilepsy, asthma, psoriasis, chronic pain, and insomnia.

Technique: *Progressive Muscle Relaxation Training*

Counseling Intention   To evoke the relaxation response through progressive muscle relaxation training (PMRT).

Description   PMRT is perhaps the most widely used of all cognitive-behavioral interventions. It is a procedure to enhance the ability to learn to relax by making the individual aware of the sensations of tensing and relaxing major muscle groups. Bernstein and Borkover (1973) provided the following directions for progressive relaxation.

Steps for Progressive Relaxation
1. Make sure that you will not be interrupted.
2. Lie down on a comfortable bed or couch, flat on your back, arms at your sides, and legs uncrossed.
3. Close your eyes gradually over a period of three to four minutes.
4. Spend only a few minutes at recognizing tensions in your muscles.
5. Never contract a muscle to relax it.
6. Do not shift your position, or try to hold still. Just let go.

If any step seems difficult, it is probably because you are holding a muscle under tension somewhere. Sensations should seem to fall away if you are relaxing properly. Relaxing muscles often feel warm at first; later, possibly they feel cool, tingly, or have no sensation.

Note: Straining and tensing your muscles before relaxing them is not progressive relaxation. In progressive relaxation, the client starts by placing enough tension on a muscle so that he or she can recognize and learn when to let go. Muscle relaxation is passive, a letting-go of all tension.

Technique: *Evoking Relaxation through Tension-Inattention*

Counseling Intention   To evoke the relaxation response through tension-inattention techniques.

Description   Steps for the tension-inattention relaxation technique were developed by White and Fadiman (1976). This technique can be learned in three to four practice sessions and assist in daily situations.

Exercise 1
1. Sit at the edge of your bed or floor.

2. Close your eyes and keep them closed for all six exercises.
3. Let your shoulders and neck be as loose as possible.
4. Rotate your head slowly in a clockwise direction four times, making the muscles still more loose.
5. Reverse direction and rotate your head in a counterclockwise direction four times.

Exercise 2
1. Lie down and raise your right foot about 12 inches.
2. Make your leg muscles as stiff and tense as possible.
3. Visualize the muscles in your leg from toes to hip. Keep your attention on them and try to make them tight and tired.
4. Hold your leg up as long as you can. Let it get so tired that you can't hold it up anymore.
5. Let your leg go completely limp and loose as you let it drop quickly.

Exercise 3
1. Raise your left leg and divert all your attention to it.
2. Now repeat all the steps for exercise two using your left leg.

Exercise 4
1. Raise your right arm, fist clenched in a salute position.
2. Stiffen and tighten the muscles.
3. Keep your thoughts on this arm only.
4. Let your arm fall limp to your side when it is completely tired.

Exercise 5
1. Immediately raise your left arm and repeat all steps as in exercise four.

Exercise 6
1. Imagine a circle about four feet in diameter on the ceiling above you.
2. Keeping your eyes closed, follow this circle with your eyes four times in a clockwise direction. Do this slowly.
3. Reverse direction and follow the circle in a counterclockwise direction.
4. Imagine a square instead of a circle.
5. Go around the square four times in each direction.
6. Lie for a few minutes and enjoy the relaxation.
7. Divert your attention from your eyes by thinking of anything pleasant.

PMRT has demonstrated effectiveness in treating insomnia, asthma, tension, headache, muscular tension, hypertension, increased heart rate, chronic anxiety, and phobias.

Perspective for the Therapist: On stress

The average American will spend 3 years sitting in meetings, 5 years waiting in lines, over 17,000 hours playing telephone tag, 4,000 hours stopped at a red light, and a lifetime trying to wind-down.

Anonymous

Technique: *Evoking Relaxation through Yoga*

Counseling Intention   To evoke the relaxation response though basic yoga.

Description   Yoga is a Hindu practice that can take any of five forms: (1) raja yoga, meditation through contemplation on universal truths; (2) jnana yoga, meditation on the nature of self; (3) karma yoga, active yoga in the service of others; and (4) bhaki yoga, meditation using prayer and chanting.

The fifth form of yoga used most in the Western world is hatha yoga. It is more often used as a form of exercise to promote good health, to alleviate stress, to energize, and to relax the body and mind. Maitland (1975) provided the following suggestions for basic yoga:

1. Let the movements compress or expand your lungs.
2. Do one, two, or three repetitions of each movement.
3. Move in both directions, clockwise and counterclockwise.
4. Keep your attention on the muscles under tension.
5. Hold your position until your muscles are extended.
6. Maintain a continuous awareness of your body as you proceed through your exercises.

Technique: *Changing One's Awareness through Silva Mind Control*

Counseling Intention   To change one's awareness from everyday consciousness via Silva Mind Control.

Description   Silva Mind Control is a process of changing one's present awakened consciousness (beta) to a lower frequency consciousness (alpha) for better problem solving and increased memory, efficiency, and creativity. The technique "uses the mind to mind itself: by first physical and mental relaxation, then affirmation, visualization, and anchoring" (Silva & Stone, 1983, p. 93). The relaxation method consists of turning the eyes upward and counting back from 10 to 1. The anchor is to put three fingers together. The vision process consists of seeing the situation first as it is; then to see the situation in the process of positive change, viewing the second image on the left to activate the right brain; and finally to see the situation resolved (Silva & Stone, 1983). This strategy has been used to accomplish personal goals, to maintain energy and enthusiasm.

Perspective for the Therapist: On breaking points

It's not the large
things that
send a man to the
madhouse . . . no, it's the
continuing series of
small tragedies
that send a man to the madhouse

not the death of his love
but a shoelace that snaps
with no time left.

Charles Bukowski
The Days Run Like Wild Horses, 1983, p. 24

Technique: *Creating Experiences through Visualization*

Counseling Intention   To use visualization to create experience in one or more sensory modes.

Description   Visualization uses the imagination to create experience. Receptive visualization works to reduce the analytical activity of the brain, allowing subconscious thoughts, emotions, ideas, or insights to emerge. A classic example of this type of visualization is having a solution to a complex problem emerge in a state of quiet. Active visualization works by giving form to thought (Gwain, 1982). An example of active visualization is creating an image of a new job or the successful transition through a stressful period. Repeated visualization works to change one's view of self. The most powerful visualizations are specific, tangible, repeated, and self-rewarding.

Technique: *Enhancing One's Mind, Behavior, and Beliefs through Affirmations*

Counseling Intention   To direct one's mind, behavior, and beliefs through positive affirmations.

Description   Inherently, beliefs present in one's mind create emotions, which influence actions, which in turn influence one's outlook on life, which fosters negative or positive self-talk. The intensity of the results or effects on one's life will be proportional to the depth of the belief and the intensity of the feeling (Helmstetter, 1986; Robbins, 1986). Changing negative beliefs and self-talk to positive beliefs and self-talk can change the circumstance of a client's life. A positive affirmation such as "I deserve this and much, much more" replaces "I'll never amount to anything."

Imagery Techniques

Imagery provides a way to communicate with the subconscious mind. When one "sees" an image in the mind, it is collaboration between the conscious and subconscious. The image seen will always be different from what others see, because it is formed from one's own memories and experiences. Imagery is like a personalized, guided dream with emotions. Everyone is capable of using imagery, but like other skills, it must be practiced. Imagery is not just visualization—it involves other senses (taste, smell, hearing, and touch) as well. Scientists are discovering that the mind actually helps maintain balance by controlling the immune system. Susceptibility to diseases increases when the normal balance becomes disturbed. Imagery helps create and maintain this balance while reducing stress. Many scientists believe that when you visualize the problems within your body, the unconscious mind then triggers your body's natural defenses.

As a counseling technique imagery can be used as a primary psychological tool for assessment, intervention, and enhancement of human potential. Over the past two decades imagery has been cited as an effective treatment medium for a wide spectrum of psychological maladies: uncovering emotional blocks or inhibiting them (Anderson, 1980); reducing anxiety, improving memory and achievement, increasing self-esteem (Lazarus, 1977; Sheikh & Sheikh, 1985); and relieving insomnia (Sheikh, 1976), depression (Schultz, 1978), obesity (Bornstein & Sipprelle, 1973), sexual malfunctioning, chronic pain (Jaffe & Bresler, 1980), and psychosomatic illness (Lazarus, 1977; Shorr, 1974; Simonton, Mathews-Simonton, & Creighton, 1978).

Currently, there is a renewed interest in imagery as a tool for counseling, with the shifting paradigm away from strict adherence to schools of counseling and psychotherapy toward a more integrated cognitive-behavioral approach. Furthermore, contemporary developments in brain research and health psychology have legitimized nontraditional approaches (Korn & Johnson, 1983). Imagery is a natural function of the human mind and does not have to be taught.

Witner and Young (1985, p. 187) outlined the areas in which imagery can be used to expand human possibilities:

- Increasing awareness of self and others.
- Future planning and career or life-style development.
- Gaining control over undesirable behavior.
- Treating illnesses.
- Improving learning, skill development, and performance.
- Reducing stress and enhancing health.
- Enhancing creativity and problem solving in everyday living.

The clinical use of imagery as a tool for therapeutic intervention was outlined by Sheikh and Jordan (1983):

1. Imagery can act as a source of motivation for future behavior. Guided imagery can produce fresh data and new solutions. Goals and solutions rehearsed through imagery during therapy can be applied more easily outside the therapeutic setting.
2. Imagery can facilitate the access to important events occurring early in one's life. Early recollections are a therapeutic component of a more Adlerian perspective to ascertain individual attitudes, beliefs, and motives.
3. Imagery provides a focus that can uncover very intense affective states or emotional reactions, fostering greater communication by moving the discussion to a more meaningful level. It also facilitates the expression of more difficult feelings. Through imagery, empathy and interpersonal relationship skills can be developed.
4. Imagery can be used to resolve dilemmas by circumventing defenses or inhibitions that may occur in verbal blockage, as well as to produce therapeutic change in the absence of any interpretation by the therapist or intellectual insight by the client.

Witmer and Young (1985) also outline a number of prerequisites for imagery development that can increase the effectiveness:

- *Readiness.* A quiet environment with few distractions, a comfortable position, and a mental device that functions as a point of focus—such as a sound, word, phrase, or a spot at which to gaze—are helpful. All imagery exercises should begin by creating a safe place in the client's imagery world (e.g., a warm beach, a special room, a quiet path). If images become too anxiety provoking or uncomfortable, the client can return to his or her safe place to process or work through threatening images.

- *Vividness.* A certain degree of vividness is essential to creating images. The greatest effectiveness is reported when multiple sensory experiences are experienced (e.g., visual, sound, or emotional components).
- *Controllability.* Imagery control ensures therapeutic effectiveness. A technique that assists in controlling the imagery is cueing—giving the person an instructional set to focus on, either the desired outcome or the process. When the outcome image is established, the mind intuitively creates a script or scenario to achieve the imagined outcome.

Cautela and McCullough (1978) concluded that control can be improved further by emphasizing to clients that (1) the imagery is theirs—they create it and they are free to change it; (2) imagining the desired response inhibits an unwanted response; and (3) keeping a log of incidents and accompanying images that evoke tension will enable them to identify or modify subsequent images.

Technique: *Wise Person Exercise*

Counseling Intention   To enable the client to experience through imagination a conversation with a wise person (Witmer & Young, 1987, p. 8).

Description   The image that appears may be a stranger, a friend, or a spiritual being. Relax and let go of all tension and worrisome thoughts. Allow the face or figure of a very wise, loving person to appear. You may ask a question. Listen and be receptive to whatever comes. You may want to hold a conversation. The wise person may have a special message for you, something you did not ask.

If you are willing to receive this, tell the wise person and wait for a response. Allow yourself to see the situation as the wise person sees it. Now see how this fits or makes sense in your life. It is time to leave the wise person. You can return at any time and find guidance and strength.

Technique: *Visualization for Physical and Mental Relaxation*

Counseling Intention   To enable the client to gain physical and mental relaxation through visualization (Witmer & Young, 1987, p. 9).

Description   Suggest the following to the client:

1. Visualize your body relaxing by using a rag doll image.
2. Visualize your favorite quiet place.
3. Blow away bad feelings and thoughts like bubbles that break or float way.
4. Imagine the light and warmth of sunlight entering your body and flowing to all parts, bringing relaxation.
5. Visualize a trip and scenes from nature (e.g., mountains, beach, woods, field, or stream).
6. Use phases that elicit heaviness, warmth, and an inner quietness.

Technique: *Imagery for Sensory Expansion*

Counseling Technique   To use imagery to deepen concentration and profound relaxation.

Description   After achieving a relaxed state, practice the following image:

Woods Scene (Fezler, 1990)

You are walking through a forest of pine trees on a beautiful summer day. See that the sky above is brilliant blue. Feel the warmth from the sun against your face. Hear the soft, low rustle of the wind through the pine boughs. Blue jays fly from branch to branch, sounding out in loud, high cackles.

Reach up and pick a pine needle. Break it in half. A drop of fluid falls from the needle onto your palm. Sniff the drop. It smells of bitter pine. Lick the drop. Taste the bitter flavor of pine. Now you come to the edge of the forest. Pass into an orchard of apples, brilliant red in the sunlight, against deep green foliage. Pick an apple. Take a jack-knife from your pocket and slice the apple in half. Beads of apple juice sparkle on the metal of the knife blade. Sniff the sweet scent of apple. Carefully lick the juice. Sweet taste of apple. Next you pass into a grove of lemon trees, yellow fruit in chartreuse leaves gleaming in the summer sun. Pick a lemon. Peel it. Smell the sour lemony fragrance of the rind. Bite into the lemon. The sour lemon juice squirts into your mouth. Your cheeks pucker, the saliva flows, as you suck the sour lemon juice. And you continue walking.

Come out of the lemon grove onto a sandy ocean beach. Dazzling turquoise water stretches as far as you can see. Smell the salt in the air. Lick your lips. You can taste the salt from the ocean spray.

> *Walk out onto the hot, dry sand. Move closer to the shimmering sea, standing where water has been splashed. Remove your shoes and socks. Feel the cold, wet sand beneath your bare feet.*
>
> *Walk back up on the beach. Lie down in the warm sand. A gentle breeze begins covering you with sand. Feel it dry and light . . . Safe secure, protected, in a warm cocoon of sand.*
>
> *Now the sun is setting on the ocean. The sky is a throbbing orange, turning fiery red on the horizon. As the sun sinks into the water, you are enveloped in a deep violet twilight. Look up at the night sky. It is a brilliant starry night. The sound of the waves, the taste and smell of the salt, the sea, the sky, and you; and you feel yourself carried upward and outward into space, one with the universe.* (pp. 99–100)

Perspective for the Therapist: On the value of self

One important element which helps people locked in their loneliness is the conviction that their real self . . . the inner self, the self that is hidden from others . . . is one which no one could love. It is easy enough to track the origin of the feeling. The spontaneous feelings of a child, his real attitudes, have so often been disapproved of by parents and others that he has come to interject this same attitude himself, and to feel that his spontaneous reactions and the self he truly is, constitute a person whom no one could love.

Carl Rogers

Technique: *Determining One's Sensory Modality*

Counseling Intention   To enable the client to explore his or her sensory imagery.

Description   Mental images can be visual, auditory, proprioceptive (feelings and skin sensations), kinesthetic (body movements), or olfactory and gustatory (smell and taste). Although visual imagery is dominant for most people, many people respond more readily to auditory, kinesthetic, or olfactory images. Weinhold (1987, p. 9) developed the following exercise to determine one's sensory modality:

1. Visual
   • Close your eyes and imagine all the colors in a box of paints or crayons—pink, orange, yellow, purple, brown, white, red, and green.
   • Close your eyes and imagine yourself walking or driving through a familiar street. Be aware of all the things that you see.

- Close your eyes a take a trip through your own house or apartment; see everything you can in each room.
2. Proprioceptive
   - Close your eyes and imagine the feel of the water on your body as you take a bath or a shower. Imagine an egg breaking in your hand; feel the slipperiness of it. Imagine holding a snowball in your bare hands, and imagine the wind nipping at your nose and ears.
3. Auditory
   - Close your eyes and imagine a church bell ringing. Imagine an orchestra or group playing or singing a favorite tune. Imagine the sound of an emergency siren.
4. Kinesthetic
   - Imagine yourself swinging on a playground swing or going in a circle on a merry-go-round.
   - Imagine yourself climbing a hill with a backpack on your back.
   - Imagine yourself dancing or playing some sport.
5. Olfactory and Gustatory
   - Imagine yourself ready to sit down to Thanksgiving dinner.
   - Imagine tasting honey or bananas on your toothpaste.
   - Imagine smelling your favorite cologne or perfume.

Guided imagery is most helpful in developing cognitive flexibility, imagination, and creativity. Zilbergeld and Lazarus (1987) found that their clients have experienced success in using visualization to deal with stressful situations and to accomplish their goals. It also can be used to rehearse mentally for events, to imagine alternative futures, to synthesize facts, and to visualize getting well.

Technique: *Favorite Quiet Place*

Counseling Intention   To help learn how to relax through imagination.

Description   Repeat to the client the following:

> *No matter where you are, you can always go to a special place in your mind. Picture a place, real or imagined, where you feel safe, calm, and happy. Close your eyes and go to that place. See yourself as free to do whatever you want. Notice everything around you. Hear the sounds. Feel what is happening to your body. Just enjoy this feeling. You can go to this place to rest, think, be alone, and feel good, no matter where you are. Slowly return to the place where your body is. Gently open your eyes. The place will always be there for your return.*

Technique: *Creative Problem Solving*

Counseling Intention   To develop problem-solving strategies through visualization.

Description   Repeat to the client the following:

Try to imagine your mind as a movie or television screen. You are the producer, actor, and viewer, all at the same time. You can allow pictures to appear spontaneously on this screen without consciously willing or controlling them.

Step 1: Relaxing. Begin to free your mind of distractions by closing your eyes or gazing at a spot in front of you. Relax your body from your head to your toes. Pay attention to your breathing, take a deep breath or two, and let go of your tension each time you breathe out. Your mind is calm and clear. You are ready to turn your attention to pictures on the screen of your mind.

Step 2: Spontaneous Imagery. Allow images or pictures to come to your mind. Let them come and go. Now picture a problem or situation that has been puzzling you. Do not force yourself to look for an answer. Just see a clear picture of the situation or problem. Open your mind to possible answers and solutions. Let them come and go. Keep picturing the problem and solution, and then wait. You will know whether one of the pictures fits your question or situation. It will feel right and you will have a tingle of satisfaction. It may be an answer to a problem.

Step 3: Directed Imagery. Continue feeling relaxed and quiet. Now you are directing the pictures. You will take charge. Put the problem or situation on your screen. Explore in your mind's eye ways you might answer the question that appears on your screen. Notice how the story ends. Create another story with a different ending. You are trying different ways to reach a solution. You see yourself doing things to find out whether they work. Store these pictures in your memory for later use. If no ideas or answers appeared, be satisfied that you were able to picture the problem. The answer may come later. Write your ideas, draw them, or tell someone else so you will remember.

When processing, sometimes answers come immediately, but other times they may need time to develop over a few days or months. All problems and questions must be explored, however, so that the mind can consider alternative and potential solutions. "Solutions to problems often are inhibited because of restrictive or convergent thinking that is emphasized in seeking the prescribed right-wrong, ready-made answer. Thinking about possibilities or divergent thought can be encouraged by picturing oneself trying a solution and considering all the possible consequences" (Witmer & Young, 1987, p. 46).

Technique: *Stress Management—Quieting Response (QR)*

Counseling Intention To provide a systematic plan to eliminate or greatly reduce stressors.

Description Quieting response (QR) is a systematic, practical technique that can be used any time. It can empower a client to gain control of a stress reaction within minutes of the event. Instruct the client to do the following:

1. Learn and practice the following steps: Recognize your stress symptoms (rapid breathing, heart palpitations, rapid heart beat, lump in throat, knot in stomach); breathe in slowly through the imaginary holes in the bottom of your feet (Byrum, 1989); begin to exhale; relax the jaw and lower tongue; permit warm air to leave through the imaginary holes in your feet; and imagine warmth and heaviness simultaneously with the exhalation as warm air descends through your neck, shoulders, arms, and chest.
2. Process why QR is an effective stress reduction technique and how it can be used in one's daily experiences.
3. Compare feelings of tension and relaxation in various muscle groups; use QR to initiate the relaxation state.

Daily Stress Reduction Tips

Naturally these will be times when these tips cannot be used, but one should try to gradually incorporate them in life where possible.

1. Add something beautiful to your life on a daily basis (e.g., flowers).
2. Do some enjoyable activities whenever possible.
3. Walk, work, and eat at a relaxed pace.
4. Take a short break after meals to relax.
5. If possible, go outside at least once per day and notice the simple things such as the weather and scenery.
6. During the day, whenever you remember, notice any tension in your body (jaw, neck, diaphragm, shoulders, etc.). Breathe deeply and gently stretch and relax any tense areas.

7. If you notice your mind racing or worrying about the past or future, take a minute to breath deeply and gently focus on something in the moment, such as your breath, the scenery, or birds.
8. Take breaks during the workday to relax.
9. Wear comfortable and loose clothing when possible. Take off your shoes when you can.
10. Avoid holding in feelings day after day, but instead find a safe place to feel, express, and embrace them.

   Some people find themselves falling back into excessively stressful habits from time to time. That is perfectly normal. Simply notice that change in a nonjudgmental way and move back to the stress reduction practices and tips that promote a healthy way of life.

Technique: *Draining—A Frustration Management Exercise*

Counseling Intention   To enhance participants' relaxation response (Glasgow, 1999).

Description   Have a small group of people tense their muscles and breath in:

1. They should then stay tense for five seconds.
2. They should start to relax, starting with the head and moving down to the feet, exhaling as they do so.
3. Repeat from steps 1 to 3 several times,
4. Once they have the knack, have them think of someone at whom they are angry or something that has frustrated them.
5. Have them tense up, thinking of the anger or frustration.
6. As they relax, tell them that the anger is draining out of them—that all emotion is leaking out of the tips of their toes and is now in a puddle at their feet.
7. Once they have drained the anger, they should stand aside, out of the puddle, and leave the anger behind.
8. Hold a discussion with the group to establish when it is appropriate to drain; have them describe how they feel; and discuss when it is wise to step aside from anger or frustration.

Technique: *Relieve Stress with the Pencil Drop*

Counseling Intention   To use an object to relieve stress (McKay & Fanning, 1999).

Description   Have participants close their eyes and get in a comfortable position.

When localized areas of high-pressure air meet low-pressure air they can spawn a whirlwind that sucks up dirt and trash and moves across the landscape spreading disorder and destruction.

When a high-pressure lifestyle meets a low ebb in energy level, an emotional whirlwind makes everything that is valued—loved ones, career, hopes, and dreams—seem like debris swirling around aimlessly. Before taking off across an emotional landscape spreading disorder and destruction, take a moment to relax and center.

When life seems like a whirlwind, the image of the calm center is important. At the exact center of a whirlwind, there is a spot of perfectly calm air. Self-talk should consist of the following: "I am the calm center of the whirlwind. I can take a moment to right myself, to return to center. At my core is a calm spot that does not turn with every gust of wind." Paradoxically, when you take your place as the calm center, the whirlwind slows, the dust settles, and your life seems more orderly and manageable.

An ordinary pencil can help find the calm center. This is something that can be done at a desk or table, when working on the bills or doing homework when there is a need to return to the calm center quickly and get on with work:

1. Pick up a pencil by the point end. Hold it very lightly between your thumb and fingertip, letting the eraser end hang down a couple of inches above the tabletop. Cradle the head in the other hand and get as comfortable as possible.
2. Breath slowly and concentrate.
3. When you are sufficiently relaxed, the pencil will slip out of your fingers and drop. That will be the sign to let go completely, to just relax and feel peaceful for two minutes.
4. Imagine the calm center of a whirlwind. Hear the cold wind whistling, everywhere but the calm center. The sun is shining. You are feeling warm and secure; imagine all cares and worries receding. The whirlwind expands and slows down. The calm center gets larger and more relaxed.
5. Continue breathing slowly, thinking about calming and relaxing all tight muscles. If a worry or doubt intrudes, think, "That's okay. I can let that go for now and relax. I'll just sit here, calm and centered, deeply, deeply relaxed."

6. Continue to enjoy the calm center for a couple of minutes. Then return to the task at hand with renewed energy, feeling calm, relaxed, and focused.

CONCLUSION

One of the most important things we can do for clients is teach them to manage stress. Stress is an unavoidable consequence of life. Fortunately, stress management is largely a learnable skill. One technique discussed to decrease the effects of stress is imagery and visualization. Thinking peaceful thoughts makes one feel relaxed. In imagining a peaceful place, clients will also distract themselves from stressful thoughts. This focus embraces the basic premise of cognitive-behavioral psychology, that feelings and behaviors are largely caused by thoughts. The best way to manage stress is to learn to change anxiety to concern. Concern means that the client has the skills and motivation to take care of real problems in life and avoid panic and anxiety. Changing feelings is largely a matter of learning to identify and change the upsetting thoughts that are the immediate cause of upset emotions.

Chapter 13

Trauma, Loss, Grief, and Post-Traumatic Stress Debriefing

Loss is a common experience that each person encounters during his or her lifetime. It does not discriminate for age, race, sex, education, economic status or nationality. Loss is a byproduct of being alive.

Kristi A. Dyer
Dealing with Death and Dying in Medical Education and Practice, 2001 (Reprinted with permission)

Nothing in life is perhaps more painful than experiencing the loss of a friend or a loved one. Even though most people experience varying degrees of loss, the grief cycle is not fully understood until it comes closer to the heart. When sudden death comes with no time for anticipation, many additional feelings are involved in the grief process. The grief work normally will be longer, lonelier, and more debilitating to lasting emotional stability because of the intensity of the anguish experienced when someone is taken suddenly or senselessly. Grief work is not a set of symptoms but rather a process of suffering that marks a transition from an old lifestyle to a new one, punctuated by numbness, denial, anger, depression, and eventually recovery. Post-traumatic loss debriefing offers a therapeutic structure to "work through" the experience of traumatic loss and accompanying stress. Talking about the death and related anxieties in a secure environment provides a means to "work through" the experience and serves to prevent destructive fantasy building. Because loss is so painful emotionally, however, our natural tendency (personally or professionally) is to avoid or to deny coming to terms with loss. Inherently, loss is a process that extends over time and more often than not has a lifelong impact.

TASKS OF MOURNING AND GRIEF COUNSELING

Life without death is meaningless . . . a picture without a frame.

John A. Wheeler

The aftermath of severe, or repeated trauma or prolonged trauma, and/or trauma that is not processed by the victim with sympathetic others, can lead to unhealthy adaptations in understanding the world, maintaining connections with others, and meeting needs in mature ways, as well as a disruption in central psychological assumption (cognitive schema) and memory processing (Nicholas & Forrester, 1999, p. 323). The tasks of mourning and grief counseling include the following:

- To accept the reality of the loss and to confront the fact that the person is dead. Initial denial and avoidance becomes replaced by the realization of the loss.
- To experience the pain of grief. It is essential to acknowledge and to work through this pain or it will manifest itself through self-defeating behavior(s).
- To adjust to an environment in which the deceased is missing. The survivor(s) must face the loss of the many roles the deceased person filled in their life.
- To withdraw emotional energy and reinvest it in another relationship. Initial grief reaction to loss may be to make a pact with oneself never to love again. One must become open to new relationships and opportunities.
- To accept the pain of loss when dealing with the memory of the deceased.
- To express sorrow, hostility, and guilt overtly, and to be able to mourn openly.
- To understand the intense grief reactions associated with the loss; for example, to recognize that such symptoms as startle reactions, including restlessness, agitation, and anxiety, may temporarily interfere with one's ability to initiate and maintain normal patterns of activity.
- To come to terms with anger, which often is generated toward the one who has died, toward self, or toward others—to redirect the sense of responsibility that somehow one should have prevented the death.

STRATEGIES TO PROCESS LOSS

The sudden, unexpected death by suicide or the sudden loss from an accidental death often produces a characteristic set of psychological and physiological responses among survivors. Persons exposed to traumatic events such as suicide or sudden loss often manifest the following stress reactions: irritability, sleep disturbances, anxiety, startle reactions, nausea, headaches, difficulty concentrating, confusion, fear, guilt, withdrawal, anger, and depression (Thompson, 1990, 1993). Post-traumatic stress disorder (PTSD) can result from three types of events: (1) natural disasters like floods, fires, earthquakes, hurricanes, and tornados, (2) accidents such as a car crash, bombing, or shootings, and (3) human actions such as rape, robbery, assault, abduction, or abuse.

Goldenson (1984) profiled stress disorder as an anxiety disorder produced by an uncommon, extremely stressful life event (e.g., assault, rape, military combat, flood, earthquake, hurricane, death camp, torture, car accident, or head trauma) and characterized by (1) reexperiencing the trauma in painful recollections or recurrent dreams or nightmares, (2) diminished responsiveness (emotional anesthesia or numbing) with disinterest in significant activities and with feelings of detachment and estrangement from others, and (3) such symptoms as heightened startle response, disturbed sleep, difficulty in concentrating or remembering, guilt about surviving when others did not (i.e., survivor guilt), and avoidance of activities that call the traumatic event to mind (p. 573).

Diminished responsiveness to one's immediate environment with "psychic numbing" or "emotional anesthesia" usually begins soon after the traumatic event. Sometimes the stress reactions appear immediately after the traumatic event, or a delayed reaction may occur weeks or months later. With acute post-traumatic stress, the counseling intention is to help the client return as rapidly as possible to full activity, especially on returning to the setting or circumstances in which the trauma occurred.

With chronic PTSD, anxiety and depression are also prevalent. The particular pattern of the emotional reaction and type of response will differ with each survivor, depending on the relationship of the deceased, circumstances surrounding the death, and coping mechanisms of the survivors. Grinspoon (1991a, b) provided 17 suggestions for counselors dealing with a client who is experiencing PTSD:

- Provide a safe environment for confronting the traumatic event.
- Link events emotionally and intellectually to the symptoms.
- Restore identity and personality.
- Remain calm while listening to horrifying stories.
- Anticipate one's own feelings or responses and coping skills—dread, disgust, anger at clients or persons who had hurt them, guilt, or anxiety about providing enough help.
- Avoid overcommitment and detachment.
- Avoid identifying with the client or seeing oneself as rescuer.
- Tell the client that change may take some time.
- Introduce the subject of trauma to ask about terrifying experiences and about specific symptoms.
- Moderate extremes of reliving and denial while the client works through memories of trauma.
- Provide sympathy, encouragement, and reassurance.
- Try to limit external demands on the client.

- During periods of client numbing and withdrawal, pay more attention to the traumatic event itself.
- Help client bring memories to light by any means possible including dreams, association, or fantasies.
- Examine photographs and old medical records; for children, employ play therapy, dolls, coloring books, and drawings.
- Employ special techniques, systematic desensitization, and implosion to eliminate conditioned fear of situations evoking memories and achieve catharsis.
- Facilitate group therapy.

TEN WAYS TO RECOGNIZE POST-TRAUMATIC STRESS DISORDER

Post-traumatic stress disorder is in many ways a normal response to an abnormal situation. Clearly, the tragedies that occurred on September 11, 2001, were unprecedented. After such a tragic event, it is likely that many will experience a variety of symptoms and emotions. Sometimes these symptoms surface several weeks or months after the tragedy in the form of PTSD. Recognizing these symptoms is the first step toward recovery and finding appropriate treatment:

1. Reexperiencing the event through vivid memories or flashbacks.
2. Feeling "emotionally numb."
3. Feeling overwhelmed by what would normally be considered everyday situations and diminished interest in performing normal tasks or pursuing usual interests.
4. Crying uncontrollably.
5. Isolating oneself from family and friends and avoiding social situations.
6. Relying increasingly on alcohol or drugs to get through the day.
7. Feeling extremely moody, irritable, angry, suspicious, or frightened.
8. Having difficulty falling or staying asleep, sleeping too much, and experiencing nightmares.
9. Feeling guilty about surviving the event or about being unable to solve the problem, change the event, or prevent the disaster.
10. Feeling fears and sense of doom about the future.

The child/adolescent assessment of post-traumatic stress (Table 13.1) can be used as a tool to normalize terrifying feelings and identify potential high-risk youth. It is important to explain that these are normal reactions to a traumatic or catastrophic event.

TABLE 13.1
Child/Adolescent Assessment of Post-traumatic Stress

Answer yes or no:
___I think about the accident more than I want to.
___I dream about the incident.
___I feel numb some of the time.
___I have difficulty talking about my thoughts and feelings.
___I get depressed easily, sometimes to the point of not wanting to live.
___I find it hard to get close to friends, teachers, and family members.
___I can't seem to make my friendships work.
___I avoid things that may remind me of the accident.
___I hardly ever feel happy.
___I feel guilty that I survived when others didn't.
___I feel scared, nervous, and jumpy.
___I look around a lot to see if something can hurt me.
___I can't sleep.
___I can't eat.
___I have trouble remembering things.
___I can't pay attention.
___I get angry and frustrated a lot.
___I worry I'll get too angry and hurt someone or something.
___I can't figure out what's bothering me.
___I feel hopeless and sad.

Source: Montgomery County Public Schools and Montgomery County Crisis Center, Blacksburg, Virginia; and Goldman, 1999. (Reprinted with permission)

THERAPEUTIC APPROACHES TO PROCESS POST-TRAUMATIC STRESS DISORDER

Both medication and psychotherapy can be helpful. The most effective treatment approaches are "cognitive-behavioral" because they focus both on the way traumatized persons view the trauma and on their resulting behavior. Exposure therapy includes systematic desensitization (training to relax in the face of frightening reminders of the trauma) and imaginable, in vivo techniques such as flooding or the process of putting the client back into the trauma psychologically. The most effective treatment for PTSD includes a variety of anxiety management training strategies. Some of these include rational emotive therapy (RET), various kinds of relaxation training, stress inoculation training, cognitive restructuring, breathing retraining, biofeedback, social skills training, and distraction techniques. Innovative therapists are successful in combining various techniques to fit the trauma and the patient's unique needs and requirements.

Post-traumatic Loss Debriefing

Post-traumatic loss debriefing is a structured approach to understand and to manage physical and emotional responses of survivors and their loss experiences. It creates a supportive environment to process blocked communication, which often interferes with the expression of grief or feelings of guilt, and to correct distorted attitudes toward the deceased as well as to discuss ways of coping with the loss. The purpose of the debriefing is to reduce the trauma associated with the sudden loss, to initiate an adaptive grief process, and to prevent further self-destructive or self-defeating behavior. The goals are accomplished by allowing for ventilation of feelings, exploration of symbols associated with the event, and enabling mutual support.

The debriefing is composed of six stages: introductory stage, fact stage, feeling stage, reaction stage, learning stage, and closure. Successful resolution and psychological well-being are dependent upon interventions that prepare individuals for periods of stress and help survivors return to their precrisis equilibrium. A debriefing should be organized 24 to 72 hours after the death. Natural feelings of denial and avoidance predominate during the first 24 hours. The debriefing can be offered to all persons affected by the loss. The tone must be positive, supportive, and understanding.

Technique: *Post-Traumatic Loss Debriefing*

Counseling Intention   To process loss and grief; to inform participants about typical stress response and implications (Figley, 1998; Schiraldi, 2000; Thompson, 1990, 1993).

Description of Introductory Stage. This stage includes brief introductions to the debriefing process and establishment of rules for the process.

- Acting as caregiver-as-facilitator, define the nature, limits, roles, and goals within the debriefing process.
- Clarify time limits, number of sessions, confidentiality, possibilities, and expectations to reduce unknowns and anxiety for survivors.
- Encourage members to remain silent regarding details of the debriefing, especially details that could be associated with a particular individual.
- Assure participants that the open discussion of their feelings in a debriefing will in no way be used against them under any circumstances.
- Give reassurances that the caregiver-as-facilitator will continue to maintain an attitude of unconditional positive regard. Reduce the survivors' initial anxieties to a level that permits them to begin talking.

Description of Fact Stage. The fact stage includes warm-up, gathering information, and recreating the event. During the fact phase, participants are asked to re-create the event for the therapist. The focus of this stage is on facts, not feelings. Encourage individuals to engage in a moderate level of self-disclosure statements, such as "I didn't know about that. Could you tell me what that was for you?" Try to achieve an accurate sensing of the survivor's world and communicate that understanding to him or her. Be aware of the survivor's choices of topics regarding the death to gain insight into their priorities for the moment. To curtail self-blaming, help survivors see the many factors that contributed to the death. Ask group members to make a brief statement regarding their role, relationship with the deceased, how they heard about the death, and circumstances surrounding the event. Have group members take turns adding in details to make the incident come to life again. This low initial interaction is a nonthreatening warm-up and naturally leads into a discussion of feelings in the next stage. It also provides a climate to share the details about the death and to prevent secrets or rumors that may divide survivors.

Description of Feeling Stage. The feeling stage includes expression of feelings surrounding the event and exploration of symbols. At this stage, survivors should have the opportunity to share the burden of feelings that they are experiencing and be able to do so in a nonjudgmental, supportive, and understanding environment. Survivors must be permitted to talk about themselves, to identify and to express feelings, to identify their own behavioral reactions, and to relate to the immediate present, the here-and-now.

An important aspect of this stage is for the caregiver-as-facilitator to communicate acceptance and understanding of the survivor's feelings. Acceptance of the person's feelings often helps him or her feel better immediately. It also can serve as a developmental transition to a healthier coping style in the future. Thoughtful clarification or reflection of feelings can lead to growth and change, rather than self-deprecation and self-pity.

Each person in the group is offered an opportunity to answer a variety of questions regarding their feelings. Often survivors will confront the emotion of anger and where their feeling is directed. It is important that survivors express thoughts of responsibility regarding the event and process the accompanying feelings of sadness.

At this stage, care must be taken to ensure that no one gets left out of the discussion, and that no one dominates the discussion at the expense of others. At times, the therapist has to do very little. Survivors have a tendency to start talking and the whole process goes along with only limited guidance from the therapist. People will most often discuss their fears, anxieties, concerns, feelings of guilt, frustration, anger, and ambivalence. All of their feelings—positive or negative, big or small—are important and need to be expressed and listened to. More importantly, this process allows survivors to see that subtle changes are occurring between what happened then and what is happening now.

Description of Reaction Phase. The reaction stage explores the cognitive and physical reactions and ramifications of the stress response. Acute reactions can last from a few days to a few weeks. Inherently, the survivor wants to move toward some form of resolution and articulates that need in terms such as "I can't go on like this anymore," "Something has got to give," "Please help me shake this feeling," or "I feel like I'm losing my mind." Typical anxiety reactions are a sense of dread, fear of losing control, or the inability to focus or to concentrate.

- The caregiver-as-therapist asks such questions as "What reactions did you experience at the time of the incident or when you were informed of the death?" and "What are you experiencing now?" These subtle questions allows them to see they are getting better day by day.
- The caregiver-as-therapist encourages clients to discuss what is going on with them in their peer, school, work, and family relationships.
- To help clarify reactions, the caregiver-as-therapist may provide a model for describing reactions, such as the focus of "ownership + feeling word + description of behavior." For example, "I am afraid to go to sleep at night since this has happened," or "I feel guilty about not seeing the signs that he was considering suicide."

Description of Learning Stage. The learning stage, for understanding of post-traumatic stress reactions to loss, is designed to assist survivors in learning new coping skills to deal with their grief reactions. It also is therapeutic to help survivors realize that others are having similar feelings and experiences. The caregiver-as-therapist assumes the responsibility to teach the group something about their typical stress response reactions. The emphasis is on describing how typical and natural it is for people to experience a wide variety of feelings, emotions, and physical reactions to any traumatic event. It is not unique but is a universally shared reaction. Critical to this stage is to be alert to danger signals to prevent negative destructive outcomes from a crisis experience and to help survivors return to their precrisis equilibrium and interpersonal stability.

This stage also serves as a primary prevention component for future self-defeating or self-destructive behaviors by identifying the normal responses to a traumatic event in a secure, therapeutic environment with a caring, trusted adult.

Description of the Closure Stage. The closure stage includes wrap-up of loose ends, questions and answers, final reassurances, action planning, referrals, and follow-up. Human crises that involve post-traumatic stress often, if debriefed appropriately, serve as catalysts for personal growth.

Phases of Recovery

Peter and Straub (1992, pp. 246–247) classified the recovery process as four phases.

1. **Emergency or Outcry Phase.** The survivor experiences heightened "fight or flight" reactions to the life-threatening event. This phase lasts as long as the survivor believes it to last. Pulse, blood pressure, respiration, and muscle activity are all increased. Concomitant feelings of fear and helplessness predominate. Termination of the event itself is followed by relief and confusion. Preoccupation centers around questions about why the event happened and the long-term consequences.
2. **Emotional Numbing and Denial Phase.** The survivor shelters psychic well-being by burying the traumatic experience in subconscious memory. By avoiding the experience, the victim temporarily reduces anxiety and stress responses. Many survivors may remain at this stage unless they receive professional intervention.
3. **Intrusive-Repetitive Phase.** The survivor has nightmares, mood swings, intrusive images, and startle reactions. Overreliance on defense mechanisms (e.g., intellectualization, projection, or denial) or self-defeating behaviors (e.g., abuse of alcohol or other drugs) may become integrated into coping behaviors in an effort to repress the traumatic event. At this juncture, the delayed stress becomes so overwhelming that the survivor may either seek help or become so mired in the pathology of the situation that professional intervention becomes necessary.
4. **Reflective-Transition Phase.** The survivor is able to put the traumatic event into perspective. He or she begins to interact positively and constructively with a future orientation and exhibits a willingness to put the traumatic event behind him or her.

> *Perspective for the Therapist: On loss and grief*
>
> *The only cure for grief is action.*
>
> George Henry Lewes

Technique: *Clinical Interventions*

Counseling Intention   To help clients through phases of grief and loss.

Description   Rando (1984) provides the following clinical interventions for caregivers when confronting dying, grief, and death.

- Be present emotionally as well as physically to provide security and support.
- Do not allow grievers to become socially isolated.
- Make certain that grievers have the appropriate medical evaluation and treatment available if symptoms warrant.
- Encourage the verbalization of feelings and recollections of the deceased.
- Help grievers identify any unfinished business with the deceased and look for appropriate ways to assist closure. (One way that comes to mind is having the client write a letter to the deceased.)
- Help grievers find a variety of new sources of personal satisfaction following the loss. Encourage grievers to be patient and not set unrealistic expectations for themselves.
- Help grievers to recognize that loss always brings about change and the need for new adjustments.
- Assist grievers in getting and maintaining a proper perspective on what the resolution of grief will mean.
- Encourage grievers, at the appropriate time, to find rewarding new things to do and people to invest in.

Technique: *Multiple Strategies to Process Grief and Loss*

Counseling Intention   To meet the diversity of needs when processing loss (Miller, 2003).

Description   Many strategies are available to help people who are mourning a loved one's death. Different kinds of losses dictate different responses, so not all strategies will suit everyone. Equally, no two people grieve alike, so what works for one may not work for another.

Carry or Wear a Linking Object. Carry something that belonged to the one who died—a keepsake, a small object, or a memento. Wear a piece of their jewelry in the same way. Look at the keepsake and remember what it signifies.

Create a Memory Book. Compile photographs that document a loved one's life. Arrange them into some sort of order so they tell a story. Add other elements such as diplomas, newspaper clippings, awards, accomplishments, and reminders of significant events. Put all this in a special binder and keep it out for people to look at if they wish. Go through it and reminisce about positive experiences of the past.

Ask for a Copy of the Memorial Service. If the funeral liturgy or memorial service held special meaning because of what was spoken or read, ask for a copy of the words. Whoever participated in that ritual will feel gratified that what they prepared was appreciated. Some people find these thoughts provide even more help weeks and months after the service.

Start a Journal. Write out thoughts and feelings. Do this at least several times a week, if not several times a day. Don't censor what is written. Let feelings flow. In time, go back over what was written and notice change and growth. Write about that, too.

Write to the Person Who Died. Write letters or other messages to the deceased, especially thoughts that were not express when that person was alive. Preserve what you write in a journal. The urge to write the deceased will eventually diminish. Initially, writing serves to release of important emotions and to provide a connection to the deceased.

Light a Candle at Mealtime. Consider lighting a taper at the table in memory of a loved one. Pause to remember the deceased and keep him or her nearby.

Create a Memory Area at Home. In a space that feels appropriate, arrange a small table that honors the person: a framed photograph or two, perhaps a prized possession or award, or something he or she had created or loved. This might be placed on a small table, a mantel, or a desk. Some people like to use a grouping of candles, representing not just the person who died but others who have died as well. In that case, a variety of candles can be arranged, each representing a unique life.

Structure Alone Time. Structure time to be alone. A large part of the grieving process involves what goes on inside—absorbing the thoughts, feelings, memories, hopes, and dreams. Allow the opportunity to go inside in order to grow inside.

Do Something the Deceased Would Enjoy. Remember the one who died in a unique way. For example, prepare a loved one's favorite dish on significant holidays. The meaning and satisfaction doesn't have to end with the death of that person.

Engage the Soul. Some people meditate, some pray, and some spend time alone in nature. Some worship with a congregation and others do it on their own. Many grieving people begin to sense that all of the human race, living and dead, are connected on a spiritual level in a way that defies understanding.

Change Some Things. As soon as it seems right, alter some things in the home environment to make clear a significant change that has occurred. Rearrange a room, replace a piece of furniture, or give away certain items that will never be used again. This does not mean to remove all signs of the one who died. It does discourage treating the home as a shrine, which would be unhealthy grieving.

Talk to the Deceased Loved One. If it helps, talk with the one who died while driving, walking, or when needing the courage to make an important decision. This self-talk serves the need to talk things over or to process unfinished conversations. This inclination to converse will eventually go away, when the time is right.

Create a Memory Quilt. Sew or invite others to sew a memory quilt. Put together a wall hanging or a bedroom quilt that remembers the important life events of the one who died. Take time and make it what it is: a labor of love.

Read How Others Have Responded to a Loved One's Death. Look at the ways others have processed grief, try Judith Viorst's *Necessary Losses* (1986), C. S. Lewis's *A Grief Observed* (1963), Lynn Caine's *Widow* (1974), John Bramblett's *When Good-Bye Is Forever* (1991), and Nicholas Wolterstorff's *Lament for a Son* (1917). There are many others. Check with a counselor or a librarian.

Reward Personal Growth. Do things that are personally rewarding. Indulge in a favorite meal or delicacy. Get a massage. Buy some flowers. Do something frivolous and soak up those moments.

Write Down Lessons Learned. The grief experience is a learning process. Reflect upon what has been learned. State it plainly and review it routinely.

> *Perspective for the Therapist: On grief and loss*
>
> *We lose not only through death, but also by leaving and being left,*
> *by changing and letting go and moving on.*
>
> Judith Viorst
> *Necessary Losses,* 1986, p. 148

Technique: *Make a "Tear Jar"*

Counseling Intention   To process grief (White, [n.d.], reprinted with permission).

Description   In the dry climate of ancient Greece, water was a precious commodity. Giving up water from one's own body, when crying tears for the dead, was considered a sacrifice. They caught their precious tears in tiny pitchers or "tear jars." The tears became holy water and could be used to sprinkle on doorways to keep out evil, or to cool the feverish. The clay tear jars were kept unpainted until the owner had experienced the death of a parent, sibling, child, or spouse. After that, the grieving person decorated the tear jar with intricate designs. This ancient custom symbolizes the transformation that takes place in people who have grieved deeply. They are not threatened by the grief of people in pain. They have been in the depths of pain themselves, and returned. Like the tear jar, they can now be with others who grieve and catch their tears.

Technique: *Resolving Grief by Remembering the Good Feelings Such as Love, Comfort, Stability, Tenderness, and Humor*

Counseling Intention   To create an "associated experience" that gives the grieving person a sense of a loved one's "felt presence" (Andreas & Andreas, 1989).

Description   The first step in resolving grief is to find out how the client represents a loved one in "felt presence." Ask the client to think of a loved one who is not physically present. Ask the client to visualize the time the valued relationship actually occurred and identify "present-felt sense of love and comfort." Use this information as a "template" to transform the grief experience into the felt presence in which the client can enjoy previously felt good feelings.

Next, have the client focus on the special qualities of the relationship that he or she had with the deceased—the love, comfort, stability, companionship, or whatever special experiences existed between them. Use the template of the felt presence to transform the loss experience into an "associated image" from which the client can reexperience the good feelings previously felt. The client regains access to all the special feelings he or she previously had with that person.

> *Perspective for the Therapist: On stages of grief*
>
> *I reject the notion that human beings, as they die, are somehow marched in lock step through a series of stages of the dying process. On the contrary . . . the emotional states, the psychological mechanisms of defense, the needs and drives, are as variegated in the dying as they are in the nondying. . . . They include such reactions as stoicism, rage, guilt, terror, cringing, fear, surrender, heroism, dependency, ennui, need for control, fight for autonomy and dignity, and denial.*
>
> Edwin Shneidman
> *Definition of Suicide*, 1985, p. 100

Loss, Crisis, and Grief: Special Considerations for Children

The intense anxiety and fear that often follow a disaster or other traumatic event can be especially troubling for children. Some may regress and demonstrate younger behaviors such as thumb-sucking or bed-wetting. Children may be more prone to nightmares and fear of sleeping alone. Performance in school may suffer. Other changes in behavior patterns may include throwing tantrums more frequently, or withdrawing and becoming more solitary. There are several things parents and others who care for children can do to help alleviate the emotional consequences of trauma.

- Spend more time with children and let them be more dependent on you during the months following the trauma. For example, allow the child to cling to caregivers more often than usual. Physical affection is very comforting to children who have experienced trauma.
- Provide play experiences to help relieve tension. Younger children in particular may find it easier to share their ideas and feelings about the event through non-verbal activities such as drawing.
- Encourage older children to discuss their thoughts and feelings with one another. This helps reduce their confusion and anxiety related to the trauma. Respond to questions in terms they can comprehend. Reassure them repeatedly that you care about them and that you understand their fears and concerns.
- Keep regular schedules for activities such as eating, playing, and going to bed to help restore a sense of security and normalcy.

Parents Should Be Alert to These Changes in a Child's Behavior
- Refusal to return to school and "clinging" behavior, including shadowing the mother or father around the house.
- Persistent fears related to the catastrophe (such as fears about being permanently separated from parents).
- Sleep disturbances such as nightmares, screaming during sleep, and bed-wetting, persisting more than several days after the event.
- Loss of concentration and irritability.
- Startling easily, and jumpy behavior.
- Behavior problems, for example, misbehaving in school or at home in ways that are not typical for the child.
- Physical complaints (stomachaches, headaches, dizziness) for which a physical cause cannot be found.
- Withdrawal from family and friends, sadness, listlessness, decreased activity, and preoccupation with the events of the disaster.

It is important to use the language of death when working with children. Stating that a loved one has "gone away," "is lost," or "is sleeping" can be very frightening to children and delays their accepting and understanding that the person will not come back. Children must have clear and concise information regarding the death of the loved one, or they may construct their own stories to fill in the holes. This is destructive fantasy building. Children must not be denied the opportunity to express their feelings in ways that are appropriate to them. There is considerable evidence of the resilience of children. Nourished by love, protection, guidance, and attention, they can spring back after even the most horrendous traumatic events (Johnson, 1998). The parent is often the most influential factor in the recovery of the child. When considering the developmental and social factors that determine the suitability of including the child in therapy, the therapist should assess the parents as carefully as the children, because the role the parent plays will determine whether their children can benefit from therapy (Nader, Dubrow, & Stamm, 1999). One of the goals for treatment of traumatized children is to help the child face the truth of what has happened. This involves enabling the child to draw, sing, dance, talk, or engage in some other form of self-expression that is also a self-soothing activity.

Technique: *How to Help a Child or Adolescent through Denial*

Counseling Intention   To open the door to confront the loss of a loved one.

Description   As a counselor or therapist, do not refute or debate the child or adolescent's current reality. Identify with the child/adolescent's feelings by saying "You really must be missing _____ now," or "You must be feeling really lonely now."

If the child doesn't want to talk, provide or suggest activities with continuity such as a scrapbook of photos or artwork portraying "the way things were then and the way things are now." Include normal routines such as home, school, family, dinner time, weekends, bedtime, time alone, and holidays.

Technique: *How to Help a Child through Denial after a Traumatic Event*

Counseling Intention   To reestablish a sense of control.

Description   Make toys available to encourage reenactment play. Dolls, puppets, building blocks, cars, fire trucks, ambulances, or other imaginative toys or props can be used to duplicate the recent crisis. Help the child to find positive outcomes in their play.

Technique: *How to Help an Older Child with Fear after a Death*

Counseling Intention   To process loss.

Description   Help older children tell their story. Discuss what happened to the deceased, and how people survive a major loss. Remind them of their support of people around them. Remind them of the strengths they used in the past when a friend moved away or a pet died.

Technique: *Providing Permission and Structure to End the Mourning Process*

Counseling Intention   To help with leaving the mourning period behind.

Description   Dealing with loss differs for each client. However, one aspect that holds true is that the closer the attachment to the deceased, the greater the loss.

1. At the appropriate time, give the child/adolescent permission to cease the mourning period.
2. Help the child/adolescent choose a ritual to say goodbye.
3. Remind the child/adolescent that the memory of the relationship will never end, just the deceased's presence.
4. Explore what has been learned from the life of the deceased.
5. Help the child/adolescent plan how to make that memory a part of his or her life, such as with a linking object.
6. Encourage a reinvestment in new or forgotten activities.

Technique: *Using a Group Mural to Deal with a Traumatic Loss Such as the Loss of a Classmate*

Counseling Intention   To integrate a tragedy in a positive way.

Description   Have children/adolescents in a group depict a common tragic event they shared. Each person's idea for inclusion in the picture should be drawn by that person. Allow the group to reach a consensus about what should be in the mural. Hang the mural in a common area and don't take it down until there is a collective discussion to remove it. This provides an opportunity to make the tragedy tangible so that survivors can integrate the loss and move on with their daily lives.

Technique: *Circle of Trust to Identify Support during Grief*

Counseling Intention   To reassure children that they have people around them whom they can count on (Goldman, 2001, pp. 109–110).

Description   The trust circle strategy (Figure 13.1) can act as a preventive tool to be used as needed to create awareness of present support during a grief period and as a vehicle for discussion and communication about thoughts, feelings, and emotions children harbor within themselves about people in their lives.

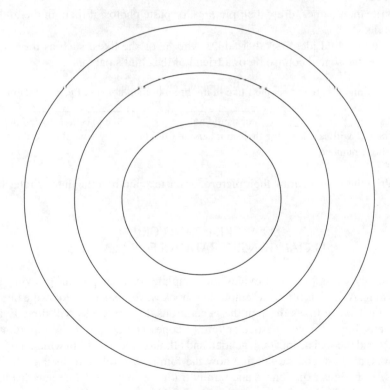

FIGURE 13.2. Circle of Trust

1. The child pastes his or her picture in the center of the circle.
2. Help the child identify people in his or her life that he or she cares about and with whom feelings can be trusted.

> I can call on these people if I need to talk or ask for something. My very most trusted people are:_____
>
> _____
>
> Their phone numbers are: _____

Have the child write these peoples' names, draw their pictures, or paste photos of them in the innermost circle.
3. Help the child identify other people who can help, such as family, friends, teachers, neighbors, coaches, or Sunday school teacher.

> There are even more people in my life I can depend on. They are:
>
> _____
>
> Their phone numbers are:_____

Write their names, draw their pictures, or paste photos of them in the middle circle.
4. Help the child identify other adults who he or she likes, such as the school nurse, the school counselor, or a friend of the child's parents.

> Sometimes there are people I like in my life, but I am not sure I can call them for help. They are: _____
> I would _____ or would not _____ like to be able to call on them. I will ask them for their numbers and tell them why I would like their phone numbers.

Write their name, draw their picture, or paste a photo in the outer circle.

LOSS, CRISIS, AND GRIEF: SPECIAL CONSIDERATIONS FOR FAMILIES

The family's loss history provides the template for their present grieving and mourning. A death is often an "emotional shock wave" experienced by the family. This shock wave flows through the generations. Previous loss will directly and indirectly impact how a particular family copes and adapts. It is important to understand the social, spiritual, gender, and ethnic contexts within which the family lives, as these contexts define how the family will relate to their grief. The family's previous experiences and family traditions regarding loss and death, as well as methods of coping, are areas that should be addressed.

- What type of losses has the family experienced? What are the dates?
- How did they or their parents/grandparents historically handle situations involving loss?
- How has the family discussed bad news?
- How has the family expressed sadness in the past?
- Are outward expressions of emotions considered a weakness? Is there a gender distinction?
- How has the family managed loss? Have they put it in the past and moved on? Have those members who wished to talk about their loss been able to talk openly?
- Do family members take on specific roles in the bereavement process?
- Is there a gender-based difference in the ways that family members cope?
- How have children been included in the bereavement process?
- What types of rituals of mourning were used in their families of origin?

Framing the Problem

Listen carefully to how family members describe both the traumatic memories and their responses as individuals and as a family. Traumatic memory management varies among individuals and within families. Some family members have vivid recollections of the traumatic event and recall it in a clear and direct manner; others either have difficulty remembering or do not wish to discuss it with others. In this early phase of treatment there are six guidelines in the treatment protocol.

1. *Telling the family's stories.* Each member of the family is encouraged to explain their experience with the trauma, focusing on the worst parts and explaining their thoughts, feelings, emotions, and kinesthetic reactions.
2. *Promoting new rules of communication.* The fundamental principle for trauma treatment is for clients to feel safe, respected, and supported so that they can tell their story, become desensitized to the trauma, and help collaboratively construct a method to enable the family cope and thrive. Drawing lessons from the traumatic event can often foster more love and respect for each other.
3. *Promoting understanding and acceptance.* Sometimes families in crisis, particularly couples, emotionally withdraw as a result of distress and the fragmented nature of family relationships. Given this challenging reality, the therapist must work to keep clients together in order to reach a level of understanding and acceptance about the trauma and the complexity of family member reactions.
4. *Listing wanted and unwanted consequences.* While the family is struggling to understand and accept what has happened to them, the therapist should attempt to also get them to articulate their incentives. Sometimes the family has

difficulty identifying a clear and reachable objective. They most often start with rather vague and broad goals, such as "to understand why this happened to us." This may not be possible under some circumstances. It is more therapeutic to help the family get along better so that they are not fighting and blaming but rather healing after the loss.

5. ***Preventing victimization and blaming.*** It is very normal and natural to simplify the situation by using a scapegoat in the family to shift the blame away from the family. It is critical to help family members express their feelings, attitudes, and physical reactions in a way that does not hurt another family member.

6. ***Shifting attention to the family.*** The therapist must strive to shift the discussion to how the family plays a role in maintaining the trauma in their thoughts, feelings, and behaviors. It is important that the family realize that the cause of the trauma may be beyond their control, but the consequences and interpersonal relationships *can* be controlled.

Creating Meaningful Rituals

Creating and participating in a ritual after the immediate time period acknowledges the loss in a way that is personally significant for the bereaved. Additionally, when there is unfinished business, issues involving other types of closure, or when the family simply wants to develop a personal family way of remembering, rituals provide a method of accomplishing these ends. Some of the saddest words in the English language are "If I had only had a chance to tell him." These words are heard countless times from the bereaved. One more chance to say goodbye, or one more opportunity for closure often haunts the bereaved for months, if not for years and generations (Cook & Dworkin, 1992). The development of the ritual must come from the client's frame of reference. It is important for clinicians to understand which religious and cultural beliefs hold particular significance for their clients and not assume that each member of the family believes in the same way. In helping the bereaved construct a meaningful ritual, the therapist may make suggestions, such as writing a letter to say goodbye, having a conversation at the grave side, or role-playing a last conversation and creating a different ending. For the ritual to have meaning, the ultimate decision and design must come from the bereaved.

Finding Closure and Preparedness

The final phase is a time for shifting to post-treatment, in which the family will return at some specified number of months as a way of assuring that the family has healed and is better prepared for life's losses. There are four useful criteria for working with traumatized families:

1. Did they reach their treatment goals?
2. Did the family develop a healing theory that all members embrace?
3. Did new rules and skills of family communications emerge?
4. Did the family experience a sense of accomplishment?

A sign of success and the end of weekly sessions is when the family members begin to act like the session is routine and regularly talk much more than the therapist. This is a sign that clients are now empowered to take back control of their lives. This places the therapist in the advantaged role of consultant, providing advice, assistance, and consultation as family members work together toward a common goal.

TAKING CARE OF THE CAREGIVERS: A NEGLECTED SURVIVAL TECHNIQUE

The helping professionals who listen to others' stories of fear, pain, and suffering may feel similar fear, pain, and suffering because they care. Helping professionals in all therapeutic settings are especially vulnerable to compassion fatigue, including emergency care workers, counselors, mental health professionals, medical professionals, clergy, advocate volunteers, and human service workers. The concept of *compassion fatigue* emerged only in the last several years in the professional literature. It represents the cost of caring about and for traumatized people.

Compassion fatigue is the emotional residue of exposure to the suffering, particularly those suffering from the consequences of traumatic events. Professionals who work with people, particularly people who are suffering, must contend not only with the normal stress or dissatisfaction of work, but also with the emotional and personal feelings for the suffering. Compassion fatigue is a state of tension and preoccupation with the individual or cumulative trauma of clients as manifested in one or more ways including reexperiencing the traumatic event, avoidance of or numbing to reminders of the event, and persistent arousal. Although similar to critical incident stress (being traumatized by something you actually experience or see), with compassion fatigue helping professionals absorb the trauma through the eyes and ears of clients. It can be thought of as secondary post-traumatic stress.

There are human costs associated with compassion fatigue. It reflects physical, emotional, and spiritual fatigue or exhaustion that takes over a person and causes a decline in his or her ability to experience joy or to feel and care for others. Compassion fatigue is a one-way street, in which individuals are giving out a great deal of energy and compassion to others over a period of time, yet aren't able to get enough back to reassure themselves that the world is a hopeful place. It's this constant outputting of compassion and caring over time that can lead to these feelings. Compassion fatigue comes from a variety of sources. Although it often affects those working in caregiving professions—nurses, physicians, mental health workers, and clergymen—it can affect people in any kind of situation or setting where they're doing a great deal of caregiving and expending emotional and physical energy day in and day out. Compassion fatigue develops over time, taking weeks, sometimes years to surface. Basically, it's a low-level, chronic clouding of caring and concern for others. Over time, the ability to feel and care for others becomes eroded through overuse of the skills of compassion. Caregivers may also experience emotional blunting, reacting to situations differently than others would normally expect.

When caregivers become emotionally drained from hearing about and being exposed to the pain and trauma of the people they are helping, self-care strategies can inhibit the fatigue of caring too much.

Self-Awareness and Self-Care

1. If you are dealing with a community tragedy, learn as much as possible about the event and deal with and articulate the powerful emotions and reactions related to the event.
2. Know your own "triggers" and vulnerable areas and learn to defuse them or avoid them.
3. Resolve your own personal issues and continue to monitor your own reactions to others' pain.
4. Be human and allow yourself to grieve when bad things happen to others. Remember that "normal responses to abnormal situations" is true for helpers as well as victims.
5. Develop realistic expectations about the rewards as well as limitations of being a helper. Set boundaries for yourself.
6. Become aware of and alter any irrational beliefs about the helping process. Develop realistic expectations about the rewards as well as the limitations of helping.
7. Balance your work with other professional activities that provide opportunities for growth and renewal.

Ask for and Accept Help from Other Professionals
1. Find opportunities to acknowledge express and work through your experience in a supportive environment. Debrief yourself regularly and build healthy support groups.

2. Seek assistance from other colleagues and caregivers who have had experience with trauma and have remained healthy and hopeful or have learned from their experience. Take their advice.
3. Delegate responsibilities and get help from others for routine work when appropriate.
4. Develop a healthy support system to protect yourself from further fatigue and emotional exhaustion.
5. Remember that most victims of trauma do grow and learn from their experiences and so can their helpers.

Live a Healthy Balanced Life
1. Eat nutritious food, exercise, rest, meditate, or pray and take care of your whole self.
2. Set and keep healthy boundaries for work. Ask yourself, "Would the world fall apart if I step away from my work for a day or a week?"
3. Think about the idea that, if you never say "no," what is your "yes" worth?
4. Find professional activities that provide opportunities for growth and renewal.
5. Take an honest look at your life before a crisis strikes. Find help to identify your obvious risks and work to correct or minimize them.
6. Find ways to provide yourself with emotional and spiritual strength for the future.
7. Develop and reward a sense of humor. Expose yourself to humorous situations. Learn to laugh, enjoy life, have healthy personal relationships, and breathe deeply.
8. Avoid chaotic situations and learn simplicity.
9. Take time to return to normal activities regularly.
10. Avoid additional stressful situations.

Specific Coping Skills for Helping Professionals

With the increased incidence of violence in our society, helping professionals will continue to be called upon to process emotionally stressful events. Holaday and Smith (1995) concluded that to protect the emotional well-being, helping professionals would benefit from five categories of coping strategies: social support, task-focused behaviors, emotional distancing, cognitive self-talk, and altruism (p. 360).

To Increase Social Support
- Work in pairs or always be within speaking distance of another helping professional to ask for assistance or for additional emotional support.
- Smile and make eye contact with peers.

- Talk to peers about the situation, especially in terms of how they are handling the stress.
- Use humor to relieve tension and anxiety.
- Give comfort through physical contact (e.g., touch, hold, or hug people who are distraught).
- Take breaks with peers; share food if available to revitalize.

To Maintain Task-Focused Behaviors

- Use problem-solving skills (i.e., think and plan about what needs to be done and take an active approach to helping).
- Generate solutions and quickly think of ways to resolve problems.
- Evaluate potential solutions. Ask: What is the most efficient thing you can do? Does it minimize harm? Identify and establish task-related priorities.
- Take action and request help if you need it.
- Focus on the task at hand. Do not be distracted by what is happening around you.
- Avoid thinking about the consequences or the long-term implications of the stressful event by focusing on what has to be done now.

To Increase Emotional Distancing

- Imagine you are an actor in a movie or think of this experience as a temporary event that will be over soon.
- Protect yourself from being overwhelmed. Block your emotions during the event and use relaxation techniques.
- Pretend the event is not really happening. Permit yourself to experience a sense of unreality, to feel as if this was happening in a dream.
- Think about other things more pleasant.
- Talk about other things with other helping professionals or talk to the person you are helping about everyday, mundane things to avoid thinking about pain, loss, and other issues.
- Try not to think of victims as people, as having children or families who will be affected. Do not look at their faces.
- Distance yourself by singing or whistling; keep moving; look off into the distance and imagine yourself there instead of where you really are.

To Manage Emotions through Cognitive Self-Talk

- Mentally prepare yourself; think about what will happen when you get to the scene. Tell yourself about the positive aspects of the work you are called on to do. Recognize that bad things happen to good people.
- Brace yourself physically. Take a deep breath, stand straight, and focus on staying in control.

- Use positive self-talk. Tell yourself you can handle it, you are strong enough to help, and you know that you are competent. Focus on your strengths, maintain an "optimistic perseverance," and become aware of self-defeating thoughts.
- Praise yourself for your contribution. Say encouraging things to yourself; tell yourself "They need me."
- Reframe your language to reduce negative impact. Change statements such as "This is horrible" to "This is challenging."
- Translate arduous tasks into meaningful ones; find a deeper meaning in your work. Do not just revive someone, "help someone get well." Celebrate with the survivors.

To Feel Better Using Altruism

- Spare others by doing more work; perform your work so that others are relieved.
- Work for those who may not be as "strong" as you are, or work for those who "cannot take it as well" as you.
- Remind yourself that it is a good thing to sacrifice for others; it feels good to help others. Be thankful for the opportunity to help.
- Put the needs of others above your own. Persevere and draw strength from adversity.

CONCLUSION

Let the person in need of comfort talk! Let him or her talk about people . . . events . . . feelings. One of the major tasks of grief is for the loss to become real. Listening to someone talk will aid this process. Each time the story is repeated, the reality becomes more realized. Listen particularly for feelings. Accept these feelings without judgment.

Hardy Clemons, *Saying Goodbye to Your Grief: A Book Designed to Help People Who Have Experienced Crushing Losses Survive and Grow Beyond the Pain*, 1999, p. 14

Suicide, homicide, violence, and terrorism have become reoccurring crises that disrupt the equilibrium of people and society. Coping skills reduce the negative effects of a stressful event. Helping professionals must be able to cope with their own post-traumatic stress. Daily crisis response team debriefings should be held to review and modify plans and communication to both promote accountability and assess any symptoms of compassion fatigue.

Chapter 14

Psychodynamic Techniques

SIGMUND FREUD AND PSYCHOANALYSIS

The central hypothesis of Freudian psychoanalysis is that human behavior is determined in large part by unconscious motives (Freud, 1961). Our personality and our actions, argued Freud, were in large part determined by thoughts and feelings contained in the unconscious. Repressed content of the unconscious inadvertently slips through into our words or deeds, resulting in what is commonly called a *Freudian slip*. If most activities are governed by the unconscious, the individual may have limited responsibility for his or her actions. Psychoanalytic/psychodynamic practitioners who use this approach tend to view psychological distress as being related to unconscious mental processes (Jacobs, 1998). Freud's contribution has been developed by others; some have followed his basic assumptions, and others have developed more independent approaches. The term "psychodynamic" offers a wider perspective, which encompasses the different analytical approaches. As Jacobs (1998) suggested, *psychodynamic* implies that the psyche (mind/emotions/spirit/self) is active, not static. These internal mental processes are dynamic forces that influence our relations with others.

The structural concept of Freud's theory of personality consisted of the id, ego, and superego. The *id* consists of everything present at birth, including instincts. The *ego* is the executive of the personality, because it controls the gateways to action, selects the features of the environment to which it will respond, and decides which needs will be satisfied and in which order. The superego is the internalized representative of the tradition values, ideals, and moral standards of society. The *superego* strives for perfection.

Under the pressure of excessive anxiety, the ego is forced to take extreme measures to relieve the pressure. These measures are called defense mechanisms, because they defend the ego against anxiety. The principle defenses are repression, projection, reaction formation, intellectualization, denial, rationalization, displacement, and regression. These defense mechanisms have crept into contemporary therapy as denial and regression. Hence, someone is in denial because they are unable to accept a tragic death, or a child regresses to a previous developmental stage as a way of dealing with a tragic death.

Defense mechanisms protect the individual from being consciously aware of a thought or feeling that he or she cannot tolerate. The defense only allows the unconscious thought or feeling to be expressed in a disguised form. For example, an individual who is angry at a demanding boss might cloak or transform that anger as follows:

Denial. You completely reject the thought or feeling: "I'm not angry with him or her!"

Suppression. You are vaguely aware of the thought or feeling, but try to hide it: "I'm going to go out of my way to be nice to him or her."

Reaction formation. You reverse the feeling: "I think she's really great!"

Projection. You project your thought or feeling onto someone else: "That man hates me." "I hate that woman."

Displacement. You redirect your feelings to another target: "I hate her secretary."

Rationalization. You come up with various explanations to justify the situation (while denying your feelings): "He's so critical because he's trying to help us succeed."

Intellectualization. You rationalize more intellectually: "This situation reminds me of how I was treated in nursery school."

Undoing. You try to reverse the feeling by doing something that indicates the opposite feeling. It may be an "apology" for the feeling you find unacceptable within yourself: "I think I'll write the boss a thank-you card."

Isolation of affect. You "think" the feeling but don't really feel it: "I guess I'm angry with her, sort of."

Regression. You revert to an old, usually immature behavior to ventilate your feeling: "Let's make prank calls to people."

Sublimation. You redirect the feeling into a socially appropriate activity: "I'm going to write a poem about anger."

Defenses may hide any of a variety of thoughts or feelings: anger, fear, sadness, depression, greed, envy, competitiveness, love, passion, admiration, criticalness, dependency, selfishness, or grandiosity.

OUTCOME STUDIES OF PSYCHOANALYSIS

There have been many, often conflicting, claims concerning the desired aim or effect of psychoanalytic treatment, as well as claims about the curative aspects of the psychoanalytic process that may bring about these changes. It is easy to be critical of psychoanalytic studies, as no definitive studies show psychoanalysis to be unequivocally effective relative to an active placebo or an alternative method of treatment. Although no methods are available to definitively indicate the existence of a psychoanalytic process, Fonagy (1999) has conducted a comprehensive analysis of outcome studies. Fonagy found that:

- Longer treatment has better outcome.
- Psychoanalysis can bring the functioning of a clinical group to the level of the normal population.
- Superiority of psychoanalysis over psychotherapy sometimes only becomes apparent some years after the treatment has ended.
- Psychoanalytic treatment can lead to a reduction in the use of psychotropic medication among inpatients.
- Long-term psychoanalytic therapy can reduce borderline symptomatology in the long run and these improvements are maintained.
- Psychoanalysis may be an effective treatment for severe psychosomatic disorders.
- More severe disturbance specifically benefits from psychoanalysis rather than psychotherapy.
- Behavioral disorders respond less well to psychoanalysis than emotional disorders.
- Younger children benefit more from psychoanalysis than older ones.
- Analytic problems are better dealt with in psychotherapy; introjective problems in psychoanalysis.
- Psychosomatic disorders respond particularly well to psychoanalysis.
- Successful psychoanalytic treatment of severe personality disorder may require a combination of supportive and expressive techniques.
- Anxiety, guilt, and idealization in the transference may be associated with successful treatment, whereas shame, humiliation, and existential anxiety are associated with failed treatments.

More recently, object relations have emerged as a psychodynamic approach to understanding human behavior, development, relationships, psychopathology, and psychotherapy. An *object relation* intuitively reflects certain truths about all human relationships, from the early relationships of infancy, to friendships, marriage, and the therapeutic relationship. Freud originally used the term *object* to mean anything an infant directs its drives toward for satiation. *Drives* are of two types: libidinal and aggressive. Accordingly, objects became a key component of Freud's drive/structural model of the human psyche.

Since Freud, however, many theorists such as Klein (1932, 1959, 1963), Winnicott (1963), Kernberg (1984), and Kohut (1959, 1971, 1977) have moved, in varying degrees, toward a relational/structural model of the psyche in which an object is the target of relational needs in human development. Within contemporary object relations theory, objects can be people (mother, father, others) or things, such as transitional objects with which we form attachments. These objects and the developing child's relationship with them are incorporated into a self, and as such become the building blocks of the self-system. This blueprint of a self-structure is formed early in life out of our relationships with the objects (significant others, and parts of significant others) around us. Once formed, the blueprint can be modified, but our basic tendency is to seek out others (friends, spouses) who will reaffirm these early self-object relationships. Psychoanalytic object relations theory focuses on the mutual influence of internalized interpersonal relations and intrapsychic conflict. Beginning with the mother-infant dyad, relationships are primary; and intrapsychic, interpersonal group experiences lay the foundation for the development of individual identity. One's unconscious striving to reenact conflicted parent-child relations emerges through a particular object choice. In summary, the term *object relations* refers to the self-structure we internalize in early childhood, which functions as a blueprint for establishing and maintaining future relationships.

> *Perspective for the Therapist: On addiction as substitution for the self-object*
>
> *[t]he addict, finally, craves the drug because the drug seems to him to be capable of curing the central deficit in his self. It becomes for him the substitute for a self-object which failed him traumatically at a time when he should still have had the feeling of omnipotently controlling its responses in accordance with his needs as if it were part of himself. By ingesting the drug he symbolically compels the mirroring self-object to sooth him, to accept him. Or he symbolically compels the idealized self-object to submit to his merging into it and thus to his partaking in its magical power. In either case, the ingestion of the drug provides him with the self-esteem which he does not possess.*
>
> Heinz Kohut
> *The Analysis of the Self,* 1971, p. 36

CARL JUNG AND ANALYTICAL PSYCHOLOGY

In Jungian psychology, the whole personality is referred to as the psyche. The psyche is made up of three components: the conscious *ego*, the *personal unconscious* and its complexes, and the *collective unconscious* and its *archetypes*. Jung also devised a typology that has been very influential. It consists of the attitudes of *extraversion* and *introversion* and the psychological functions of *thinking, feeling, sensing,* and *intuiting.* Extroverts turn their attention to the outside world with an active interest in people and the events around them. Introverts are more absorbed in their private world, tend to be less sociable, and lack confidence in dealing with other people.

Technique: *Childhood Memories*

Counseling Intention To understand the dynamics and significance of childhood memories.

Description Write down one or two early childhood memories. Create a title for each memory, as if they were a newspaper article with a headline that captures its essence. Process the dynamics and significance of childhood memories with the following questions:

1. Does the memory reveal important themes in your past as well as present life? The title of the story often helps clarify the nature of your relationships with significant others, predominant issues, conflicts, emotions, and attitudes.
2. Is the memory accurate? Are the details of the memory meaningful? Do they come from other memories? Is this memory really a composite of several memories?
3. How would significant others remember the event? If there are differences from how you remember it, what is the meaning of those differences? Why do people remember the same event differently? What does it say about them?
4. Do memories accurately depict reality, or subjectively "create" the past? Is there really a "reality" at all?

Technique: *Specific Tactics for Dismantling Old Traumas*

Counseling Intention To provide the opportunity to process past childhood traumas.

Description Some traumas will be released by sound. A person may need to let loose with a ferocious scream that reverberates up from the depth of the body. There are all kinds of sound deep in the heart of traumas and no list can be adequate. Rather, a given individual needs to be given permission to express, with sound, what is deep within the body. Another tactic is for the person to tell the trauma to you all over again while occasionally taking breaths as if he or she was on a seashore enjoying nature. Sometimes the person needs to do deep breathing and have the body experience, for a new redeeming time, what needed to be felt long ago and far away. An individual can:

- Yell it out.
- Breathe it out.
- Emotionally express it out.
- Imagine it away.

Process with questions that need to be asked about each of these five feelings: Is there any sadness still left back there? Anger? Fear? Happiness? Excitement? Tenderness?

Technique: *Visualize an Elevator Descending to an Earlier Age*

Counseling Intentions   To capture old memories.

Description   Visualize an elevator with 21 floors. The buttons on the elevator number from 1 to 18, which represent the first 18 years of your life. Push a button and feel yourself descend to that "floor," to an age in your life. When the elevator doors open, step out to the floor and remember yourself at that age.

1. Retrieve a memory of yourself at that age. Take whatever memory comes to you about that particular age. It can be as simple as a dress or suit you wore, a remembered snapshot, a particular smell, or music.
2. Get back on the elevator and push a lower button. Visualize yourself going down gently and safely. When the door opens, step out into that age and re- trieve another memory. Bring it back with you and get onto the elevator again.
3. Push a button lower than six. If possible go down in the elevator as far as one or two or even "B" for the basement (or born). Feel yourself descend slowly, floor by floor, into the safe darkness. When the elevator stops, get out and walk around and see what comes to you.
4. Choose one of the earlier memories to work with. When you have retrieved a memory that seems important to you, stay with it and keep visualizing it.
   - "Where are you?"
   - "Who's with you?"
   - "How are you feeling?"
   - "What kinds of colors and shapes do you see around you?"
   - "What sounds and smells?"
   - "What are you most aware of?"
5. Stay with the scene until you have retrieved buried details. Continue to watch the scene with eyes closed and focus on the detail of events:
   - "What is going on around you? What did you notice that you didn't notice before?"

- "What can you hear being said by others?"
- "At what point does the scene end?"

6. Return to the elevator and come back slowly to the surface, bringing with you the memories you retrieved.
7. Get back on the elevator, allow the doors to close and push the button marked 21. Feel the elevator rise. Take your time returning. Before opening your eyes, ask yourself these questions:
   - "Why is this particular memory important to me?"
   - "What does it still evoke in me?"
8. Now try to capture in writing the things you saw, heard, and felt. Tell your story as a very young child would see it:
   - Focus on one short incident, something that happens in minutes.
   - Keep the child's point of view.
   - Use present tense as if it's happening in the moment.

Technique: *The Shadow Exercise*

Counseling Intention   To identify suppressed parts of identity (Suler, 2003, www.rider.edu/~suler/psycyber).

Description   Think of someone you know whom you don't like very much. Maybe you even hate this person. On a piece of paper, write down a description of that person. Write down what it is about this individual's personality that you don't like. Be as specific as you can.

Draw a box around what you have written—and at the top of the box write "My Shadow." What you have written down is some hidden part of yourself— some part that you have suppressed or hidden. It is what Jung would call your *shadow*.

Maybe it's a part of you that you fear, can't accept, or hate for some reason. Maybe it's a part of you that needs to be expressed or developed in some way. Maybe you even secretly wish you could be like that person you hate.

Process how suppressed parts of ourselves are projected onto others, and how we sometimes choose these "hated" people for close relationships.

Technique: *I-Ching*

Counseling Intention   To gain self-insight (Suler, 2003, www.rider.edu/~suler/psycyber).

Description   The I-Ching is one of the cornerstone texts of Chinese taoism. It consists of 64 "hexagrams," each hexagram being an image or symbol that applies to a specific but complex social, psychological, and/or spiritual situation. Consult the I-Ching as if it were a wise advisor and oracle. After posing a question about an issue or situation in life, toss coins or randomly sort short sticks; the resulting configuration points to a corresponding hexagram in the I-Ching. The hexagram will help clarify current situations, state of mind, and predict the future outcome, as well as offer advice.

Carl Jung was fascinated by the I-Ching, and proposed "synchronicity" as the actual mechanism by which one's mind, the coins or sticks, and the hexagrams become interconnected. Synchronicity occurs when two events that are related in meaning occur at the same time without being the cause of the other. For example, a person may dream of the death of a relative, and learn later that the relative died at the same time he or she had the dream. Mental telepathy, clairvoyance, and other forms of paranormal experiences can be explained by the principle of synchronicity.

Technique: *Show and Tell*

Counseling Intention   To discover more about personal identity and sense of self (Suler, 2003, www.rider.edu/~suler/psycyber).

Description   Ask members to bring in some personal item that is important to them—an item that reveals something significant about their identity (in psychoanalytic psychology terms, a *self object*). Give feedback about what they think the item says about the member, as well as share how they relate to the other members self objects.

THE SUBCONSCIOUS AND ALTERED STATES OF CONSCIOUSNESS

Perspective for the Therapist: On inner personalities

We know that, although we seem to be individuals, we are actually plural beings. Each of us has a great multitude of distinct personalities coexisting within one body, sharing one psyche. It is these inner personalities that appear to us in our dreams as persons.

Robert A. Johnson
Inner Work, 1989, p. 211

TECHNIQUE: *Understanding Our Dreams*

Counseling Intention   Interpersonal/intrapersonal insight.

Description   Dreams have been part of the human psyche since before recorded time. The scientific studies of dreaming and dream content that have accumulated gradually over the past 50 years do not support any of the ideas about dreams that are specifically "Freudian" or "Jungian," but they do support the general notion that many dreams have meaning in the sense of coherence, correlations with other psychological variables, and connections with waking thoughts (Domhoff, 1996; Fisher & Greenberg, 1977, 1996; Foulkes, 1985, 1999). In the networks of the brain, dreaming makes connections more broadly than waking. Dreaming also conceptualizes a dominant emotion. This is demonstrated most clearly in dreams after trauma: the trauma resolves, but can still be seen in dreams under stress, pregnancy, and other situations where the dominant emotional concern is known.

Three general ideas remain from Freudian and Jungian theory after sifting through the scientific evidence developed by empirical dream researchers. First, dreaming is a cognitive process that draws on memory schemas, episodic memories, and general knowledge to produce reasonable simulations of the real world (Antrobus, 1993; Foulkes, 1985, 1999), with due allowance for the occasional highly unusual or extremely memorable dream (Bulkeley, 1999; Hunt, 1989; Knudson & Minier, 1999; Kuiken & Sikora, 1993). Second, dreams have psychological meaning in the sense of coherency, correlations with other psychological variables, and correspondences with waking thought (Domhoff, 1996; Foulkes, 1985; Hall, 1953b). Third, the unusual features of dreams, such as unlikely juxtapositions, metamorphoses, and impossible acts, may be products of figurative thought (Hall, 1953a; Lakoff, 1997). Other aspects of dreaming in the literature include:

- Traumatic dreams that reflect a preoccupation with problems we have not resolved.
- Recurrent dreams are most often reported to begin in childhood.
- The most frequent content theme of recurrent dreams is being attacked or chased.
- Anxiety dreams feature the dreamer being threatened or pursued.
- Recurrent dreams are often reported to begin at times of stress, such as the death of a loved one, separation from parents, or the divorce of parents.
- Recurrent dreams are very similar to the dreams of post-traumatic stress disorder.
- Dreams relate to our emotional preoccupations.
- People dream about emotional hang-ups, fixations, and unfinished personal business.

- Dreams objectify that which is subjective, they visualize that which is invisible, they transform the abstract into the concrete, and they make conscious that which is unconscious.

> *Perspective for the Therapist: On dream content*
>
> *The dream's fantastic theater is the place in which the many varied sides of the self show. All figures, events, and even locations appearing in a dream may be aspects of the self, exhibited in a disguised form. And even though other people, sometimes completely unfamiliar, appear and perform in the dream, in the last analysis they all represent aspects of the dreamer.*
>
> Ilan Kutz
> *The Dreamland Companion,* 1993, p. 142

Dream Work: Writing Dreams Down

A dream is a personal letter to one's self. It might be helpful to record the following types of information:

1. Record anything remembered about the dream itself, even if only fragments.
2. Record small details in the dream, even if they seem insignificant. Record the feelings or sensations experienced during the dream.
3. Record events from life that come to mind when thinking about the dream.
4. Record the thoughts that were mindful when falling asleep.

Record any other thoughts, feelings, memories, or sensations that arise when reflecting on the dream.

The Hall/Van de Castle System of Dream Interpretation

The Hall/Van de Castle system is an application of the general methodological strategy called *content analysis*. Content analysis is an attempt to use carefully defined categories and quantitative methods to extract meaning from a "text," or dream report (Figure 14.1). The original Hall/Van de Castle system consisted of eight general categories, most of which are divided into two or more subcategories. Those eight general categories are:

1. Characters (subdivided into animals, humans, and mythical figures)
2. Social Interactions (subdivided into friendly, aggressive, and sexual)
3. Activities (often analyzed in terms of physical and nonphysical activities)
4. Striving: Successes and Failures

5. Misfortunes and Good Fortunes
6. Emotions (anger, apprehension, sadness, confusion, and happiness)
7. Physical Surroundings: Settings and Objects
8. Descriptive Elements (modifiers, temporality, and negativity)

The Hall/Van de Castle system in effect treats a dream report as a story or play in which there are:

- A cast of characters (animals, men and women, friends, strangers)
- A series of social interactions (aggressive, friendly, sexuality)
- Activities (thinking, talking, running)
- Successes and failures
- Misfortune and good fortune
- Emotions (happy, sad, embarrassed)
- One or more settings (indoors vs. outdoors, familiar vs. unfamiliar)
- Objects (chairs, cars, streets, body parts)
- Descriptive modifiers (tall, fast, crooked)
- Temporal references
- Elements from the past
- Food and eating references

There are almost no elements in a dream report that cannot be classified somewhere, and some fit into more than one category (e.g., hugging someone is both a friendly interaction and a physical activity). Then, too, parts of categories can be used, or two or more categories can be combined to create new indicators (e.g., the degree to which the dreamer initiates aggressive, friendly, and sexual interactions, as opposed to being the recipient of such actions, can be thought of as a measure of "assertiveness" in dream reports). Table 14.1 and Figure 14.2 present an overall view of the various coding symbols employed for characters.

TABLE 14.1
Hall/Van de Castle System: Summary of Coding Symbols

Number	Sex		Identity		Age
1 individual	M male	F father	I infant		A adult
2 group	F female	M mother	Y family members		T teenager
3 individual dead	J joint	X parents	R relative		C child
4 group dead	I indefinite	B brother	K known		B baby
5 individual imaginary	T sister	P prominent			
6 group imaginary	H husband	O occupational			
7 original form	W wife	E ethnic			
8 changed form	A son	S stranger			
	D daughter	U uncertain			
	C child				

Source: Domhoff, G.W., College Eight, UCSC, Santa Cruz, CA dreamresearch.net. 9/22/02. Reprinted with permission.

Age _____

Gender _____

Date Today _____

We would like you to write down the last dream you remember having, whether it was last night, last month, or last year.

- First please tell us the date this dream occurred: _____.
- Then tell us what time of day you think you recalled it: _____.
- Then tell us where you were when you recalled it: _____.

Please describe the dream exactly and as fully as you remember it. Your report should contain, whenever possible: a description of the setting of the dream, whether it was familiar to you or not; a description of the people, their age, sex, and relationship to you; and any animals that appeared in the dream. If possible, describe your feelings during the dream and whether it was pleasant or unpleasant. Be sure to tell exactly what happened to you and the other characters during the dream. Continue your report on the other side and on additional sheets if necessary.

FIGURE 14.1. Recording a Dream

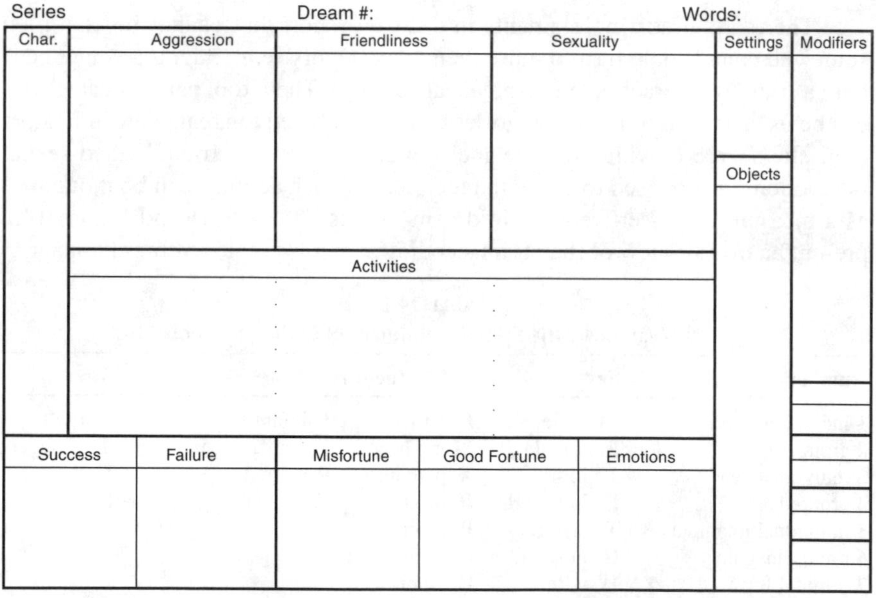

FIGURE 14.2. Hall/Van de Castle System: Recording Dreams

Source: Domhoff, G.W., College Eight, UCSC, Santa Cruz, CA dreamresearch.net. 9/22/02. Reprinted with permission.

HYPNOTHERAPY

With its ability to enhance the power of suggestion, hypnosis has been found effective for a variety of problems that hinge on emotions, habits, and even the body's involuntary responses. It is also helpful against anxiety, tension, depression, phobias, and compulsions, and can sometimes help break an addiction to smoking, alcohol, or drugs. It has successfully alleviated an amazing range of symptoms, including those of asthma, allergy, stroke, multiple sclerosis, Parkinson's disease, cerebral palsy, and irritable bowel syndrome. It can control nausea and vomiting from cancer medications, reduce bleeding during surgery, steady the heartbeat, and bring down blood pressure. It has helped some people lose weight, control severe morning sickness, or gain much relief from muscle spasms and even paralysis.

People who have undergone hypnosis describe their experiences in very different ways (Farthing, 1992, p. 349):

> *"I felt as if I were 'inside' myself; none of my body was touching anything . . ."*
>
> *"I was very much aware of the split in my consciousness. One part of me was analytic and listening to you [the hypnotist]. The other part was feeling the things that the analytic part decided I should have."*

Hence, it is very difficult to arrive at a single definition for the state of hypnosis. It appears that consciousness has been altered; however, how hypnosis occurs, they way it is experienced, and even susceptibility vary from one person to another. Ways of measuring susceptibility for hypnosis include some of the following exercises:

- *The eye-roll test.* Open the eyes wide, then roll them up. Then lower the eyelids without rolling the eyes down. Ability to complete these tasks is not, however, a foolproof predictor of the ability to be hypnotized.
- *The light test.* Stare at a small spot of light in a dark room. Most people will be convinced that the light is moving, but those who see it change direction most frequently are supposedly the best subjects for hypnosis.
- *The lemon test.* Some therapists ask first-time patients to imagine looking at, feeling, picking up, and slicing a lemon in half. They must then picture themselves squeezing some of the juice into a container, smelling it, and drinking a little. Those who are aware of salivating after performing the exercise once (or, in some cases, more than once), are likely to be better candidates than those who do not salivate more than usual.

The therapist can use several techniques to put the client into a hypnotic trance.

- Asking the client to watch a moving object as it swings back and forth, then suggesting in a monotonous, soothing voice that your eyes are getting so heavy you can't keep them open.
- Telling the client to concentrate on the therapist's voice as he gives you instructions.
- Having the client count backward slowly from 30 to 0.

When performing self-hypnosis, sit or lie in a quiet, comfortable place, such as your favorite chair. Then try to relax completely, letting all your muscles go limp and allowing all tension to flow away. To induce the hypnotic trance, or focused state of mind, imagine walking down a long path or descending a long staircase; concentrate on an object and breathe slowly and deeply; count backward from 10 to 0; repeat over and over that your eyes are heavy, your limbs are numb, or your face is warm or cool; or repeat a word or phrase. Once you have achieved a hypnotic state, tell yourself how you want to feel, or listen to a tape on which you have recorded the message. To wake up, count slowly upward from 0 to 10, or reverse the image you used to put yourself under—for example, walk up the staircase. Tell yourself you will awaken feeling wonderful.

One of hypnotherapy's greatest benefits may be its ability to reduce the effects of stress. Many physicians and psychologists believe that the mind has a direct impact on physical well-being. According to this theory, tension, anxiety, and depression can undermine immunity and compromise your health, while a positive attitude can reinforce the immune system, enabling it to better fight infections, toxins, and other immune system invaders. Hypnosis can alleviate stress by putting you into a relaxed state, offering positive suggestions, and ridding the mind of negative thoughts. As tension in your muscles and even your blood vessels recedes, the theory goes, your circulation improves and your entire body feels healthier.

Technique: *Four Ways to Reach a State of Inner Peace*

Counseling Intention   To maintain a state of calm and to relax effortlessly.

Description   Sometimes maintaining inner peace is not convenient. Here are four ways to achieve inner peace that can be used anywhere.

1. Peripheral vision
Look at the opposite wall and find a point that is straight ahead and a little above eye level. Continue to look at this point in soft focus throughout this exercise. After you have concentrated for a while on this point, the rest of the room should go a little dark, vague, or fuzzy, creating a kind of tunnel vision.

Keep your eyes on that point, and begin to broaden the field of vision and notice more and more of what is at either side of that point, so that attention is given to what you see out of the corners of the eyes on each side. By staying in peripheral vision, notice that breathing has moved lower down in the chest and may be slowed down or become deeper; that the muscles of the face have relaxed, especially the jaw muscles. To relax even more, stay in peripheral vision until both hands and feet become warmer.

Peripheral vision seems to activate the parasympathetic nervous system, the part of your nervous system that produces a calming effect. It allows the mind, body, and emotions to come back into balance.

Peripheral vision is particularly useful when speaking in public, its calming effect enables the speaker to see the whole audience; become more aware of any little movements they make; and gauge how they are reacting. There is only a need to go into peripheral vision a little way to contact that deep reserve of peace and tranquility.

2. Centering

Particular attention to the body has a big effect on feelings and perceived strength. This is recognized in the ancient traditions of yoga and the martial arts.

Begin by paying attention to a point that is a few inches below the navel, and halfway between the front and the back to the center of the body. At the same time look straight ahead and go into peripheral vision. Let the body relax, and make sure the knees aren't locked. The ability to maintain this focus on the center of the body can be done anywhere. Focusing on the center point eliminates anxiety and is useful for confrontations and pressure situations.

3. Project an energy bubble

Imagine a bubble of energy projecting out from the central point and surrounding the body like science fiction force field. Everything stressful that happens outside this bubble bounces off and away from the central point, instilling a calm inside the bubble. So the more stressful it is on the outside, the calmer it is on the inside. The unconscious mind doesn't distinguish between imagination and reality. Being shielded from chaos becomes not imagination but reality. This is another resource for dealing with pressure situations. When giving a presentation, extend the energy bubble all the way out to the back and side walls of the room, and then pull it in slightly to embrace and include the whole audience. The audience will notice the difference.

4. Float up above yourself

Sometimes in emotionally fraught situations it can be a good idea to detach from the circumstances to calm down and get things in perspective. A good way to do this is to float up above the situation.

Imagine floating out of the body, higher and higher, and looking down at yourself. Float up until you reach a height at which you are completely comfortable. You'll notice that the higher up you float, the more detached you feel.

You can do this with memories or with imagined future situations as well. If the memory involves other people, float up above the memory of yourself as you interact with them. Observe the scene as a whole system—notice how they react to what you do and say, and how you react to what they do and say. What do you learn from this new perspective?

BREATHWORK

Breathwork is a term used increasingly by practitioners who use breathing techniques where the focus is on the breath. By freeing the breath one learns to breathe through difficult or uncomfortable experiences and feelings. Often energy from a denied experience is freed up to move through the body to be released. The aftereffects of this can be an enormous sense of relief. Old patterns of holding on begin to gently break up and a new sense of aliveness enters as the breath anchors oneself in the present. Breathwork is about reconnecting—embracing and integrating all aspects of ourselves. This includes unresolved feelings (pleasant and unpleasant) or surrounding events (recent, biographical/childhood events, birth process events, past lives). This includes the client's events kept buried in his or her subconscious minds, which can have significant impact on our psychological and physical health. Such a process, while difficult at times, can be tremendously healing. Use of the breath and a sincere willingness to feel whatever comes up are the keys to accessing these unresolved issues. The process involves using the breath and sometimes other techniques as a way to get beyond our ego and defenses and locate issues in the subconscious mind (often reflected in the body as tightness or energy blockages) that need to be felt, embraced, and integrated. There is no need to direct the mind to specific events, as the breath will take the person where he or she needs to go.

Technique: *Breath Work*

Counseling Intention   To become more relaxed through breathing.

Description   A few nice deep breaths can be so relaxing. It can be a quick and easy stress reliever. It can be done at any time, and it is not visible to others.

The client will feel less stressed, and will be able to handle things more easily. Clients who are stressed tend to take short little breaths rather than deep, relaxing ones. Try the following:

- Sit down or lie down.
- Inhale slowly and say to yourself, "*I am . . .*
- Exhale slowly and say to yourself, "*. . . relaxed.*"

Breathing is not something done. Rather it is something that is allowed. Allow breathing to occur smoothly and naturally.

Technique: *Experiencing a Full Breath*

Counseling Intention   To extract life force from the air.

Description   It is not possible or necessary to fully expand the lungs with every breath, but it is vital in heightening awareness to experience how a really complete breath feels. This exercise uses the lungs to capacity, and extracts great amounts of "life force" from the air. Because breathing is normally unconscious but can be controlled consciously, changing your breathing, or just becoming aware of it, is an easy way to change your physiological state.
    Try this exercise sitting, standing, or lying down.

1. Exhale deeply, contracting the belly.
2. Inhale slowly and expand the abdomen.
3. Continue inhaling and expand the chest.
4. Continue inhaling and raise the shoulders up toward the ears.
5. Hold for a few comfortable seconds.
6. Exhale in reverse pattern, slowly. Release shoulders, relax chest, contract the abdomen.
7. Repeat.

This exercise will require gentle practice so that inhalation and exhalation become smooth and balanced. Beginners should only do it two or three times continuously.

CONCLUSION

All the techniques in this chapter represent an emphasis on the unconscious and altered states of consciousness for client self-understanding and interpersonal mastery. The influence of the unconscious on human behavior cannot be minimized, nor can the influence of childhood trauma and the importance early relationships. Dreamwork, breathe work, hypnosis, and meditation are techniques that focus on reaching a level of higher consciousness and inner peace.

Chapter 15

Eclectic Techniques for Use with Family Systems and Family Development

My Declaration of Self-Esteem
I AM ME

In all the world, there is no one else exactly like me
Everything that comes out of me is authentically me
Because I alone chose it—I own everything about me
My body, my feelings, my mouth, my voice, all my actions,
Whether they be to others or to myself—I own, my fantasies,
My dreams, my hopes, my fears—I own all my triumphs and
Successes, all my failures and mistakes. Because I own all of
Me, I can become intimately acquainted with me—by so doing
I can love me and be friendly with me in all my parts—I know
There are aspects about myself that puzzle me, and other
Aspects that I do not know—but as long as I am
Friendly and loving to myself, I can courageously
And hopefully look for solutions to the puzzles
And for ways to find out more about me—However I
Look and sound, whatever I say and do, and whatever
I think and feel at a given moment in time is authentically
Me—If later some parts of how I looked, sounded, thought
And felt turn out to be unfitting, I can discard that which is
Unfitting, keep the rest, and invent something new for that
Which I discarded—I can see, hear, feel, think, say, and do
I have the tools to survive, to be close to others, to be
Productive to make sense and order out of the world of
People and things outside of me—I own me, and
therefore I can engineer me—I am me and

I AM OKAY

Virginia Satir, *Self-Esteem*, 1975, p. 12
(Reprinted with permission)

In the past two decades, family therapy from a systems perspective has gained momentum as an innovative force in counseling. It has profoundly influenced therapeutic interventions in the lives of client and their families (Schafer, Briesmeister, & Fitton, 1984; Stanton, 1984). Marriage and family therapists treat clients with a wide array of disorders in various stages of crisis. Treatment typically involves not only the individual, but may draw upon the strengths and dynamics of the family system for working toward problem resolution. The issues marriage and family therapists face are complex and run the course of the life cycle, from childhood and adolescent issues to difficulties faced by the aging population. The goal is not only to resolve the immediate problems presented for treatment, but also to build a foundation of wellness and to understand and accept transgenerational issues. Marriage and family therapy is one of the nation's most rapidly advancing disciplines. Academic and professional study areas include human development; personality theory; psychopathology; assessment, diagnosis treatment, and intervention methods in marriage and family therapy; family life cycle and development; interactional and behavioral patterns; cross-cultural, minority, and gender issues; human sexuality; research design, methods, and statistics; and ethics and professional studies. Marriage and therapists can be found at the cutting edge of development knowledge in mental health. Marriage and family therapists work with:

- Families facing depression, major mental illness, or emotional disorders.
- Custody mediation for families facing divorce.
- The alcohol or drug abuser and his or her family.
- Persons with chronic illness and disability and their families.
- Crime victims struggling to reclaim their lives, and their family members.
- Patients and the family members who care for them.
- HIV-positive individuals, people living with AIDS, and their family members.
- Veterans, firemen, police officers, emergency medical technicians seeking counseling following a devastating traumatic event.
- Military personnel and their family members.
- Families facing possible loss of their children to out-of-home placement.
- The homeless and homeless mentally ill.
- Abuse victims and perpetrators.
- Immigrants adjusting to a new life in the United States.
- Adolescents at risk for incarceration (and their families).
- Families in the foster care system.
- Providing treatment alternatives to prison.

Systems theory, for example, provides both a conceptual and practical framework for organizing diagnostic information and evaluating presenting problems. Family systems theory is appropriate when evidence of family dysfunction exists.

Fundamentally, the systems theoretical framework views the family as a self-regulating system joined together by unspoken rules whose purpose is to maintain itself. Psychological symptoms are perceived as manifestations of a dysfunctional family. The focus of treatment becomes the family system, not the problem or symptomatic family member. The goal of counseling and family therapy is to engender human and systematic growth.

Therapists always have understood that the problems they deal with arise largely in families and take their form from family relationships. A number of theoretical models have evolved with their respective counseling techniques. Many therapists, however, are eclectic and use the model and technique most appropriate for a particular family and treatment setting. A brief synopsis of 11 models follows.

1. *Psychodynamic*—an object relations approach to family therapy pioneered by Ackerman (1958) and originally described by Fairbairn (1967) and Klein (1959) and applied to marital relationships by Dicks (1967). It views dysfunction as the result of inappropriate behavioral attempts to work out issues of the past. Since the 1980s there has been a resurgence of interest in psychodynamics among family therapists, spurred on by object relations theory and self-psychology integrating depth psychology and systems theory (Kirschner & Kirschner, 1986; Nichols, 1987; Sander, 1989).

2. *Family Systems Therapy*—focuses on the importance of differentiation, relationships between generations, transgenerational dysfunctions (such as alcoholism), and triangulation (Bowen, 1978; Kerr, 1980), with a focus on multigenerational family systems, i.e., how interlocking triangles connect one generation to the next. The idea of intergenerational conditions has been very influential in the counseling field. According to Bowen (1971, 1974, 1975), the major problem in families is emotional fusion. The fundamental solution is differentiation. The triangle is the primary focus of analysis in both principle and practice. Like Freud, Bowen believed the important impact of early family relationships. The primary relationship between the self and parents is described as a triangle and has major implications for life.

3. *Experiential Family Therapy*—Designed to change family members, families are treated as groups of individuals more than systems. Interpersonal change and growth is emphasized more than problem solving. Therapists seek intense emotional awareness, expressive techniques, and interventions that take the form of self-disclosure, teasing, sarcasm, humor, personal confrontation, paradoxical intention, and modeling (Duhl, 1983; Duhl & Duhl, 1981).

4. *Comunications*—describes pathology manifested in dysfunctional communication patterns (Bateson, 1972; Jackson & Weakland, 1961; Satir, 1967; Satir & Baldwin, 1983). Treatment focuses on changing interpersonal interaction patterns to promote growth and to increase self-esteem, conflict resolution, and new adaptive responses to dysfunctional communication.

5. *Structural Family Therapy*—views family dysfunction as a consequence of family structure (Haley, 1976, 1984; Minuchin, 1974; Taylor, 1984). Wisdom and insight come only after structural change. Structural family theory has become one of the most widely used conceptual models in the field. The fundamental tenet of this approach is that every family has a structure that is revealed only when the family is in action. The basic structural concepts are boundaries, subsystems, alignments, and complementarity. Therapists take into account the individual family and social context, providing a clear organizing framework for understanding and healing families.

6. *Systems*—emphasizes the influence of networks of relationships upon individuals. Relationships can be understood as any unit of interaction or communication between individuals.

7. *Strategic Intervention*—a brief treatment model of therapeutic change designed by the Akerman Institute, Haley (1976, 1984), and Selvini-Palazzoli (1978). Strategic intervention is aimed at changing the powerful family rules in families that are particularly resistant to change.

8. *Transactional Analysis*—created by Eric Berne (1961, 1964), deals with aspects of the personality that other techniques may exclude: the behavioral, the interpersonal, and the intrapsychic. It is a contractual form of therapy that focuses on ego states of parent, adult, child, and aspects of rescripting for redecision and change.

9. *Multiple-Family Group Therapy*—proposed by Bahatti, Janakiramariah, and Channabasvanna (1982), employs multiple family group therapy as a means for establishing support and help to a family. The family benefits through an extended family living experience. Mutual support and belongingness are common goals; the entire group serves as a resource for problem solving, generating alternatives, and developing action plans for change.

10. *Cognitive-Behavioral Family Therapy*—is used primarily to teach parents how to apply learning theory to control their children; to help parents substitute positive for aversive control; and to diminish anxiety in couples with sexual problems. Treatment is usually time limited and symptom focused, based on social learning theory. Behaviorists have developed a wealth of reliable and valid diagnostic and assessment methods and applied them to evaluation, treatment planning, and monitoring progress and outcomes.

11. *Narrative Therapy*—is organized around two simple metaphors: a client's personal narrative and social construction (i.e., challenging the notion of an objective basis for knowledge shaped by culturally shared assumptions). By challenging rigid and pessimistic versions of events, therapists make room for flexibility, optimism, and hope. The strategies of narrative therapy fall into three stages: (1) recasting the problem as a misfortune by focusing on the effects rather than the causes; (2) finding exceptions or partial triumphs over the misfortune and instances of successful experiences; and (3) some

kind of public ritual to reinforce new and preferred interpretations (Brunner, 1991; Freedman & Combs, 1996; White & Epston, 1990; Zimmerman & Dickerson, 1996).

As families journey through developmental stages, coping skills during important transitions may become impaired (Klimek & Anderson, 1988). Members of dysfunctional families can become fixated in self-perpetuating pathological patterns. Common characteristics of such families may include the following:

* One or more symptomatic members
* Blurred generational boundaries
* Confused communication patterns
* Overprotection
* Enmeshment
* Denial
* Inability to resolve conflict
* Submerged tension
* Scapegoating
* Low tolerance for stress
* Fragmented, disjointed, isolated individuals
* Noncohesive, pseudo-closeness
* Skewed relationships, for example, isolation of one member
* Extreme positions by all members in an effort to differentiate
* Lack of respect for individual differences.

In response to these pathological tendencies, Notarius & Markman (1993, pp. 272–273) offer these simple truths to promote respect and understanding among couples:

Simple truth 1: Each relationship contains a hidden reservoir of hope.
"I know that we can work it out."
"I know he or she means well."
"He's not intentionally trying to be difficult."
Simple truth 2: One put-down will erase 20 acts of kindness.
"With anger, I'll rarely get what I want."
"Criticism is rarely constructive."
"One put-down a day will keep the doctor in business."
Simple truth 3: Little changes in you can lead to huge changes in the relationship.
"Partner change follows self-change."
"Make a little behavior change today for a big feeling change tomorrow."
Simple truth 4: It's not the differences between partners that cause prob-

lems but how the differences are handled when they arise.

"When it doubt, listen and relate—don't suggest and resolve."

"When we are happy, our differences didn't matter. I won't let them matter now, either."

Simple truth 5: Men and women fight using different weapons but suffer similar wounds.

"We're both human."

"We need to work together as a team."

Simple truth 6: Partners need to practice relationships skills in order to become good at them.

"Practice makes perfect, and to err is human."

"Better talk is a path, not a destination."

These tenets serve to anchor couples into a philosophy of relating to one another, to promote communication, respect, and mutual problem solving.

Technique: *Lifeline*

Counseling Intention The purpose of the Lifeline is to assist individuals and couples in examining their past and present and making projections for the future (Coleman, 1998, p. 52).

Description

1. Draw a Lifeline of yourself. The Lifeline should be how the client perceives his or her self. The line can take a variety of shapes and forms, dips and valleys.
2. Begin somewhere in the past, and project to some point into the future. The client should start with his or her earliest memory, and project to at least one year from the current date.
3. Note that significant events that have shaped the client's life.
4. For clarification use the following symbols to further illustrate the Lifeline:

    ! = a risk or chance the client took.

    X = an obstacle, something (or someone) that prevented the client from getting or doing what he or she wanted.

    O = a decision made for the client by someone else.

    + = a positive, satisfying, or appropriate decision.

    − = a negative, unsatisfying, or inappropriate decision.

    ? = a decision that the client anticipates in the future (i.e., up to two years from now).

Discuss the Lifeline in detail. The therapist should ask for feedback and clarification of various events and statements made on the Lifeline.

Technique: Constructing a Compromise
That Both Parties Can Live With

Counseling Intention To get both partners to yield a little and find their common ground so that they can arrive at a compromised position on an issue. These strategies work with solvable problems (Gottman, 1999, p. 233).

Description In this exercise, spouses work together to try to develop a common way of thinking about an issue and start to construct a compromise that they can both live with. They should ask their partner these questions:

1. How can we understand this issue? Can we develop a compromised view?
2. What are common feelings or the most important feelings here?
3. What common goals do we have?
4. What methods can we agree upon for accomplishing these goals?

Technique: *Sharing Meaning in Family Rituals*

Counseling Intention To build or strengthen shared meaning around rituals (Gottman, 1999, p. 261)

Description Couples explore the following questions to develop their own family rituals:

1. How do we eat dinner? What is the meaning of dinner time? How was dinner time done in each of our families growing up?
2. How should we part at the beginning of each day? What was it like in our families growing up? How should our reunions be?
3. How should bedtime be? What was it like in our families growing up? How do we want this time to be?
4. What is the meaning of weekends? What was it like in our families growing up? What should they be like?

Questions can continue regarding vacations, holidays, sickness, time alone, work, children, and so on.

> *Perspective for the Therapist: On familiarity and contempt*
>
> *The more intensively the family has stamped its character upon the child, the more [the child] will tend to feel and see its earlier miniature world again in the bigger world of adult life.*
>
> Carl Jung

Technique: *Building Shared Meaning in Family Roles*

Counseling Intention To build shared meaning around roles (Gottman, 1999, p. 262).

Description Couples explore the following questions to develop their own family roles:

1. How do you feel about your role as husband or wife? What does that role mean to you? How did your father or mother view this role? How are you similar or different? How would you like to change this role?
2. How do you feel about your role as a father or mother? What does it mean to you? How did your father or mother view this role? How are they similar or different? How would you like to change this role?

Questions continue focusing on issues such as role as son or daughter, as work and career, as friend to others, in the community, and how to achieve balance among all of these responsibilities.

BLENDED OR STEPFAMILY CONFIGURATIONS

The "blended family" or "stepfamily" is no longer an aberration in American society: It's a norm. Today, more than 33 percent of all U.S. children are expected to live in a stepfamily before age 18. Born of conflict and loss, newfound commitments and often abrupt transitions, these families confront a multitude of lifestyle adjustments and challenges. Children of stepfamilies face a higher risk of emotional and behavioral problems and are less likely to be resilient in stressful situations, psychologists' research has found. Walsh (1992) identified four basic categories of issues in remarriage or stepfamilies: (1) initial family issues, (2) developing family issues, (3) feelings about self and others, and (4) adult issues. Within the four categories, he cited 20 major issues that are significant contributors to family disharmony. Counselor sensitivity to these concerns may lead to more accurate assessments and more timely interventions (p. 714).

Initial Family Issues
1. Name to call the new parent—issues of power and authority.
2. Affection for the new parent and absent parent—issues of loyalty or allegiance.
3. Loss of natural parent—issues of loss and grief.
4. Instant love of new family members—issues of emotional bonding.

5. Fantasy about the old family structure—Parental reconciliation fantasies, especially for children whose identification with the absent parent is strong.

Developing Family Issues

6. Discipline by the stepparent—issues of being inattentive, disengaged, or overly restrictive.
7. Confusion over family roles—issues of role assignments in cultural, personal, and legal spheres creating ambiguity.
8. Sibling conflict—issues of stepsibling relationships.
9. Competition for time—issues about contact with absent parent, competition of the custodial parent, and jealously of the stepparent.
10. Extended kinship network—issues of expectations, different values and lifestyles, belongingness, and visitations during significant holidays.
11. Sexual conflicts—loosening of sexual boundaries.
12. Changes over time—issues of remarriage, organization, and boundaries.
13. Exit and entry of children—influence on home, school, and peer relations of children shuttling between their permanent home and the home of the noncustodial parent.

Feelings about Self and Others

14. Society's acceptance of the remarriage family.
15. The connotation of stepfamily.
16. Individual self-concept and lower self-esteem.

Adult Issues

17. Effects of parenting on the new marital relationship.
18. Financial concerns and obligations.
19. Continuing adult conflict from previous relationships and communication with children.
20. Competition of the noncustodial parent in child-rearing and over material possessions.

Successful family transitions must confront all these issues.

> *Perspective for the Therapist: On taking responsibility for our actions as parents*
>
> *We all carry our parents around inside us. Their presence is always felt, still nagging, praising, threatening, judging, and advising. The extent that our parents were wise and loving, their presence is useful, as well as pleasant company... When parents are unwise, insensitive, harsh, unloving, or misguided, their presence is detrimental.*
>
> Jack Lee Rosenberg and Majorie L. Rand

Technique: *Counseling Techniques for Dysfunctional Families*

Counseling Intention To help family members demonstrate how they normally deal with situations.

Description Anderson (1988) capsulated several techniques that can be useful in assessing how families work together, their developmental stage, and their real versus presenting problem.

> *Sequencing.* Ask questions such as who does what, when? When the kids are fighting, what is the mother or father doing?
>
> *Hypothetical questions.* Who would be most likely to stay home if a child became ill? Which child can you visualize living at home as an adult?
>
> *Scaling reports.* On a scale of most to least, compare one another in terms of anger, power, neediness, and happiness.
>
> *Family map.* Organize information about the generational development of the family that reveals the transmission of family rules, roles, and myths (Bowen, 1978).
>
> *Tracking.* How does the family deal with a problem? "What was it like for you when *X*?" rather than "How did you feel when *X*?" Such questions help keep the focus on the family rather than on the individual.
>
> *Sculpting.* Create a still picture of the family that symbolizes relationships by having members position one another physically. This technique can be used to cut through defenses and helps nonverbal members express themselves.
>
> *Paradoxical intervention.* Instruct the family to do something unexpected; observe how the family changes by rebellion or noncompliance. This is often most appropriate with highly resistant or rigid families.

Technique: *The Family Safety Watch*

Counseling Intention To provide a family network for crisis intervention; to provide an intervention strategy for self-destructive behavior.

Description The Family Safety Watch (Stanton, 1984) is an intense intervention strategy to prevent self-destructive behavior of a family member (e.g., a suicidal adolescent). The safety watch also can apply to such problems as child abuse, self-mutilation, eating disorders, and drug or alcohol abuse. The procedure is as follows.

Family members conduct the watch. They select people to be involved in the watch from among their nuclear family, extended family, and network of family friends. An around-the-clock shift schedule is established to determine what the adolescent is going to do with his or her time over a 24-hour period—that is, when he or she is to sleep, eat, attend class, do homework, play games, or view a movie—according to a structured, planned agenda.

The intervention team leader consults with the family in (1) determining what the family resources and support systems are, (2) figuring out ways for involving these support systems in the effort (e.g., "How much time do you think Uncle Harry can give to watching your son/daughter?"), (3) designing a detailed plan for the safety watch, and (4) figuring out schedules and shifts so that someone is with the at-risk child 24 hours per day.

A backup system also is established so that the person on watch can obtain support from others if he or she needs it. (A cardinal rule is that the child must be within view of someone at all times, even when in the bathroom or when sleeping.) The family is warned that the at-risk youth may try to manipulate situations to be alone (e.g., pretend to be fine) and that the first week will be the hardest.

A contractual agreement is established that if the watch is inadvertently slackened or compromised and the at-risk youth makes a suicide attempt or tries to challenge the program in some way, the regime consequently will be tightened. This is a therapeutic move that reduces the family's feeling of failure should a relapse occur during the year.

The primary goal of the watch is to mobilize the family to take care of their "own" and feel competent in doing so. With tasks surrounding the watch, the family, adolescent, and helping professionals (as a team) collaborate in determining what the adolescent must do in order to relax and ultimately to terminate the watch. Task issues should focus around personal responsibility, age-appropriate behavior, and handling of family and social relationships, such as the following:

1. Arise in the morning without prompting.
2. Complete chores on time.
3. Substitute courteous and friendly behavior for grumbling and sulking.
4. Talk to parents and siblings more openly.
5. Watch less TV and spend more time with friends and significant others.

The decision to terminate the watch is made conjointly by the family and the therapeutic team. It is contingent upon the absence of self-destructive behavior as well as the achievement of an acceptable level of improvement in the other behavioral tasks assigned to the adolescent. If any member of the therapeutic team feels there is still a risk, the full safety watch is continued.

This approach appeals to families because it makes them feel potent and useful, and reduces the expense of an extended hospital program. It also reestablishes the intergenerational boundary, opens up communication within the family, reconnects the nuclear and extended families, and makes the adolescent cared for and safe. In addition, it functions as a "compression" move that pushes the youth and family members closer together and holds them there and awaits the rebound or disengagement that almost inevitably follows. This rebound is often a necessary step in bringing about appropriate distance within enmeshed subsystems, opening the way for a more viable family structure—a structure that does not require a member to exhibit suicidal or self-destructive behavior.

Technique: *Airing Grievances Constructively*

Counseling Intention To provide a constructive way to build a new relationship.

Description The following guidelines provided by Bach and Wyden (1968) are designed to provide a constructive way of rebuilding relationships between couples. It can be adapted for any two people with conflict or resentment toward each other. Make an appointment to confront each other. Many conflicts and accompanying dialogue are unproductive because only one individual is ready to confront the issues and the other may refuse to fight. Designating a time without distractions provides a more equitable advantage.

- Take turns expressing resentments. Let one person talk for five minutes without interruption. Reciprocate the process.
- When all issues are presented, have your partner repeat the concerns as you outlined them. Check for understanding. Reciprocate the process.
- Clearly state your expectations of each other—the behavior you will not resent.
- Determine together if your expectations are realistic, negotiable, or both. Then proceed with a mutually satisfactory agreement about the future. Be as specific as possible about compromises and expectations.

Technique: *Exercises to Open Communication*

Counseling Intention Satir (1967) provided a strategy for helping couples reach a deeper level of communication and understanding.

Description Instruct couples to do the following:

- Stand back to back and talk to each other. This simulates what frequently occurs when one partner wants to talk finances or schedules and the other is reading the newspaper, fixing dinner, or otherwise preoccupied.

- Stand face to face, and look at each other without talking. What do you think your partner is thinking and feeling? When discussing, check for the accuracy of your perception.
- Now eyeball each other, and communicate without talking. See how much more communication gets through.
- Close your eyes and communicate without talking.
- Eyeball each other and talk without touching.
- Use all forms of communication (talk, touch, look at each other).

Most couples find it difficult to argue with each other without looking away or withdrawing physically. Touch and eye contact creates more intimacy.

Technique: *The Total Truth Exercise*

Counseling Intention To acknowledge pent-up feelings (Marston, 1994).

Description Releasing pent-up feelings can help gain control of emotions. The total truth technique helps free excess emotional baggage in conflictual relationships. Write a letter to the person with whom you have a conflict to express the full range of your emotions, starting with anger and ending with forgiveness. If you proceed to the section on forgiveness, but still have feelings of anger or sadness, go back to the angry part of your letter and keep writing until you feel free of that particular emotion.

Anger and Resentment
> I'm angry that . . .
> I hate it when . . .
> I'm fed up with . . .
> I resent it when . . .
> I can't stand it when . . .

Hurt
> I feel hurt when . . .
> I feel rejected when . . .
> I feel sad when . . .
> I feel jealous about . . .
> I feel disappointed about . . .

Fear
> I feel scared when you . . .
> I feel scared that you don't . . .
> I'm afraid that . . .

I feel insecure about . . .
I'm afraid that I . . .

Remorse and Regret
I'm sorry that . . .
I regret that I . . .
Please forgive me for . . .
I didn't mean to . . .
I feel sad that . . .

Wants
All I ever wanted was . . .
I want you to . . .
I wish that . . .
I deserve . . .
I want us to . . .
What I really want is . . .

Love and Forgiveness
I forgive you for . . . and I forgive myself for . . .
What I love most about you is . . .
I understand that . . .
I appreciate you for . . .
Thank you for . . .

This exercise can be used when a client feels stuck in emotions. Feelings need to be expressed in order to be released and for healing to occur. This is a safe and highly effective method for releasing and confronting feelings.

Technique: *Actualizing Individual Strengths*

Counseling Intention To actualize the positive strengths of partners or family members.

Description Abraham Maslow maintained that we should be more concerned with enhancing a person's potential rather than dwelling their weaknesses. The following exercise will identify the positive strengths of people in the group.

> *Step 1.* Each person writes his or her name on a slip of paper; one person's name is chosen at random. A volunteer takes notes on the strengths seen in this person.

Step 2. The person who has been chosen expresses to the family all the strengths he sees in himself.

Step 3. The person who has been chosen then asks the group, "What other strengths or potentialities do you see in me? What do you see keeping me from using these strengths?"

Step 4. The members now share with this person their perception of his strengths and blocks.

Step 5. The members then fantasize what this person would be like if he were using these strengths in the next five years.

Step 6. The volunteer gives the notes to the chosen person, who discusses how the session has been of value to him. The same procedure may be repeated for another person.

Technique: *Enhancing Interpersonal Communication*

Counseling Intention To actively listen to what another person is saying.

Description Demonstrate the art of listening to the couple or family.

Step 1. Before person A can respond to person B or begin a new topic, A must repeat what B has said.

Step 2. B must confirm that A has rephrased what he or she said (and felt) before A can make his or her point.

Step 3. The counselor then asks the group if any person thinks B communicated something (verbally or nonverbally) that A did not hear, or if anyone has a different interpretation of what A said. A should check this with B; that is, A should tell B what he heard to see if this is what B meant to communicate.

Process that we usually hear only part of what another person says and then begin to form our own response, counterargument, or rebuttal. We often respond to the *words* people express rather than their *feelings*.

Technique: *Using Confrontation to Improve Relationships*

Counseling Intention To enable couples to express honest feelings of anger in a safe way.

Description Each couple or family takes turns to discuss the following:

- "The things you do to make me angry are . . ."
- "The things you do that most block our relationship are . . ."
- "The things you do to improve the relationship are . . ."

Each individual is provided with the opportunity to confront each other. Process whether the confrontation exercise enabled them to express honest feelings of anger in a safe way.

Technique: *An Exercise to Deescalate Conflict*

Counseling Intention To create more positive communication.

Description (1) Identify the issues that are causing the conflict. (2) Discuss the pain and concerns of the issue. (3) Identify the consequences of each other's actions. (4) The offender in the relationship asks for forgiveness and apologizes. (5) The offended agrees to forgive and not use the issue in the future, or bring up the past in the present. (Note: Bringing up the past is disrespectful.) The offender agrees to change his or her behavior.

Technique: *Problem Solving for Couples*

Counseling Intention To resolve conflict and disagreements.

Description Nine ways to resolve conflicts in relationships:

1. *Show respect.* Don't belittle your mate or call him or her names.
2. *Focus on the problem.* Describe behavior, not aspects of the other's personality.
3. *Tackle one problem at a time.* Stay on task and don't bring in other issues.
4. *Use a time out.* When losing control, call for a time out and resume discussing the issue later.
5. *Listen for the feelings under the words.* Everything discussed is important and should be valued.
6. *Don't try to be a mind reader.* Clarify what your partner thinks and feels.
7. *Try to see your partner's point of view.* Validate your partner's feelings by acknowledging his or her viewpoint.
8. *Try to solve the problem.* Say: "What can we do to solve the problem?" and "I am willing to do the following . . ." Say it and do it.
9. *Forgive and accept each other.*

Technique: *How to Conduct a Couples Meeting*

Counseling Intention To air grievances without conflict (Notarius & Markam, 1993, p. 204).

Description The following guidelines can foster a climate of respect and shared understanding:

1. *Make a date.* Set up a regular weekly time for half an hour to talk with each other.
2. *Focus on the problem.* Sit down face to face with no distractions (i.e., no children, television, computer, or telephone) and talk about one subject at a time.
3. *Use the speaker-listener tool.* Decide what will be talked about and who is the speaker. Write on a piece of paper the world "FLOOR." Rotate the FLOOR back and forth and speak only when the FLOOR is in possession. The speaker should keep his or her statements short so that the listener can follow them.
4. *Don't blame and attack.* Remember the problems that interfere with a more positive relationship are between the couple. The clients should focus on how each feels and their role in the problem.
5. *Reserve the right to take a break.* When the discussion starts to not go well (e.g., one partner starts to blame, attack, or escalate the conflict), either partner can call stop to the action. At that point in the meeting, agree to stop talking and pick up the conversation again within 24 hours.

Technique: *Using the Speaker-Listener Tool in a Couples Meeting*

Counseling Intention To provide structure in expressing concerns to one another (Notarius & Markam 1993, pp. 208–209).

Description The following speaker-listener tool provides structure and outlines expectations for couples as they seek to resolve problems

Step 1: One partner, as speaker, states his or her thoughts, feelings, or concerns about issue or event X and then asks politely for the other partner to show understanding.

Step 2: The listener tries to communicate a sincere understanding of the speakers thoughts and feelings about event X without being defensive, apologizing for any role he or she may have had in X, or dismissing what the speaker has to say by simply saying "I understand." (This promotes respect between each other.) The listener concludes by asking the speaker, "Is that how you are feeling?" giving the speaker a chance to clarify anything that the listener might have missed. The listener is directed not to introduce his or her side of the matter until the roles switch and he or she is the speaker.

Step 3: If the speaker feels the listener has sincerely understood, it should be acknowledged: "Yes, that's how I'm feeling." Steps 1 and 2 continue until feelings about event *X* are understood. Partners then may switch roles and carry on the same steps. Better talking skills can also be enhanced with the following responsible speaker guidelines:

1. The client should share his or her side of things.
2. The client should keep statements short and not deliver a long, detailed monologue.
3. The client should use declarative sentences, not questions that entrap his or partner by blaming or attacking and escalating conflict.
4. The client should be polite.

Technique: *Let's Make a Date*

Counseling Intention To provide more enjoyable activities in a couple's life (Notarius & Markam, 1993).

Description Clients should make a list of fun activities to be enjoyed during an agreed-upon time period.

- Plan a surprise weekend for your spouse/lover, making sure the other person does not know the destination.
- Spend a night at a bed-and-breakfast.
- Go on a one-day cruise to nowhere.
- Learn a new sport or game to play together (e.g., golf lessons, tennis lessons, dance lessons, backgammon, or sailing).
- Take a limo ride to a favorite restaurant.
- Go browsing through antique shops.
- Decide not to watch television for a week. Tape the shows and watch them all at one sitting, leaving more time for fun activities.
- Pack a picnic dinner and watch the sun set.
- Leave love notes, candy, or other surprises in his or her briefcase or purse.

The list is endless and can be individualized to couples' needs and resources.

Technique: *Listening for Understanding*

Counseling Intention To improve communication between partners.

Description The following listening skills can improve communication:

> *Paraphrase:* Restate what you heard your partner say by restating what she said in your own words.
>
> *Clarify:* Ask questions and ask for clarification on anything that is not understood. Ask you partner to explain his feelings.
>
> *Constructive feedback:* Tell your partner what your reaction is to what has been said. Feedback must be immediate, honest, supportive, and something that the person can legitimately change.

Technique: *Receiving Family Feedback*

Counseling Intention To provide structured exercises for feedback from family members.

Description Lewis and Streitfeld (1970) provided the following strategies to solicit feedback from members of the family.

- **Stranger on a Train.** Imagine that a stranger is coming to visit you. He has never met your family, and someone is to meet him at the train. How would each member of your family describe the others? Be specific, go beyond what they might be wearing to a personality or behavioral trait.
- **Biography.** Imagine that somebody is writing a biography of each member of your family. When interviewed, what would each member say about the other— likes/dislikes, turn-ons/turn-offs, values/goals, and so on.
- **Self-portrait.** After everyone has had a chance to describe everyone else, describe yourself.
  1. How would you tell someone to find you at the station? What would you tell your biographer?
  2. Discuss the differences that turn up between self-impressions and family's impressions of you. What have you found out about yourself?
- **Family Adjectives.** If you could choose just one adjective to describe each member in your family, what would it be? Check for discrepancies and congruencies among family members.

- **Sculpturing.** Go up to each member of the family in turn, and arrange his or her body in a position that you feel characterizes him or her. Give the sculpture a title.
- **Family Classified.** Write a classified ad for your ideal family (e.g., "father wanted" and "daughter wanted") in which you describe, in 20 or 30 words, what you would like in a family member. Compose the ad in which you list your attributes. Describe the kind of relative you are and how you may improve. Examples follow:

Father Wanted

"To be more involved with teenager. Be attentive, warm, and understanding. Let daughter be herself and trust her more. Listen without putting others down or without shouting."

Daughter Available

"Warm and concerned about others when not hassled. Has made mistakes but is willing to learn. May be strong willed and assertive, but very honest."

Perspective for the Therapist: On relationships

For me, anything that gives new hope, new possibilities and new positive feelings about ourselves will make us more whole people and thus more human, real and loving in our relationships with others.

If enough of this happens, the world will become a better place for all of us. I matter. You matter. What goes on between us matters.

Since I always carry me with me, and I belong to me, I always have something to bring to you and me—new resources, new possibilities to cope differently and to create anew.

Virginia Satir

Technique: *Time-limited Intercommunication*

Counseling Intention To treat marital discord; to achieve more equitable levels of understanding and communication.

Description The couple is instructed to set aside at least three separate, hour-long appointments each week for prescribed communication. A timer is set for five minutes. During those five minutes, the first speaker discusses any topic of choice. The listener may not interrupt. The listener may take notes in preparation for a rebuttal, but no verbal response may occur until the five minutes elapse and the timer sounds.

The timer is set for another five minutes and the other partner repeats the process under the same ground rules. Each partner has six five-minute intervals in which to talk and six to attend to the other person's verbalizations. At the end of the hour, the couple is to embrace each other and to cease further communication on the issues until the next one-hour appointment.

Technique: *The Simulated Family Approach*

Counseling Intention To explore family roles and gain insight into one's behavior and its effect on others.

Description The various family members simulate each other's behaviors; for example, the daughter plays the father, the father plays the stepson. The members may also be asked to pretend they are a different family. The therapist and family discuss how they differ from or identify with the roles they project.

Technique: *"Family Sayings"*

Counseling Intention To encourage self-awareness, expectations, and transgenerational belief systems.

Description Every family has its own favorite expressions, belief system, slogans, warnings, or counsel. Have members list all the repetitive expressions they recall from their childhood. For example, "Father knows best" may be interpreted as you have no opinion of your own; "What will the neighbors think?" may be interpreted as not to let anything tarnish our public façade; or "One man's trash is another man's treasure" may be warning not to discard anything!

Have members list all the repetitive expressions that they can recall from childhood. Process the underlying messages. What values do they represent? How do they influence growth or impede independence?

Technique: *Family Sculpture*

Counseling Intention To assess communication and relationships.

Description Ask someone in the family to describe a typical family argument, and then have the person sculpt the argument by placing each family member in appropriate positions—complete with gestures, facial expressions, and touch. This can be followed by asking each of the other members how he or she would change it and letting each make the changes.

Technique: *"All Tied Up"*

Counseling Intention To better understand the complexity of relationships and crossed transactions.

Description Each family member takes some long ropes, one for each of the others in the family, and ties all the ropes around his or her waist. Next, instruct them to tie one rope to each of the other family members. Process the resulting tension and mass of ropes to help the family understand the complexity of its relationships and crossed transactions.

Technique: *Constructing a Family Genogram*

Counseling Intention To recognize closed/distant relationships, transgenerational issues, enmeshed boundaries, communication patterns, family rituals, and family dysfunctions.

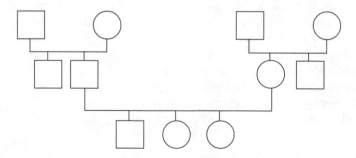

FIGURE 15.1. Genogram

Description The genogram (Figure 15.1) is a format for constructing a family tree which can provide a structure as a diagnostic and treatment technique (Wachtel, 1982). It reflects the clinical perspective that the self originates with a family context. Systems models, self-psychology, and object relations theories all hold that personal identity is intricately intertwined with the intergenerational family—past, present, and future (Bowen, 1978; Erlanger, 1990; Kohut, 1971; Scharf & Scharf, 1987). Transgenerational issues play an important role in family dynamics. Families have different "scripts," and in any one family there can be several sets of directions and expectations.

The genogram provides an enormous amount of information in a relatively short period of time. There are three types of genograms: (1) the basic genogram, (2) the distance genogram, and (3) the details genogram. The basic genogram focuses on individuals, gender, date of birth, career, marriage, divorce, remarriage, or death. The distance genogram focuses on interpersonal relationships within family systems. The details genogram provides a more comprehensive diagram of a family over three generations, focusing on personality traits, unusual circumstances, family themes, family roles, traditions, belief systems, and interpersonal hierarchies.

A number of therapeutic aspects can occur when completing a genogram. First, the process of creating a genogram provides a focus for the interview while fostering an empathic relationship between the client and the counselor. Second, the genogram may take the focus off the identified client and subtly reframe the situation as a "family problem." Third, the genogram provides a natural framework for a life review, presenting problems in wider context while identifying psychological resources that may link the past with the future. Another analysis could include a distance genogram to identify emotional links as well as generational lines. The counselor also may want to focus on a client's relationships or family "scripts." In any one family there may be several sets of directions.

Group Variation

1. Have everyone in the group bring in their family diagram.
2. Create a circle in the middle of the room and place them there.
3. Have everyone close his or her eyes and move into meditative awareness.
4. Ask everyone to call in the favorite beings they use for support.
5. Ask that the negative energies, bonds, entities, and issues represented in each family diagram be released and transmuted into the universe for the good of all concerned.
6. Ask each participant to silently request that any particular problems she or he is aware of in his or her family be healed, or any particular person needing healing receive it.
7. Imagine the light burning away negativity and bringing healing and protective energies to each family.

8. Know that the healing energy you have sent to the family diagram will be transmitted to everyone in it.
9. When you are ready, open your eyes.

Technique: *Developing a Family History*

Counseling Intention To see how family members evaluate the impact of major events in the family (Richardson, 1987).

Description Using index cards, chronologically list the major events in the history of the family. Beside the dates, list any major world events that coincide with family events. Also, note the impact that any particular event had on the family.

Have the client show the cards to as many family members as he or she can. Can the client account for any discrepancies in the dates that different family members assign to different events? How do different family members evaluate the impact of major events on the family?

Technique: *Helping Survivors of Abuse*

Counseling Intention To help cleanse the survivor of negative family energy.

Description Have everyone write down on small pieces of paper the names of family members who hurt them, or with whom they feel they have negative ties. Have one participant put his or her pieces of paper in the trash can, and then set them on fire. As the papers burn, tell that person to imagine the negative energies, issues, and improper bonds going up to the universe with the rising smoke. When the paper is burnt, empty the cauldron. Ashes should be given back to the participant to be disposed of as she wishes. Once everyone is finished, affirm that the negative energies of the family members listed and burned are now as ephemeral as the smoke.

Technique: *Draw a Rose*

Counseling Intentions   To help survivors of abuse project themselves in a rose.

Description Bring out a large piece of paper for each member of the group and a box of crayons. Ask them, "If you were a rose, what would you look like?" Have them draw a picture of the rose they would be. When everyone is done, have everyone hold their pictures up so that all can view them. Isn't it interesting how many different interpretations can be made of a rose? Are some roses in pots and some out in nature? Are some big and others small and timid-looking? Do some have thorns and others not? Did some people draw an environment for their rose or is the rose alone in the picture? Are some roses growing by walls, trees, or some other protected situation? Now ask each member to present the picture to the group, telling the others why they drew the rose the way they did. How the pictures are drawn can provide clues to each person's self-image. What insights can the group provide about each picture? Let the group have fun with their interpretations, but each artist should have the final say about what a picture means.

INTERACTIVE THERAPEUTIC APPROACHES: FILIAL PLAY THERAPY

Filial play therapy is a psychoeducational intervention model in which the therapist trains and supervises the parents as they hold special child-centered play sessions with their own children. Parents are viewed as partners in the therapeutic process and the primary change agents for their own children. A combination of family therapy and filial play therapy can serve to eliminate presenting problems, improve parent-child relationships, and strengthen the family system. Filial play therapy has been used successfully with many child and family problems such as aggression, anxiety, depression, abuse/neglect, single parenting, adoption/foster care, relationship problems, divorce, family substance abuse, oppositional behaviors, toileting difficulties, attention problems, trauma, chronic illness, stepparenting, and multiproblem families. It can be used individually or in groups for prevention, intervention, or remediation. Families who have participated in filial therapy often continue their special play sessions, reporting that both children and parents truly benefit from this therapeutic approach. A filial therapy playroom looks much like a child-centered play therapy room. A variety of toys that can be used in imaginative and expressive ways by children are scattered in an inviting manner around the playroom.

Family-Related and Nurturance Toys
- Doll family (mother, father, brother, sister, baby)
- Doll house/furniture
- Puppet family and animal puppets
- Baby doll
- Dress-up clothes
- Baby bottles
- Container with water
- Bowls for water
- Kitchen dishes

Aggression-Related Toys
- Bop bag
- Dart guns with darts
- Small plastic soldiers and/or dinosaurs
- 6- to 10-foot piece of rope
- Foam aggression bats

Expressive and Construction Toys
- Crayons or markers and drawing paper
- Play-Doh, Sculpey, or other modeling substance
- Sand tray with miniature toys
- Plastic telephones
- Scarves or bandanas
- Blocks or construction toys
- Heavy cardboard bricks
- Blackboard
- Mirror
- Masking tape
- Magic wand
- Masks

Other Multiuse Toys
- Cars, trucks, police cars, ambulances, fire trucks, school buses
- Playing cards
- Play money
- Ring-toss or similar game
- Doctor's/nurse's kit

Technique: *Interactive Techniques for Working with Children*

Counseling Intention To build rapport and enhance relationships.

Description Interactive techniques with children can include therapeutic game play (Corder, 1986; Nickerson & O'Laughlin, 1982; Schaefer & Reid, 1986; Serok, 1986), stories and metaphors (Brooks, 1985, 1987; Gardner, 1986) and role-play and simulation (Larrabee & Wilson, 1981; Renard & Sockol, 1987).

Games

The use of games as a structured therapeutic tool in child therapy is beginning to gain momentum within professional circles. Many counselors are familiar with psychologically therapeutic games such as the "Talking, Feeling, and Doing Game" (Gardner, 1986) and the "Ungame" (Parker Brothers). Checkers or chess also can be used as either a diagnostic or a therapeutic tool. By observing how the child plays the game, the counselor can gain insight into the child's attitude, viewpoint, and behavior toward self and others.

The counselor can use the interaction during the game as a means for making therapeutic comments and suggestions. The counselor also may use the context of the game to make interpretations of children's behavior, thought patterns, and feelings. For example, Gardner (1986) revealed that children who lack self-esteem may hesitate to play checkers because they are afraid they may lose. Rather than risk ineptitude, they may suggest a game of chance such as blackjack.

Kottman (1990) found that games can provide the counselor with a therapeutic tool for deepening the therapeutic relationship in a relatively short period of time. Playing games allows a safe manner of expression for feelings, thoughts, and attitudes. It also offers a structured format for exploring children's concerns and interactional patterns. Games like checkers or chess also can be used to encourage children and to help them learn and assimilate new behaviors.

Stories and Metaphors

Stories and metaphors can facilitate the expression of threatening emotions with a minimum of risk to the child. One method that the counselor may find useful is the mutual storytelling technique (Gardner, 1986). Gardner developed this technique to communicate with children using their own language and to help them gain insight into their own behavior and interactions. In the mutual storytelling technique, the counselor tells the child that they are going to do a Make-Up-a-Story Television Program. To start this television program, the child must tell a story, with a beginning, middle, and an end. The child invents the characters, the setting, the themes, and the plot of the story. The counselor listens to the story, attempting to grasp the symbolic meaning of the setting, the characters, and the plot. Then the counselor chooses one or two important ideas from the original story and tells a different story, using the same setting and characters. The characters in the counselor's story, however, should resolve their differences in a more mature, adaptive way than do the characters in the original story (Kottman, 1990).

In the creative characters technique, Brooks (1987) used stories to represent different aspects of a child's interpersonal life, such as self-esteem, relationships, beliefs, values, feelings, learning style, and coping style. The counselor audiotapes the beginning of the story before the counseling session. The counselor establishes characters, setting, and some general themes in the beginning story. Each story contains significant characters that represent the child and significant others in the child's life. The counselor takes on the active role of key character (such as "wise owl" or "superhero") to communicate to the child about the dynamics of the problem situation and about possible alternative solutions to difficulties (Brooks, 1987). After the initial segment of the story in which the structure for the setting and characters is established, the child becomes the storyteller, responsible for the plot and themes from his or her point of view. Many times, simply by listening to the child describe various significant others, the counselor can generate metaphors that "will resonate with the client's inner world and a significant level of understanding will be established" (Brooks, 1985, p. 765). Kottman (1990) maintained that "communication through metaphors allows children to experience and express threatening emotions directly. This sanctioned distancing may help decrease some of the stress involved in the counseling process and convert resistance to cooperation" (Kottman, 1990, p. 142).

Role-Play and Simulation

Role-play and simulation provide a means for trying new skills or creating self-awareness in a nonthreatening manner. Renard & Sockol (1987) have suggested that creative dramatics (role-playing and simulations) can be used by counselors to promote thinking, learning, and social skills:

1. Increasing one's ability to communicate feelings and thoughts.
2. Developing listening skills, concentration, and the ability to observe and discuss.
3. Fostering imagination, spontaneity, and visualization skills; encouraging increased originality, flexibility, and elaboration of thinking; creating an atmosphere in which children can begin to feel successful; sharpening abilities in cooperation, planning, decision making, and evaluating; and having fun.

Using simulations and role-playing, the counselor frames an initial situation, outlines any rules that have implications in the situation, and asks the child to act out the particular situation. After the entire interaction is completed, the counselor processes the experience with children, focusing on reactions and observations. Simulations and role-plays have been successful for promoting peer-pressure refusal skills, communication, feeling-processing skills, decision-making skills, moral dilemmas, skills for establishing positive behavior, and assertiveness, family relationship, or interpersonal skills.

Technique: *How to Resolve Family Conflicts*

Counseling Intentions   To resolve conflict collaboratively.

Description   Clarify the problem. The parent moderator should introduce the general nature of the problem, then use the "go around" technique to get each person's view of the problem.

1. Go Around Questions: What is the problem as you see it? How does it affect you? What is your contribution to the problem?
2. These are challenging questions. The family should listen to each speaker with respect and an attempt at understanding. Avoid interrupting or becoming defensive.
3. The moderator should write down the points of agreement and disagreement as they arise.
4. Brainstorm solutions. Go around as many times as necessary to come up with a list of possible solutions to the problem. Don't analyze the solutions now; just write them all down.
5. Go through the list of possible solutions to narrow them down to the best solution for all family members.
6. Use the "go around' technique to get each person's view on what is the best solution for everyone. Ask "Which of these do you think is the best solution? Why? Is it fair to everyone?"
7. Select the best solution. Get commitment from each person to make the solution work.
8. Decide what each person will do to implement the solution. This is the time to come up with responsibilities, rewards, limits, consequences, and other agreed upon commitments.
9. Go around one more time with each family member stating what specific action they will take to solve the problem.

Technique: *The Family Floor Plan*

Counseling Intention   To identify information in a nonthreatening way; to use as a diagnostic tool about the family system (Coopersmith, 1980).

Description   Parents might be asked to draw the family floor plan for the family of origin. Information across generations is then gathered in a nonthreatening manner, focusing on meaningful issues related to one's past.

Another adaptation of this technique is to have members draw the floor plan for their nuclear family. The importance of space and territory is often revealed in the family floor plan. Levels of comfort between family members, space accommodations, and rules are often revealed. Indications of enmeshment, differentiation, operating family triangles, and subsystems often become evident.

Technique: *Reframing*

Counseling Intention To join with the family and offer a different perspective on presenting problems (Sherman & Fredman, 1986).

Description Reframing involves taking something out of its logical context and placing it in another category. For example, a mother's repeated questioning of her daughter's behavior after a date can be seen as *genuine caring and concern* rather than a *nontrusting* parent. Through reframing, a negative often can be reframed into a positive.

Technique: *Tracking*

Counseling Intention To join the therapy process with the family (Minuchin & Fishman, 1981).

Description   The therapist listens intently to family stories and carefully records events and their sequence. Through tracking, the family therapist is able to identify the sequence of events operating in a system that is keeping it the way it is. What happens between point A and point B or C to create D can be helpful when designing interventions.

Technique: *Family Sculpting*

Counseling Intention To re-create the family system (Duhl, Kantor, & Duhl, 1973).

Description Family sculpting provides for re-creation of the family system, representing family members' relationships to one another at a specific period of time. The therapist can use sculpting at any time in therapy by asking family members to physically arrange the family. Adolescents often make good family sculptors, as they are provided with a chance to nonverbally communicate thoughts and feelings about the family.

Technique: *Family Photos*

Counseling Intention To provide a wealth of information about past and present functioning.

Description One use of family photos is to go through the family album together. Verbal and nonverbal responses to pictures and events are often quite revealing. Adaptations of this method include asking members to bring in significant family photos and discuss reasons for bringing them, and locating pictures that represent past generations. Through discussion of photos, the therapist often more clearly sees family relationships, rituals, structure, roles, and communication patterns.

Technique: *Draw Your Family Table*

Counseling Intention To have family members examine the impact of their family of origin and/or current family dynamics on their personality and interpersonal dynamics (Trotzer, 1986).

Description

1. On a large sheet of paper, draw the shape of the table your family ate at when you were growing up, between the ages of 7 and 18.
2. Place members of your family around the table in their usual places, using squares to represent males and circles to represent females. Identify each person by name and role (e.g., mother, brother, grandfather).
3. By each member of the family at the table write a descriptive phrase or comment that describes each family member's personality.
4. On the surface of the table, write descriptors (words or phrases) that describe the atmosphere of the family and what it was like living with that family.
5. Have each member share his or her table with the group. Process the impact of the family of origin.

Technique: *Family-O-Gram*

Counseling Intention To examine communication dynamics in the family (Trotzer, 1986).

Description Using the family table drawing, have a group member represent each person at the table, including the client who drew the table. Have the person who drew the table give a verbal description of each family member and specify *typical statements that family members would make*. Each "family member" is to remember the statement and present it in the character of the family member described.

1. Once the description and statements have been assigned, place the person who drew the table in the center and form the other members around him or her in the manner depicted by the family table.
2. Starting with a parent figure, have the table's drawer face that person and make eye contact. When the drawer does this, the family member must make the statement in character. The table drawer then rotates to the next person on the right, repeating the procedure until each family member has given his or her statement to the table drawer in the center. Repeat the rotation at least three times without interruption.
3. After three rotations, have the family members move in closer to the table drawer in the center. Instruct him or her to close his or her eyes and then have all the family members make their statements once, trying to get the attention of the table drawer in the center.

   After 15 to 20 seconds, stop the procedure and process the experience with the table drawer. Process the experience with all participants.

Technique: *Family Choreography*

Counseling Intention   To reflect real and ideal family relationships.

Description In family choreography, arrangements go beyond initial sculpting; family members are asked to position themselves as to how they see the family and then to show how they would like the family situation to be. Family members may be asked to reenact a family scene and possibly resculpt it to a preferred scenario. This technique can help a stuck family and create a lively situation.

Technique: *Family Council Meetings*

Counseling Intention To assign families homework to follow through on therapy between sessions.

Description   Family council meetings are organized to provide specific times for the family to meet and share with one another. The therapist might prescribe council meetings as homework, in which case a time is set and rules are outlined. The council should encompass the entire family, and any absent members have to abide by decisions. The agenda may include any concerns of the family. Attacking others during this time is not acceptable. Family council meetings help provide structure for the family, encourage full family participation, and facilitate communication.

Technique: *Strategic Alliances*

Counseling Intention To encourage a family member to change.
Description This technique, often used by strategic family therapists, involves meeting with one member of the family as a supportive means of helping that person change. Individual change is expected to affect the entire family system. The individual is often asked to behave or respond in a different manner. This technique attempts to disrupt a circular system or behavior pattern.

Technique: *Positive Action Tags: Using Therapeutic Symbols in Family Therapy*

Counseling Intention To reveal how the lack of given virtues cause family disruption, disrespect, and dysfunction (Cox, 1973).

Description

1. Have a family member discuss how he or she would have felt if a given virtue had been extended and attempt to get others to discuss how they felt a given virtue was withheld from the situation (e.g., when someone was impatient).
2. Find a phrase, poem, passage, or virtue that articulates interpersonal dignity (e.g., virtues such as self-discipline, compassion, responsibility, friendship, work, courage, perseverance, honesty, loyalty, or faith).

3. Have small metal plates made (like army dog tags) and place them on neck chains. Instruct each family member to wear their "positive action tag" for one week and agree to practice the virtue on the tag every day with all other family members. Dad, for example, agrees to practice "compassion," mom agrees to practice "patience," and daughter agrees to practice "respect."
4. At the next family session, have each family member discuss their experience with practicing their designated virtue on their positive action tag and how it felt practiced on them.
5. Have family members exchange positive action tags for the following week. Tags are exchanged by drawing them out of a hat. Family members have no choice in the tag they get.

Technique: *Getting Rid of the Seven Deadly Habits of Unhappy Couples*

Counseling Intention To help clients see that all purposeful behavior is chosen and to understand *choice theory* (Glasser, 1999).

Description Choice theory explains that, because clients can only control their own behavior, when a client is having difficulty with another person he or she try to choose behaviors that would bring them closer. The therapist explains that there are seven deadly external control habits that eventually will destroy the happiness in any relationship. It is almost certain that they are both using one or more of these habits in their marriage: (1) criticizing, (2) blaming, (3) nagging, (4) complaining, (5) threatening, (6) punishing, and (7) rewarding to control or bribe.

Assign homework to the couple that they should complete separately, writing down examples of when each uses one or more of the seven habits consistently in their marriage.

Once they believe they understand the difference between using external control language and choice theory language, they should together discuss how they could rewrite the examples they had written down. Their task would be to change their words from external control to choice theory language. Process how their lives and their marriage will improve significantly.

Technique: *Mission and Legacy*

Counseling Intention To encourage couples to write about some aspects of their life and personality that will help them as spouses to understand each other better (Gottman, 1999, p. 211).

Description "Imagine that you are standing in a graveyard looking at your own tombstone. Think of the epitaph you would like to see there. Imagine your own obituary in the newspaper following your death. Write this obituary of yourself— it does not have to be brief. How do you want people to think of your life, to remember you?

"Next, write the mission statement for your life. What are you trying to accomplish? What is your larger struggle? What is you dream? What legacy would you like to leave this world when you die?

"What are your life dreams? What is that you definitely want to do in your life that you have not yet fulfilled? This can be creating something or on an experience that you want to have, such as learning to sail, climbing a mountain, or parachuting out of an airplane."

Process that involvement in what is wanted most is a process of becoming. "What kind of person do would you like to be? What have been your struggles in trying to become that person?"

Technique: *Deposits in an Emotional Bank Account— Stress-reducing Conversations*

Counseling Intention To enhance the couple's ability to create a peaceful home by learning how to have a stress-reducing conversation on a daily basis (Gottman, 1999, p. 214).

Description "Tell the couple that this exercise deals with the management of daily external stress, like job stress. Ask spouses to commit to having a conversation like this one every day, for at least 20 minutes at the end of the day. Ask the spouses to discuss a recent or upcoming stress in each of their lives that is not related directly to a marital issue (i.e., upcoming visit from toxic in-laws, or a business venture). They take turns, allowing about 15 minutes for each. In the last five minutes of the exercise, ask the partners to discuss how and when they could build in this kind of conversation into each day."

Technique: *Diffusing Physiological Arousal by Taking a Structured Break*

Counseling Intention To introduce a "withdrawal ritual" or "time out" procedure in the marriage to manage stress (Gottman, 1999, p. 231).

Description Have the couple discuss the following questions. There is no blaming.

1. What makes me feel flooded (overwhelmed)? What are the feelings inside me when this happens? What am I thinking usually?
2. How do I typically bring up issues or complaints?
3. Do I store things up?
4. Is there anything I can do that soothes you?
5. Is there anything I can do to soothe myself?
6. What signals can be developed for letting the other know when one of us is feeling flooded? Can we take breaks? (This is the most important part of the exercise.)

Technique: *Working as a Team: The Paper Tower*

Counseling Intention To help the couple work as a team by turning toward each other rather than away from one another, and giving and accepting influence in an equitable sharing of power on a task that is unrelated to marital issues (Gottman, 1999, p. 293).

Description The couple is given a box containing assorted materials such as newspapers, magazines, construction paper, tape, sparkling glue, magic markers, stickers, straws, string, stapler, and anything else to make the box interesting. They are instructed to build a paper tower. It must be tall, strong, and beautiful, and has to be able to stand unsupported. They can earn up to 25 points for size, 25 points for strength, and 50 points for beauty. The points are awarded by the therapist, who also gives the spouses feedback on how they worked together as a team. The most influential team member is the one who draws out the other, asks questions, and gives support, rather than the one who dominates.

Technique: *Solution-Focused Family Techniques*

Counseling Intention Identify and amplify solution patterns (deShazer, 1982, p. 42).

Description Increase cooperation by accepting the clients' goals framed in a realistic, positive way. Maintain an overtly supportive, accepting therapeutic stance. Stay solution-focused:

1. Initial changes are small.
2. Clients' intermittent return to problem talk is not a failure.
3. Measure success by goal attainment, not by number of sessions.

Ask solution-focused questions and expand the answers with the following questions:

1. Exceptions: "What things are different when the problem is not happening?"
2. Miracles: "Let's pretend a miracle occurred while you were sleeping. What would you notice when you awoke that would tell you the problem was gone?"
3. Scaling: "On a scale of 1 to 10, where are you now? What would you prefer? What could you do to advance 1 point?"
4. Coping: "What do you do to keep things from being worse? How did you get through such a difficult thing?"
5. Increasing readiness to notice change: "It will be interesting to see how things change for the better this week."
6. Solution tasks: "Between now and the next time we meet, notice what is going right that you do not want to change (p. 42)."

Technique: *Mapping Your Emotional Relationships*

Counseling Intention To map out changes in emotional relationships over a life span (Richardson, 1987, p. 18).

Description Draw a diagram, using circles for females and squares for males of your family of origin when you were 12 years old. Include each family member and yourself. Place them either close or distant to each other, depending on what you think the emotional relationships were at that time in your life. See Figure 15.2 for an example.

Draw a similar diagram for ages 16 and 21. Note any changes of relationships over the years. Draw a diagram of your present relationship with your family of origin. Then draw a diagram of your current family of spouse and children, if any. Are there any similarities or differences in these family diagrams?

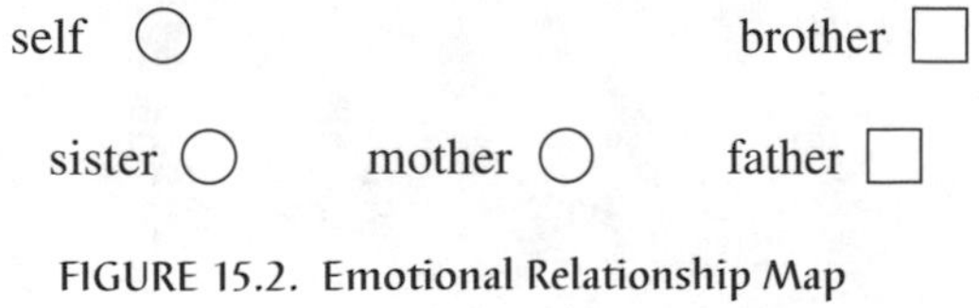

self ○   brother □

sister ○   mother ○   father □

FIGURE 15.2. Emotional Relationship Map

CONCLUSION

The typical family relationship has changed dramatically in the last two decades. Currently 22% of children in America are born out of wedlock. Family organizational structures include blended, common-law, single parent, communal, serial, polygamous, cohabitational, and homosexual (Goldenberg & Goldenberg, 1985). One of the latest family structures is that of skip-generation parents— grandparents who are raising their children's children. Taken in perspective, these kinds of family relationships are having a tremendous impact on schools, communities, childcare, health care, and the workforce. With changing demographics and the accompanying diversity, it becomes even more futile to rely on one model as an all-inclusive intervention approach with families. With the focus on healthy family functioning, therapists cannot allow themselves to be limited to a prescribed operational procedure, a rigid set of techniques or set of hypotheses. Therefore, creative judgment and personalization of application are encouraged.

References

Ackerman, N. (1958). *The psychodynamics of family life.* New York: Basic Books.

Akeroyd-Guillory, D. (1988). A development view of anorexia nervosa. *The School Counselor, 36,* 24–33.

Albee, G. W. (1982). Preventing psychopathology and promoting human potential. *American Psychologist, 37,* 1043–1050.

Alberti, R. E., & Emmons, M. L. (1986). *Your perfect right: A guide to assertive living* (5th ed.). San Luis Obispo, CA: Impact.

Allen, D. M. (1988). *Unifying individual and family therapies.* San Francisco: Jossey-Bass.

American Psychiatric Association. (1994). *Diagnostic and statistical manual of mental disorders* (4th ed.). Washington, DC: Author.

Anderson, D. (1992). A case for standards of counseling practice. *Journal of Counseling and Development, 71*(2), 22–26.

Anderson, A. E., & Hay, A. (1985). Racial and socioeconomic influences in anorexia nervosa and bulimia. *International Journal of Eating Disorders, 4,* 479–487.

Anderson, E. M., & Lambert, M. J. (1995). Short-term dynamically oriented psychotherapy: A review and meta-analysis. *Clinical Psychology Review, 9,* 503–514.

Anderson, M. (1988). *Counseling families from a system perspective.* Ann Arbor, MI: ERIC/CAPS Digest.

Anderson, R. F. (1980). Using guided fantasy with children. *Elementary School Guidance & Counseling, 15,* 39–47.

Anderson, S. A., & Russell, C. S. (1982). Utilizing process and content in designing paradoxical interventions. *American Journal of Family Therapy, 10,* 48–60.

Andreas, C., & Andreas, S. (1989). *Heart of the mind.* Moab, UT: Real People Press.

Andrews, J. D. W. (1989). Integrating visions of reality: Interpersonal diagnosis and the existential vision. *American Psychologist, 44*(5), 803–817.

Antrobus, J. (1993). Dreaming: Could we do without it? In A. Moffitt, M. Kramer, & R. Hoffman (Eds.), *The functions of dreaming* (pp. 549–558). Albany, NY: SUNY Press.

Apolinsky, S. R., & Wilcoxon, S. A. (1991). Symbolic confrontation with women survivors of childhood sexual victimization. *The Journal of Specialists in Group Work, 16*(2), 85–90.

Aponte, H. J., & Van Deusen, J. M. (1981). Structural family therapy. In A. S. Gurman & D. P. Kniskern (Eds.), *Handbook of family therapy* (pp. 116–134). New York: Brunner/ Mazel.

Armeniox, L. (2000). Dance therapy recognized as counseling specialty. *The National Certified Counselor, 17*(1), 3.

Arrindell, W. A., Sanderman, W. J., Hogeman, J. H., Pickersgill, M. G., Kwee, G. T., Van der Molen, H. T., & Lingsma, M. M. (1990). Correlates of assertiveness. *Advances in Behavior Research and Therapy, 12,* 153–182.

Asay, T. P., & Lambert, M. J. (1999). The empirical case for the common factors in therapy: Quantitative findings. In M. A. Hubble, B. L. Duncan, & S. Miller (Eds.), *The heart and soul of change* (pp. 33–55). Washington, DC: American Psychological Association.

Attneave, G. S. (1990). A network model for helping. *Journal of Mental Health Counseling, 12*(1), 24–30.

Babensee, B. A., & Pequette, J. R. (1982). Perspectives on loss: A manual for educators. P.O. Box 1352, Evergreen, CO 80301.

Bach, G. R., & Wyden, P. (1968). *The intimate enemy.* New York: William Morrow.

Bahatti, R. S., Janakiramariah, N., & Channabasvanna, S. (1982). Group interaction as a method of family therapy. *International Journal of Group Psychotherapy, 32,* 103–113.

Bankoff, E. A., & Howard, K. I. (1992). The social network of the psychotherapy patient and effective psychotherapeutic process. *Journal of Psychotherapy Integration, 2*(4), 273–294.

Barbanell, L. (1997). Clinical report: The management of resistance using time-out technique. *International Journal of Group Psychotherapy, 47*(4), 509–512.

Barker, P. (1985). *Using metaphors in psychotherapy.* New York: Brunner/Mazel.

Bartlett, D., Kaufman, D., & Smeltekop, R. (1993). The effects of music listening and perceived sensory experiences on the immune system. *Journal of Music Therapy, 30,* 194–209.

Bateson, G. (1972). *Steps to an ecology of mind.* New York: Random House.

Bauer, M. S., & McBride, L. (2002). *Structured group psychotherapy for bipolar disorder.* New York: Springer.

Bayles, F. (2000, April 13). War on an eyesore that wrecks city life. *USA Today,* p. 3A.

Beck, A. T. (1976). *Cognitive therapy and emotional disorders.* New York: International Universities Press.

Beck, A. T., & Emery, G. (1985). *Anxiety disorders and phobias: A cognitive perspective.* New York: Basic Books.

Bednar, R. L., & Kaul, T. (1978). Experiential group research. In S. L. Garfield & A. E. Bergin (Eds.), *Handbook of psychotherapy and behavior change* (2nd ed., pp. 66–82). New York: Wiley.

Bedrosian, R. C., & Beck, A. T. (1980). Principles of cognitive therapy. In M. J. Mahoney (Ed.), *Psychotherapy process* (pp. 115–135). New York: Plenum.

Beitman, B. D. (1994). Stop exploring! Start defining the principles of psychotherapy integration: Call for a consensus. *Journal of Psychotherapy, 4*(3), 203–228.

Beitman, B. D. (1997). A model of psychotherapy for the 21st century. *Psychiatric Times, 14*(4), 202–210.

Belfer, P. L., Munoz, L. S., Schacter, J., & Levendusky, P. G. (1995). Cognitive behavior therapy for agoraphobia and panic disorder. *International Journal of Group Psychotherapy, 45*(2), 185–205.

Belkin, G. S. (1988). *Contemporary psychotherapies* (2nd ed.). Monterey, CA: Brooks/ Cole.

Bellack, A. S., & Hersen, M. (1988). *Behavioral assessment: A practical handbook* (3rd ed). New York: Pergamon.

Benson, H. (1974). Your innate asset for combating stress. *Harvard Business Review, 52,* 49–60.

Bent, R. J., Putman, D. G., Kiesler, D. J., & Nowicki, S., Jr. (1976). Correlates of successful psychotherapy. *Journal of Counseling and Clinical Psychology, 44*(149), 120–125.

Berger, C. R. (1985). Social power and interpersonal communication. In M. L. Knapp & G. R. Miller (Eds.), *Handbook of interpersonal communication* (pp. 439–499). Beverly Hills, CA: Sage.

Bergin, A. E., & Lambert, M. J. (1978). The evaluation of therapeutic outcomes. In S. L. Garfield & A. E. Bergin (Eds.), *Handbook of psychotherapy and behavior change: An empirical analysis* (2nd ed., pp. 139–190). New York: Wiley.

Bergman, J. S. (1985). *Fishing for barracuda: Pragmatics of brief systemic therapy.* New York: W. W. Norton.

Bernard, M. E., Kratochwill, T. R., & Keefauver, L. W. (1983). The effects of rational-emotive therapy and self-instruction training on chronic hair pulling. *Cognitive Therapy and Research, 7,* 273–280.

Berne, E. (1961). *Transactional analysis in psychotherapy: A systemic individual and social psychiatry.* New York: Grove Press.

Berne, E. (1964). *Games people play: The psychology of human relations.* New York: Grove Press.

Berne, E. (1972). *What do you say after you say hello? The psychology of human destiny.* New York: Grove Press

Bernstein, D. A., & Borkover, T. D. (1973). *Progress relaxation training: A manual for the helping professionals.* Champaign, IL: Research Press.

Bettelheim, B. (1976). *The uses of enchantment.* New York: Knopf.

Beutler, L. E., & Clarkin, J. (1990). *Systematic treatment selection: Toward targeted therapeutic interventions.* New York: Brunner/Mazel.

Beutler, L. E., Clarkin, J. F., & Bongar, B. (2000). *Guidelines for the systematic treatment of the depressed patient.* New York: Oxford University Press.

Beutler, L. E., Crago, M., & Arizmendi, T. G. (1986). Research on therapist variables in psychotherapy. In S. L. Garfield & A. E. Bergin (Eds.), *Handbook of psychotherapy and behavior change* (3rd ed., pp. 257–310). New York: Wiley.

Beutler, L. E., Goodrich, G., Fisher, D., & Williams, R. E. (1999). Use of psychological tests/instruments for treatment planning. In M. Maruish (Ed.), *Use of psychological testing for treatment planning and outcome assessment* (2nd ed., pp. 81–113). Hillsdale, NJ: Lawrence Erlbaum.

Blades, S., & Girualt, E. (1982). The use of poetry therapy as a projective technique in counseling and psychotherapy. Paper presented at the meeting of the California Personnel and Guidance Association, San Francisco. (ERIC Document Reproduction Service No. ED 213 040.)

Blatner, A. (1988). *Acting-in: Practical applications of psychodrama methods.* New York: Springer.

Blatner, A. (2000). *Foundations of psychodrama: History, theory and practice* (4th ed.). New York: Springer.

Bloch, S., & Crouch, E. (1985). *Therapeutic factors in group psychotherapy.* Oxford: Oxford University Press.

Blocher, D. H. (1974). *Developmental counseling* (2nd ed.). New York: Ronald.

Blocher, D. H. (1987). On the uses and misuses of the term theory. *Journal of Counseling and Development, 66,* 67–68.

Blocher, D. H. (1989). The interactional view: Family therapy approaches of the mental research institute. In A. S. Gurman & D. P. Kriskerr (Eds.), *Handbook of family therapy* (pp. 267–309). New York: Brunner/Mazel.

Bloom, B. L. (1981). Focused single-session therapy: Initial development and evaluation. In S. H. Budman (Ed.), *Forms of brief therapy* (pp. 66–82). New York: Guilford.

Blum, M. D. (1988). *The silent speech of politicians.* San Diego: Brenner Information Group.

Boldt, S. (1996). The effects of music therapy on motivation, psychological well-being, physical comfort, and exercise endurance of bone marrow transplant patients. *Journal of Music Therapy, 33*(3), 164–188.

Bornstein, P. H., & Sipprelle, C. N. (1973, April 6). *Clinical applications of induced anxiety in the treatment of obesity.* Paper presented at the Southeastern Psychological Association Meeting, Atlanta, Georgia.

Boscolo, L., Cecchin, G., Hoffman, L., & Penn, P. (1987). *Milan systemic family therapy: Conversations in theory and practice.* New York: Basic Books.

Bowen, M. (1971). Family therapy and family group therapy. In H Kaplan & B. Sadock (Eds.), *Comprehensive group psychotherapy* (pp. 106–136). Baltimore: Williams & Wilkins.

Bowen, M. (1974). Toward the differentiation of self in one's family of origin. In F. Andres & J. Lorio (Eds.), *Georgetown Family Symposium* (Vol. 1, pp. 222–242). Washington, DC: Department of Psychiatry, Georgetown University Medical Center.

Bowen, M. (1975). Family therapy after twenty years. In S. Arieti (Ed.), *American handbook of psychiatry* (Vol. 5). New York: Basic Books.

Bowen, M. (1976). Family reaction to death. In P. Gueerin (Ed.), *Family therapy: Theory and practice* (pp. 335–348). New York: Gardner.

Bowen, M. (1978). *Family therapy in clinical practice.* New York: Jason Aronson.

Bowlby, J. (1982). *Attachment.* (2nd ed.). New York: Basic Books.

Bower, S. A., & Bower, G. H. (1976). *Asserting yourself: A practical guide for positive change.* New York: Addison-Wesley.

Boy, A. V., & Pine, G. J. (1983). Counseling: Fundamentals of theoretical renewal. *Counseling and Values, 27,* 248–255.

Brabeck, M. M., & Welfel, E. R. (1985). Counseling theory: Understanding the trend toward eclecticism from a developmental perspective. *Journal of Counseling and Development, 63*(6), 343–348.

Bramblett, J. (1991). *When good-bye is forever: Learning to live again after the loss of a child.* New York: Ballantine.

Brammer, L. M., & Shostrum, E. L. (1968). *Therapeutic psychology: Fundamentals of actualization counseling and psychotherapy.* Englewood Cliffs, NJ: Prentice-Hall.

Brammer, L. M., & Shostrum, E. L. (1977). *Therapeutic psychology: Fundamentals of counseling and psychotherapy* (3rd ed.). Englewood Cliffs, NJ: Prentice-Hall.

Brammer, L. M., & Shostrum, E. L. (1982). *Therapeutic psychology: Fundamentals of counseling and psychotherapy* (4th ed.). Englewood Cliffs, NJ: Prentice-Hall.

Brand, A. G. (1987). Writing as counseling. *Elementary School Guidance and Counseling, 21*(4), 247–283.

Bricker, D. C., & Young, J. E. (1993). *A client's guide to schema-focused cognitive therapy.* New York: Cognitive Therapy of New York.

Brigman, G., & Earley, B. (1990). *Peer helping: A training guide.* Portland, MA: J. Weston Walch.

Brooks, R. (1985). The beginning sessions of child therapy: Of messages and metaphors. *Psychotherapy, 22,* 761–769.

Brooks. R. (1987). Storytelling and the therapeutic process for children with learning disabilities. *Journal of Learning Disabilities, 20,* 546–550.

Brooks-Gunn, J., Burrow, C., & Warren, M. P. (1988). Attitudes toward eating and body weight in different groups of female athletes. *International Journal of Eating Disorders, 7,* 749–757.

Brown, N. W. (1996). *Expressive processes in group counseling.* Westport, CT: Praeger.

Bruner, J. S. (1991). The narrative construction of reality. *Critical Inquiry, 18*(1), 1–21.

Budman, S. H. (Ed.). (1981). *Forms of brief therapy.* New York: Guilford.

Budman, S. H. (1992). Models of brief individual and group psychotherapy. In J. L. Feldman & R. J. Fitzpatrick (Eds.), *Managed mental health care: Administrative and clinical issues* (pp. 231–248). Washington, DC: American Psychiatric Press.

Bulkeley, K. (1999). *Visions of the night: Dreams, religion, and psychology.* Albany, NY: State University of New York Press.

Burgoon, J., David, H., Buller, B., & Woodall, W. G. (1989). *Nonverbal communication: The unspoken dialogue.* New York: Harper & Row.

Burlingame, G. M., & Fuhriman, A. (1987). Conceptualizing short-term treatment: A comparative review. *Counseling Psychologist, 15*(4), 557–595.

Burns, D. D. (1989). *The feeling good handbook: Using the new mood therapy in everyday life.* New York: William Morrow.

Butler, A. C., & Beck, J. S. (2000). Cognitive therapy outcomes: A review of meta-analyses. *Journal of the Norwegian Psychological Association, 37,* 1–9.

Butler, P. E. (1981). *Talking to yourself: Learning the language of self-support.* San Francisco: Harper & Row.

Byrum, B. (1989). New age training technologies: The best and the safest. In J. W. Pfeiffer (Ed.), *The 1989 Annual: Developing human resources* (pp. 79–89). San Diego, CA: University Associates.

Caine, L. (1974). *Widow.* New York: Morrow.

Canfield, J., & Wells, H. C. (1976). *100 ways to enhance self-concept in the classroom: A handbook for teachers and parents.* Englewood Cliffs, NJ: Prentice-Hall.

Cantwell, D. P., & Carlson, G. A. (1983). *Affective disorders in childhood and adolescence.* New York: Spectrum.

Caple, R. B. (1985). Counseling and the self-organization paradigm. *Journal of Counseling and Development, 64,* 173–178.

Carkhuff, R. R., & Berenson, B. G. (1967). *Beyond counseling and psychotherapy.* New York: Holt, Rinehart & Winston.

Carrington, P. (1977). *Freedom in meditation.* Kendall Park, NJ: Pace Educational Systems.

Carroll, M. R., & Wiggins, J. (1990). *Elements of group counseling: Back to the basics.* Denver: Love Publishing.

Cautela, J., & McCullough, L. (1978). Covert conditioning: A learning-theory perspective on imagery. In J. L. Singer & K. S. Pope (Eds.), *The power of human imagination* (pp. 227–254). New York: Plenum.

Cavanagh, M. E. (1982). *The counseling experience.* Monterey, CA: Brooks/Cole.

Christiansen, A., Johnson, S. M., Phillips, S., & Glassgow, R. E. (1980). Cost efficiency in family behavior therapy. *Behavior Therapy, 11,* 208–226.

Clemons, H. (1999). *Saying goodbye to your grief: A book designed to help people who have experienced crushing losses survive and grow beyond the pain.* Macon, GA: Smyth & Helwys Publishing.

Coady, N. (1991). The association between complex types of therapist interventions and outcomes in psychodynamic psychotherapy. *Research on Social Work Practice, 1,* 257–277.

Coady, N. (1996). A reflective/inductive model of practice: Emphasizing theory building for unique cases versus applying theory to practice. In G. Rogers (Ed.), *Social work field education: Views and visions* (pp. 139–151). Dubuque, IA: Kendall/Hunt.

Coleman, V. D. (1998). Lifeline. In H. G. Rosenthal (Ed.), *Favorite counseling techniques.* Washington, DC: Accelerated Development.

Cook, A. S., & Dworkin, D. S. (1992). *Helping the bereaved: Therapeutic interventions for children, adolescents, and adults.* New York: Basic Books.

Cook, E. P. (1987). Characteristics of the biopsychosocial crisis of infertility. *Journal of Counseling and Development, 65,* 465–470.

Coppersmith, E. (1980). The family floor plan: A tool of training, assessment, and intervention in family therapy. *Journal of Marital & Family Therapy, 6,* 141–145.

Corbishly, M. A., & Yost, E. B. (1985). Therapeutic homework assignments. *The School Counselor, 33,* 21–28.

Corder, B. (1986). Therapeutic games in group therapy with adolescence. In C. E. Schaefer & S. E. Reid (Eds.), *Game play: Therapeutic use of childhood games* (pp. 279–290). New York: Wiley.

Corey, G. (1986). *Theory and practice of counseling and psychotherapy.* Monterey, CA: Brooks/Cole.

Corey, M. S., & Corey, G. (1987). *Groups: Process and practice* (3rd ed.). Monterey, CA: Brooks/Cole.

Corsini, R. J. (1989). Introduction. In R. J. Corsini & D. Wedding (Eds.), *Current psychotherapies* (4th ed., pp. 1–16). Itasca, IL: Peacock.

Corsini, R. J., & Wedding, D. (1989). *Current psychotherapies* (4th ed.). Itasca, IL: Peacock.

Cox, R. H. (1973). *Religious systems and psychotherapy.* Springfield, IL: Charles C Thomas.

Crawford, T., & Ellis, A. (1989). A dictionary of rational-emotive feelings and behaviors. *Journal of Rational-Emotive and Cognitive Therapy, 7,* 3–28.

Crose, R. (1990). Reviewing the past in the here and now: Using Gestalt therapy techniques with life review. *Journal of Mental Health Counseling, 12*(3), 279–287.

Cummings, N., & Sayama, M. (1995). *Focused psychotherapy: A casebook of brief, intermittent psychotherapy throughout the life cycle.* New York: Brunner/Mazel.

Daniluk, J. C. (1988). Infertility: Intrapersonal and interpersonal impact. *Fertility and Sterility, 49,* 1123–1125.

Daniluk, J. D. (1991, March/April). Strategies for counseling infertile couples. *Journal of Counseling and Development, 69*(4), 317–320.

Davis, J. M. (1985). Suicidal crises in schools. *School Psychology Review, 14*(3), 313–322.

Davis, H., & Fallowfield, L. (1991). *Counselling and communication in health care.* Chichester, England: Wiley.

Dehouske, E. J. (1979). Original writing: A therapeutic tool in working with disturbed adolescents. *Teaching Exceptional Children, 11,* 66–70.

Dell, P. F. (1981). Some irreverent thoughts on paradox. *Family Process, 20,* 37–42.

de Shazer, S. (1978). Brief therapy with couples. *International Journal of Family Counseling, 6,* 17–30.

de Shazer, S. (1979). The confusion technique. *American Journal of Family Therapy, 7,* 23–30.

de Shazer, S. (1982). *Patterns of brief family therapy.* New York: Guilford.

de Shazer, S. (1985). *Keys to solutions in brief therapy.* New York: Norton.

de Shazer, S. (1988). *Clues: Investigating solutions in brief therapy.* New York: Norton.

de Shazer, S. (1991). *Putting difference to work.* New York: W. W. Norton.

Devi, I. (1963). *Renew your life through yoga.* New York: Prentice-Hall.

DeVito, J. A., & Hecht, M. L. (1990). *The nonverbal communication reader.* Prospect Heights, IL: Waveland Press.

Dicks, H. (1967). *Marital tensions.* New York: Basic Books.

Dies, R. R. (1983). Clinical implications of research on leadership and in short-term group psychotherapy. In R. R. Dies & K. R. Mackenzie (Eds.), *Advances in group psychotherapy* (pp. 27–78). New York: International Universities Press.

Dies, R. R. (1994). The therapist's role in group treatments. In H. S. Bernard & K. R. MacKenzie (Eds.), *Basics of group psychotherapy* (pp. 60–99). New York: Guilford.

Dies, R. R, & Dies, K. T. (1993). The role of evaluation in clinical practice: Overview and group treatment illustration. *International Journal of Group Psychotherapy, 43,* 77–105.

Dinkmeyer, D. (1988). Marathon family counseling. *Individual Psychology: Journal of Adlerian Theory, Research, and Practice, 44,* 210 215.

Dinkmeyer, D. C., & Losoncy, L. E. (1980). *The encouragement book: Becoming a positive person.* Englewood Cliffs, NJ: Prentice-Hall.

Dinkmeyer, D. C., Pew, W. L., & Dinkmeyer, D. C., Jr. (1979). *Adlerian counseling and psychotherapy.* Monterey, CA: Brooks/Cole.

Dobyns, S. (1997). *Best words, best order: Essays on poetry.* New York: St. Martins Griffini.

Dohrenwend, B. S., & Dohrenwend, B. P. (1985). Life stress and psychopathology. In H. Goldman & S. I.Goldston (Eds.), *Preventing stress related psychiatric disorders* (DHHS Pub. No., ADM 85-1366, pp. 37–51). Rockville, MD: NIMH.

Domhoff, G. W. (1996). *Finding meaning in dreams: A quantitative approach.* New York: Plenum.

Downing, J. (1988). Counseling interventions with depressed children. *Elementary School Counselor, 22*(3), 296–301.

Dryden, W. (1987). *Current issues in rational-emotive therapy.* London: Croom Hehm.

Duhl, B. S. (1983). *From the inside out and other metaphors.* New York: Brunner/Mazel.

Duhl, B. S., & Duhl, F. J. (1981). Integrative family therapy. In A. S. Gurman & D. P. Knniskern (Eds.), *Handbook of family therapy* (pp. 236–258). New York: Brunner/Mazel.

Duhl, F. S., Kantor, D., & Duhl, B. S. (1973). Learning space and action in family therapy: A primer of sculpting. In D. Bloch (Ed.), *Techniques of family psychotherapy: A primer* (pp. 119–139). New York: Grune & Stratton.

Dunlap, K. (1946). The technique of negative practice. *American Journal of Psychology, 55,* 270–273.

Duttweiler, P. C. (1984). The internal control index: A newly developed measure of locus of control. *Educational and Psychological Measurement, 36*(2), 209–226.

Dyer, W. W., & Vriend, J. (1977). *Counseling techniques that work.* New York: Funk & Wagnall.

Dysinger, B. J. (1993). Conflict resolution for intermediate children. *The School Counselor, 40*(4), 113–118.

Edwards, S. S., & Kleine, P. A. (1986). Multimodal consultation: A model for working with gifted adolescents. *Journal of Counseling and Development, 64*(9), 598–601.

Egan, G. (1975). *The skilled helper: A model for systematic helping and interpersonal relating.* Pacific Grove, CA: Brooks/Cole.

Egan, G. (1990). *The skilled helper: A systematic approach to effective helping* (4th ed.). Pacific Grove, CA: Brooks/Cole.

Eibl-Eibesfeldt, I. (1970). *Ethology: The biology of behavior.* San Francisco: Holt, Rinehart, & Winston.

Eisenberg, G. M. (1981). Midtherapy training: Extending the recent system of pretherapy training. *Dissertation Abstracts International, 41,* 2754B.

Ekman, P. (1980). *The face of man: Expressions of universal emotion in a New Guinea village.* Garland STPN Press.

Ekman, P. (1992). *Telling lies.* New York: W. W. Norton

Ekman, P. (1998). Commentaries. In Darwin, C. (1872). *The expression of the emotions in man and animals* (3rd ed.). New York: Oxford University Press.

Elias, M. J. (1989). Schools as sources of stress to children: An analysis of causal and ameliorative influences. *Journal of School Psychology, 27,* 393–407.

Ellis, A. (1962). *Reason and emotion in psychotherapy.* New York: Lyle Stuart.

Ellis, A. (1973). *Humanistic psychotherapy: The rational-emotive approach.* New York: McGraw-Hill.

Ellis, A. (1975). *How to live with a neurotic.* North Hollywood, CA: Wilshire Books.

Ellis, A. (1979). The theory of rational-emotive therapy. In A. Ellis & J. M. Whiteley (Eds.), *Theoretical and empirical foundations of rational-emotive therapy* (pp. 33–60). Monterey, CA: Brooks/Cole.

Ellis, A. (1985). Expanding the ABC's of rational-emotive therapy. In M. J. Mahoney & A. Freeman (Eds.), *Cognition and psychotherapy* (pp. 313–323). New York: Plenum.

Ellis, A. (1988). *How to stubbornly refuse to make yourself miserable about anything, yes anything.* New York: Kensington.

Ellis, A. (1989). Comments on my critics. In M. E. Bernard & R. DiGiuseppe (Eds.), *Inside rational-emotive therapy: A critical appraisal of the theory and therapy of Albert Ellis* (pp. 199–260). San Diego, CA: Academic Press.

Ellis, A. (1990). How can psychological treatment aim to be briefer and better? The rational-emotive approach to brief therapy. In J. K. Zeig & S. G. Gilligan (Eds.), *Brief therapy: Myths, methods, and metaphors* (pp. 291–302). New York: Brunner/Mazel.

Ellis, A. (1992). Group rational-emotive and cognitive-behavioral therapy. *International Journal of Group Psychotherapy, 42*(1), 63–80.

Ellis, A., & Dryden, W. (1990). The basic practice of RET. In W. Dryden (Ed.), *The essential Albert Ellis* (pp. 145–183). New York: Springer.

Ellis, A., & Harper, R. A. (1975). *A new guide to rational living.* Hollywood, CA: Wilshire.

Ellis, A., Sichel, J., Yeager, R., DiMattia, D., & DiGiuseppe, R. (Eds.). (1989). *Rational-emotive couples therapy.* New York: Pergamon.

Emery, G. (1981). *A new beginning: How you can change your life through cognitive therapy.* New York: Simon & Schuster.

Emery, G., & Campbell, J. (1986). *Rapid relief from emotional distress.* New York: Fawcett Columbine.

English, H. B., & English, A. C. (1958). *A comprehensive dictionary of psychoanalytic terms.* New York: McKay.

Erickson, M. (1954). Special techniques on brief hypnotherapy. *Journal of Clinical and Experimental Hypnosis, 2,* 109–129.

Erlanger, M. A. (1990). Using the genogram with the older client. *Journal of Mental Health Counseling, 12*(3), 321–336.

Ewer, R. F. (1968). *Ethology of mammals.* New York: Plenum.

Fagan, J., & Shepherd, I. L. (1970). *Gestalt therapy now: Theory, techniques, applications.* New York: Harper & Row.

Fairbairn, W. R. D. (1967). *An object relations theory of personality.* New York: Basic Books

Fals-Stewart, W., & Lucente, S. (1994). Behavioral group therapy with obsessive-compulsives: An overview. *International Journal of Group Psychotherapy, 44,* 35–51.

Falvey, E. (1989). Passion and professionalism: Critical rapprochements for mental health research. *Journal of Mental Health Counseling, 11,* 86–105.

Farthing, C. W. (1992). *The psychology of consciousness.* Englewood Cliffs, NJ: Prentice-Hall.

Fezler, W. (1990). *Imagery for healing, knowledge, and power.* New York: Simon & Schuster.

Fiebert, M. S. (1983). *Ways of growth* (3rd ed.). Lexington, MA: Ginn.

Figley, C. R. (1998). Burnout as systemic traumatic stress: a model for helping traumatized family members. In C. R. Figley (ed.), *Burnout in families: The systemic costs of caring* (pp. 15–28). Boca Raton, FL: CRC Press.

Fisch, R., Weakland, J. H., & Segal, L. (1983). *The tactics of change: Doing brief therapy.* San Francisco: Jossey-Bass.

Fisher, J., & Byrne, D. (1975). Too close for comfort: Sex differences in response to invasions of personal space. *Journal of Personality and Social Psychology, 32,* 15–21.

Fisher, S., & Greenberg, R. (1977). *The scientific credibility of Freud's theories and therapy.* New York: Basic Books.

Fisher, S., & Greenberg, R. (1996). *Freud scientifically appraised.* New York: Wiley.

Fluegelman, A. (Ed.). (1976). *The new games book.* Garden City, NY: Doubleday.

Foa, E. B., Stekette, G. S., & Ascher, L. M. (1980). Systematic desensitization. In A. Goldstein & E. B. Foa (Eds.), *Handbook of behavioral interventions: A clinical guide* (pp. 46–63). New York: Wiley.

Fodor, I. G. (1987). Cognitive behavior therapy: Evaluation of theory and practice for addressing women's issues. In M. A. Douglas & L. E. Walker (Eds.), *Feminist therapies: Integration of therapeutic and feminist systems* (pp. 91–117). Norwood, NJ: Ablex.

Fonagy, P. (1999). Report prepared by the Research Committee of the International Psychoanalytic Association at the request of the President Editor and Chair. London: International Psychoanalytic Associations.

Foulkes, D. (1985). *Dreaming: A cognitive-psychological analysis.* Hillsdale, NJ: Lawrence Erlbaum.

Foulkes, D. (1999). *Children's dreaming and the development of consciousness.* Cambridge, MA: Harvard University Press.

Frankl, V. (1960). Paradoxical intention. *American Journal of Psychotherapy, 14,* 520–535.

Frayn, D. H. (1992). Assessment factors associated with premature psychotherapy termination. *American Journal of Psychotherapy, 46,* 250–261.

Free, M. L., Oei, T. P. S., & Sanders, M. R. (1991). Treatment outcome of a group cognitive therapy program for depression. *International Journal of Group Psychotherapy, 41,* 533–547.

Freeman, A., & DeWolf, R. (1989). *Woulda, coulda, shoulda.* New York: Silver Arrow Books.

Freedman, J., & Combs, G. (1996). *Narrative therapy: The social construction of preferred realities.* New York: Norton

Freud, S. (1961). *The psychopathology of everyday life.* New York: Signet. (Original work published 1901)

Friedlander, M. L., (1981). The effects of delayed role induction on counseling process and outcome. *Dissertation Abstracts International, 43,* 3887–3888B.

Fuhriman, A., & Burlingame, G. M. (1990). Consistency of matter: A comparative analysis of individual and group process variables. *The Counseling Psychologist, 19*(1), 6–62.

Fuhriman, A., Paul, S. C., & Burlingame, J. C. (1986). Electic time-limited therapy. In J. C. Norcross (Ed.), *Handbook of eclectic psychotherapy* (pp. 48–62). New York: Brunner/Mazel.

Gardner, R. (1986). The game of checkers in child therapy. In C. E. Schaefer & S. E. Reid (Eds.), *Game play: Therapeutic use of childhood games* (pp. 215–232). New York: Wiley.

Garfield, S. L. (1980). *Psychotherapy: An eclectic approach.* New York: Wiley.

Garfield, S. L., & Bergin, A. E. (Eds.). (1986). *Handbook of psychotherapy and behavior change* (3rd ed.). New York: Wiley.

Garner, D. M., & Garfinkle, P. E. (1980). Socio-cultural factors in the development of anorexia nervosa. *Psychological Medicine, 10,* 647–656.

Gaston, L., Marmar, C. R., & Thompson, L. (1988). Relation of patient pretreatment characteristics to the therapeutic alliance in diverse psychotherapies. *Journal of Consulting and Clinical Psychology, 56,* 483–489.

Gaushell, W. H., & Lawson, D. M. (1989). Using a checksheet with misbehaviors in school: Parent involvement. *The School Counselor, 36*(6), 208–214.

Gelso, C. J., & Carter, J. A. (1985). The relationship in counseling and psychotherapy: Consequences, components, and theoretical antecedents. *The Counseling Psychologist, 13,* 155–243.

Gentner, D. S. (1991). A brief model for mental health counseling. *Journal of Mental Health Counseling, 13*(1), 58–68.

Gibson, R. L., & Mitchell, M. M. (1990). *Introduction to counseling and guidance* (3rd ed.). New York: Macmillan.

Gill, S. J., & Barry, R. A. (1982). Group focused counseling: Classifying the essential skills. *The Personnel and Guidance Journal, 60*(5), 110–118.

Ginter, E. J. (1988). Stagnation in eclecticism: The need to recommit to a journey. *Journal of Mental Health Counseling, 10,* 3–8.

Ginter, E. J. (1989). Slayers of monster watermelons found in the mental health patch. *Journal of Mental Health Counseling, 11,* 77–85.

Givens, D. B. (2002). *Dictionary of gestures, signs and body language.* Spokane, WA: Center for Nonverbal Studies Press

Gladfelter, J. (1990). Integrated psychotherapy. In J. K. Zeig & M. M. Munion (Eds.), *What is psychotherapy?* (pp. 336–340). San Francisco: Jossey/Bass.

Gladfelter, J. (1992). Redecision therapy. *International Journal of Group Psychotherapy, 42*(3), 319–334.

Glasgow, A. (1999). Sample activities: Anger management exercise: Draining. URL: http:www.therapeuticresources.com/sampleactivity.html [Accessed: January 1, 2003]

Glasser, W. (1982). Interview by D. B. Evans, What are you doing? An interview with William Glasser. *Personnel and Guidance Journal, 61,* 460–462.

Glasser, W. (1985). *Control theory.* New York: Harper & Row.

Glasser, W. (1999) *The language of choice theory.* New York: HarperCollins.

Gleick, J. (1988). *Chaos: Making a new science.* New York: Penguin.

Goldenberg, I., & Goldenberg, H. (1985). *Family therapy: An overview.* Monterey, CA: Brooks/Cole.

Goldenson, R. M. (1984). Post-traumatic stress disorder. In *Longman dictionary of psychology and psychiatry.* New York: Longman.

Goldfriend, M. R. (1982). Toward the delineation of therapeutic change principles. *American Psychologist, 35,* 991–999.

Goldman, D. J. (1976). Meditation helps break the stress spiral. *Psychology Today, 9*(9), 82–84.

Goldman, D. J., & Schwartz, G. E. (1976). Meditation as an intervention in stress reactivity. *Journal of Consulting and Clinical Psychology, 44,* 456–466.

Goldman, L. (2001). *Breaking the silence: A guide to helping children with complicated grief—suicide, homicide, aids, violence and abuse.* New York: Brunner-Routledge.

Goleman, D. (1999). *Emotional intelligence.* New York: Bantam.

Gonzales, M., Jones, D, Whitely, R. M., & Whitely, J. M. (1988). *The AACD stress management manual.* Alexandria, VA: American Counseling Association.

Goodman, J. (1985). *Turning points: New developments in values clarification* (vol. 1). Saratoga Springs, NY: Creative Resource Press.

Gottman, J. M. (1999). *The marriage clinic: A scientifically-based marital therapy.* New York: W.W. Norton.

Greenberg, L. S., & Safran, T. D. (1987). *Emotion in psychotherapy.* New York: Guilford Press.

Grencavage, L. M. & Norcross, J. C. (1990). Where are the commonalities among the therapeutic common factors? *Professional Psychology: Research and Practice, 21,* 372–378.

Grieger, R. (1986). *A client's guide to rational-emotive therapy.* Charlottesville, VA: University Press.

Grinspoon, L. (Ed.). (1991a, February). Post-traumatic stress: Part I. *Harvard Mental Health Letter, 7*(8), 1–4.

Grinspoon, L. (Ed.). (1991b, March). Post-traumatic stress: Part II. *Harvard Mental Health Letter, 7*(9), 1–4.

Gruen, D. S. (1993). A group psychotherapy approach to postpartum depression. *International Journal of Group Psychotherapy, 43*(2), 191–203.

Guidano, V. F., & Liotti, G. (1983). *Cognitive processes and emotional disorders.* New York: Guilford.

Gwain, G. (1982). Active visualization: Creating what you want. *Professional Psychology: Research and Practice, 13,* 211–216.

Haley, J. (1963). *Strategies of psychotherapy.* New York: Grune & Stratton.

Haley, J. (Ed.). (1967). *Advanced techniques of hypnosis and therapy: Selected papers of Milton H. Erickson.* New York: Grune & Stratton.

Haley, J. (1973). *Uncommon therapy.* New York: W. W. Norton.

Haley, J. (1976). *Problem solving therapy.* San Francisco: Jossey-Bass.

Haley, J. (1984). *Ordeal therapy: Unusual ways to change behavior.* San Francisco: Jossey-Bass.

Hall, C. S. (1953a). A cognitive theory of dream symbols. *The Journal of General Psychology, 48,* 169–186.

Hall, C. S. (1953b). A cognitive theory of dreams. *The Journal of General Psychology, 49,* 273–282. Abridged version in M. F. DeMartino (Ed.). (1959). *Dreams and personality dynamics* (pp. 123–134). Springfield, IL: Charles C Thomas.

Hall, E. T. (1968). Proxemics. *Current Anthropology,* pp. 83–108.

Hamachek, D. E. (1992). *Encounters with the self.* London: Thomas Learning.

Hamilton, J. A., & Harberger, P. (Eds.). (1992). *Postpartum psychiatric illness.* Philadelphia: University of Pennsylvania Press.

Handly, R., & Neff, P. (1985). *Anxiety and panic attacks: Their cause and cure.* New York: Ballantine.

Hansen, J., Stevic, R., & Warner, R. (1986). *Counseling: Theory and process* (4th ed.). Boston: Allyn & Bacon.

Hansen, J.C., Warner, R.W., & Smith, E.J. (1980). *Group counseling: Theory and practice* (2nd ed.). Chicago: Rand McNally.

Hare-Mustin, R. (1976). Paradoxical tasks in family therapy: Who can resist? *Psychotherapy: Theory, Research, & Practice, 13,* 128–130.

Harris, T. A. (1969). *I'm OK—You're OK.* New York: Harper & Row.

Hay, L. L. (1987). *You can heal your life.* Carlsbad, CA: Hay House, Inc.

Heider, J. (1985). *The Tao of leadership.* Atlanta, GA: Humanics New Age.

Hellman, C. A., Morrison, B. K., & Abramowitz, L. M. (1986). The stress of therapeutic work. *Journal of Mental Health Counseling, 8,* 36–40.

Helmstetter, S. (1986). *What to say when you talk to yourself.* New York: Pocket Books.

Henry, W. P., Schacht, T. E., & Strupp, H. H. (1986). Structural analysis of social behavior: Application to a study of interpersonal process in differential psychotherapeutic outcome. *Journal of Counseling and Clinical Psychology, 54,* 27–31.

Herr, E. L. (1989). *Counseling in a dynamic society: Opportunities and challenges.* Alexandria, VA: American Association of Counseling and Development.

Hershenson, D. B., Power, P. W., & Seligman, L. (1989a). Mental health counseling theory: Present status and future prospects. *Journal of Mental Health Counseling, 11,* 44–69.

Hershenson, D. B., Power, P. W., & Seligman, L. (1989b). Counseling theory as a projective test. *Journal of Mental Health Counseling, 11,* 273–279.

Hill, C. E., Helms, J. E., Spiegal, S. B., & Tichenor, V. (1988). Development of a system for categorizing client reactions to therapist interventions. *Journal of Counseling Psychology, 35,* 257–306.

Hill, C. E., & O'Grady, K. (1985). List of therapeutic intentions illustrated in a case study with therapists of varying theoretical orientations. *Journal of Counseling Psychology, 32,* 3–22.

Hill, H. (1992). Fairy tales: Visions for problem resolution in eating disorders. *Journal of Counseling and Development, 70,* 584–587.

Hofling, C. K. (1979). An instance of psychotherapy continued by correspondence. *Bulletin of the Menninger Clinic, 43,* 393–412.

Holaday, M., & Smith, A. (1995). Coping skills training: Evaluating a training model. *Journal of Mental Health Counseling, 17*(3), 360–367.

Hollis, J. W., & Wantz, R. A. (1986). *Counselor preparation 1986–1989: Programs, personnel, trends* (6th ed.). Muncie, IN: Accelerated Development.

Horvath, A. O., & Greenberg, L. S. (1994). *The working alliance: Theory, research, and practice.* New York: Wiley.

Howard, K. I., Orlinsky, D. E., & Lueger, R. J. (1994). The design of clinically relevant outcome research: Some considerations and an example. In M. Aveline & D. A. Shapiro (Eds.), *Research foundations for psychotherapy practice.* New York: Wiley.

Howard, M., Nance, D. W., & Myers, C. (1986). *Adaptive counseling and therapy: A systematic approach to selecting effective treatments.* San Francisco: Jossey-Bass.

Howe, L. W., & Howe, M. M. (1975). *Personalizing education: Values clarification and beyond.* New York: Hart.

Hsu, L. K. G. (1989). The gender gap in eating disorders: Why are eating disorders more common among women? *Clinical Psychology Review, 9,* 393–407.

Hughes, E. F. (1991). *Writing from the inner self.* New York: HarperCollins.

Huxley, A. (1946). *Silence, liberty and peace.* London: Fellowship of Reconciliation/Harpers, p. 24.

Hunt, H. (1989). *The multiplicity of dreams: Memory, imagination, and consciousness.* New Haven: Yale University Press.

Hynes, A. M., & Wedl, L. C. (1990). Bibliotherapy: An interactive process in counseling older persons. *Journal of Mental Health Counseling, 12*(3), 288–302.

Ivey, A. E. (1973). Demystifying the group process: Adapting microcounseling procedures to counseling groups. *Educational Technology, 13,* 27–31.

Ivey, A. E. (1986). *Developmental therapy: Theory into practice.* San Francisco: Jossey-Bass.

Ivey, A. E. (1989). Mental health counseling: A developmental process and profession. *Journal of Mental Health Counseling, 11,* 26–35.

Ivey, A. E. (1990). *Developmental strategies for helpers: Individual, family, and network interventions.* Pacific Grove, CA: Brooks/Cole.

Ivey, A. E., & Goncalves, O. F. (1988). Developmental therapy: Integrating developmental processes into clinical practice. *Journal of Counseling and Development, 66,* 406–413.

Ivey, A. E., & Rigazio-DiGilio, S. A. (1991). Toward a developmental practice of mental health counseling: Strategies for training, practice, and political unity. *Journal of Mental Health Counseling, 13*(1), 21–36.

Ivey, A. E., & Simek-Downing, L. (1980). *Counseling and psychotherapy: Skills, theories, and practice.* Englewood Cliffs, NJ: Prentice-Hall.

Jacobs, E. (1988). *Use of creative techniques and props in individual and group counseling.* Breckenridge, CO: American School Counselors Association (ASCA) Elementary/Middle School Guidance Conference.

Jacobs, M. (1998). *The presenting past: The core of psychodynamic counseling and therapy.* Buckingham, London: Open University Press.

Jacobson, N. S., & Margolin, G. (1979). *Marital therapy: Strategies based on social learning and behavior exchange principles.* New York: Brunner/Mazel.

Jackson, D. P., & Weakland, J. H. (1961). Conjoint family therapy: Some considerations on theory, technique, and results. *Psychiatry, 24,* 30–45.

Jaffe, D. T., & Bresler, D. E. (1980). Guided imagery: Healing through the mind's eye. In J. E. Shorr, G. E. Sobel, P. Robin, & J. A. Connella (Eds.), *Imagery: Its many dimensions and applications* (pp. 253–266). New York: Plenum.

Jakubowski, R., & Lange, A. J. (1978). *The assertive option: Your rights and responsibilities.* Champaign, IL: Research Press.

Jamison, K. R. (1995). *An unquiet mind.* New York: Alfred A. Knopf.

Johnson, C., & Maddi, K. (1986). The etiology of bulimia: Biopsychosocial perspectives. In S. Feinstein (Ed.), *Adolescent psychiatry, developmental and clinical issues* (Vol. 13, pp. 253–273). Chicago: University of Chicago Press.

Johnson, K. (1998). *Trauma in the lives of children: Crisis and stress management techniques for counselors, teachers, and other professionals.* Alameda, CA: Hunter House.

Johnson, W. Y., & Wilborn, B. (1991). Group counseling as an intervention in anger expression and depression in older adults. *The Journal of Specialists in Group Work, 16*(3), 133–142.

Kahler, A. A. (1974). *Organization and instructional problems of beginning teachers of vocational agriculture.* Ames: Iowa State University, Department of Agricultural Education.

Kalafat, J. (1990). Adolescent suicide and the implications for school response programs. *The School Counselor, 37,* 5, p. 359–369.

Kaplan, K. J. (1985). A response to Gilbert's comments. *Transactional Analysis Journal, 15,* 144–145.

Kaplan, K. J. (1987). Jonah and Narcissus. Self-integration versus self-destruction in human development. *Studies in Formative Spirituality, 8,* 33–54.

Kaplan, K. J. (1988). TILT: Teaching individuals to live together. *Transactional Analysis Journal, 18,* 220–230.

Kaplan, K. J. (1990). TILT for couples: Helping couples grow together. *Transactional Analysis Journal, 20,* 229–244.

Kaplan, K. J. (1998). *TILT: Teaching individuals to live together.* Philadelphia: Brunner-Mazel.

Kaplan, K J., Capace, N. K., Clyde. J. D. (1984). A bidimensional distancing approach to transactional analysis: A suggested revision of the OK corral. *Transactional Analysis Journal, 15,* 114–119.

Keat, D. B. (1985). Child-adolescent multimodal therapy: Bud the boss. *Journal of Humanistic Education and Development, 23,* 183–192.

Keat, D. B. (1990). Change in child multimodal counseling. *Elementary School Guidance and Counseling, 24*(4), 192–198.

Kelly, K. R. (1988). Defending eclectism: The utility of informed choice. *Journal of Mental Health Counseling, 10,* 210–213.

Kelly, K. R. (1991). Theoretical integration is the future for mental health counseling. *Journal of Mental Health Counseling, 13*(1), 106–111.

Kernberg, O. (1984). *Severe personality disorders.* New Haven. Yale University Press.

Kerr, M. (1980). Emotional factors in physical illness: A multigenerational perspective. In R. R. Sagar (Ed.), *Georgetown family symposia: Vol. 4 (1977–78)* (pp. 47–63). Washington, DC: Georgetown University.

Kerr, M., & Bowen, M. (1988). *Family evaluation: An approach based on Bowen theory.* New York: W. W. Norton.

Kettlewell, P. W., Mizes, J. S., & Wasylsyshyn, N. A. (1992). A cognitive-behavioral group treatment of bulimia. *Behavior Therapy, 23*(4).

Kipper, D. A. (1992). The effects of two kinds of role playing on self-evaluation of improved assertiveness. *Journal of Clinical Psychology, 48*(23), 246–250.

Kirschner, D., & Kirshner, S. (1986). *Comprehensive family therapy: An integration of systemic and psychodynamic treatment models.* New York: Brunner/Mazel.

Klein, M. (1932). *The psychoanalysis of children.* New York: Delacorte Press/Seymour Lawrence.

Klein, M. (1959). *Our adult world and its roots in infancy.* London: Tavistock.

Klein, M. (1963). *Our adult world and other essays.* London: Heinemann Medical Books.

Klerman, G., & Weissman, M. (1985). Affective responses to stressful life events. In H. Goldman & S. Goldston (Eds.), *Preventing stress-related psychiatric disorders* (DHHS Pub. No. ADM 85-1366, pp. 55–76). Rockville, MD: NIMH.

Klier, J., Fein, E., & Genero, C. (1984). Are written or verbal contacts more effective in family therapy? *Social Work, 29,* 298–299.

Klimek, D., & Anderson, M. (1988). *Inner world, outer world: Understanding the struggles of adolescence.* Ann Arbor, MI: The University of Michigan. (ERIC Clearinghouse on Counseling and Personnel Services No. ED 290 118)

Knapp, M. L., & Hall, J. A. (1992). *Nonverbal communication in human interaction* (3rd ed.) New York: Holt, Rinehart & Winston.

Knaus, W. J. (1974). *Rational emotive education: A manual for elementary school teachers.* New York: Institute for Rational Living.

Knudson, R. M., & Minier, S. (1999). The on-going significance of significant dreams: The case of the bodiless head. *Dreaming, 9*(4), 235–245.

Kohut, H. (1959). Introspection, empathy, and psychoanalysis. *Journal of the American Psychoanalysis Association, 7,* 459–483.

Kohut, H. (1971). *The analysis of the self.* New York: International Universities Press.

Kohut, H. (1977). *The restoration of the self.* New York: International Universities Press.

Kohut, H. (1984). *How does analysis cure?* Chicago: The University of Chicago Press.

Kolb, D. L., Beutler, L. E., Davis, C. S., Crago, M., & Shanfield, S. (1985). Patient and therapist process variables relating to dropout and change in psychotherapy. *Psychotherapy: Theory, Research, and Practice, 22,* 702–710.

Korn, E. R., & Johnson, K. (1983). *Visualization: The use of imagery in the health professions.* Homewood, IL: Dow-Jones/Irwin.

Kottman, T. (1990). Counseling middle school students: Techniques that work. *Elementary School Guidance and Counseling, 25*(2), 138–145.

Kranzow, K. (1973). Deliberate psychological education. *The Personnel and Guidance Journal, 48*(6), 72–78.

Krumboltz, J., & Krumboltz, H. (1972). *Changing children's behavior.* New York: Prentice-Hall.

Krumboltz, J. D., & Thoresen, C. E. (1976). *Counseling methods.* New York: Holt, Rinehart, & Winston.

Kuiken, D., & Sikora, S. (1993). The impact of dreams on waking thoughts and feelings. In E. A. Moffitt, E. M. Kramer et al. (Eds.), *The functions of dreaming* (pp. x, 610). Albany, NY: State University of New York Press.

L'Abate, L., & Weeks, G. A. (1978). A bibliography of paradoxical methods in psychotherapy of family systems. *Family Practice, 17,* 95–98.

Lakoff, G. (1997). How unconscious metaphorical thought shapes dreams. In D. Stein (Ed.), *Cognitive science and the unconscious* (pp. 89–120). Washington, DC: American Psychiatric Press.

Lambert, M. J. (1989). The individual therapist's contribution to psychotherapy process and outcome. *Clinical Psychology Review, 9,* 469–485.

Lambert, M. J. (1992). Psychotherapy outcome research: Implications for integrative and eclectic therapist. In J. C. Norcross & M. R. Goldfried (Eds.), *Handbook of psychotherapy integration* (pp. 94–129). New York: Basic Books.

Lambert, M. J. (1996). Tracking patient progress on a session-by-session basis. *Behavioral Healthcare Tomorrow, 45*(3), 48–50.

Lambert, M. J., Shapiro, D. A., & Bergin, A. E. (1986). The effectiveness of psychotherapy. In S. L. Garfield & A. E. Bergin (Eds.), *Handbook of psychotherapy and behavior change* (pp. 111–141). New York: Wiley.

Lampropoulos, G. K. (2000). Evolving psychotherapy integration: Eclectic selection and prescriptive applications of common factors in therapy. *Psychotherapy, 37*(4), 285–297.

Larrabee, M., & Wilson, B. (1981). Teaching teenagers to cope through family-life simulations. *The School Counselor, 28,* 117–123.

Lazarus, A. A. (1967). In support of technical eclecticism. *Psychological Reports, 21,* 415–416.

Lazarus, A. A. (1971). *Behavior therapy and beyond.* New York: McGraw-Hill.

Lazarus, A. A. (1976). *Multimodal behavior therapy.* New York: Springer.

Lazarus, A. A. (1977). *In the mind's eye: The power of imagery for personal enrichment.* New York: Rawson.

Lazarus, A. A. (1981). *The practice of multimodal therapy.* New York: McGraw-Hill.

Lazarus, A. A. (1985). *Casebook of multimodal therapy.* New York: Guilford.

Lazarus, A. A. (1992). The multimodal approach to the treatment of minor depression. *American Journal of Psychotherapy, 86*(1), 50–56.

Lazarus, A. A. (1993). *The practice of multimodal therapy.* Baltimore: Johns Hopkins University Press.

Lazarus, A. A., Beutler, L. E., & Norcross, J. C. (1992). The future of technical eclecticism. *Psychotherapy, 29,* 11–20.

Lazarus, A. A., & Mayne, T. I. (1990). Relaxation: Some limitations, side effects, and proposed solutions. *Psychotherapy, 27*(2), 261–266.

Lazarus, R. S., & Folkman, S. (1984). Coping and adaptation. In W. D. Gentry (Ed.), *The handbook of behavioral medicine* (pp. 378–384). Chicago: Science Research Associates.

Leedy, J. J. (Ed.). (1985). *Poetry as healer: Mending the troubled mind.* New York: Vanguard Press.

Lehar, S. (2002). *The world in your head: A Gestalt view of the mechanism of conscious experience.* Mahwah, NJ: Lawrence Erlbaum Associates.

LeShan L. (1974). *How to meditate.* New York: Bantam Books.

Leveton, E. A. (1992). *A clinician's guide to psychodrama.* New York: Springer.

Levitsky, A., & Perls, F. S. (1973). The rules and games of gestalt therapy. In J. Fagan & I. L. Shephard (Eds.), *Gestalt therapy now* (pp. 140–149). Palo Alto, CA: Science and Behavior Books.

Lewis, C. S. (1963). *A grief observed.* Greenwich, CT: Seabury Press.

Lewis, H. R., & Streitfield, H. S. (1970). *Growth games: How to tune in yourself, your family, your friends.* New York: Bantam Books.

Lewy, A. J., Sack, R. L., & Miller, L. S. (1987). Antidepressant and circadian phase-shifting effects of light. *Science, 235,* 352–354.

Lieberman, M., Yalom, I., & Miles, M. (1973). *Encounter groups: First facts.* New York: Basic Books.

Liebman, M. (1986). *Art therapy for groups.* Cambridge, MA.: Brookline.

Linden, W., & Wen, F. K. (1990). Therapy outcome research, health care policy, and the continuing lack of accumulated knowledge. *Professional Psychology: Research & Practice, 21,* 482–488.

Linehan, M. M. (1993). *Cognitive-behavioral treatment of borderline personality disorder.* New York: Guilford.

Link, P. W., & Darling, C. A. (1986). Couples undergoing treatment for infertility: Dimensions of life satisfaction. *Journal of Sex and Marital Therapy, 12*(1), 46–59.

Lipscy, M., & Wilson, D. (1993). The efficacy of psychological, educational, and behavioral treatment: Confirmation from meta-analysis. *American Psychologist, 48,* 1181–1209.

Luborsky, L., Cruts-Cristoph, P., Mintz, J., & Auerbach, A. (1988). *Who will benefit from psychotherapy: Predicting therapeutic outcomes.* New York: Basic Books.

Luborsky, L., Singer, B., & Luborsky, L. (1975). Comparative studies of psychotherapies. *Archives of General Psychiatry, 32,* 995–1008.

Lundholm, J. K., & Littrell, J. M. (1986). Desire for thinness among high school cheerleaders: Relationship to disordered eating and weight control behaviors. *Adolescence, 21,* 573–579.

Madanes, C. (1981). *Strategic family therapy.* San Francisco: Jossey-Bass.

Maharishi, M. Y. (1972). *The science of living and the art of being.* New York: Signet.

Mahlstedt, P. P. (1985). The psychological component of infertility. *Fertility and Sterility, 43*(3), 335–346.

Mahoney, M. J. (1977). Reflections on the cognitive learning trend in psychotherapy. *American Psychologist, 32,* 5–13.

Mahoney, M. J., & Gabriel, T. J. (1987). Psychotherapy and the cognitive sciences: An evolving alliance. *Journal of Cognitive Psychotherapy: An International Quarterly, 1,* 39–59.

Main, A. P., & Roark, A. E. (1975). A consensus method to reduce conflict. *Personnel and Guidance Journal, 53,* 754–759.

Maitland, R. (1975). *Essentials of meditation.* Lakemont, GA: CSA Press.

Malan, D. (1975). Psychodynamic changes in untreated neurotic patients. *British Journal of Psychiatry, 32,* 110–126.

Maltz, M. (1960). *Psychocybernetics.* Englewood Cliffs, NJ: Prentice-Hall.

Manley, L. (1986). Goals of misbehavior inventory. *Elementary School Guidance and Counseling, 21,* 160–162.

Mann, J. (1973). *Time-limited psychotherapy.* Cambridge, MA: Harvard University Press.

Mann, J. (1981). The core of time-limited psychotherapy: Time and the central issue. In S. H. Budman (Ed.), *Forms of brief therapy* (pp. 25–42). New York: Guilford.

Marcer, D. (1986). *Biofeedback and related therapies in clinical practice.* Rockville, MD: Aspen Publishers.

Marquis, J., Morgan, W., & Piaget, G. (1973). *A guidebook for systematic desensitization* (3rd ed.). Palo Alto, CA: Veterans Workshop.

Marshall, W. L., Gauthier, J., Christie, M. M., Currie, D. W., & Gordon, A. (1977). Flooding therapy effectiveness, stimulus characteristics, and the value of brief in vivo exposure. *Behavior Research and Therapy, 15,* 79–87.

Marston, S. (1994). *The divorced parent.* New York: William Morrow.

Marziali, E. A. (1992). People in your life. Development of a social support measure for predicting psychotherapy outcome. *Journal of Nervous Mental Disorders, 175*(6), 327–338.

Maultsby, M. C. (1975). *Help yourself to happiness.* New York: Institute for Rational Living.

Mazza, N. (1981). The use of poetry in treating the troubled adolescent. *Adolescence, 16,* 403–408.

McBride, M. C., & Martin, G. E. (1990). A framework or eclecticism: The importance of theory to mental health counseling. *Journal of Mental Health Counseling, 12,* 495–505.

McEwan, K. L., Costello, C. G., & Taylor, P. J. (1987). Adjustment to infertility. *Journal of Abnormal Psychology, 96*(2), 108–116.

McKay, M. J., & Fanning, P. (1999). Sample activities: An exercise from The Daily Relaxer. URL: http:www.therapeuticresources.com/sampleactivity.html [Accessed: January 1, 2003]

McKay, M., Davis, M., & Fanning, P. (1983). *Messages: The communication skills book.* Oakland, CA: Harbinger.

McMahon, R. J., & Forehand, R. (1984). Parent training for the noncompliant child: Treatment, outcome, generalization, and adjunctive therapy procedures. In R. F. Dangel & R. A. Polster (Eds.), *Parent training: Foundations of research and practice* (pp. 47–67). New York: Guilford.

McMullin, R. (1986). *Handbook of cognitive therapy techniques.* New York: Norton Press.

McMullin, R., & Giles, T. (1981). *Cognitive behavior therapy: A restructuring approach.* New York: Grune & Stratton.

Mehrabian, A. (1971). *Silent messages.* Belmont, CA: Wadsworth.

Meichenbaum, D. (1977). *Cognitive behavior modification: An integrated approach.* New York: Plenum.

Meichenbaum, D., & Meichenbaum, A. (1974). *Cognitive behavior modification.* Morristown, NJ: General Learning.

Messor, S. B., & Boals, G. F. (1981). Psychotherapy outcome in a university-based psychology training clinic. *Professional Psychology, 12*(6), 785–793.

Miller, J. (2001). Grief tips. URL: http:www.wilowgreen.com/cust_AdviceDisplay.asp? TextTypeID=31&List=Grief [Accessed: January 2, 2003]

Miller, J. E. (2003). *Grief tips.* Fort Wayne, IN: Willowgreen Publishing.

Miller, W. R., Brown, J. M., Simpson, T. L., Handmaker, N. S., Bein, T. H., Luckie, L. F., Montgomery, H. A., Hester, R. K., & Tonigan, J. S. (1995). What works? A methological analysis of the alcohol treatment outcome literature. In R. K. Hester & W. R. Miller (Eds.), *Handbook of alcoholism treatment approaches: Effective alternatives* (2nd ed., pp. 12–14). Boston: Allyn & Bacon.

Milne, D. (1986). *Training behavior therapists: Methods, evaluation and implementation with parents, nurses, and teachers.* Cambridge, MA: Brookline Books.

Minuchin, S. (1974). *Families and family therapy.* Cambridge, MA: Harvard University Press.

Minuchin, S., & Fishman, H. (1981). *Techniques of family therapy.* Cambridge, MA: Harvard University Press.

Mitchell, J., Pyle, R. Eckert, E., Hatsukami, D., Pomeroy, C., & Zimmerman, R. (1990). A comparison study of antidepressants and structured intensive group psychotherapy in the treatment of bulimia nervosa. *Archives of General Psychiatry, 47,* 149–157.

Mole, J. (2002). Decoding body language: The four basic modes of body language in business. URL: http://www.johnmole.com articles18.htm [Accessed: January 5, 2003]

Monroe, C., Borzi, M. G., & Burrell, R. D. (1992). Communication apprehension among high school dropouts. *The School Counselor, 39*(4), 273–280.

Monti, P. M., Rohsenow, D. J., Colby, S. M., & Abrams, D .B. (1995). Coping and social skills training. In R. K. Hester & W. R. Miller (Eds.), *Handbook of alcoholism treatment approaches: Effective alternatives* (2nd ed., pp. 221–241). Boston: Allyn & Bacon.

Moreno, J. L. (1975). *The theatre of spontaneity,* vol. 1. New York: Beacon Press.

Morris, D. (1994). *Bodytalk: The meaning of human gestures.* New York: Crown Publishers.

Morris, R., & Kratochwill, T. (1983). *Treating children's fears and phobias: A behavioral approach.* New York: Pergamon Press.

Morse, C., & Dennerstein, L. (1985). Infertile couples entering an in vitro fertilization program: A preliminary survey. *Journal of Psychosomatic Obstetrics and Gynecology, 4,* 207–209.

Morse, L. A. (1987). Working with young procrastinators: Elementary school students who do not complete assignments. *Elementary School Guidance and Counseling, 21*(3), 259–268.

Mosak, H. H. (1971). Lifestyle. In A. G. Kelly (Ed.), *Techniques for behavior change* (pp. 74–84). Springfield, IL: Charles C. Thomas.

Moos, R. H. (1990). Depressed outpatients' life contexts, amount of treatment and treatment outcome. *Journal of Nervous Mental Disorders, 178*(2), 105–112.

Myers, R. (2000). The family chip system. Villa Park, CA: Child Development Institute. URL:http://www.practicalparent.org.uk/chip.htm [Accessed: January 5, 2003]

Nader, K., Dubrow, K., & Stamm, B. H. (Eds.). (1999). *Honoring differences: Cultural issues in the treatment of trauma and loss.* Philadelphia: Brunner/Mazel.

Nance, D. W. (1995). *How therapists ACT: Cases combining major approaches to psychotherapy and the adaptive counseling model.* Washington, DC: Accelerated Development.

Nance, D. W., & Myers, P. (1991). Continuing the eclectic journey. *Journal of Mental Health Counseling, 13*(1), 119–130.

Nelson, R. C. (1990). *Choice awareness: A systematic eclectic counseling theory.* Minneapolis, MN: Educational Media Corporation.

Nelson, R. L. (1992). Spa in counseling. *Journal of Counseling and Development, 71*(2), 214–220.

Nicholas, M., & Forrester, A. (1999). Advantages of heterogeneous therapy groups in the psychotherapy of the traumatically abused: Treating the problem as well as the person. *International Journal of Group Psychotherapy, 49*(3), 323–328.

Nichols, M. P.(1987). *The self and the system.* New York: Brunner/Mazel.

Nicholson, R. A., & Berman, J. S. (1983). Is follow-up necessary in evaluating psychotherapy? *Psychological Bulletin, 93,* 261–278.

Nickerson, E., & O'Laughlin, K. (1982). The therapeutic use of games. In C. E. Schaefer & K. J. O'Conner (Eds.), *Handbook of play therapy* (pp. 174–187). New York: Wiley.

Norcross, J. C. (Ed.). (1986). *Handbook of eclectic therapy.* New York: Bruner/Mazel.

Norcross, J. C., & Goldfried, M. R. (Eds.). (1992). *Handbook for psychotherapy integration.* New York: Basic Books.

Norcross, J. D., & Prochaska, J. O. (1983). Clinician's theoretical orientations: Selection, utilization and efficacy. *Professional Psychology: Research and Practice, 14,* 197–208.

Notarius, C., & Markman, H. (1993). *We can work it out: Making sense of marital confict.* New York: Putnam.

Novaco, R. W. (1975). *Anger control: The development and evaluation of an experimental treatment.* Lexington, MA: Lexington Books/DC Heath.

Oberkirch, A. (1983). Personal writings in psychotherapy. *American Journal of Psychotherapy, 37,* 265–272.

O'Hanlon,W., & Weiner-Davis, M. (1989). *In search of solutions: A new direction in psychotherapy.* New York: W. W. Norton.

Ohlsen, M. M. (1977). *Group counseling.* New York: Holt, Rinehart, & Winston.

Ohlsen, M., Horne, A., & Lawe, C. (1988). *Group counseling* (3rd ed.). New York: Holt, Rinehart, & Winston.

Okum, B. F. (1990). *Seeking connections in psychotherapy.* San Francisco: Jossey-Bass.

O'Malley, S. S., Suh, C. S., & Strupp, H. H. (1983). The Vanderbilt Psychotherapy Process Scale: A report of the scale development and a process outcome study. *Journal of Consulting and Clinical Psychology, 51,* 581–586.

Omizo, M. M., & Omizo, S. A. (1988). The effects of participation in group counseling on self-esteem and locus of control among adolescents from divorced families. *The School Counselor, 36*(1), 54–58.

Orlinsky, D. E., & Howard, K. I. (1986). Process and outcome in psychotherapy. In S. L. Garfield & A. E. Bergin (Eds.), *Handbook of psychotherapy and behavior change* (pp. 311–381). New York: Wiley.

Palmer, D., & Hampton, P. T. (1987). Reducing broken appointments at intake in a community mental health center. *Community Mental Health Journal, 23,* 76–78.

Patterson, C. H. (1986). *Theories of counseling and psychotherapy* (4th ed.). New York: Harper & Row.

Peiser, I. (1982). Similarity, liking, and missed sessions in relation to psychotherapy outcome. *Dissertation Abstracts International, 42,* 4587B.

Pelletier, K. R. (1980). *Holistic medicine.* New York: Delacorte.

Perls, F. S. (1969). *Gestalt therapy verbatim.* Lafayette, CA: Real People Press.

Peterson, S., & Straub, R. L. (1992). *School crisis survival guide: Management techniques and materials for counselors and administrators.* West Nyack, NY: Center for Applied Research in Education.

Piper, W. E., McCallum, M., & Azim, H. (1992). *Adaptations to loss through short-term group psychotherapy.* New York: Guilford.

Pollack, H. B., & Slan, J. B. (1995). Reflections and suggestions on leadership of psychotherapy groups. *International Journal of Group Psychotherapy, 45*(4), 507–519.

Polster, E., & Polster, M. (1973). *Gestalt therapy integrated.* New York: Random House.

Powers, R. L., & Haln, J. M. (1977). Creativity in problem-solving: The double dialogue technique. *Individual Psychologist, 14*(1), 22–32.

Prochaska, J. O., & Prochaska, J. M. (1994). A transtheoretical model of change for addictive behaviors. In M. Gossop (Ed.), *Psychological treatment for addictive behaviors* (pp. 222–242). Barcelona, Spain: Cevron.

Prochaska, J. O., DiClemente, C. C., & Norcross, J. C. (1992). In search of how people change. *American Psychologist, 47*(9), 1102–1114.

Progoff, I. (1975). *At a journal workshop: The basic text and guide for using the intensive journal process.* New York: Dialogue House Library.

Purkey, W. W., & Schmidt, J. J. (1990). *Invitational learning for counseling and development.* Ann Arbor, Michigan: ERIC/CAPS Select.

Rako, S., & Mazer, H. (Eds.). (1983). *Semrad: The heart of a therapist.* Northvale, NJ: Jason Aronson.

Rando, T. A. (1984). *Grief, dying, and death: Clinical interventions for caregivers.* Cambridge, IL: Research Press.

Rathus, S. A., & Nevid, J. S. (1977). *BT: Behavior therapy strategies for solving problems in living.* New York: Signet.

Redd, W. H., Porterfield, A. L., & Andersen, B. L. (1979). *Behavior modification.* New York: Random House.

Renard, S., & Sockol, K. (1987). *Creative drama: Enhancing self-concepts and learning.* Minneapolis: Educational Media.

Rhyne, J. (1970). The gestalt art experience. In J. Fagan & I. Lee (Eds.), *Gestalt therapy now* (pp. 274–284). New York: Harper & Row.

Rich, P. (1999). *The healing journey through grief: Your journal for reflection and recovery.* New York: Wiley.

Richardson, R. W. (1987). *Family ties that bind.* Bellingham, WA: Self-Counsel Press.

Richmond, V. James, P., McCroskey, C., & Payne, S. K. (1991). *Nonverbal behavior in interpersonal relations* (2nd ed.). Englewood Cliffs, NJ: Prentice-Hall.

Rimm, D., & Masters, J. (1979). *Behavior therapy: Techniques and empirical findings* (2nd ed.). New York: Academic Press.

Roark, A. E. (1978). Interpersonal conflict management. *Personnel and Guidance Journal, 57,* 400–402.

Roback, H. B., Moore, R. F., Bloch, F. S., & Shelton, M (1996) Confidentiality in group psychotherapy: Empirical findings and the law. *International Journal of Group Psychotherapy, 46*(1), 117–135.

Roberts, C. G., & Guttormson, L. (1990). *You and stress: A survival guide for adolescence.* Minneapolis, MN: Free Spirit Press.

Robertson, M. H. (1995). *Psychotherapy education and training: An integrative perspective.* Madison, CT: International Universities Press

Robbins, A. (1986). *Unlimited power: The new science of personal achievement.* New York: Fawcett Columbine.

Rogers, C. R. (1980). *A way of being.* Boston: Houghton Mifflin.

Rogers, C. R. (1961). *On becoming a person. A therapist's view of psychotherapy.* Boston: Houghton Mifflin.

Rogers, C. R. (1986). Client-centered therapy. In I. Kutash & A. Wolf (Eds.), *Psychotherapist's casebook: Theory and techniques in the practice of modern therapies* (pp. 197–208). San Francisco: Jossey-Bass.

Rohrbaugh, M., Tennen, H., & Eron, J. (1982). Paradoxical interventions. In J. H. Masserman (Ed.), Current psychiatric therapies (vol. 21, pp. 89–124). New York: Grune & Stratton.

Romen, A. (1981). *Self-suggestion and its influence on the human organism.* Armonk, NY: M. E. Sharpe.

Rosenthal, N. E. (1989). *Light therapy: Treatment of psychiatric disorders, Vol. 3.* Washington, DC: American Psychiatric Association, Task Force on Treatment of Psychiatric Disorders.

Rosenthal, N. E., Carpenter, J. P., & James, S. P. (1986). Seasonal affective disorders in children and adolescence. *American Journal of Psychiatry, 143,* 356–358.

Rosenthal, N. E., Sack, D. A., Gillin, J. C., Lewy, A. J., Goodwin, F. K., Davenport, Y., Mueller, P. S., Newsome, D. A., & Wehr, T. A. (1984). Seasonal affective disorder: A description of the syndrome and preliminary findings for light therapy. *Archives General Psychiatry, 41,* 72–80.

Rosenthal, N. E., & Wehr, T. A. (1987). Seasonal affective disorders. *Psychiatric Annals, 17*(10), 664–669.

Rychlak, J. F. (1985). Eclecticism in psychological theorizing: Good and bad. *Journal of Counseling and Development, 63*(6), 351–353.

Sabatino, J. A., & Smith, L. M. (1990). Rational self-analysis. *Journal of Counseling and Development, 69,* 167–172.

Safran, J. (1990). Towards a refinement of cognitive therapy in light of interpersonal theory: 11. Practice. *Clinical Psychology Review, 10,* 107–115.

Safran, J. C., Segal, Z. V., Vallis, T. M., Shaw, B. F., & Samstag, L. W. (1993). Assessing patient suitability for short-term cognitive therapy with an interpersonal focus. *Cognitive Therapy and Research, 17,* 23–38.

Salzer, L. (1986). *Infertility: How couples can cope.* New York: G. K. Hall.

Sanders, F. M. (1989). Marital conflict and psychoanalytic therapy in the middle years. In J. Oldham & R. Liebert (Eds.), *The middle years: New psychoanalytic perspectives.* New Haven: Yale University Press.

Sapir, E. (1931). "Communication." *Encyclopedia of the Social Sciences, New York,* 4, 78–81.

Satir, V. (1967). *Conjoint family therapy.* Palo Alto, CA: Science and Behavior Books.

Satir, V. (1975). *Self esteem.* CA: Celestial Arts.

Satir, V., & Baldwin, M. (1983). *Satir step by step: A guide to creating change in families.* Palo Alto, CA: Science and Behavior Books.

Schaefer, C. E., & Briesmeister, J. M. (Eds.). (1989). *Handbook of parent training: Parents as co-therapists for children's behavior problems.* New York: Wiley.

Schaefer, C. E., Briesmeister, J. M., & Fitton, M. E. (1984). *Family therapy techniques for problem behavior of children and teenagers.* San Francisco: Jossey-Bass.

Schaefer, C. E., & Reid, S. (Eds.). (1986). *Game play: Therapeutic use of childhood games.* New York: Wiley.

Schaefer, D. (1987). *Choices and consequences: What to do when a teenager uses alcohol and drugs.* Minneapolis: Johnson Institute Books.

Scharf, D., & Scharf, J. S. (1987). *Object relations family therapy.* Northvale, NJ: Jason Aronson.

Scheidlinger, S. (1995). The small healing group—A historical overview. *Psychotherapy,* 32(4), 657–668.

Scheidlinger, S. (1997). Group dynamics and group psychotherapy revisited: Four decades later. *International Journal of Group Psychotherapy,* 47(2), 141–159.

Schinfeld, J. S., Elkins, T. E., & Strong, C. M. (1986). Ethical considerations in the management of infertility. *Journal of Reproductive Medicine,* 31(11), 1038–1042.

Schiraldi, G. R. (2000). *The post-traumatic stress disorder sourcebook: A guide to healing, recovery, and growth.* Los Angeles: Lowell House.

Schmich, M. (1997, June 1). Advice, like youth, probably just wasted on the young. *Chicago Tribune.* URL:http:www.chicagotribune.com/news/columnists/chi-970601sunscreen.column [Accessed: January 1, 2003]

Schriner, C. (1990). *Feel better now: 30 ways to handle frustration in three minutes or less.* Rolling Hills Estates, CA: Jalmar Press.

Seligman, M. E. P. (1995). The effectiveness of psychotherapy: The *Consumer Reports* study. *American Psychologist,* 50, 965–974. [http://www.apa.org/journals/seligman.html]

Seltzer, L. F. (1986). *Paradoxical strategies in psychotherapy: A comprehensive overview and guidebook.* New York: Wiley.

Selvini-Palazzoli, M. (1978). *Paradox and counterparadox.* New York: Jason Aronson.

Selvini-Palazzoli, M., Boscolo, L., Cecchin, G., & Prata, G. (1974). The treatment of children through brief therapy of their parents. *Family Process, 13,* 429–442.

Selvini-Palazzoli, M., Boscolo, L., Cecchin, G., & Prata, G. (1978). *Paradox and counterparadox: A new model in the therapy of the family in schizophrenic transaction.* New York: Aronson.

Serok, S. (1986). Therapeutic implications of games with juvenile delinquents. In C. E. Schaefer & S. E. Reid (Eds.), *Game play: Therapeutic use of childhood games* (pp. 311–329). New York: Wiley.

Sexton, T. L., & Whiston, S. C. (1991). Review of the empirical basis for counseling: Implications for practice and training. *Counselor Educations and Supervision, 30*(6), 330–354.

Shapiro, D., & Shapiro, D. (1982). Meta-analysis of comparative therapy outcome studies: A replication of refinement. *Psychological Bulletin, 92,* 581–604.

Sheikh, A. A. (1976). Treatment of insomnia through eidetic imagery: A new technique. *Perceptual and Motor Skills, 43,* 994.

Sheikh, A. A., & Jordan, C. S. (1983). Clinical uses of mental imagery. In A. A. Sheikh (Ed.), *Imagery: Current theory, research, and application* (pp. 391–435). New York: Wiley.

Sheikh, A. A., & Sheikh, D. S. (Eds.). (1985). *Imagery in education.* Farmingdale, NY: Baywood Publishing.

Sherman, R., & Fredman, N. (1986). *Handbook of structural techniques in marriage and family therapy.* New York: Brunner/Mazel.

Shneidman, E. (1985). *Definition of suicide.* New York: Wiley.

Shorr, J. E. (1974). *Psychotherapy through imagery.* New York: Intercontinental Medical.

Sifenos, S. P. (1979). *Short-term dynamic psychotherapy: Evaluation and technique.* New York: Plenum.

Sifenos, S. P. (1981). Short-term anxiety-provoking psychotherapy: Its history, technique, outcome, and instruction. In S. H. Budman (Ed.), *Forms of brief therapy* (pp. 45–80). New York: Guilford.

Silva, J., & Stone, R. B. (1983). *The Silva mind control method for business managers.* Englewood Cliffs, NJ: Prentice-Hall.

Simkin, J., & Yontef, G. M. (1984). Gestalt therapy. In R. Corsini (Ed.), *Current psychotherapies* (3rd ed., pp. 61–82). Itasca, IL: Peacock.

Simon, G. M. (1989). An alternative defense of eclecticism: Responding to Kelly and Ginter. *Journal of Mental Health Counseling, 11,* 280–288.

Simon, G. M. (1991). Theoretical eclecticism: A goal we are obligated to pursue. *Journal of Mental Health Counseling, 13*(1), 367–378.

Simon, S. B., Howe, L. W., & Kirschenbaum, H. (1972). *Values clarification: A handbook of practical strategies for teachers and students.* New York: Hart.

Simonton, O. C., Mathews-Simonton, S., & Creighton, J. S. (1978). *Getting well again.* Los Angeles: Tarcher.

Slaveney, P. R., & McHugh, P. R. (1987). *Psychiatric polarities: Methodology and practice.* Baltimore: Johns Hopkins University Press.

Smith, D. (1982). Trends in counseling and psychotherapy. *American Psychologist, 37,* 802–809.

Sowa, C. J. (1992). Understand clients'perceptions of stress. *Journal of Counseling & Development, 71*(2),179–183.

Spinelli, E. (1994). *Demystifying therapy.* London: Constable

Spitzer, R. L., Endicott, J., & Robins, E. (1978). Research diagnostic criteria: Rationale and reliability. *Archives of General Psychiatry, 35,* 773–782.

Spivack, G., Platt, J., & Shure, M. (1976). *The problem-solving approach to adjustment.* San Francisco: Jossey-Bass.

Squires, R. L., & Kagen, D. M. (1985). Sex-role and eating behaviors among college women. *International Journal of Eating Disorders, 4,* 539–548.

Stanton, M. D. (1981). *Strategic approaches to family therapy.* New York: Brunner/Mazel.

Stanton, M. D. (1984). Fusion, compression, diversion, and the workings of paradox: A theory of therapeutic/systemic change. *Family Process, 23,* 135–167.

Stefanowski-Harding, S. (1990). Suicide and the school counselor. *The School Counselor, 37*(5), 328–336.

Stockton, R., & Morran, D. (1982). Review and perspectives of critical dimensions in therapeutic small group research. In G. M. Gazda (Ed.), Basic approaches to group psychotherapy and group counseling (3rd ed., pp. 47–68). Springfield, IL: Charles C Thomas.

Striegel-Moore, R., Silberstein, L. R., & Rodin, J. (1986). Toward and understanding of risk factors for bulimia. *American Psychologist, 41,* 246–263.

Strupp, H. H. (1981). Clinical research, practice and the crisis of confidence. *Journal of Consulting and Clinical Psychology, 49,* 216–219.

Strupp, H. H., & Bergin, A. E. (1969). Some empirical and conceptual bases for coordinated research in psychotherapy. *International Journal of Psychiatry, 7,* 68.

Suler, J. R. (1996). Teaching clinical psychology: Family sociograms. URL: http://p24601.rider.edu/sites/suler/sociogram.html. [Accessed: January 1, 2003]

Szmukler, G. I., Eisler, I., Gillies, C., & Hayward, M. E. (1985). The implications of anorexia nervosa in a ballet school. *Journal of Psychiatric Research, 19,* 177–181.

Talmon, M. (1990). *Single session therapy.* San Francisco: Jossey-Bass.

Taub, D. E., & McLorg, P. A. (1989). Anorexia nervosa and bulimia. In H. Tierney (Ed.), *Women's studies encyclopedia: Vol. I. View from the sciences* (pp. 101–121). Westport, CT: Greenwood.

Taylor, J. W. (1984). Structured conjoint therapy for spouse abuse cases. *Social Casework, 65,* 11–18.

Teusch, R. (1988). Level of ego development and bulimics' conceptualizations of their disorder. *Internal Journal of Eating Disorders, 7,* 607–615.

Thiessen, I. (1983). Using fairy tales during hypnotherapy in bulimerexia and other psychological problems. *Medical Hypnoanalysis, 4,* 139–144.

Thompson, R. A. (1990, February). Strategies for crisis management in the schools. *National Association of Secondary School Principals Bulletin, 14*(6), 54–58.

Thompson, R. A. (1993). Post-traumatic stress and post-traumatic loss debriefing: Brief strategic intervention for survivors of sudden loss. *The School Counselor, 34,* 133–138.

Tillett, R. (1984). Gestalt therapy in theory and practice. *British Journal of Psychiatry, 145,* 231–235.

Towers, D., Wollum, S., Dow, E., Senese, R., Ames, G., Berg, J., & McDonald, T. (1987). *Metaphor as a tool for counselors.* Paper presented at the Annual Convention of the American Association for Counseling and Development, New Orleans. (ERIC Document Reproduction Service No. ED 285096)

Treadwell, T., Kumar, V. K., & Collins, L. (1997). Spontaneity scale: Reliability and validity. *Journal of Group Psychotherapy, Psychodrama, and Sociometry, 48,* 57–65.

Treadwell, T., Kumar, V. K., Stein, S., & Prosnick, K.(1997). Sociometry: Tools for research and practice. *Journal for Specialists in Group Work, 22,* 52–65.

Treadwell, T., Kumar, V. K., Stein, S., & Prosnick, K. (1998). Sociometry: Tools for research and practice. *International Journal of Action Methods, Psychodrama, Skill Training and Role Playing,* 45–52.

Trotzer, J. P. (1986). *Marriage and family: Better ready than not.* Muncie, IN: Accelerated Development.

Truax, C. B., & Carkhuff, R. R. (1967). *Towards effective counseling and psychotherapy.* Chicago: Aldine.

Tschuschke, V., & Dies, R. R. (1994). Intensive analysis of therapeutic factors and outcome in long-term inpatient groups. *International Journal of Group Psychotherapy, 44,* 185–208.

U.S. Department of Health and Human Services. (1999). *Mental Health: A Report of the Surgeon General—Executive Summary.* Rockville, MD: U.S. Department of Health and Human Services, Substance Abuse and Mental Health Services Administration, Center for Mental Health Services, National Institutes of Health, National Institute of Mental Health.

Valentine, D. P. (1986). Psychological impact of infertility: Identifying issues and needs. *Social Work in Health Care, 11*(4), 61–69.

Van De Riet, V., Korb, M. P., & Gorrell, J. J. (1980). *Gestalt therapy: An introduction.* New York: Pergamon.

Vargas, M. F. (1986). *Louder than words: An introduction to nonverbal communication.* Ames, IA: The Iowa State University Press.

Viost, J. (1986). *Necessary Losses.* New York: Simon & Schuster.

Vriend, J. (1985). *Counseling powers and passions: More counseling techniques that work.* Alexandria, VA: American Association of Counseling and Development.

Vrugt, A., & Kerkstra, A. (1984). Sex differences in nonverbal communication. *Semiotica, 50,* 1–41.

Wachtel, E. R. (1982). The family psyche over three generations: The genogram revisited. *Journal of Marriage and Family Therapy, 8,* 335–343.

Wachtel, P. L. (1977). *Psychoanalysis and behavior therapy: Toward an integration.* New York: Basic Books.

Wachtel, P. L. (1987). *Action and insight.* New York: Guilford.

Waldo, M. (1985). A curative factor framework for conceptualizing group counseling. *Journal of Counseling and Development, 64*(1), 46–52.

Walen, S. R., DiGiuseppe, R., & Wessler, R. L. (1980). *A practitioner's guide to rational emotive therapy.* New York: Oxford University Press.

Walsh, W. M. (1992). Twenty major issues in remarriage families. *Journal of Counseling and Development, 70*(6), 200–203.

Walter, J. L., & Peller, J. E. (1992). *Becoming solution focused in brief therapy.* New York: Brunner/Mazel.

Walters, V. (1981). The living school. *RETwork, 1*(1), 136–144.

Ward, D. E. (1983). The trend toward eclecticism and the development of comprehensive models to guide counseling and psychotherapy. *Personnel and Guidance Journal, 62,* 154–157.

Wassmer, A. (1978). *Making contact: A guide to overcoming shyness, making new relationships and keeping those you have.* New York: Dial Press.

Waters, V. (1982). Therapies for children: Rational emotive therapy. In C. R. Reynolds & T. B. Gutkin (Eds.), *Handbook of school psychology* (pp. 216–232). New York: Wiley.

Watzlawick, P., Beavin, J. H., & Jackson, D. D. (1967). *Pragmatics of human communication.* New York: W. W. Norton.

Watzlawick, P., Weakland, J., & Fisch, R. (1974). *Change: Principles of problem formation and problem resolution.* New York: W. W. Norton.

Weakland, J., Fisch, R., Watzlawick, P., & Bodin, A. M. (1974). Brief therapy: Focused problem resolution. *Family Process, 13,* 141–168.

Weeks, G. R., & L'Abate, L. (1982). *Paradoxical psychotherapy: Theory and practice with individuals, couples, and families.* New York: Brunner/Mazel.

Weight, L. M., & Noakes, T. D. (1987). Is running an analog of anorexia? A survey of the incidence of eating disorders in female distance runners. *Medicine and Science in Sports and Exercise, 19,* 213–217.

Weinhold, J. (1987). Altered states of consciousness. *Journal of Humanistic Psychology, 12,* 14–17.

Weinrach, S. G. (1991). Selecting a counseling theory while scratching your head: A rationale-emotive therapist's personal journey. *Journal of Mental Health Counseling, 13*(3), 367–378.

White, J., & Fadiman, J. (Eds.). (1976). *Relax: How you can feel better, reduce stress, and overcome tension.* New York: Dell/Confucian Press.

White, P. G. (n.d.). The legend of the tear jar. URL: http:www.webhealing.com/articles/tearjar1.htm [Accessed: January 1, 2002]

White, M., & Epston, D. (1990). *Narrative means to therapeutic ends.* New York: Norton.

Wickman, S.A. (1999). *Making something of it: An analysis of the conversation and language of Carl Rogers and Gloria Lakoff.* Unpublished doctorial dissertation, Southern Illinois University, Carbondale.

Wickman, S. A., Daniels, M. H., White, L. J., & Fesmire, S. A. (1999). A "primer" in conceptual metaphor for counselors. *Journal of Counseling and Development, 77,* 389 394.

Wilde, G. (1992). *Rational counseling with school-aged populations: A practical guide.* Muncie, IN: Accelerated Development.

Wilde, G. (1996). *Treating anger, anxiety, and depression in children and adolescents: A cognitive-behavioral perspective.* Washington, DC: Accelerated Development.

William T. Grant Commission on Work, Family & Citizenship. (1988). *The forgotten half: Pathways to success for America's youth and young families.* New York: William T. Grant Foundation.

Williams, W. C., & Lair, G. S. (1991). Using a person-centered approach with children who have disabilities. *Elementary School Guidance and Counseling, 25*(3), 194–203.

Witmer, J. M., & Young, M. E. (1985). The silent partner: Uses of imagery in counseling. *Journal of Counseling and Development, 64*(3), 187–190.

Witmer, J. M., & Young, M. E. (1987). Imagery in counseling. *Elementary School Guidance and Counseling, 22*(1), 5–15.

Woodman, M. (1985). *The pregnant virgin: A process of psychological transformations.* Toronto, Canada: Inner City.

Wolpe, J. (1982). *The practice of behavior therapy* (3rd ed.). New York: Pergamon.

Wolterstorff, N. (1987). *Lament for a son.* Grand Rapids, MI: Eerdmans.

Wright, J., Coley, S., & Corey, G. (1989). Challenges facing human services education today. *Journal of Counseling and Human Service Professions, 3*(2), 3–11.

Yalom, I. D. (1985). *The theory and practice of group psychotherapy.* New York: Basic Books.

Yapko, M. (1986). Hypnotic and strategic interventions in the treatment of anorexia nervosa. *American Journal of Clinical Hypnosis, 28,* 224–232.

Young, J. E. (1999). *Cognitive therapy for personality disorders: A schema-focused approach* (3rd ed.) Sarasota, FL: Professional Resource Press.

Ziegler, D. J. (1989). A critique of rational-emotive theory of personality. In M. E. Bernard & R. DiGiuseppe (Eds.), *Inside rational-emotive therapy: A critical appraisal of the theory and therapy of Albert Ellis* (pp. 27–45). Orlando, FL: Academic Press.

Zilbergeld, B., & Lazarus, A. (1987). *Mind power.* Boston: Little, Brown.

Zimbardo, P. G. (1977). *Shyness: What it is and what to do about it.* Menlo Park, CA: Addison Wesley.

Zimstrad, S. W. (1989). Brief systemic therapy for families of the close head injured: Therapy with two hands. *Cognitive Rehabilitation, 7*(3), 26–28.

Zimmerman, J., & Dickerson, V. (1996). *If problems talked: Narrative therapy in action.* New York: Guilford.

Zirpoli, T. J., & Melloy K. J. (1993). *Behavior management: Applications for teachers and parents.* New York: MacMillan.

Index